CHRISTIANITY & WESTERN THOUGHT

A History of Philosophers,
Ideas & Movements

Alan G. Padgett &
Steve Wilkens

VOLUME 3

JOURNEY TO POSTMODERNITY IN THE 20TH CENTURY

IVP Academic

An imprint of InterVarsity Press
Downers Grove, Illinois

InterVarsity Press
P.O. Box 1400, Downers Grove, IL 60515-1426
World Wide Web: www.ivpress.com
E-mail: email@ivpress.com

InterVarsity Press® is the book-publishing division of InterVarsity Christian Fellowship/USA®, a movement of students and faculty active on campus at hundreds of universities, colleges and schools of nursing in the United States of America, and a member movement of the International Fellowship of Evangelical Students. For information about local and regional activities, write Public Relations Dept., InterVarsity Christian Fellowship/ USA, 6400 Schroeder Rd., P.O. Box 7895, Madison, WI 53707-7895, or visit the IVCF website at <www.intervarsity.org>.

Design: Cindy Kiple

Images: Florence in 1480. Detail from "Catena Map." Museo di Firenze com'era, Florence, Italy. Scala/Art Resource, NY

ISBN 978-0-8308-3857-8

Printed in the United States of America ∞

Library of Congress Cataloging-in-Publication Data

Brown, Colin, 1932-
  Christianity and western thought Vol. 1/Colin Brown
    p.   cm.
  Includes bibliographical references.
  ISBN 0-8308-1752-2
    1. Christianity—Philosophy. 2. Faith and reason—History of doctrines. 3. Philosophy—History. 1. Title.
  BR100.B6483 1990   *89-48564*
                                                              CIP

| P | 19 | 18 | 17 | 16 | 15 | 14 | 13 | 12 | 11 | 10 | 9 | 8 | 7 | 6 | 5 | 4 | 3 | 2 | 1 |
| Y | 25 | 24 | 23 | 22 | 21 | 20 | 19 | 18 | 17 | 16 | 15 | 14 | 13 | 12 | 11 | 10 | 09 |

To our children,
Luke & Lindsey, Zoe & Zachary
with love from two proud and thankful fathers

Acknowledgments

A series like this one does not come to fruitful completion without the guidance and help of a large number of people and institutions. Rodney Clapp, then at IVP, first agreed to have us finish the series started by Colin Brown, and Jim Hoover has seen this project through with patience and grace. Steve would like to thank Azusa Pacific University for library assistance in research and for providing two Accomplished Scholar Awards that offered important release time for research and writing. In addition, he is grateful to colleagues at Azusa Pacific who shared their expertise and were patient sounding-boards. Both of us are grateful for the love our wives and children have shown us over the long years which have gone into this project. Alan started his research for this volume while on a summer faculty seminar in 1996 led by Merold Westphal at Calvin College. He is grateful for that stimulating beginning, the wonderful people who were part of the seminar and the excellent opportunity provided by Calvin and the Pew Charitable Trust.

Other aspects of the work were written at Luther Seminary, which is a wonderful place to fulfill one's passion for research and teaching. My research assistant, Sarah Dahl, read through every chapter, making helpful and sometimes humorous comments and corrections, and also created the index. Others who read through chapters include our faculty secretary Victoria Smith, my friend Phil Rolnick and two anonymous reviewers for IVP. We are grateful for their support of our project. Alan is also grateful to the library staff at Luther Seminary for their expert help in procuring sometimes very obscure works. The substantial support of a full year's sabbatical went a very long way in giving Alan the time and resources needed to finish this project. Much of the last part of the book was written while at the University of Notre Dame, as a Crosson Fellow in the Center for Philosophy of Religion. It's hard to imagine a more ideal location for reading, arguing about, writing and in general doing philosophy. My thanks to several friends from my time at Notre Dame who read over or discussed chapters with me, including Kevin Hart and Nick Trakakis. We are both very grateful to all these people and institutions which helped make this book possible. Both Steve and Alan think that any remaining problems you may still find in this book should be blamed on the other author.

We are also grateful to God who has blessed us in so many ways, beyond what we can name or number, most particularly in the gift of four wonderful children, to whom we dedicate this work

Introduction

The book that lies before you is the continuation of and final volume in the series *Christianity and Western Thought*. Our purpose remains the same as before, namely, an overview and introduction to Western thought from a Christian point of view. While we do not cover theology as fully as in previous volumes (there simply was no time or space) we remain interested as Christian scholars in the thought of the great philosophers of the twentieth century. What did these women and men believe, and how does their thought engage the Christian worldview? What are the implications of these philosophies for the ongoing task of church mission, worship and scholarship? We hope this volume meets the needs of students, pastors and general readers for a narrative introduction to the fascinating developments in Western philosophy in the twentieth century. We make no pretensions to neutrality, but come to twentieth-century philosophy as disciples of Christ Jesus.

Western culture in the nineteenth century went through many changes and upheavals, but nothing compared to our own time. We now look back to the nineteenth century as an era of relative stability and progress, when many people believed in reason, science and the inevitable triumph of the human spirit. The machine age and industrialization gave people hope in the future. Great systems of thought arose to give shape to this optimism. Philosophers such as Nietzsche and Schopenhauer, generally pessimistic concerning the human race, were swimming against the stream in their own day. Today many thinkers look back on them as prophets.

Two major events changed the character of Western culture forever, shattering both intellectual systems and general optimism: World War I and World War II. These long and bloody battles, in which the new technologies brought massive death and destruction, profoundly shaped

twentieth-century Western culture. In fact, both the nineteenth and twentieth centuries were inaugurated by war: the nineteenth century, with its
relative stability in Europe, began with the defeat of Napoleon and
redrawing of European boundaries at the Congress of Vienna (1814-
1815). Culturally, the nineteenth century continued with its stability and
belief in reason and progress until the outbreak of World War I (1914).
The struggles and sufferings of the "war to end all wars" created the cultural crisis that shattered the complacency of the West, ushering in the
twentieth century.

Loss of Faith in Science, Self and Society

No unified, coherent account of the West's response to the two world
wars, and the immense changes they wrought, will ever be fully satisfactory. There is a dizzying array of responses and denials to be found in
twentieth-century art, literature, philosophy and religion. Much of this
response occurs not only in reply to the devastation of war, economic
depression, neocolonialism and revolution, but also to a crisis of reason.
The Enlightenment held to the power of reason and believed in progress
based on human rationality and science. However, world war unforgetta-
bly demonstrated the inherent evil possible even in the most technological and "rational" society. Reason, science and technology were revealed
to have a dark side, or at best, to be morally neutral: they can be used to
help alleviate suffering or, in the wrong hands, to greatly increase
human suffering and oppression. The atomic bomb stands as the most
potent symbol of the destructive power of new technology. So the moral
ambiguity—some would say the moral bankruptcy—of science and reason created a cultural crisis. The history of Western thought in the twentieth century is a history of response to this crisis.

Along with a loss of faith in reason and science, the twentieth century has witnessed a loss of faith in the human self (or consciousness)
and in society as a whole. The Enlightenment view of the self was
grounded in confidence in reason and morality. It was thought that
human consciousness (especially the power to reason and moral
responsibility) gave people an obvious superiority to animals and the
natural world: rational men (and later, women) can band together to
create the good society, based upon democracy, rational political struc-

tures, technology and rational moral behavior. Examples of such confidence in humanity are found in Locke's political philosophy, Hegelian idealism and the utilitarianism of John Stuart Mill.

World war and devastation—ironically begun by just such rational, technological societies—destroyed much of Western confidence in humanity and society. They undermined faith in human consciousness and morality. Are we really any better than the beasts? Less certain, too, was any confidence in human society as a place of progress, peace and understanding. Aren't the nations destroying themselves with ever more devastating skill? As usual, the artists grasped and expressed this loss of faith before philosophers and theologians. The brilliant poem "The Waste Land" is an outstanding example of just the crisis we are describing. Written by T. S. Eliot in 1922, it helped set the agenda for twentieth-century English-language poetry. In the first part of the poem, "The Burial of the Dead," Eliot's description of London's financial district (the City) echoes Dante's first glimpses beyond the gates of Hell in the *Inferno:*

Unreal City,

Under the brown fog of a winter dawn,

A crowd flowed over London Bridge, so many,

I had not thought death had undone so many.

Sighs, short and infrequent, were exhaled,

and each man fixed his eyes before his feet.[1]

Eliot was for many years a professional, working in London; these lines depict work and society, the City, as unreal and as a place of death. In an earlier poem, "Preludes," Eliot reflects upon the transitory, scattered nature of the human self that inhabits this society:

You tossed a blanket from the bed,

You lay upon your back and waited;

You dozed, and watched the night revealing

The thousand sordid images

Of which your soul was constituted;

They flickered against the ceiling.[2]

The soul is reduced to a mere flickering of images, sordid and dirty, a reflection of the modern city's harsh and impermanent landscape.

Eliot is hardly the only poet or artist to describe this modern angst.

The Irish poet W. B. Yeats begins "The Second Coming" (1921) with this unsettling vision:

> Turning and turning in the widening gyre
> The falcon cannot hear the falconer;
> Things fall apart; the center cannot hold;
> Mere anarchy is loosed upon the world,
> The blood-dimmed tide is loosed, and everywhere
> The ceremony of innocence is drowned;
> The best lack all conviction, while the worst
> Are full of passionate intensity.[3]

The falcon has lost all connection with the falconer—nothing remains to control its flight. The universe has no center, no order. Things fall apart, and anarchy is loosed upon the world. The story of philosophy in the twentieth century is a narrative of Western culture responding to, or articulating, this same sense of anarchy.

The Story of Philosophy in the Twentieth Century

It is always difficult to write about our own century, even when it is over. We lack distance and historical perspective. Only the passage of time allows people to reflect upon the past, to discover the essential ingredients of culture, to gain insight into the why and how of events. With the passage of time comes the wisdom to distinguish the really important from the merely interesting. Still, the longest journey begins with the first step. We must do our best to understand our own century, sure in knowledge that other, later scholars will correct our myopia.

Our story begins in central Europe, in German-speaking intellectual circles. In response to the challenge of Kant, Hegel and idealism, several thinkers began to insist that philosophy must return to its scientific foundations. The most important of these turn-of-the-century philosophers was Gottlob Frege (1848-1925). All of his highly technical publications are in the area of logic and mathematics. Although his work received almost no recognition in his lifetime, he contributed to our story through those he influenced.

Frege is the first philosopher of our century to make the "linguistic turn," that is, to argue that (1) philosophy can only proceed by a careful analysis of the symbols used in expressing propositions, and (2) that the meaning of a symbol (or word) is its use in a formula (or sentence). Mathematics, Frege argued, is not based upon the inner psychology of the mind, but on external considerations of the symbol system of language. He influenced two philosophers whose works helped establish the two streams of Western philosophy in our century: Bertrand Russell in analytic philosophy, and Edmund Husserl in phenomenology. These men in turn influenced two philosophers who stand at the center of our story. Both Frege and Russell influenced Ludwig Wittgenstein, while Husserl had a major impact on Martin Heidegger. With Heidegger and Wittgenstein we reach philosophers whose work is arguably the most influential in our century. The two streams in which they stand are the two schools or movements into which Western philosophy is typically divided: the analytic and continental approaches.

Early in the century, analytic philosophers Bertrand Russell and G. E. Moore in Cambridge rejected the idealism then popular in British philosophy. Russell began his career in the philosophy of mathematics and logic, and it is due to him that Frege's work became well-known. With Moore, he established a new manner of proceeding in philosophy, which focused on the careful analysis of the sentences in which philosophers expressed their ideas in order to expose the underlying logic of what was being said. Frege, Russell and Wittgenstein (at this early point in his career) all agreed that the ambiguities of language had led traditional philosophy into logical blunders and pseudoproblems. Only careful, exacting, logical analysis could possibly help philosophy out of the blind alley of ordinary language.

A similar school of thought was growing in Austria, known as the Vienna Circle. The work of these German-speaking thinkers was brought to the English-speaking world by A. J. Ayer in a widely influential tract, *Language, Truth and Logic* (1936). These logical positivists, as they became known, also held that a careful, logical analysis of language was the only way forward in philosophy. In addition, they insisted that the meaning of a proposition is only found in its method of empirical verification. They were, like Hume, empiricists in their epistemology and skeptical of any positive claims to metaphysical knowledge.

The style of philosophy at Cambridge and Vienna, which we now call analytic, dominated philosophy in the English-speaking world for much of our century. Traditional metaphysics was almost wholly forsaken, while logic, philosophy of mathematics and philosophy of science were the new dominant concerns. Idealism, once so influential, had been swept from the field. The other major philosophical movement in our century is continental, which begins with phenomenology. These terms, methods and ideas will be covered more fully in the rest of our book.

The continental tradition in the twentieth century tends to circle around Husserl's student Martin Heidegger. Heidegger's early work examined consciousness, as Husserl did, with a special focus on human Being that is conscious. In his central work, *Being and Time* (1927), he argued that knowledge of reality must begin with an investigation of the knower, that is, of human Being (*Dasein* in German, roughly meaning human existence in the world). Heidegger was also concerned with meaning, but focused on the meaning of human Being and of the world we live in, rather than simply the meaning of words. Yet *Being and Time* is pregnant with important insights for hermeneutics. He argued that traditional metaphysics had to be overcome, in order to clear the way for Being to speak. In his later thought, Heidegger focused more explicitly on language, and his work had a profound effect upon the philosophy of language and hermeneutics. The turn to human Being as the ground of knowledge (as opposed to the stable Cartesian *ego*), alongside the general concern with the loss of center and loss of self during and after World War I, helped spark the rise of existentialism.

Existentialism was more of an attitude or trend than a specific style or method of philosophy. Building upon the work of Heidegger and other philosophers, existentialists investigated the meaning of human existence. They held (for the most part) that existence and freedom were basic. Human Being cannot be reduced to an object for empirical, scientific inquiry. They rejected the quest for scientific foundations in philosophy and for a rational basis for ethics. Each individual is unique and faces unique situations: only she can discover, for herself, what authentic existence means for her. We cannot be dictated to by structures, institutions or religions. To rely upon such external authorities for the meaning of our lives is "bad faith." Existentialism had a tremendous impact on Western culture, and we will look in some detail at its influence on Christian theology. The influence of existentialism extended beyond philosophy proper, to include the fine arts, literature and psychology as well as theology.

Existentialism represents a general reaction against reason, science and logical analysis. Following Heidegger, thinkers of this type rejected the pretensions of traditional metaphysics. No universal, scientific, rationalist approach to life can possibly be authentic or address my deepest personal (i.e., existential) needs. This general rejection of Enlightenment rationalism continues to the end of the century and expands to other movements.

Alongside Heidegger a key philosopher of the age was Ludwig Wittgenstein. Through arduous analysis and reflection upon his own earlier work, Wittgenstein changed completely the character of his philosophy and, with it, the analytic tradition. In his later work, Wittgenstein withdrew his belief in abstract propositions and pure logic as the basis of truth. Instead, he turned to an analysis of language that focused on the use of sentences in actual life. The notion of an ideal, logically pure language—such that mathematics purports to be—is an illusion. Meaning comes from use by a speaking community, in the actions of real life. We must pay attention to the way words are actually used in various contexts, in what he called "language games." By ignoring how language is grounded in many forms of life, philosophers have committed numerous errors. The goal of the philosophy therefore becomes therapeutic, rather than cognitive: we help thinkers overcome the errors that language has led them into. This behavioral, communal approach to meaning was just as detrimental to traditional metaphysics as logical positivism had been. It also served to undermine the logical program of Russell and Frege, and their more abstract, propositional notions of meaning and truth. Wittgenstein moved much closer to a kind of pragmatism in the philosophy of language.

Along with the work of the later Wittgenstein, the philosophy of W. V. Quine and other logical pragmatists effectively undermined the confident faith in logical analysis characteristic of early analytic philosophies. This loss of confidence reaches its acme in the work of the popular American pragmatist Richard Rorty. Rorty insists that the history of Western philosophy is a dead end, a quest for objective truth that is doomed to failure. Enlightenment faith in reason must be rejected for the "bad faith" it was, and a pluralistic, relativistic and pragmatic approach to truth

and meaning must take its place. Rorty is the parade example of postmodern analytic philosophy.

Recent French philosophy provides another example of postmodernity. The work of Michel Foucault and Jacques Derrida, sometimes
described as "poststructuralist," exerts a powerful hold over Western
intellectuals, especially in the humanities and human sciences. Foucault
and Derrida were both influenced by French structuralism, but ended up
rejecting and radically undermining the structuralist claim to a universal
science of language, self and society. Foucault was primarily a social philosopher and historian. Like Wittgenstein and the logical pragmatists, he
insists on the social and cultural foundations of all sciences, worldviews
and philosophies. Furthermore, following the influence of Marx and
Nietzsche, Foucault sees the hand of power and class behind the domination of a scientific program, a philosophy or a worldview. Humans
construct such meaning systems for the purpose of social organization,
and they must be understood in their social and historical contexts. Such
a historicist approach calls into question any notion of "truth" for science, philosophy or theology.

Like Foucault, Derrida learned the questions and concerns of his
teachers only to radically undermine their results. Derrida's work in philosophy focuses on language. He emphasizes the great distance that he
finds between language and Being or "presence." Derrida finds Being to
be under "erasure" in the text, and the author to be dead—any appeal to
some inner authorial intention as a norm for meaning is futile. Rather,
texts are a fabric of the traces of Being, referring to an endless play of
possible meanings. Thus meaning is endlessly deferred, and *differánce* (as
we will see) becomes the leitmotif of Derrida's philosophy.

Clearly, the story of Western philosophy in the twentieth century is a
story of great change. The century began with the attempt to ground philosophy in reason and create a scientific approach to philosophical
issues. However, much popular and intellectual culture abandoned faith
in the power of reason and science to discover certain truth about reality
or to establish human control over it. In both the analytic and the phenomenological traditions, philosophers undermined the rationalism of
earlier founders. By the end of the century postmodern philosophies,
with their emphasis on the social construction of reality and the relativity

of all claims to truth and meaning, dominated many academic disciplines. It does seem as if indeed the center did not hold.

Continental vs. Analytic?

This brief sketch of twentieth-century philosophy is a simplification. It is also possible, again as a help for the beginner, to create a scheme or typology by which the different movements and thinkers can be compared and contrasted. The most common such classification is between philosophers in the continental tradition and those in the analytic tradition: many surveys of philosophy group thinkers into either Anglo-American or continental categories. While we agree with the basic idea of this division (which in reality is based upon content rather than geography) the names are unfortunate. Many so-called continental thinkers can be found in Great Britain and North America; likewise, Anglo-American philosophy actually originates on the continent and still has important representatives in German-speaking countries. So the major problem with these names is that they give a false impression of geographical division where none in fact exists. We prefer the name "analytic" for the so-called Anglo-American school. The continental approach is more difficult to name with a nongeographical term, since so many views are represented. We are forced to keep this name for such schools as phenomenology, hermeneutics, structuralism, Marxism, critical theory and post-structuralism. In any case, it is the standard term which students of Western thought will encounter, so we will use it as well.

As our brief story indicates, analytic philosophies represent movements of thought concerned with exact reasoning, especially science, mathematics and logic. There is a tendency in this type of philosophy to respond to the loss of confidence in reason and science. It is no accident that the "grandfather" of analytic philosophy is also the father of modern logic: Frege. Analytic philosophies include such movements as logical positivism, linguistic analysis and logical pragmatism.

What are normally called continental philosophies center on concerns that Hegel raised in his *Phenomenology of Spirit*. It includes the issues of human consciousness, reason, society, culture and the nature of the reality we inhabit. Thinkers of this type are the heirs (and critics) of Kant and Hegel, without whom their works can scarcely be understood.

The concerns of logic, truth, natural science and the clarification of concepts take a definite second place to human consciousness or human Being, with its roots in society and the world. The most influential of the continental thinkers in our century has been Martin Heidegger. While both schools discuss language, and it is common to speak of a "linguistic turn" in philosophy during our century, this rubric nevertheless can mask fundamental differences. We will discuss these movements more fully in chapters to come.

Theology in the Twentieth Century

What impact has philosophy made upon theology in the twentieth century? This is a vital question which for the most part we have been forced to ignore in this book. The main theological parts concern the development of dialectical theology and Thomism, which we do cover to some degree. A full and complete analysis of twentieth-century theology is beyond the scope of this third volume. Thinkers such as Karl Barth or Karl Rahner, therefore, will be introduced to the extent that they respond to the major issues in twentieth-century Western thought and in some ways shape the discussion. No attempt at a survey of theology is made for our brief introduction. That does not mean the present writers think that theology is unimportant. On the contrary, it is a sign of the importance we attach to theology that we insist it have its own, fuller analysis—an analysis beyond the scope of the present work.[4]

1. SCIENCE, PHILOSOPHY AND THE DEMISE OF IDEALISM

F ollowing the work of Kant, the philosophy of idealism dominated the intellectual world of the nineteenth century. In the shift from the nineteenth to the twentieth century, however, this dominance began to slip. Students of Western culture usually attribute this to the culture shock of World War I and the Great Depression. This is no doubt correct, in terms of popular culture. The worldview of idealism could not survive the grim realities of such violence and suffering. However, the intellectual roots of the demise of idealism can be found in the soil of the nineteenth century. In this chapter we will examine some philosophers whose work helped bring an end to the dominance of idealism in the West.

The story begins at the end of the nineteenth century with the work of several scholars who are the springs from which the torrent of anti-idealism eventually flowed. All of these men were trained in the nineteenth century, but became important and influential voices for twentieth-century philosophy. All of them wished to reclaim the "scientific" character of philosophy, hearkening back to the philosophical ideals of the Enlightenment, and to interpret the sciences from a philosophical perspective. Yet their understanding of the scientific character of philosophical work was quite distinct from their Enlightenment forbears.

The first of these thinkers is Charles S. Peirce, whose work in logic and epistemology formed the foundation of American pragmatism, logic and semiotics (the study of signs and symbols). Peirce's work has already been canvassed in volume two of this series, and need not be revisited here. We should note, however, that he very much wanted philosophy to model the methods of the natural sciences, and his work formed one of the sources of the anti-idealist tendencies at the turn of the century. Peirce, who died in 1914, was especially influential in America. Two philosophers from the other side of the Atlantic, Bertrand Russell and G. E. Moore, will be the subject of our next chapter. Unlike the three Anglo-Americans (Peirce, Russell and Moore) the three thinkers we shall now cover all hail from Europe. They are Gottlob Frege (1848-1925), Edmund Husserl (1859-1938) and Henri Bergson (1859-1941).

Frege is the founder of modern logic and the grandparent of contemporary analytic philosophy. Husserl, who was influenced by Frege, is the founder of phenomenology, which later led to existentialism and the dominant philosophical schools on the continent. Bergson was considered by many to be the greatest philosopher of his day, and he is the first major voice in process philosophy in the twentieth century. His understanding of the relationship between science and philosophy also influenced French existentialism. The work of these men, then, provides the origins of philosophy in the twentieth century and gives shape to the general rejection of idealism that took place as the nineteenth century gave way to the twentieth.

Frege

It would be difficult to overestimate the importance of Gottlob Frege for philosophy in the twentieth century.[1] Frege's work is of central importance in logic, philosophy of mathematics and the philosophy of language. His publications in logic are the most important work in the field since Aristotle and form the basis for all modern formal logic. His work in the philosophy of mathematics is one of the greatest single contributions in Western history, while his essays in the philosophy of language provide the starting point for contemporary work on this topic. Ironically, however, his significant work was almost totally ignored by his contemporaries. When they did read it, they usually misunderstood it. Let us hope we can do better!

Gottlob Frege (1848-1925) spent his entire academic career in the mathematics department of the University of Jena.[2] His written work, and his lectures, focused almost entirely on logic, while he also wrote on the topics of mathematics and the philosophy of language.[3] Frege wanted to create a clear, unambiguous foundation for arithmetic. He believed he could show, in a rigorous argument from axioms, that all arithmetic reduces to logic (this view is now known as "logicism"). This attempt failed, as was rigorously demonstrated by Kurt Gödel (1906-1978) in his famous "incompleteness theorem."[4] But it was a magnificent defeat! For even in the attempt, Frege achieved one of the greatest contributions to logic and mathematics by any individual in Western history.

Because he was interested in rigorous argument, Frege insisted that there is a kind of objective thought which sentences express. Careful logical analysis can show the similarities in sentences that might look, at first glance, to be different. For example, take these two sentences: "Aristotle was the teacher of Alexander," and "Alexander was taught by Aristotle." On a purely grammatical level, these appear to be different ideas represented by different subjects and predicates. But Frege demonstrated that they nevertheless express the same logical thought. He created a formal, symbolic calculus to express relationships between subject and predicate, or in terms which Frege borrowed from mathematics, between a "function" and its "arguments." This insight, and the idea of a formal system of signs to express such logical connections, is the foundation of all modern formal logic and Frege's greatest contribution.

Frege's logicism and his philosophy of mathematics are now out-of-date. But his philosophy of language is still the object of serious study and an area of research where he made significant advances.[5] Where previous philosophers of language had spoken vaguely of "meaning," Frege introduced a very significant distinction between "sense" and "reference" as elements of the meaning of a sentence.[6] This allows for a distinction between the grammatical or "ordinary" meaning of a sentence and the objects that the sentence is about. Roughly, the sense is concerned with the meaning or informative content of a statement, while the reference is what the statement is about. This may seem an elementary distinction, but in fact it is central to the philosophy of language.

He also insisted, rightly we now believe, that the meaning of a word is only found in the context of its use in a sentence.[7] Most philosophers of language before Frege located the meaning of a word in the inner, mental idea of the speaker, a view which Frege called "psychologism." Frege rejected the notion that the meaning of a sentence resides in some inner, mental intention or psychological state. Rather, the meaning of a word derives from the way it is used in public language. Meaning, then, is objective and can be investigated in a scientific way. Frege believed that his logical analysis did just that. Careful logical analysis of a sentence is necessary, therefore, if a truly scientific approach to knowledge and meaning is to have any hope of proceeding.

Frege's work, along with that of others, inspired a whole school of thought which we now call "analytic philosophy." These philosophers tend to focus on language as the best way to advance philosophical reflection. Complex phenomena must be broken down into simpler parts and their relationships laid bare. It is only through an analysis of language, assisted by logic and careful reasoning, that such an investigation of thought and experience can rightly proceed. Like Frege, this philosophical school takes its cue from mathematics and science. They hope that the difficult problems of philosophy, and of our knowledge of the world, can be answered through clear analysis and rigorous logical argument. This school replaced idealism as the dominant force in English speaking philosophy in the twentieth century.

During his own lifetime, Frege did have a significant influence on the work of several major philosophers in the analytic tradition, most notably Bertrand Russell, Ludwig Wittgenstein and the Vienna Circle. A full discussion of the collapse of idealism would include the work of these thinkers; however, we shall postpone a consideration their work until a later chapter, since they belong more fully and obviously to the twentieth century.[8]

Husserl

In addition to Russell and Wittgenstein, Frege also had some influence on his contemporary Edmund Husserl (1859-1938).[9] Like Frege and Russell, Husserl wanted to reestablish rigorous philosophical research upon solid scientific foundations. Like them he rejected Hegelian idealism in favor of a new approach, more in keeping with mathematics and rational certainty. Husserl called this new approach "phenomenology," borrowing a term from the Greeks and from Hegel. This approach proved to be the single most important and influential one in the continental philosophical tradition.

Husserl was born in Prossnitz, then located in Austria. He studied at German and Austrian universities, and like Frege, Russell and Whitehead, began his work in mathematics. Like them, his interests turned to philosophy. After earning a Ph.D. in mathematics from the University of Vienna in 1883, Husserl attended lectures in philosophy, including those of Franz Brentano. His first published work in philosophy was *Philosophy of Arithmetic*, vol. 1 (1891).[10] This book based numerical truths on empirical, psychological events in the human mind, such as counting and believing. Upon further reflection, Husserl found this position to be too "psychological," that is, too subjective. Frege's long, critical review of this book must have reinforced this conviction.[11] At several points in his life Husserl decided that the foundations of his approach to philosophy needed to be rethought from the beginning. Like Frege, he wanted to establish philosophy upon solid logical and rational or scientific grounds. The result of this labor was his first important work, *Logical Investigations* (1900-1901).[12] This book was well accepted and established Husserl's reputation. He then expanded his phenomenological analysis beyond the merely mathematical, logical and linguistic to the broad areas of the world as experienced and the subject who experiences. His next major publication was *Ideas Pertaining to a Pure Phenomenology and to a Phenomenological Philosophy* (vol. 1, 1913).[13] Husserl also published a kind of manifesto of his approach to philosophy, "Philosophy as a Rigorous Science" about this time (1911).[14] It was partly on the basis of this work that he eventually received a full professorate in philosophy at the University of Freiburg in 1916, after lecturing in philosophy at other German universities. Husserl soon became the most respected thinker of his day in German philosophy.

Husserl remained at Freiburg for the rest of his professional career. Because of pressure from the Nazis, Husserl was forced to retire early in 1928, on account of his Jewish descent. Nevertheless, he continued to work hard at establishing the foundations of philosophical science and developing his phenomenological method. In 1929 he published his *Formal and Transcendental Logic*, another analysis of logic and transcendental phenomenological method.[15] He also gave two sets of technical lectures in France, Vienna and Prague; these were published as *Cartesian Meditations* (1931), and then the final major work in his lifetime, *The Crisis of*

European Sciences and Transcendental Phenomenology (1936).[16] As a Jew Husserl was denied public activities such as lectures and professional conferences in his own country, so of necessity he spoke and published his work abroad. Each of these major publications was subtitled as an "introduction" to phenomenology, and indeed, most of Husserl's life was devoted to establishing secure, scientific grounds for philosophy and for knowledge in general. After suffering for some months with pleurisy, Husserl died on April 27, 1938 just before the outbreak of the Second World War.

Much of Husserl's work in philosophy was in manuscript form at his death. As the work of a Jew (even though Husserl was of Protestant faith), this material could have been destroyed. However, a Belgian Catholic follower of his thought, Fr. Herman Leo van Breda, traveled to Vienna and with no little effort and the help of Belgian political leaders he managed to smuggle the bulk of his work out (including Frau Husserl, Husserl's private library and even some furniture!). Van Breda then established the Husserl Archives at the University of Leuven, which has since published Husserl's complete work in modern critical editions and a complete English translation.[17]

Husserl's thought went through several stages, but there is a core viewpoint found in his work from the publication of *Ideas* I to *The Crisis of European Sciences* (1913-1936). We will here focus on these mature works. Even so, Husserl's philosophy is difficult to expound in a short space.[18] This is no doubt because it is both technical and almost wholly devoted to philosophical method. He insisted that philosophy be established on scientific, rational foundations. Husserl argued that philosophy is not based upon empirical studies, and so is not based upon the natural or social sciences. Rather, a pure, rational foundation for philosophy (and therefore for all knowledge, since philosophy is the most basic of the sciences) can only be found in a rigorous, scientific analysis of the bases of knowledge.[19] Husserl believed he had found such a method in phenomenology, that is, the rigorous analysis of experience to discover both its grounds, and the categorical or rational structures which govern experience. Husserl was thus a follower of both Descartes and Kant. Like Descartes, Husserl was interested in renewing the investigation of the foundations of knowledge, based upon a fresh inquiry into the origins of experience. Like Kant, Husserl argued that experience (or consciousness) is structured by certain conceptual categories, which he argued could be laid bare by careful phenomenological analysis.

The major difference between Husserl on the one hand, and Kant and Hegel on the other, has to do with the type of idealism they espoused. Husserl argued, *contra* Kant (who held that we cannot know the things-in-themselves), that the immediate experience of consciousness, the object as intended by conscious reflection, was normally a guide to the objects themselves or the "thing." Of course such things can only be known as objects of consciousness, and therefore of human intention. He wrote:

> All perceiving and imagining is, on our view, a web of partial intentions, fused together in the unity of a single total intention. The correlate of this last intentions the thing, while the correlate of its partial intentions are *the thing's parts and aspects*. Only in this way can we understand how consciousness reaches out beyond what it actually experiences. It can, so to say, mean beyond itself, and its meaning can be fulfilled.[20]

We should note the use of "intention" in this quotation. Husserl borrows this concept from Brentano, who taught that all consciousness is a "consciousness-of" something. I don't just remember or judge, for example: I remember *something*, I judge that *something* is true. Consciousness thus can, and *intends* to, reach beyond itself to things. The ideal meanings or "noemata" we find in the object of consciousness normally leads us to the thing. This intention is not always fulfilled, however, because sometimes we are conscious of objects that do not exist. An example would be a botanist who is developing a new color of rose which does not yet exist. That specific rose is an object of consciousness, intended by the botanist, but not (yet!) a thing. Thus Husserl is no idealist in the usual sense. He called his viewpoint *transcendental idealism*.

When he used transcendental idealism to describe his philosophy, he did not mean to deny the reality of objects, but to affirm the structural quality of the reasoning process that gives shape to our perception and the absolute grounding of perception in the transcendental ego.[21] In fact, he was critical of both idealism (in the Hegelian sense) and empiricism. Instead he argued that the objects as presented to consciousness are structured by the knowing subject. These structures or categories are revealed only through transcendental phenomenological analysis. A naïve empiricism, therefore, must also be ruled out. Of course, Husserl also insisted that his philosophy was "empirical" in the best sense; that is, it was based on careful study of the objects themselves as presented to consciousness. "But to judge rationally or scientifically about things signifies to conform to the things themselves or to go from words and opinions back to the things themselves, to consult them in their self-givenness and to set aside all prejudices alien to them."[22]

Through phenomenological analysis, the very essence of the things themselves, which he called *eidos* (Greek for "idea" or "form") is available to reason. "The essence (Eidos) is a new sort of object. Just as the datum of individual or experiencing intuition is an individual object, so the datum of eidetic intuition is a pure essence."[23] However, in order to pay attention to the way objects are presented to consciousness, it is necessary (Husserl argued) to "bracket" any and all presuppositions about them, including the idea that they exist. As a rigorous science, phenomenology must be utterly without presuppositions. Husserl thus follows Descartes in arguing that we must question everything heretofore accepted as "real." This means, for Husserl, that I must suspend my judgments about direct experience in order to carefully attend to the experience itself. Husserl called this the philosophical posture the *epoche*, or suspension of belief (borrowing another Greek word).[24] One interesting result of such a suspension is Husserl's conception of the knowing self.

We have seen that Husserl was a follower of Descartes in some ways, wishing to begin with a presuppositionless, rigorous foundation for knowledge. He was more of a Kantian in his view of the self, however. For according to Husserl, phenomenological analysis and the *epoche* reveal that even if the world I experience changed radically, or was even annihilated, "the being of consciousness . . . would not be touched."[25] The mind or self exists in a way that is independent of the particularities of consciousness and experience. At the same time his phenomenological analysis of the *self as embodied knower* including empathy, motion and the self in everyday life (all in *Ideas* II) puts to rest any charge of simplistic mind-body dualism in his thought.[26]

Husserl moderated his views somewhat over time with regard to the self and its history. In *The Crisis of the European Sciences*, he specifically discussed the concepts of history and of our surrounding "life-world." Both of these moderate the singularity and the pure subjectivity of reason and perception for the mature Husserl. He argued against what are typically called a priori truths: "The supposedly completely self-sufficient logic which modern mathematical logicians think they are able to develop, even calling it a truly scientific philosophy, namely, as the universal, *a priori*, fundamental science for all objective sciences, is nothing but naïveté."[27] But even when he recognizes the character of the life-world as contextualizing our claims to knowledge, he still believes that there are "general structures" that pertain to any and all life-worlds. These structures do not change in different times and cultures; but exactly what these unchanging foundations of our "horizon" are is difficult to spell out clearly. One example Husserl did work out himself was a phenomenology of our internal consciousness of time, a universal element of the human life-world.[28]

In his concern for uncovering the objective foundations of knowledge in the midst of history and the life-world, Husserl did point out the problem of my own personal history as a philosopher. This history provides a set of prejudices and filters through which I encounter the world. It is the job of phenomenological analysis to overcome these prejudices and see the world as it is presented to consciousness in its self-givenness. Because the fundamental structures of the life-world do not vary across cultures, Husserl avoids relativism, while recognizing the historical and social character of consciousness. He insists that real, scientific and transcendental knowledge is possible, as long as it is "traced back" to the prelogical ground upon which everything makes sense, namely, the structures of consciousness, the life-world and the ego.[29]

Husserl's philosophical work shaped the character of Western thought. If the greatness of a teacher is measured by his students, Husserl was very great indeed. He founded the methods and concerns of continental philosophy, even when those after him disagreed with his work. Martin Heidegger, one of the giants of twentieth-century thought, was his most important student. But many French thinkers such as Maurice Merleau-Ponty, Jean-Paul Sartre, Paul Ricoeur, Emmanuel Levinas and Jacques Derrida all cut their philosophical eye-teeth on Husserl, while at the same time they modified, transformed or deconstructed his methods.[30] The phenomenological method has been adopted by philosophers and social scientists across the world. At the same time, Husserl has only a few real followers for his carefully developed, logical methodology. The broad idea of a phenomenology of human consciousness was accepted, but the content and conclusions of Husserl's work were overshadowed by Heidegger and the French phenomenologists.

Bergson

The third philosopher we will introduce here is French. In his day Henri Bergson (1859-1941) was one of Europe's most famous and influential intellectuals. Although not as important as Frege or Husserl, books and articles about him number in the thousands.[31] Today his work is for the most part rarely studied or discussed.[32] Yet he has an important role to play in the development of Western thought in the nineteenth and twentieth centuries. His work paved the way for French existentialism as well as for process philosophy and theology.[33]

Bergson was born in Paris on October 18, 1859, and his life revolved around his academic career.[34] He was of Jewish ancestry, which became problematic after the Germans occupied Paris. His father was Polish, but his mother was English, and Bergson was fluent in the English tongue. He showed his early intellectual promise at the *lycée* (a French preparatory school), where he excelled in mathematics. He then attended the famous École Normale Supérieure (ENS) where he distinguished himself again, moving to philosophy and earning his doctorate in 1889. His doctoral thesis, "An Essay on the Immediate Data of Consciousness," translated into English as *Time and Free Will*, is the first of his four major books.[35] This work sets out the main themes of Bergsonian philosophy, paying attention to human consciousness and our experience of time. Like Frege and Husserl, Bergson was interested in the philosophical interpretation of mathematics and science. "What I wanted," he wrote of his own philosophical journey, "was a philosophy which would submit to the control of science and which in turn could enable science to progress."[36] Early on, Bergson was very much influenced by biology, evolution and the philosophy of Spencer.[37] However, in his dissertation he gives particular attention to the new science of psychology.

In 1896 Bergson published his second major book, *Matter and Memory*. In this work he developed a novel conception of the mind-body relationship and began his reflections on cosmology and the nature of the world. After lecturing in various provincial lycées, Bergson returned to Paris in 1898 and was appointed to the chair of modern philosophy at the Collège de France. The Collège is an outstanding academic institution where professors have no students, but lecture to the general educated public. Bergson's lectures were very popular, packing the lecture halls hours before his appointed time. He attracted all types of people in fashionable Paris, not just academics, and was considered an outstanding and stimulating speaker. The French philosopher Gabriel Marcel wrote of "the feeling of inner expansion that Bergson awoke in all of us. . . . At the Collège de France it seemed to me that I was never present at one of his classes without being stirred by the hope that a revelation would be given me."[38] During this period—roughly 1900-1925—many considered him to be the most significant philosopher of the day. He published *Creative Evolution* in 1907, the book which brought him worldwide fame. It is still his most famous work, in which he fully develops his philosophical interpretation of the natural world and of natural science, especially biology and evolution.

Bergson was elected to the French Academy in 1914, the same year that his books were put on the Index of Prohibited Works by the Holy Office (thus demonstrating his influence on French Catholic intellectuals). To top it all, in 1927 he was awarded the Nobel Prize in literature (contrary to all that is sacred and sensible, there is no Nobel Prize in philosophy).

During World War I, Bergson began to devote himself to international affairs. He made a diplomatic visit to the United States, hoping to convince President Wilson to join the war against the Central powers. After the war, he continued to work in international organizations, in the hope of fostering peace and cooperation among nations. He was appointed the first president of the International Commission for Intellectual Cooperation by the League of Nations, but had to resign in 1925 due to ill health. He also resigned from his philosophy chair in 1921, for the same reason. During this time, Bergson's crippling arthritis made intellectual work extremely difficult. Yet he managed to publish essays and two books, one of which was devoted to a discussion of relativity theory in dialogue with Einstein.[39] His most important work of this period, and the last of his major books, was about ethics and religion: *The Two Sources of Morality and Religion* (1932). In this volume he works out the implications of his philosophical approach for ethics and the philosophy of religion.

Bergson's work as a philosopher is known for its clarity, style and sweeping use of metaphors and illustrations. His critics claim that his work lacks logical rigor. Many of his main ideas are indeed unclear, even ambiguous, and much of his work does lack a certain precision. Yet Bergson's philosophical style is tantalizing, stimulating and suggestive: logical precision is sacrificed to rhetorical power and literary style. But surely there is room in Western literature for both types of philosophy.

In considering the philosophy of Bergson, or "Bergsonism," one is struck by the consistency of his system. The totality of his work fits together well. It is a holistic interpretation of human freedom, knowledge, science, the material world, society, morality and religion. But what is the central idea, the root metaphor, of Bergsonism? He answered that question himself, in a letter to a Danish colleague: the intuition of duration.[40] Explaining this phrase will send us into the heart of Bergson's philosophy.

As early as his 1889 dissertation, Bergson took pains to distinguish scientific, abstract knowledge from immediate, direct experience. The human mind is a development from primitive instinct and has a very practical, pragmatic end. The focus of human *intelligence* is on discerning objects in space, understanding the world around us and meeting practical goals. From this abstract, reflective and practical knowledge comes mathematics and modern science. Bergson argues that both math and science are fundamentally *spatial* in nature. Each requires an element of measurement, and therefore of spatial "picturing" of the object. Symbols are the means whereby intelligence communicates this space-based knowledge and understands the world. Thus the symbolic and spatial is basic to our human analysis of the world we live in, or in terms of modern psychology, of the human self.

On the other hand, Bergson argues, there is another approach to reality that is direct and immediate: *intuition*. By intuition we grasp the dynamic, temporal aspect of reality which mathematics and science are incapable of communicating. This intuition is qualitative, while intelligence is quantitative. Intuition grants us knowledge of the most basic aspect of reality: its constant flux. Intelligence abstracts what we call "solid objects" out of this dynamic, constantly changing process. Intelligence, moreover, communicates its spatial abstractions through symbols, while intuition is nonsymbolic, immediate knowledge that must be experienced oneself to be known: it cannot be communicated through symbolic expressions. As Bergson writes in his *Introduction to Metaphysics* (1903), "The inner life is all this at once: variety of qualities, continuity of progress, and unity of direction. It cannot be represented by images. But it is even less possible to represent it by *concepts*, that is, by abstract, general or simple ideas."[41] When we communicate the direct knowledge we have through intuition, then it automatically becomes conceptual, abstract and therefore no longer real intuition. It becomes intelligence.

An example may help us understand this distinction. Let us say we are standing in awe of a great work of art, perhaps a painting. Analysis can deliver a great deal of scientific knowledge about the painting: it can measure the light waves and colors found on the canvas; it can weigh the painting and measure its dimensions; we can even examine the painting under great magnification, to see how each color is used and how each brush stroke adds to the picture. But none of this abstract, intellectual work can convey the direct experience of a great work of art. Only direct, immediate intuition can do that—and we find that when we try to convey this experience through words, symbols or concepts, the essence of the experience is lost. So it is, Bergson believed, with our apprehension of all reality. Reality itself is a dynamic system which can only be fully grasped through a combination of intuition and intellect.

Based on this distinction, Bergson insists on two things. First, reality is a dynamic process which he calls "duration." The abstract, mathematical understanding of time as a fourth "dimension" is just a mathematical model. It fails to grasp the true essence of reality, which is in constant flux. Bergson insists on this understanding of reality against a background of more static interpretations of physics and physical reality. Second, scientific knowledge is limited. It is based on intelligence, which is only one of two ways of approaching reality. The other way, intuition, is equally valid and even more vital for human knowledge. This leaves room for another type of knowledge, other than and supplemental to science, namely philosophy. In Bergson's own words, "Metaphysics, then, is the science which claims to dispense with symbols."[42] By "dispense with symbols" Bergson means that metaphysics and philosophy proceed on the basis of intuition rather than intelligence.

Bergson's views were subject to criticism by rationalistic philosophers who followed the positivism of Comte and others,[43] which was a major intellectual force in France during the turn of the century. Bergson was in his day the greatest opponent of that naïve scientism which rejects any form of knowledge other than a "scientific" one. It would be false to characterize his philosophy on these grounds (as many did) as "anti-intellectual" or "anti-scientific." Bergson was pointing out, rightly in our view, the limitations of a scientific and mathematical approach to reality. This does not mean he was against science. On the contrary, he was a superior mathematician and spent his life interpreting and seeking to understand science. Nevertheless, he insisted that human knowledge can and must move beyond the merely scientific and intellectual. This point was taken over and extended by existentialism in the next generation of French thinkers.

A well-known example of his approach to science and philosophy is his most famous book, *Creative Evolution* (1907). In this work, Bergson accepts the general character of evolution, but he rejects the notions of random chance and materialism usually associated with it. He also rejects a deterministic understanding of evolution, which he calls "finalism." Instead, he develops a version of "vitalism," that is, the idea that there is a vital principle or impulse (in French, *élan vital*) which gives direction to natural selection and to the evolution of life and intelligence. Life has its own original direction and force, even when it is divided and multi-formed, growing over time into many different organisms. Bergson sees evolution as closer to a work of art than a machine. Like art, life cannot be predicted from its origins and component parts. But Bergson leaves open (or at least really never solves in this text) the question of the exact nature of this *élan vital*.[44] That is left for his last major work.

Bergson continued to be interested in the interpretation of science in the years following the publication of *Creative Evolution*. For example, he published a dialogue with Einstein concerning the proper interpretation of relativity theory, *Duration and Simultaneity* (1922).[45] But his major work for this period takes its cue from the social sciences rather than from the physical. Perhaps because of the religious or spiritual implications of his view of evolution, Bergson devoted his last major work to the issue of the role of religion and morality in human life and society.[46] The goal of *The Two Sources of Morality and Religion* was to interpret the social-scientific study of religion, arguing for individual freedom and creativity. He argued that careful sociological and psychological study of religion leads to the view that humans can experience, through intuition or "mysticism," the creative force or *élan vital* that Bergson identified with the Creator God.

In this text, Bergson distinguishes between an open society and a closed one.[47] A closed society is rigid, highly structured and turned in upon itself (recall that Bergson was writing these words during the rise of Fascism in Europe). Open societies, on the other hand, are dynamic and open to all people and to all other societies. The open society is characterized by creativity, community and the ethics of love.

There are also two types of religion—static and dynamic—that parallel the two types of societies. Static religion is also rigid, closed and rule-based. Static religion (like animal memory, or the mechanics of evolution) is subject to scientific, intelligent analysis. Bergson agrees that such religious institutions are based on social and psychological need (such as the fear of death, or the need for social order). But there is also dynamic religion, that is, a religion which is open, creative and mystical (or intuitive). Dynamic religion arises from an intuitive, mystical contact with the *élan vital*, now openly identified with God. "In our eyes," he wrote, "the ultimate end of mysticism is the establishment of a contact . . . with the creative effort which life itself manifests. This effort is of God, if it is not God himself."[48]

No doubt much of Bergson's philosophy is rather uncritical and imprecise. It leaves many questions unanswered. Yet his books are creative and suggestive. Real insights are often expressed in lucid prose. While we cannot, for example, accept the whole of his view of God, it is striking that a philosopher such as Bergson should end up, in the evolution of his thought, close to Christianity.[49] Bergson's philosophy was very popular in its day, and his influence has been significant. His insistence that human Being can only be known through direct, inner intuition (rather than external, scientific analysis) found its way into existentialism. French existentialist thinkers likewise insisted that static "things" are not the true essence of reality, but rather life and "existence" takes priority over any "essence." Finally, Bergson's philosophy of science and his theology bore fruit in process philosophy, as we shall shortly discover.

2. LOGIC AND LANGUAGE: EARLY ANALYTIC PHILOSOPHY

Early twentieth-century thinkers from the continent, along with the American C. S. Peirce, provided roots for the development of Western thought throughout the century. However, little has been said thus far about British philosophy, and this deficiency must now be addressed. In this chapter we will trace the rise of the analytic school from its roots in Vienna and Cambridge. In particular, we shall have a chance to survey the work of Bertrand Russell, G. E. Moore, the early Wittgenstein and the Vienna Circle. Although each held a distinctive philosophy, they were united in their insistence that idealism was false and that the way forward for philosophy lay in careful philosophical analysis and attention to the circumstances in which truth can be expressed.

Despite their many differences, there are interesting similarities in the thinking of Moore, Russell, the early Wittgenstein and the Vienna Circle. The analytic school of philosophy they founded was and is empiricist in its biases; that is, they followed in the footsteps of Locke and Hume by insisting that all knowledge about the world (as opposed to logical truths) comes through the senses. While Moore did not use the new symbolic logic developed by his friend Russell to any great degree, the others (Russell, Wittgenstein and the members of the Vienna Circle) were convinced that only a scientific—and that meant logical and empirical—approach to philosophical problems had any hope of a rational solution to the difficulties of the past. In particular, the new logic could show where ordinary language had confused and mislead philosophers in the past. Only careful analysis could "show the fly the way out of the fly-bottle" (Wittgenstein) and clarify the pseudo-problems of philosophy. The concerns of logic dominate the analytic tradition; yet in the history of British philosophy, the earliest of these "analytic" scholars was, by all accounts, G. E. Moore.

Moore

One of the most important philosophers of the twentieth century, George Edward Moore (1873-1958), led the way in the transition from British idealism to analytic philosophy in the English-speaking world.[1] With his friend and colleague Bertrand Russell, Moore transformed the way philosophy is done in Anglo-American circles.[2] His insistence on clarity, his dogged determination to ask the right question, his method of "analysis" and his refusal to countenance "nonsense" were tremendously influential in the early part of our century.

Moore was born in 1873 near London, and went through the normal public school education, which consisted for the most part in classics. He then advanced to Cambridge, where he planned to major in classics, in 1892. "I came up to Cambridge expecting to do nothing but Classics there, and expecting that also, all my life long, my work would consist in teaching Classics to the Sixth Form of some Public School—a prospect to which I looked forward with pleasure."[3] Such a life, however, was not to be. Instead, Moore joined a venerable (and secret) debating society known as the Cambridge Conversazione Society, or "The Apostles."[4] This intellectual and stimulating group included philosophy professors and lecturers, which sparked Moore's interest in the subject. Many of Moore's friends at Cambridge were members of this society, and he was elected a member himself in his second year. His friendship with Bertrand Russell, also an Apostle, was the catalyst which caused him to change his career from classics to philosophy; Moore ended up with first class honors in both subjects for his B.A.

In this early period, both Moore and Russell were idealists, following in the tradition of F. H. Bradley and the British Neo-Hegelians.[5] It was Moore who, after finishing his B.A. and earning a six-year "prize" fellowship at Trinity College, led the way out of idealism and into a Platonic and pluralistic realism. Reflecting on this move many years later, Russell wrote that Moore took the lead in the rebellion, and I followed with a sense of emancipation. Bradley had argued that everything that common sense believes in is mere appearance; we reverted to the opposite extreme, and thought that *everything* is real that common sense, uninfluenced by philosophy or theology, supposes real. With a sense of escaping from prison, we allowed ourselves to think that grass is green, that the sun and the stars would exist if no one was aware of them, and also that there is a pluralistic timeless world of Platonic ideas. The world which had been thin and logical, suddenly became rich and varied and solid.[6]

Moore published his second prize dissertation as "The Nature of Judgment" (1899).[7] Having previously published papers that were idealist in nature, at only twenty-six Moore was already undermining the philosophy of his teachers through his own careful, analytical work. Like Frege and Husserl, Moore insisted that our judgments of true and false are exclusive of any inner psychological states. Contrary to most British empirical thought, especially J. S. Mill, Moore argued that logic is not an empirical science. "From our description of a judgment, there must, then, disappear all reference either to our mind or to the world."[8] At the turn of the century, Russell and Moore believed that truth was based upon Platonic concepts or objects of thought which exist independently of our minds, and for some concepts, even of space and time (what Kant called a priori truths). They were realists of a Platonic sort at this early stage, rather than materialists. Moore's "concepts" included all sorts of things. Yet this early view did undermine idealism, which insisted that mental reality or ideas are the foundation of all truth. Against this view, Moore was an ontological pluralist, that is, he held that there were many distinct parts of reality.

Our previous discussion of the demise of idealism was clearly incomplete without the early work of Moore and Russell. Yet Moore is distinct from Frege, Husserl and Bergson in that he arrived at his position through logic and the careful analysis of propositions, rather than through any interest in the natural sciences.

Near the end of his fellowship at Trinity, Moore published two works that brought him world-wide fame, his *Principia Ethica* and "The Refutation of Idealism," both published in 1903.[9] These works establish two of

Moore's lifelong interests: ethics and the philosophy of mind (or philosophical psychology). His famous article attacks the proposition that to exist is to be perceived (*esse est percipi*, in Berkeley's famous Latin phrase), a view Moore found to be essential to idealism. He attacked this idea by distinguishing between acts of consciousness and the objects of consciousness.[10] If I look at a blue ball, the sensation of blueness which I see is different from the act of consciousness by which I see the blue ball. Moore will later call this first thing, the sensation itself, "sense-data." Because there is a difference between this object of consciousness and the phenomenon of consciousness itself, it cannot be the case that the claim "to be is to be perceived" holds for all perceived things. The *act* of perception that senses the ball, and *what* is seen—the blueness and roundness of the ball itself—are different, according to Moore.

Moore's work in the philosophy of perception reminds one, in some respects at least, of Husserl. Indeed, Moore found Husserl's position (as mediated through the Husserlian psychologist Dr. Messer) to be the most important he had encountered on this subject. He also found that Husserl's teacher, Brentano, had anticipated many of his arguments in the area of ethics. When Moore gave lectures on philosophical psychology in 1909, he sounded very much like a phenomenologist.[11] But Moore's interest in philosophical psychology focused almost wholly on perception, and he soon developed his famous "common sense" approach to our knowledge of the external world. Nevertheless, Moore remained a very careful analyst of mental experience, especially in the area of sense perception. In fact, he gave annual lectures on the philosophy of mind until his retirement in 1939.

Another 1903 work, *Principia Ethica*, was Moore's most famous book among his own contemporaries. Like his earlier work on judgment, in this book Moore argues against psychologism and subjectivism. The concept of moral goodness, he insists, cannot be reduced to mere psychological states such as pleasure; hedonism and classical utilitarianism are both guilty of such reductionism in Moore's view. The key to these arguments is something Moore calls the "naturalistic fallacy." He insists that goodness itself cannot be reduced or analyzed into any other concept. It is simple and *sui generis*, its own kind of thing and not another; in fact, the motto of Moore's book is a quote from Bishop Butler: "Everything is what it is and not another thing." Morality cannot be reduced to a description of the way the world is; what ought to be is different from what is. The naturalistic fallacy is the false move from "is" to "ought," that is, from the way the world is to what ought to be. With this argument Moore also rebuffs idealist ethics, which based the good on metaphysical properties. The good, for Moore, can never be reduced to or explained by factual or metaphysical truths.

Moore's ethics in this book is Platonic; the good is outside of time and space, objective but not reducible to matter or psychological experience. What is good is intrinsically good, worth having for its own sake. There may be many such goods in human life; Moore discusses artistic experience and friendship as illustrations. In decisions of moral duty Moore advocates a kind of Platonic or idealist utilitarianism: act in a way that brings the greatest number of highest goods for all concerned. Even with this limited end, however, it can be difficult to judge what our moral duty is in a particular situation. "It now remains to insist that, even with regard to these immediate effects, we can only hope to discover which, among a few alternatives, will *generally* produce the greatest balance of good in the immediate future."[12] Moore's arguments had the effect of undermining any absolute rule-based ethics.

Moore's book was very well received and discussed among his Cambridge friends, especially the Apostles and a group of London intellectuals, writers and artists known as "The Bloomsbury Club." This latter group included a number of Apostles as well, such as the philosopher and economist John Maynard Keynes, along with other bright and influential artists, critics and thinkers (e.g., the novelist Virginia Woolf and her husband). Through his influence in Cambridge and London, Moore became a famous figure in British intellectual life. His book was amazingly popular among the educated readership of Great Britain and throughout the English speaking world for a number of potential reasons. It may have been because Moore made space for a variety of "goods" in life, including art. It may have been because Moore undermined any strict ethics of commandments such as one associates with Victorian culture. Perhaps, too, Western thought needed some kind of objective grounds for ethics apart from Christian belief in God, which Europe was in the process of discarding (as, indeed, almost all of the

Apostles did). Perhaps all of these motives were at work in making *Principia Ethica* so widely read and discussed. Leonard Woolf describes the attraction of this text in his autobiography:

> Moore's distinction between things good in themselves or as ends and things good merely as means, his passionate search for truth in his attempt in *Principia Ethica* to determine what things are good in themselves, answered our questions, not with the religious voice of Jehovah from Mount Sinai or Jesus with his Sermon from the Mount, but with the more divine voice of plain common-sense.[13]

Moore left Cambridge in 1904 when his fellowship at Trinity expired. He was wealthy enough to continue his philosophical research on the basis of private means. Between the years of 1904-11 he read widely in philosophy, including a careful study of Russell's work. Moore's ontology evolved during this period from a Platonic pluralism to a common sense realism. This view was worked out in reflections on various philosophers, including phenomenologists Russell, Thomas Reid, William James and Hume. Of these, no doubt Russell was the most important, as Moore himself acknowledged: "I should say that I certainly have been more influenced by him than by any other single philosopher."[14] In his 1905 lecture on the nature of objects of perception, Moore began to argue that we have good grounds for affirming the reality of the objects we perceive around us, although we cannot explicitly prove that they exist. In his 1909 essay on Hume's philosophy, he asserts that those who believe in external objects are just as warranted in their belief as the skeptic is in his disbelief that we know they exist.[15]

In 1911 Moore returned to Cambridge, where he was to spend the rest of his active philosophical life, becoming professor in 1925. The studies of his earlier period resulted in two famous papers, setting forth his common sense realism: "A Defense of Common Sense," which appeared in a volume surveying British philosophy; and his lecture to the British Academy, "Proof of an External World."[16] Moore here follows Reid in defending our "common sense" view of the world, but in a way that differs significantly from Reid himself. In both of these lectures, Moore rejects fully the idealism of his teachers. Unlike the idealists, he asserts that direct perception gives us good grounds for claiming that we know certain things exist, such as our own body. In fact, Moore claims to know such truisms as "other humans have bodies" with *certainty*. He is unclear on the grounds of this certainty and never really answers this question to anyone's satisfaction, including his own. Yet his position is a wise move against skepticism. Any epistemological stance may be uncertain and in need of correction, Moore can claim; however, that does not mean we don't know simple things such as: these words are printed on a page; or, I have a body. The question of *what basis* we have for such claims is not as important as the fact (if it is a fact) that we do know them. Moore thus concluded his lecture to the British Academy: "I can know things, which I cannot prove; and among things which I certainly did know, even if (as I think) I could not prove them, were the premises of my two proofs" (i.e., two human hands exist).[17] The simple premises of common sense are at least as certain as any argument the skeptic may make against them.

Moore's teaching and publication helped define analytic philosophy in the Anglo-American tradition. While he published few works, his papers and books were very influential. His teaching and its influence on a whole generation of thinkers was just as important, if not more so. The golden age of Cambridge philosophy was the 1930s when Moore, Wittgenstein (who succeeded Moore in 1939 as professor) and Russell were all active, and philosophers from across the world came to study with them.

Russell

Any adequate study of the life of either Russell or Moore will necessarily include the other man. The two were friends and coworkers for years, and together they reshaped the face of Anglo-American philosophy. However, their philosophies and methods were distinct. Of the two, it was Bertrand Russell (1872-1970) who was the more famous.[18] He epitomized in the view of most scholars what it meant to be an analytic philosopher. It was Russell who attracted the young Wittgenstein to Cambridge, and it was Russell who was awarded the Nobel Prize for literature in 1950. From the reception of his *magnum opus, Principia Mathematica* (1910-1913) until his death, Russell was the most famous living philosopher in the English speaking world.[19]

Russell came from an aristocratic and "free-thinking" family.[20] His grandfather was Lord John Russell, who was twice prime minister and elevated by Queen Victoria to earldom. Lord John introduced the landmark Reform Bill of 1832 and is generally remembered for his progressive politics. Bertrand Russell's father and mother were likewise controversial and progressive; for example, they were devoted to such causes as women's suffrage and birth control. When he was two, young Bertrand lost first his mother and sister, then his father. He was raised by his conservative grandparents, rather than the freethinkers that his parents named in their will.

In many ways Russell's social philosophy and ethics mirrored the views of his deceased parents in rebellion against the traditional Victorian values of his grandparents. Russell did not like the conservative politics and ethics of his grandparents, nor their Christian religion. Like his parents, Russell had a lifelong interest in ethics and politics, often taking liberal stands on controversial issues, and much of his voluminous writing was devoted to such topics.[21] Later in life, Bertrand Russell the philosopher became the third Earl Russell. He continued to be interested in politics and got involved in the social issues of his day, including sexual ethics, pacifism and nuclear disarmament.

While Russell published books and essays in many subjects, and indeed had an enormous literary output, his most impressive and highly lauded work was in the area of symbolic logic and the philosophy of mathematics.[22] Russell tells us he became interested in philosophy through consideration of religion and mathematics.[23] Math was his earliest and longest-lived academic love. During his early life with his grandparents, he considered and rejected arguments for the existence of God and at the same time fell in love with mathematics. He went to Trinity College in Cambridge University at the age of eighteen and studied mathematics for three years. After meeting Moore and some of the other Apostles (including Whitehead, who was his math teacher) Russell turned to the "moral sciences" (i.e., philosophy). Russell earned a First Class in both mathematics and moral sciences at Cambridge—an early sign of his intellectual gifts. Early in his philosophical studies he was attracted to idealism, being influenced especially by Bradley and McTaggart. But with Moore, Russell soon led a worldwide revolt again Anglo-American idealism, changing the history of philosophy for the twentieth century.[24]

Russell's contributions to logic and the foundations of mathematics are his greatest contributions and the work which made him in his lifetime the most famous and respected English-speaking philosopher in the world. This work is very technical, and like Frege's, of interest mostly to specialists. Here we can only indicate some of the goals and effects of his labors in logic.

Independently of Frege, Russell began a work in logicism, that is, in the reduction of mathematics to logical truths. Russell was a classical foundationalist, looking for certain knowledge. It bothered him when some mathematical proof was sloppy or unsound. He believed that by rigorously showing that arithmetic reduced to logical laws, he could find certain truth in at least formal domains of knowledge. Later he encountered Frege's work and was influenced by it (as well as critical of it).

The *Principia Mathematica* was Russell's greatest work and his major contribution to logic and the philosophy of mathematics. At this early stage in his career, Russell believed that logical truths were a part of the world. In 1919 he wrote: "Logic is concerned with the real world just as truly as zoology; though with its more abstract and general features."[25] Later the early work of his brilliant student Wittgenstein would change his mind on this matter. Russell would then come to believe the common view today, namely that logical truths are tautologies that can tell us nothing of the real world. As to the dream of reducing mathematics to logic, in 1931 the brilliant Austrian mathematician and logician, Kurt Gödel, demonstrated that this dream was in fact logically impossible.[26] The influence of Russell's work in logic, therefore, remains one of the many significant advances he made while pursuing a goal that eventually eluded him.

One very influential "spin-off" of Russell's logical work was his so-called theory of descriptions for proper nouns, names and the like.[27] In his early work, Russell was not particularly interested in language. Like Frege, Russell saw language as a clumsy tool, which should be corrected and replaced by a logically pure, symbolic language. He believed that clean, sharp, symbolic logic could solve many of the problems created by the blunt instrument of ordinary language. One such problem, to take only one example, has to do with reference. Sometimes the objects referred to in sentences do not exist, or are just plain silly. Are these propositions true or false, or neither? For example, consider this sentence: "The present King of France is bald." Our immediate response must be, "This is false!" since there is no reigning monarch in France. However, notice this: the negation of this sentence would be, "The present King of France is not bald." And this proposition looks just as wrong as the first one! Yet, logic dictates that the negation of a false proposition must be true. What's gone wrong here?

Russell argued that denoting words, like "the golden mountain," "the President of the United States" or "Harry's wife," do not really refer to objects at all. Rather, denoting words can and should be logically translated into descriptions. Russell held that "even proper names, as a rule, really stand for descriptions."[28] Russell thought that such troublesome elements of ordinary language could be analyzed away into clean logic. So, to return to our bald monarch, "The present King of France is bald" can be analyzed logically into the following conjunction of simple propositions: there is one and only one X who is presently a King of France, and who is bald. This conjunction can (and should) be written in symbolic logic. Now it turns out that, logically, if any part of a conjunction of propositions is false, then the whole thing is false. Because "there is an X who is King of France" is false, so is the whole description. So, after careful logical analysis, we see that the proposition "The present King of France is bald" is indeed false: not the sentence itself, but rather the symbolic translation which Russell insists is its true meaning. The important, and at the time (1905) revolutionary idea in all of this is that ordinary language must be translated into symbolic logic (at least in some cases) in order to evaluate its truth.

But what about the other sentence, "The present King of France is not bald"? That ordinary sentence translates, according to the theory of descriptions, into the following conjunction of propositions: "there is one and only one X who is presently a King of France, and who is not bald." A little reflection shows that this conjunction, too, is false. What this thought experiment reveals is not that the same proposition can be both true and false: Russell denied this, and indeed his theory was created to assist in this denial. Rather, it shows, according to Russell, that ordinary language is hopelessly confused and must be translated into symbolic logic—"analyzed"—in order to determine its truth value. Arguments such as these created the very idea of "analytic philosophy."

Russell called his philosophy "logical atomism."[29] By this he meant that the world can be arranged into logically simple facts for analysis, something like "This patch of color is red." These simple facts can be known directly through experience. Here we see the empiricism that Russell inherited from earlier British philosophers coming into its own, over against the idealism of his youth. These logically simple facts combine to create complex truths that describe reality. Therefore, to test the truth of any complex idea we need a symbolic logical analysis of the supposed truth, which we analyze into its simple or "basic" propositions. We can then test the simple propositions to see if they are true. We can see, then, that Russell used the new symbolic logic to propose new solutions to difficult philosophical problems. For many thinkers of his generation, this was the very definition of analytic philosophy.

Russell's contributions to logic and epistemology gained for him an international reputation. However, his radical political and religious views kept him from several important academic posts. For example, City College in New York offered Russell a chair in philosophy in 1940, only to be blocked in the courts by conservative popular opinion, including that of several prominent clergymen.[30] This only brought Russell greater fame and appreciation among academics generally. From 1941 to 1943 he lectured to a more popular audience in Philadelphia; these lectures eventually became his bestselling book, *A History of Western Philosophy* (the last chapter of which, like Hegel's history a century earlier, culminates in the author's own philosophy!). In 1944 he returned to Cambridge and was elected a fellow for life of Trinity College. His most important philosophical works in this latter period of life were in epistemology, especially *An Inquiry into Meaning and Truth* (1940) and *Human Knowledge: Its Scope and Limits* (1948). He died in 1970, widely acclaimed as perhaps the greatest philosopher of his time.

Russell on Christianity. Russell was certainly the most famous English-speaking philosopher of his day. He used the weight of his reputation as a philosophical genius to forward a number of political, ethical and religious causes. He is in fact remembered by many Christians as the author of a famous essay, "Why I Am Not a Christian" (1927). While philosophy of religion is one area where he made no original contributions, because his criticism of Christianity has become well known some brief remarks on his views of God and religion are in order.

Russell spent his life searching for certainty. He found it, to his mind, in logic, mathematics and natural science. Russell's rather naïve scientism was a result of his belief in systematic doubt: "the whole subject [of this book] is the product of Cartesian doubt. I observe that men err, and I ask myself what I must do to avoid error."[31] Only science, logic and mathematics provide sources of certain knowledge; therefore, only what they teach can be really known. It doesn't require much reflection to see that religious and ethical propositions will, in this kind of scientism, be found wanting. Russell thought that religious ideas cannot be supported by science, logic and fact; therefore they cannot be held with certainty—that is, they cannot serve as solid sources for knowledge about reality. This also applies to ethics. In fact, this insistence landed Russell in a strange position. As Wayne Booth has brilliantly demonstrated, his own epistemological dogmas contradicted his most precious and passionately held intellectual values, including his valuation of science.[32] Russell's naïve scientism put him in a position of performative contradiction within the vast corpus of his work: he held very strongly a number of beliefs (e.g., fear as such is bad, or rigorous thought is valuable) which other parts of his philosophical writings did not allow him to assert as known. Russell's response to this seems to have been to resort to bluff and bluster, that is, to use his position as a famous philosopher to make blanket assertions that, when examined, have little or no evidence in their favor. This is true of much of his popular essays and lectures on religion, ethics and politics. E. S. Brightman, in discussing Russell's philosophy of religion, correctly saw that in his criticisms of Christianity, "he impresses one here as being more concerned to reject than to define, more concerned to express his dislike for Christianity than to present an explanation of what Christianity is."[33] For example, it just plain false that "the Christian religion, as organized in its churches, has been and still is the principle enemy of moral progress in the world."[34]

If we ignore Russell's rhetoric, forgive his naïve scientism and overlook his bully-pulpit tactics in expressing his own feelings about religion and ethics, is there anything left of his critique of Christianity? Yes, indeed. Christians have been too ready to dismiss the objections of their critics over the centuries. We would do well to listen to Russell's criticisms of Christianity, since they represent areas of life and thought that need improvement. What is more, his views have become standard fare in our culture. Russell's views on religion, for better or worse, were and are very popular, perhaps even becoming the standard perspective of our modern world: religion and values are a matter of personal, private opinion, not of knowledge and reason.

Russell's first attack on religion is a moral one. Organized religion has retarded progress in both knowledge (especially science) and social ethics. Standard examples of this include the Catholic Church's silencing of Galileo and the Crusades. Now I believe Russell greatly exaggerates things in his criticism of the church. But rather than be defensive, let us acknowledge that the church has indeed made many moral errors in the past. The record of the Christian church is a mixed one, with some good and some bad, rather than the completely unsavory picture that Russell paints. Russell in fact has little evidence in favor of his sweeping claims about the church inhibiting moral and scientific progress. Contrary to Russell, there are many wonderful things the world owes to Christianity and to the Bible. However, the record of sin, stupidity and hatred is there in church history for all to read as well. Let us acknowledge these facts, and seek to overcome them in the present and future life of the church.

At the same time, we would level a similar charge against Russell's religion of science and "facts." While we will not make the sweeping claim that science has always led to destruction, death, arrogance and the devastation of the earth, there can be no doubt that science and technology have often done so. Science has a record of evil too. No human institution—religious, scientific, political—of any long duration is free of sin, corruption and abuse.

The second of Russell's charges is against the Bible, specifically against the moral excellence of Jesus. He objects that Jesus was not uniformly a good man. Against the biblical picture of Christ, Russell objects to the teachings on hell, the cursing of the fig tree, the condemnation of his enemies and the teaching about the unpardonable sin. Here I think that Russell seems ignorant of the vast literature surrounding the proper approach to biblical interpretation. His remarks are glib, off the cuff and unscientific—that is, they proceed without reference to an entire body of knowledge compiled by academic, sophisticated biblical studies. For example, Jesus' teachings on hell must be understood in terms of the

general way the afterlife was discussed in his own day. His stories, parables and metaphors used the everyday world of his time as the substance
out of which he created his teachings. Further, even to approach Jesus'
sayings along these lines would be only the barest beginning of an adequate, scientific approach to interpreting the biblical teachings about
judgment and afterlife. Literature on this subject fills many shelves of the
library at Cambridge University, yet Russell eschews such academic considerations for a simplistic, even naïve, reading of the texts. One gets the
impression he is not really interested in finding out what Christians have,
for centuries, replied to just the kind of objections he makes. There is not
much for us to learn here from Russell, I'm afraid.

The final problem Russell names shows more promise, and it is epistemological. Religious faith has no evidence, he claims. There is a famous
episode, reported later by others, in which a woman asked Russell at a
party what he would say to God if, upon dying, he were to meet his
Maker. "Not enough evidence," Russell replied; "I would say to God,
'more evidence.'"[35] Russell was certainly wrong to think that belief in God
and immortality were the central tenets of Christian faith. Yet belief in a
God surely is part of that faith. And even if Russell's dogmatism of doubt
and "proof" must be rejected, the call for some evidence in favor of
belief is not unreasonable.

Russell reviews the arguments for the existence of God in several
places, at different times of his life, yet always with the same result: we
have no reason to believe there is a God.[36] There is no sound evidence
that he exists, according to Russell. Our first response returns to the criticisms of Russell's approach to religion and ethics made by Wayne Booth.
Why should the believer doubt that God exists, just because no evidential,
public, rational proof can be given? After all, as Alvin Plantinga has
argued, is it just as hard to "prove" that other humans have minds as to
"prove" that God exists?[37] The problem here is with Russell's Cartesian
approach to epistemology, that is, to his principle of doubt. It may well be
that belief in God is "properly basic" without need of empirical justification, as is my belief that Sally has a mind, or that the universe did not
begin five minutes ago (with all the evidence of age built in, including
our own memories).[38]

A further reply to Russell is that his overview of the arguments is weak.

Once again, we find that Russell too easily dismisses views that he doesn't like, without bothering to examine sophisticated, scholarly versions of the arguments. For example, Russell is satisfied to recycle this old chestnut in his discussion of the cosmological argument: if everything must have a cause, then who created God?[39] In a famous radio debate with the Catholic philosopher F. C. Copleston, Russell was not able to get away with anything so simplistic. But his responses, even then, were weak. For example, in keeping with his logicism, Russell insisted that only analytic propositions are necessary, not things.[40] But that is simply a piece of sheer prejudice on his part. After all, certain *things* are impossible (like a ball that is both red and green all over at the same time). If certain *things* are impossible, then by rigorous logic, it follows that, possibly, certain *things* are necessary. In other words, if the logical category of *impossible* can apply to things, then it must be the case that *possible* and *necessary* may apply to them also.

Yet even here we can learn from Russell. While Christians do not believe in God because of arguments (here Plantinga is surely right), nevertheless some kind of public argument can and should be made in favor of ideas implicit in the Christian faith. And here, as in Russell's day, Christian intellectuals have work to do. In the broad intellectual culture of the West the case still needs to be made for faith on rational grounds and in response to the (often rather confused) criticisms of atheists. During Russell's lifetime, Christian philosophers had a lot of work to do, explaining clearly and logically what evidence there might be in favor of some Christian ideas, and also explaining the relationship between religious faith, religious language and empirical evidence. This much, at least, was a serious challenge from analytic philosophy to Christian thought. How Christians responded will be the subject of the last section of this chapter, as well as a later chapter on Christian philosophy.

In conclusion, we should listen carefully to Russell's complaints against Christianity. Christians who ignore their critics are acting rather foolishly. Still, in the long run, most of his so-called arguments against Christian faith are open to serious question. If all that Christianity has against it are the arguments marshaled by Russell, the case for Christianity must be quite strong.

The Early Wittgenstein

After Russell and Moore came the final member of the Cambridge triumvirate of world-famous philosophers in the early part of the twentieth century: Ludwig Wittgenstein (1885-1951).[41] Wittgenstein's fame and influence are great, and his work has come to eclipse that of his teachers at Cambridge, Moore and Russell. One could even argue that Wittgenstein is one of the two most important philosophers in the twentieth century, the other being Martin Heidegger.[42] His ideas, publications and influence developed in two distinct stages, usually called the "early" and the "later" Wittgenstein.[43] Because the early Wittgenstein is so closely linked to Russell and the Vienna Circle, we will discuss his early life and work in this chapter, canvassing the further development of his thought a little later on.

Wittgenstein is associated with Cambridge philosophy, but he was originally from Vienna. Born into one of the leading families of the Austro-Hungarian Empire, Wittgenstein's father was a wealthy, powerful captain of industry and a major patron of the arts, while his mother was a cultured woman of taste and a trained concert pianist. From a large family with Jewish ancestry, Wittgenstein was raised in luxury, beauty and artistic excellence. All of his brothers and sisters were given the finest education and expected to achieve greatness. All of the brothers but two committed suicide. This background can help explain much of the intense character of Wittgenstein's personality and some elements of his philosophical style.[44]

Wittgenstein was taught first by private tutors, then sent to learn practical, technical subjects at a *Realschule* in Lintz (where Adolf Hitler was, coincidentally, also a student). He then attended Manchester University, which had a strong reputation in engineering and the natural sciences. Wittgenstein was interested in the new technology of aeronautics and designed a new type of propeller. It was during these studies that he became interested in mathematics and then in the foundations of mathematics. This led him to Russell's *The Principles of Mathematics*, a book that was to change the young man's life.

This encounter with the philosophy of mathematics was to prove decisive. Wittgenstein never did anything halfway. He was seized by his interest in, and genius for, the new symbolic logic that Frege, Russell and Whitehead had just developed. During the summer vacation of 1911,

Wittgenstein traveled to Jena to visit the elderly Frege. Frege in turn sent him to study with Russell.

The next term Wittgenstein began to show up at Russell's (very small) lectures at Trinity College, Cambridge. He deeply admired Russell and began to pester him about logic and the foundations of mathematics at all hours of the day and night. Russell saw promise in the young man and encouraged it. Wittgenstein told his friends that this encouragement saved his life (he had been thinking of suicide while a student at Manchester).

It was Wittgenstein's goal to create a work of philosophical genius—or give up philosophy. He did not have any formal training in the history of philosophy and generally found the work of prior thinkers to be "rubbish" (a word he used a great deal). He became Russell's protégé and greatly impressed Moore. They began to treat him as their equal. Learning that he was indeed capable of world-class work in logic, Wittgenstein threw himself into the task. Never one to do anything small, he believed he could solve all the main problems in logic. In order to isolate himself for this great work, so as to better concentrate, Wittgenstein decided to leave England. He lived in a small hut for two years, about as far from European civilization as one could get and still be in Europe: Skjolden, Norway. Yet such was his reputation for genius that Moore visited him there and took notes on his progress in logical theory.[45] However, Wittgenstein's arrogance and bad temper upon not being allowed to apply for a B.A. ruptured their friendship.

A strong sense of internal duty to his own inner sense of right lies behind many of Wittgenstein's odd ways and decisions. At this point in his life, this sense of duty led him back to Austria. World War I had begun, and Wittgenstein volunteered for service. Even though he could easily have served as an officer, he decided to forsake the kind of preference his family could obtain for him. He served as a front-line enlisted man but continued to carry around with him his notes on logical problems. This terrible war affected an entire generation, including Wittgenstein, who was never quite the same again.

Wittgenstein bought the only book left in a small bookstore during the war: Tolstoy's *The Gospels in Brief*. It became one of his favorite books, and from his diary we know he considered himself a Christian. However, he was a loner and never joined any church. His kind of religion was entirely private, and in fact mostly ethical. In many ways Wittgenstein's approach to religion resembled that of Kant: the essence of religion is a strict duty-based morality. Both Kant and Wittgenstein held traditional dogmatics in contempt. Systematic theologians claim to know, they believed, far more than any human rightly could.

Wittgenstein's approach to war service was in line with his strict, dutiful ethics. He took a very dangerous job near the front lines and was captured by the Italians. While in prison camp he wrote one of the greatest philosophical masterpieces of the twentieth century: the *Tractatus Logico-Philosophicus* (1921). This was the only philosophical book that Wittgenstein published during his lifetime; his other masterpiece, the *Philosophical Investigations*, was prepared for publication just after his death. After the war, Wittgenstein adopted Tolstoy's idealistic attitude toward work and wealth, and he gave away the entirety of his huge fortune (he was probably the wealthiest single male in Europe at the time). Ironically, he was thus unable to financially support the publication of his great work. Without Russell's intervention, who also agreed to write a preface, the book might not have come out. Russell's friend C. K. Ogden agreed to publish the work in the series he edited, "International Library of Psychology, Philosophy and Scientific Method." The German publication (1921) of the *Tractatus* was filled with errors, and Ogden agreed to publish a German-English edition.[46] Wittgenstein was fortunate to find in Ogden a careful, patient editor who made numerous corrections, wrote many letters asking for explanations and translated the work himself.[47]

The *Tractatus* is indeed a work of great genius. Like many great works, its interpretation is still a matter of no little debate.[48] Wittgenstein believed not only that he had solved the major problems of the new logic developed by Frege, Russell and Whitehead, but of traditional philosophy as a whole, such as metaphysics and ethics. In the preface, he wrote: "The book deals with the problems of philosophy and shows, as I believe, that the method of formulating these problems rests on the misunderstanding of the logic of our language. . . . I am, therefore, of the opinion that the problems have in essentials been finally solved." In the *Tractatus* Wittgenstein believed he has solved the problems of logic, and at the same time, the problems of traditional philosophy such as metaphysics and ethics. He was all of thirty-two years old at the time.

What are the main teachings and insights of this rather slim volume? One goal, in the area of logic, was to show that the truths of logic are all tautologies: they tell us nothing about the world. Frege, Russell and Whitehead had held that the truths of logic they were developing were the most general facts about the universe; Russell in particular accepted the results of Wittgenstein's argument, but was also quite disappointed (he tended to give up on formal logic after this).

But while the *Tractatus* is a work in logic, its primary thrust is not merely logical, but metaphysical and even ethical, as Wittgenstein himself remarked.[49] Wittgenstein's purpose was to demonstrate the limits of language, or better, of meaningful language, and to show the underlying logic of our speech. His arguments are presented in a series of numbered propositions, borrowing the structure of *Principia Mathematica*. One says "arguments," but in fact the work is very sparse and sharp: almost like a surgeon's scalpel, cutting to the root of the issue and using short aphorisms or sayings more than arguments in any traditional sense.

Wittgenstein makes two basic distinctions in his early philosophy: between sense and nonsense, and between saying and showing. An understanding of these two distinctions will get us to the heart of the early Wittgenstein. He follows Russell in believing that atomic facts, or states of affairs, are the basic elements of reality: "The existence and non-existence of states of affairs is reality" (2.06).[50] A state of affairs, in turn, is a combination of objects in the world (2.01). We use language, then, to "picture" or model states of affairs to ourselves (2.1). A proposition is a logical model of a particular state of affairs (4.023). A thought is a logical picture of facts (3). A true proposition shows the way the world is (2.222). The totality of propositions is language (4.001).

For the early Wittgenstein, then, meaningful language is a logical "picture" or blueprint of reality: "The picture is a model of reality" (2.12). Sense or meaning comes from the elements of the proposition depicting possible states of affairs. "What a picture represents is its sense" (2.221). This is Wittgenstein's famous "picture theory of language." The propositions of language give us a blueprint, in logical space, of objects in a particular state. If this state obtains, then the proposition is true; if it does not obtain, then the proposition is false. The truths of logic, on the other hand, have no sense because they don't give us a description of any state of affairs in the world of objects (which is the only world there is according to the *Tractatus*). That is why logical propositions have no sense: they are true because they are tautologies, or false because they are a contradiction (4.462).

Thus the truths of logic, along with logically contradictory statements, have no sense. This "no-sense" is not the same thing as nonsense, however; nonsense for Wittgenstein means that a sentence is a pseudo-proposition, which looks like it says something but its logical analysis is meaningless. A sentence may therefore look like a proposition and not be one.

Take as an example the sentence, "The universe has a purpose." Such a sentence cannot be divided into elementary propositions which describe states of affairs. Thus, this sentence in fact says nothing: it is nonsense. It tries to say what can only be shown. This second distinction is just as important for the *Tractatus*. Certain things that are important can only be shown; they cannot be said. For example, the way in which propositions manage to create blueprints of the world can only be shown, it cannot be said. "What expresses *itself* in language, *we* cannot express by means of language. Propositions *show* the logical form of reality. . . . What *can* be shown *cannot* be said" (4.121 and 4.1212). For Wittgenstein, therefore, analysis demonstrates that only empirical or purely logical propositions are meaningful.

What, then, of ethics or religion? Is their language nonsense? Wittgenstein believed that such important matters can be lived, but not talked about. "The sense of the world must lie outside of the world" (6.41) and therefore cannot be expressed in meaningful language. Likewise, "It is clear that ethics cannot be put into words" (6.421). That which is beyond the world can be *shown*, but it cannot be *said*. For Wittgenstein, clearly, the best worship of God would be in silence.

This position is not a new one. Early Christian theologians, following Neoplatonic views, held that God is beyond human speech. Their position is called negative or apophatic theology. To take a famous example, the first Western book on the study of signs and symbols (semiotics) was a book on how to rightly interpret the Bible: Augustine's *On Christian Teaching*. In it the great theologian remarks that the being of God is beyond human speech.[51] Wittgenstein takes this apophatic approach to anything transcendent, anything beyond the physical world, such as religion, ethics and aesthetics. This leads Wittgenstein to the famous final proposition of the book: "Whereof one cannot speak, thereof one must be silent." This echoes his claim in the preface: "The whole sense of the book might be summed up in the following words: what can be said at all can be said clearly, and what we cannot talk about we must pass over in silence."

But what of the sentences that make up the *Tractatus* itself? Must they be described as nonsense too? Take, for example, Wittgenstein's assertion that "what can be said at all can be said clearly." Does this describe a fact, some logical form of objects in the world? Clearly not, and yet Wittgenstein believed it was the "whole sense" of his book. Thus the book itself is not science, but philosophy, and therefore nonsense. Wittgenstein knew this was the case. In the penultimate paragraph he wrote, "My propositions serve as elucidations in the following way: anyone who understands me eventually recognizes them as nonsensical." What the *Tractatus* gives us, then, is not facts but rather a whole new way of seeing the world: "He must surmount these propositions; then he sees the world rightly" (6.54). Wittgenstein firmly believed his propositions were true: "the *truth* of the thoughts that are here communicated seems to me unassailable and definitive" (preface). Yet, his thoughts are not about the world; rather, they help us to see the world the right way. They are an attempt to say what cannot be said, what in fact can only be shown.

Having served in the war, been released from concentration camp, given away his vast fortune and solved the problems of philosophy, Wittgenstein turned to "useful" work: he became an elementary school teacher. His great *Tractatus* was misunderstood by many readers, even Russell and Frege. Those who most appreciated and understood it either worked with the author (such as F. P. Ramsey) or were members of his own culture, of turn-of-the-century Vienna. Such were the members of the so-called Vienna Circle and of the movement of thought—logical positivism—which they began.

The Vienna Circle

Logical positivism is the name given to a movement in analytic philosophy which began in Europe in the early part of the twentieth century. In some ways, analytic philosophy was identified with logical positivism for a good part of this century. Also known as "logical empiricism," this movement is associated with the work of the "Vienna Circle," headed by Moritz Schlick (1882-1936).[52] These thinkers were inspired by the logical work of Frege, Russell and the early Wittgenstein, and they were very much in favor of a fully scientific approach to philosophical problems. Like their predecessors, they believed that a real solution to the problems and confusions of philosophy was at hand through logical analysis and conceptual clarification.

Schlick came to Vienna in 1922 as a professor of the philosophy of science, at the urging of the "Ernst Mach Society" which formed the core of the Vienna Circle.[53] Schlick soon formed a regular seminar for discussion, and under his direction this group of like-minded empiricists had a positively evangelistic zeal for promoting their views. Members of the Circle included mathematicians, physicists and social scientists, as well as philosophers. Among the members of the group, Rudolf Carnap (1891-1970) and Kurt Gödel (1906-1978) stand out for their significant contributions to philosophy and mathematics. A similar group began in Berlin, calling itself the "Society for Empirical Philosophy." Its most important members were Hans Reichenbach (1891-1953) and Carl Hempel (1905-1997).[54] The two schools began to publish their own journal, *Erkenntnis* (German for "knowledge") in 1930, which was edited by Reichenbach and Carnap. In 1929 they called the first of several international philosophy conferences "for scientific philosophy" and "for the Unity of Science." Members of both the Vienna and Berlin group, and like-minded philosophers such as A. J. Ayer (1910-1989), spread the doctrines of logical positivism throughout the world. Schlick was very much interested in Wittgenstein and considered him a great genius. However, Wittgenstein himself was not a member of the Vienna Circle and was critical of logical positivism.

The rising conflict in Europe brought hardship to the members of the Circle. Its work was suspect and eventually suppressed. Many fled central Europe for English-speaking countries, especially America. Schlick himself was shot on the very steps of the University of Vienna by an insane student. However, the diaspora of positivist thinkers out of Austria and

Germany had a major impact on English language philosophy throughout the world. With its "scientific" approach, its similarity to the "logical atomism" of Russell and some elements of the early Wittgenstein, and its evangelistic zeal and certainty, logical positivism of various sorts dominated English-speaking philosophy for a good part of this century.

The tenets of logical positivism are laid out in the manifesto of the Vienna Circle, "The Scientific World Outlook" (1929):

Scientism. Science is the best, or only, form of rational knowledge.

Logical Analysis. The new formal logic, developed by Frege, Russell, Whitehead and the early Wittgenstein is a pure instrument to analyze the often confusing and ambiguous sentences of natural language.

The Verification Principle. The meaning of a proposition is its means of verification. In other words, a sentence expresses a meaningful idea (statement, proposition) if and only if (a) it is true or false by logical factors alone (a tautology, an analytic statement); or, (b) it can be verified by sensory experience. This is an expression of the general empiricism of the movement.

The Unity of Science. Since observable things are the only basis for rational knowledge (apart from mathematics and logic), natural and social science must progress toward a pure, scientific language which will describe all true facts about the world.[55]

It was the avowed purpose of this movement to sweep all metaphysical claims from the field of rational knowledge. Neither Wittgenstein nor Russell held to the final two points (the Verification Principle and the Unity of Science), but they are characteristic of the Vienna Circle and of logical positivism in general. An English version of the teachings of the Vienna Circle was published by A. J. Ayer as *Language, Truth and Logic* (1936), a very popular and influential work.[56]

The Vienna Circle, in its exuberance and evangelistic zeal, was overly simplistic in its solution to difficult problems. This much even members of the Circle admitted over time. In particular, the unity of all empirical science and the verification criterion of meaning were eventually abandoned or radically altered. These changes can be seen in the work of the most influential and important member of the Vienna Circle, Rudolf Carnap (1891-1970).

Carnap was born in 1891 in Germany and studied in Freiburg and

Jena.[57] He was a student of Frege, who introduced him to the new symbolic logic. Originally Carnap studied physics and mathematics but became interested in the foundations of math, logic and science. He was an enthusiastic follower of Frege, Russell and the early Wittgenstein and came to Vienna in 1926 on Schlick's invitation, where he soon became an important member of the group. Carnap escaped Nazi domination late in 1935 and arrived at the University of Chicago, where he taught for many years. There he helped make logical positivism the dominant approach in English speaking philosophy, becoming the world's leading member of that school of thought. Carnap followed Frege in seeing ordinary language as too vague and imprecise for scientific philosophy. He worked on the question of what the logic of a purely formal, scientific language would be. Carnap's logical system of scientific language was in fact neutral with respect to the reality of the external world; nevertheless, he held that metaphysical questions were in fact "pseudo-questions" based on an improper logical analysis of ordinary language. For Carnap, a meaningful language was one that could be translated into a pure, clean, logically constructed language. "Every sentence of the language of science is translatable into a sentence concerning observable properties."[58] He gradually refined the verification criterion from its early and rather too simplistic form. This was necessary because the criterion excluded many important scientific truths, including general scientific laws.

For example, take the most famous law in modern physics: $E=mc^2$. This law does not report an observation. It is based very loosely on "experience"; how then can it be "verified" by direct observation? Problems like this forced logical positivists to loosen up their criterion of meaning. As Carnap himself wrote, "these features [of the Vienna Circle] caused a certain rigidity, so that we were compelled to make some radical changes in order to do justice to the open character and the inevitable uncertainty of all factual knowledge."[59] Carnap eventually developed the criterion of "significance" for rational language, in which a term or concept was scientifically meaningful if and only if it is defined by observation, or if nonobservable, is embedded in a theory that is testable by observation, and the term actually does some work in creating the test for the theory.[60] This very weak concept of "verification" allows for many terms or objects that would earlier have been rejected as "metaphysical." Nevertheless, even this weak conception of "significance" left little room for speech about God or theology as meaningful, rational discourse. Carnap insisted throughout his life that confirmation by evidence is the hallmark of science and that metaphysics is composed mostly of "pseudo-statements."[61]

Karl Popper (1902-1994) was an important early critic of the work of the Circle, which he attended from time to time. Born in Vienna and a student at its University, Popper eventually published his own philosophy of science in the Circle's series of monographs, *The Logic of Scientific Discovery*. While following the Circle in its scientism and empirical methods, Popper developed his own criterion for genuine science. He noted that "positivists, in their anxiety to annihilate metaphysics, annihilate natural science along with it. For scientific laws, too, cannot be logically reduced to elementary statements of experience."[62] Therefore, he insisted that what distinguished science from pseudoscience is not a criterion of meaning, but the criterion of falsification. A theory or proposition is scientific if, among other things, it is open to being falsified by experience, especially by experiment. Like the full members of the Circle, Popper too left Vienna, in his case, for New Zealand. He later settled in England where he became an influential and much respected philosopher of science.

Among logical positivists for whom English was a native tongue, A. J. Ayer was the most famous and influential.[63] His short book introducing the "new" approach is the most important philosophical tract of the movement, at least in the English speaking world. Indeed, *Language, Truth and Logic* (1936) is often identified with logical positivism in its purest form. Ayer modified the verification principle in response to counter-examples—like sentences about past facts—which created problems for the simple and early notion. Ayer's first statement of the principle, however, is clear and precise: "I require of an empirical hypothesis, not indeed that it should be conclusively verifiable, but that some possible [!] sense-experience should be relevant to the determination of its truth or falsehood."[64] Notice that sensations play a purely hypothetical role in determining whether an empirical statement is meaningful. As this book makes clear (much clearer than the difficult works of the Vienna Circle), the implications of the verification criterion of meaning were vast and sweeping. The so-called truths of ethics, metaphysics and theology alike were, on this principle, neither true nor false, but simply meaningless. "We may accordingly define a metaphysical sentence as a sentence which purports to express a genuine proposition, but does, in fact, express neither a tautology nor an empirical hypothesis. And as tautologies and empirical hypotheses form the entire class of significant propositions, we are justified in concluding that all metaphysical assertions are nonsensical."[65] Since moral, metaphysical and religious statements are not verifiable through sense experience, and they are not true by logic alone, they cannot be meaningful.

While not all analytic philosophers from 1930 to 1970 (the heyday of logical positivism) would accept every tenet of the Vienna Circle's sweeping program, the general issue of how religious language could possibly be meaningful—much less true!—was pressed hard by analytic philosophers. While not all analytic philosophers accept the various verification principles, which were subject to serious criticism, they were empiricist in their epistemology. How could theologians and believing philosophers respond to this claim?

This problem was pressed by Antony N. Flew in a very influential book of readings exploring the meaning of the new logical empiricism for theology. "What would have to occur or to have occurred to constitute for you a disproof of the love of, or the existence of, God?"[66] Flew followed Karl Popper in a "falsification" criterion for cognitive meaningfulness. Such an approach seemed to undermine the rationality of belief in God.

The Logic of Religious Language
In sweeping terms, one could argue that analytic philosophy of religion began as a response to the challenge of logical positivism. Here we limit the discussion to the decades when logical positivism was king, withholding further developments in philosophy of religion for later in this work. Some theologians simply ignored the problem, seeing it as a technical difficulty of no lasting importance, or simply irrelevant to theology. This is certainly not the case, as traditional theology itself knew well. The logical positivists raised an important issue: how shall we understand religious language? This is a question theologians can ignore only at their

intellectual peril. The issue of the empirical foundations of religious language, especially the meaningfulness of that language as well as its truth or falsity, and the various uses that religious symbols, rules, statements and prayers are put to, are important theological problems in their own right. Greek and Latin theologians of the past spent centuries discussing them and similar problems.

A second possibility was to accept the verification criterion, or something like it, and reinterpret religion so as to make it meaningful. This usually led to some kind of behavioral interpretation of religion which reduced it to ethics.[67] However, religion is in fact more that ethics, which makes this result problematic. John Hick (1922-) made a different move. He argued that religious language is "verified" in the next life, a view few accepted.[68] A third position was to insist that the methods of logical positivism were fine for factual knowledge, but to contend that belief in God is not a simple matter of empirical fact. Faith involves seeing the world in a certain way, adherents of this view argued, and living one's life in the light of that viewpoint. Ian T. Ramsey (1915-1972) was an early exponent of this move.[69] This response became even more plausible in light of Wittgenstein's later philosophy of language, a development we will cover later in this book. Because he was very critical of his own early work and that of the logical positivists, and because he came to ground meaning in its use (which he termed "language-games" and "forms of life"), it became possible to see religious belief, language and practice as part of a meaningful "language-game" like other human pursuits.

A final response was to loosen the strictness of the verification principle to allow some room for both metaphysics and theology, while accepting the general empiricist challenge to provide evidence for theism. This response came from philosophers influenced by traditional Christian philosophy, such as F. C. Copleston, E. L. Mascall and Austin Farrer, and from process theologians like Charles Hartshorne. They continued to insist that religious language was meaningful, in response to empiricist philosophy of language. They also developed more clear and precise arguments for the existence of God. A full expression of this position was later provided by Richard Swinburne.

The eventual demise of logical positivism in midcentury opened the door to completely new epistemologies within analytic circles. This situation allowed Christian philosophers such as Alvin Plantinga to propose epistemologies much more friendly to religious belief. We will return to these developments later in this work, in a section on analytic philosophy of religion.

Conclusion

The developments within the analytic tradition began with the Vienna Circle and the early positivists. While positivism as a movement is passé, there are a number of characteristics of the analytic tradition which began with these early pioneers and have never really left the tradition. The emulation and honoring of science, for example, is still a part of this tradition. There is a concern for careful, logical analysis and explication of argument based upon evidence. Clarity, rationality and logical rigor are still valued virtues within the Euro-American analytic school of philosophy.

While analytic philosophy grew out of, and still flourishes on, the continent of Europe, so-called continental philosophy has been dominated by other schools of thought. The schools or movements characteristic of continental thought are phenomenology and existentialism. To their beginnings, and especially the work of Heidegger, we must now turn our attention.

3. THE MEANING OF BEING: HEIDEGGER AND GERMAN EXISTENTIALISM

M*artin Heidegger was arguably the most influential philosopher of the* century on the continent. His has certainly been the most lasting and powerful voice. This is true despite his many detractors, his loss of favor among some philosophers, and despite the fact that Husserl, his teacher, developed the methodology which Heidegger employed. Heidegger, as we shall see, provided a major impetus to both existentialism and postmodern thought. His work stimulated the development of hermeneutic theory as well. But how did the student of Husserl become the wellspring of existentialism? The answer to this question turns out to be rather more complicated than it might first appear.

Heidegger had many influences upon his philosophical development besides Husserl. Among the German philosophers in the generation before him, Wilhelm Dilthey is particularly significant for the development of hermeneutics and the question of meaning in the human world. He had no small influence upon Heidegger. Since we have not discussed Dilthey previously, we will pause here to briefly canvass his main ideas before we turn to Heidegger himself.

Dilthey
Wilhelm Dilthey (1833-1911) suffers from relative neglect compared to many of the predecessors of current continental thought such as

Nietzsche or Kierkegaard.[1] The Spanish philosopher Ortega y Gasset exaggerates when he calls him "the most important philosopher in the second half of the nineteenth century," but Dilthey's work deserves more study that it usually receives in the history of philosophy.[2]

Like many philosophers of his time and culture, Dilthey went to the university to study theology, but his interest in history and philosophy soon turned him away from the ministry. He studied at Berlin during the great years of Hegel and Schleiermacher, and his work is indebted to both.[3] Dilthey was very much influenced in his studies by the rise of historical consciousness in German culture, of which Hegel is such a brilliant representative. Later Dilthey returned to take up Hegel's own chair in philosophy at Berlin.

Dilthey's great ambition as a philosopher was to give solid philosophical ground to the human sciences, or *Geisteswissenschaften*, just as Kant had done for the natural sciences. To this end, he wanted to write a "Critique of Historical Reason" to match Kant's great *Critique of Pure Reason*. Dilthey was never able to achieve his ambition or finish this project. His first attempt was published in 1883 as an "Introduction to the Human Sciences."[4] Much of his writings come to us as articles, lectures, introductions and unpublished manuscripts. But his attempt, and the ideas and directions he came to in the struggle to give scientific grounding to the human or social sciences, were influential in German intellectual circles.

Dilthey grounded the study of human beings upon the study of life: "Life as a starting-point and abiding context provides the first basic feature of the structure of the human studies; for they rest on experience, understanding and knowledge of life."[5] He rejected any attempt to know the human based upon the model and methods of the natural sciences. On the natural science model, physics is typically taken as the exemplary mode of learning about the world. This natural-scientific model has in fact dominated American social scientific thought. But Dilthey argued that natural science and metaphysics are both mere abstractions from life. Human beings must be studied as living, thinking beings, and therefore in life itself. For this reason, he grounded the social sciences on history and hermeneutics. Because human beings are fundamentally historical in nature, the historical approach to the study of human cultures is central.

Following Hegel, Dilthey saw each culture in history as the objective or external product of its mind or spirit. Thus art, music, government, religion and philosophy must all be understood in their historical context. The task of understanding, then (following Schleiermacher), is to reconstruct the lived experience of the age, as expressed in its objective products such as language, art or legal systems. Dilthey clearly saw the scientific problem of the social sciences: how can such a subjective reconstruction be scientifically objective?[6] He never fully answered this question; however, he was convinced that it has to do with what he called understanding; that is, with the science of interpretation or hermeneutics:

> Understanding is the rediscovery of the I in the Thou; the mind redis-
> covers itself at ever higher levels of connectedness; this sameness of
> the mind in the I and the Thou and in every subject of a community,
> in every system of culture and, finally, in the totality of mind and uni-
> versal history, makes the working together of the different processes
> in the human studies possible.[7]

The human sciences study cultural artifacts and human behaviors, including speech. The quest to understand these "objectifications of life" must, he argued, be rule-governed.[8] He needed a new epistemology that would not take mathematics or the natural sciences as its model. In Husserl's *Logical Investigations* (1901), Dilthey found that the new phenomenology provided him with the inspiration and foundation he was seeking, as well as the closest approximation to his goal of a critique of historical reason. His unfinished manuscript, "The Formation of the Historical World in the Human Sciences" was the fullest expression of this goal.[9] In this late work, Dilthey argued that hermeneutics provides the key epistemological difference between the natural sciences and the social or human sciences, since it is the task of hermeneutics to study meaning. Meaning is a fundamentally human phenomenon, and the study of meaning is therefore the key to the human sciences.

> Only in the world of the mind—which is active, responsible, and self-
> determined, which moves within us—and in it alone has life its value,
> its goal, and its meaning. . . . In the human sciences we are dealing
> with states, churches, institutions, customs, books, and works of art; in
> such facts, as in man himself, there is always the reference from an

outer sensible side to one withdrawn from the senses, and therefore inner.[10]

Dilthey argued that the human sciences must proceed in an historical manner, setting forth the "worldviews" created by different people in various ages and cultures. Dilthey was very interested in the historical analysis of various types of worldviews, for this reason.[11] Human experience, expression and understanding are fundamentally historical. Life is something that takes place in time. Therefore meaning, too, is temporal.

> The course of life is something temporal. . . . The present is the filling of a moment of time with reality; this is experience, in contrast to the memory of it, or to the wishes, hopes, expectations and fears about something which may be experienced in the future. . . . The smallest unit which we can describe as an experience is whatever forms a meaningful unit in the course of a life. . . . Thus we come face to face with the category of meaning."[12]

The historical analysis of the systems of human life-experience, expressed in various objectifications of life in societies, is the central task of the social or human sciences as Dilthey came to see them. Dilthey's philosophy of life and his work on the foundations of the social sciences provided an important stimulus to continental thought. This was particularly true in two areas of philosophy dealing with meaning: hermeneutics and existentialism.

Dilthey and Husserl mutually influenced and responded to one another, including some philosophical correspondence. In his important lecture, "Philosophy as a Rigorous Science," Husserl critiqued Dilthey's work as too historical and unscientific compared to his own approach.[13] But he studied Dilthey's work with his students in Freiburg and among them was the young Martin Heidegger. Dilthey's work had no small influence upon Heidegger's philosophical development, especially before 1930.[14] As we shall see, Heidegger did indeed take up some of the key themes of Dilthey (especially hermeneutics, life and time), but in a radically new way.

Heidegger

Martin Heidegger (1889-1976) was the most important and influential continental philosopher of his age.[15] Like Kant before him, prior thought leads up to Heidegger, and philosophy after him looks back to his work (at least on the continent).[16] Heidegger changed the shape of Western thought. Yet he has also been derided as a quack philosopher, a supporter of Hitler and an author of incomprehensible drivel.[17] These dismissals cannot withstand careful and unbiased investigation into his work. Heidegger's is a major philosophical voice in the twentieth century, and it cannot be casually dismissed with a wave of a logical hand.

Heidegger's great work *Being and Time* (1927) burst forth like a supernova in the constellation of continental philosophy. The book has had tremendous impact, not only in the creation of existentialism and the development of philosophy, but also the philosophical domain altogether, among theologians, novelists, literary critics, sociologists and psychologists. In this work Heidegger turns our attention again to a traditional metaphysical question: "What is being?" or "What is it to be?" At the same time he focused on the meaning of *human* being (which he called Dasein). But who was this particular human being, Martin Heidegger, and where did he come from?

Heidegger grew up and worked in southern Germany, where he spent almost all of his life.[18] He loved the mountains and forests of his native land, especially the Black Forest where he had a mountain cabin in Todtnauberg. Born in the small town of Messkirch in 1889, Heidegger was at first a Catholic scholar and attended the university to study for the priesthood and the Jesuit order. In this early period as a Christian scholar Heidegger first began to think "the question of Being."[19] At age eighteen, the precocious and hard-working young student was given by his headmaster a book too difficult for him at the time: *On the Various Meanings of Being According to Aristotle* by Franz Brentano. For the rest of his intellectual career, Heidegger sought to think clearly about Being, and in doing so transformed Western thought.

Heidegger entered the University of Freiburg to study theology. He would spend most of his academic career there. Because of a heart condition, and perhaps a lack of vocation, Heidegger had to leave his studies for the priesthood in 1911. He had already been attracted to philosophy, including the work of Husserl, and now began more advanced studies. During this period ("the young Heidegger") he was a Catholic philosopher, and he remained (as far as he was concerned) a kind of "outsider"

Catholic all of his life. As a sign of this, we note that he asked for and was given a Catholic burial in his parish church of St. Martin in 1976.[20]

His studies in philosophy earned him a Ph.D., and he continued on at Freiburg with the required higher doctorate (habilitation). His habilitation thesis (1915) was on meaning and the categories of being in Duns Scotus. Heidegger pursued his interest in ontology through a careful study of the great medieval philosopher, along lines suggested by Husserl's phenomenology. However, the Great War of 1914 soon interrupted the young philosopher's development.

Heidegger's heart condition and his religious vocation (at least formally) allowed him to enter the army reserves at first. But in 1915 he was called into full-time duty as a postal censor and meteorologist for the army. We know very little of how the war affected him, but he must have had time to think through some important questions of life. In the middle of his war service (1915-18) he married a Protestant, Elfriede Petri, and by canon law could not remain an official member of the Catholic Church. Upon his return to academia in 1918, he soon declared to a Catholic theologian friend that he had broken free intellectually of "the Catholic System," by which he meant Scholastic and Neo-Thomistic theology and philosophy.[21] This break also coincided with an intensive period of investigation into Christianity, especially through mystical and Protestant writers.

Heidegger's lectures on the phenomenology of religion were not published in his lifetime.[22] But we now know that Heidegger embarked upon a serious investigation into Catholic mystics and other Christian theologians and philosophers. He was particularly interested in the most primitive layers of religious experience, that is, what lay underneath it, and he sought a nondogmatic, "pretheoretical" reality which gives rise to religious experience. He rejected in the strongest terms the traditional metaphysics of Thomistic thought, which he characterized as the "dogmatic, casuistical pseudo-philosophy" of "Catholicism."[23] To this end Heidegger studied and lectured upon Paul, Luther, Kierkegaard, Dostoevsky and Schleiermacher, and also investigated Catholic mystical theologians such as Meister Eckhart and Teresa of Avila. These religious investigations provided key themes for his later philosophical development. Indeed, we might see Heidegger's later philosophy as a kind of "mysticism of Being" in which Being takes on a role similar to that of God in mystical, negative or apophatic theology (the *via negativa*).[24] Heidegger also continued his careful study of Aristotle and of Neo-Kantian philosophy, all of which contributed to the development of his thought as he worked toward *Being and Time*.

Heidegger was passed over for the chair in Catholic philosophy, but was able to work full time at Freiburg as assistant to Husserl. The young academic joined in the new school of phenomenology and began to lecture on this topic. He was well received among students and gained the reputation of a philosophical lecturer of brilliance and insight. German philosophy students elsewhere began to hear "rumors of a hidden king."[25] His lectures and studies at this time prepared the way for his magnum opus of 1927. In the meantime, however, Heidegger moved to Marburg (with Husserl's assistance), where he became friends with the great New Testament theologian Rudolf Bultmann, as well as other scholars. With Bultmann he began to investigate the earliest Greek philosophers, the pre-Socratics, and they collaborated in many other ways. He lectured on the pre-Socratics at Marburg as well as on Plato, Aristotle, Aquinas, Kant and Leibniz. Heidegger published his master work near the end of the Marburg period; *Being and Time* was originally a very long article, dedicated to Husserl and published in a journal that he edited. It became "perhaps the most celebrated philosophical work which Germany has produced in this century," and certainly stands as Heidegger's masterpiece.[26] On the strength of this work, he was able to move back to Freiburg (again, with Husserl's help), becoming a full professor and taking up the master's own chair of philosophy in 1928.

Dasein and the question of Being. After steeping himself in the "new" method of phenomenology and spending several years considering the question of Being and matters of philosophical method, Heidegger published a "First Half" of his investigation into the meaning of Being. It was meant to be a kind of methodological prolegomena to a fundamental ontology. We cannot provide here a complete exposition of its many themes and arguments, but can only give a few indications of the chief points, new terminology and novel perspectives which Heidegger introduced into Western ontology.[27]

The task of translating *Being and Time* is a difficult one, for Heideg-

ger introduces many novel terms and fractures the German language
with strange spellings, new words and odd hyphenations in order to
press home his points. An example of this is the key term *Dasein*. In
ordinary German, this word simply means "to exist" or "be present."
Heidegger adopts it as his special word for *human* being and sometimes
hyphenates it as *Da-sein* to emphasize the meaning of "being-there."[28]
This emphasis accompanies his insistence that human being is not an
abstract nature or essence, but something real, something that is *there*.
With linguistic complexities like these, one can understand why this
work was not available in an English translation until thirty-five years
after its original publication!

As we might expect from the title, the leitmotiv of this book is Being.
Heidegger's interest in early Greek philosophy—those thinkers who initiated the entire philosophical preoccupation with Being—dates back to
his first encounter with the meaning of being in Aristotle at eighteen
years of age. This trend is part of the warp and woof of his entire philosophy.[29] It is fitting, then, that his great work begins with a quotation from
Greek. This sentence from one of Plato's dialogues must have leapt from
the page at Heidegger, for in it the Stranger (with typical Socratic irony)
expresses his perplexity as to the meaning of the word *being*, while also
noting that others seem rather too confident about what it means.[30] In a
way, this is exactly what Heidegger's book is about.

In order to clarify the meaning of Being, Heidegger insisted on
greater philosophical precision in phenomenology. He radically rejected
as flawed all previous ontology, and in fact called for a "destruction of the
history of ontology."[31] All previous attempts to understand Being are confused and conflicted, and therefore Heidegger must begin afresh. But
where to begin? Heidegger makes the Kantian move of beginning with
the one who knows, or in this case, the one who asks the question of
Being. That one is Dasein, that is, the human being. Heidegger likewise
has no patience for previous philosophical methods. He is not interested
in a scientific or purely abstract set of propositional truths about beings
(or humans for that matter). Instead, he calls for a hermeneutical
approach, an "Interpretation of Dasein," rather than the science of
anthropology. Only a phenomenological interpretation can engage and
unravel the dynamic reality of human Being in the world.

At the same time, Heidegger rejects the notion of some Cartesian, pre-suppositionless investigation into ontology. "Every inquiry is a seeking. Every seeking gets guided beforehand by what is sought."[32] Neither philosophy nor science is pure, abstract or neutral. There is no such thing as a "view from nowhere" (as Thomas Nagel puts it). All of us begin with a perspective and with biases, which guide our investigation of the object at hand. This argument, now a commonplace in our intellectual milieu, can be traced back to the introduction to *Being and Time*.

Heidegger turns, therefore, from ontology itself to a "fundamental analysis of Dasein," that is, an "existential analytic." For him this meant an analysis of human existence itself from within existence, as opposed to the static and abstract propositions of traditional ontology. The reason for this turn to the human is clear: "Thus to work out the question of Being adequately, we must make a being [or entity]—the inquirer—transparent in his own Being."[33] Only human beings reflect—as part of their very existence—upon the meaning of what it is to exist. Thus Heidegger must investigate Dasein as the ground of ontology. This turn to the human, and the manner in which he carries it out, is the main origin of existentialism in the twentieth century.

Heidegger insists that we must study Dasein in its *facticity,* that is, in the actuality of our existence, as well as in its "everydayness." He joins Dilthey, Bergson and many other philosophers of his day in rejecting the abstractions of prior schools of thought. We must get back to the reality, the true and living being, as the basis for philosophical inquiry. For Dilthey this was "life," and for Bergson it was "duration" or "vital force." In Heidegger's existential analysis, it is the facticity and everydayness of Dasein. By "facticity" Heidegger means the reality of its existence, which is prior to and the proper basis for ontology: the "factual objective presence" of Dasein.[34] He therefore calls this "preontological" mode of being the existence of Dasein.[35] He rejects the metaphysical ontology of the past, claiming he is uninterested in some objective description of the metaphysical properties of the human animal. Heidegger is not seeking a science of Dasein, but rather its interpretation, that is—following Dilthey—a *hermeneutical* approach to human existence.

Heidegger makes several key distinctions that are necessary to understand his ontology and his hermeneutics of existence. In the first place,

he distinguishes between Being and beings or entities. Heidegger wishes
to prepare us simply to ask the question of Being. For this we must set
aside our focus on particular things and look at sheer existence itself,
Being itself. Following classical Greek thought, he distinguished between
Being (which according to Aristotle is not a genus) and particular
things.[36] In fact, wonder at the sheer fact of Being lies as the heart of
Heidegger's philosophical work. But this wonder is only possible when
we see the difference between Being and things (beings). This is *the* fundamental ontological distinction, and one he presses home throughout
his philosophical work. This distinction carries through to the distinction
he makes between what is ontic (having to do with the study of particular
things) and what is ontological (having to do with being per se). Finally,
regarding Dasein—that peculiarly human mode of Being—Heidegger
distinguishes between the *existentiell* and the existential. The particulars
of existence encountered by Dasein are *existentiell* whereas the existential
denotes Dasein's fundamental, *a priori* possibilities. To grasp this difference, let us take an example from Shakespeare.

When Macbeth struggles with the question of whether or not to murder King Duncan, that is a particular anxious moment for one individual
(Act I, scene vii). A scientific knowledge of anthropology or of humanity
in general is of no help to Macbeth in making his dread decision! His
problem is something *existentiell*—do I follow the laws of honor and duty
that lend order to the world, or do I violate them in order to recreate my
own order? Like Macbeth in the play, all of us are "thrown" into the situations that make up our life. The context of our life and of specific situations is part of the very structure of our being in the world. So the fact of
our thrownness is *existential*—it is something we humans have in common. What Heidegger seeks, then, is an existential analytic of Dasein, not
an *existentiell* one.

Heidegger discerns three characteristics of Dasein in his analysis: facticity, existentiality and fallenness. The facticity of Dasein is the sheer
givenness of our human situation. We do not choose to exist, nor do we
have any control over the initial situation of our lives, or as Heidegger
says, of our Being-in-the-world. Dasein is always already Being-*in*-the-
world and Being-*with*-the-world. We are, in the famous words of Howard
the Duck, "trapped in a world we never made." The "world" in this case is

not just a physical environment, but is what Husserl will later call the "life-world." In the everydayness of our existence, we find ourselves already enmeshed with our life-world. Things, animals, people and our "stuff" are not merely abstract objects to us in our day-to-day existence. Rather, in Heidegger's analysis, items in the world are already part of our project, of our "dealings" in the world.[37] This is what gives them their meaning for us. The equipment in our world, then, is "ready-to-hand," revealed to us as what it is for us and for our project in the world.[38] We find ourselves, then, already caught up in the world. We are "thrown" into our world, without choosing all of its characteristics. This is what Heidegger meant by our facticity.

Second, the existentiality of Dasein means that there is no "generic" form of being-there. Rather, each person owns their particular way of life, their own Dasein, within the manifold possibilities for human Being. The possibilities are general, but the particular character of my own being is mine alone. This is another reason that a science of Dasein is impossible. Third, Heidegger argues that Dasein can be authentic or inauthentic. We can either grasp the true character of our existence or allow the world to drown out the clarity of our true being. We start, Heidegger believed, in a form of inauthentic being. He called this "fall-enness," a word with clear overtones of the Fall and original sin.[39] As part of our thrownness we find ourselves "absorbed" in the world, stuck in a rut of action and so forgetting about Being. This, according to Heidegger, is the human condition.

Have you ever felt stuck in a rut, doing the same things over and over again without meaning or thought? Do we not sometimes call our work a "rat race" for just this reason? For how many of us is our labor truly meaningful and fulfilling, enhancing our humanity? Many people feel trapped in their lives, unable to escape from the deadening repetition of daily existence. This is exactly what Heidegger is pointing to. "Dasein's absorption in the 'they' and its absorption in the 'world' of its concern, make manifest something like a *fleeing* of Dasein in the face of itself."[40] There is one way out of this mindless absorption: dread. Dread, anxiety or "angst" provides a clearing in which Dasein can come to itself. In dread one can see the true possibilities of his existence; she can see her way free of the rat race. Heidegger seems to be saying that it is only when things get really out of hand (or really messed up) that a person can think clearly about his own existence. The most important of these moments of clarity is one's reflection upon death. For after all, says Heidegger, human Being is ultimately being-toward-death. For this reason he can write elsewhere, "Only in dying can I to some extent say absolutely, 'I am.'"[41]

What is revealed, then, to Heidegger's analysis of authentic Dasein, in the clarity provided by dread and death? According to him, Dasein reveals itself as *care*. We care about others and about ourselves. And since our existence is radically historical, this care always and everywhere has a temporal structure. Thus "Dasein's Being finds its meaning in temporality."[42] In our care for the world and our projection of ourselves into the possibilities of Being, we await the future, retain the past and make present our concerns.[43] It is care, then, which gives Dasein its temporal structure.

This brief sketch of Heidegger's masterwork, of course, fails to do it full justice. One has to engage the arguments and structure of the work itself, often with the help of commentaries and specialized dictionaries. And in the end, his work is incomplete. Heidegger planned three parts for his major investigation of ontology. He only completed the first half of the first part. But even in this preliminary investigation, he broke new ground and posed new possibilities for philosophical reflection. Existentialism develops out of this hermeneutic of Dasein, and philosophy in the West is given a new direction and focus.

The later Heidegger. The most politically charged debate about Heidegger after his death has been his involvement with the National Socialist (Nazi) Party. We cannot here enter into the whole of this acrimonious debate, but neither can we completely ignore it. Karl Löwth (a Jewish philosopher and sometime student of Heidegger's) is surely right in suggesting that the philosophical development of the "later Heidegger" (his third phase) is partly an intellectual response to the disillusionment that grew out of his involvement with National Socialism, and of the War in general.[44] His "turn," or third phase, was already under way in the early 1930s, but his response to Nazism is a part of his overall philosophical development. Thus no student of Heidegger's philosophy can ignore his political involvement.

There are certain facts about Heidegger's political life which have come to light in recent years, and which illumine this dark period of his life.[45] One thing is clear: Heidegger was not always fully honest about his involvement in the Nazi party, even in his official reports. For one thing, despite what he and his defenders have sometimes written, Heidegger embraced fully and willingly the National Socialist "revolution" as early as 1932. Careful historical research into unpublished letters, diaries and papers reveals that Heidegger was already a Nazi sympathizer before he ever joined the party. He leaned upon the party's support to help him be elected rector of the University of Freiburg in 1933. He did not seek this post reluctantly, but out of his own political schemes. He only openly became a party member after his election, since membership would have undermined his prospects among the full professors. His infamous lecture as rector, "On the Self-assertion of the German University" (1933), is clearly in line with (and uses the political catchphrases of) National Socialism.[46] It seems Heidegger thought he could become a kind of spiritual or philosophical leader to the movement. Even when, years later, he reprinted his lectures which allude to, or support, National Socialism, he never apologized or denounced his membership.[47]

Heidegger was interested in the "spiritual" side of German fascism and in a few years became disillusioned with the brutish leaders of the movement. A hint of this can be seen, for example, in his 1935 lectures, *An Introduction to Metaphysics*. Near the end of the published version (1953), Heidegger complains about "the works that are being peddled about nowadays [1935] as the philosophy of National Socialism but have nothing whatever to do with the inner truth and greatness of this movement."[48] Heidegger soon learned to scorn the "intellectual" leadership of the Nazis. His disillusionment with politics, the horrors of the war and of German defeat worked to push Heidegger away from politics, society and the academic world. He spent even more time in his mountain cabin at Todtnauberg. In his philosophy, he retreated more into poetry and mysticism, and became even more pessimistic about the mass of humanity and philosophy's ability to ask the question of Being. He came to see science and technology, as well as philosophy and metaphysics, as detrimental to society and authentic human existence—but also as fated by the history of Being. His experience with politics helped to shape (but did not begin,

nor determine) the direction he took after 1935. This "turn" in his philosophical journey is known as "the later Heidegger."

After Heidegger left the rectorship, he began to distance himself from
the Nazi leadership. He refused to sack two deans of the University who
were openly against the Nazi regime, and resigned his post in 1934.
Returning to his classes in philosophy, Heidegger refused to open with
the mandatory German salute *("Heil Hitler!")* and was critical of some elements of National Socialism. He was expelled from the University into
national service in 1944 to dig ditches and do other menial labor for the
last months of the war. After the Allied victory, Freiburg fell under
French control. As part of the denazification of the University, Heidegger
was suspended from teaching duties for five years. In 1950 he was reinstated as a working full professor. By this time he had become world
famous as the "father of German existentialism," much to his consterna-
tion, as he rejected existentialism both as a label and a philosophy. He
continued to teach and work in relative isolation from the rest of the
world, giving the occasional lecture or seminar, until his final retirement
in 1967.

Making sense of the later Heidegger has become a kind of cottage
industry among continental philosophers. The meaning of his later,
more cryptic writings is a continuing matter of debate among experts.
One point seems clear enough. These later writings are not just a jumble
of sentences, nor a random collection of sayings (although on the face of
things they might give this impression!). Rather, Heidegger developed a
coherent perspective, however much he struggled to express it, and we to
grasp it. Despite everything, Heidegger remained focused upon Being.

One of the earliest indications, to the reading public, of this turn in
Heidegger's development is the postscript he added to *What Is Metaphysics?* in 1943.[49] Six years later, he added a long foreword to this same
book.[50] Taken together, they indicate his new attitude and perspective
toward philosophy and metaphysics. First of all, metaphysics has become
something less central. Now, to achieve true insight into Being, we must
"overcome" metaphysics. "Metaphysics thinks about beings as beings. . . .
Metaphysical representation owes this sight to the light of Being. The
light itself, i.e., that which such thinking experiences as light, does not
come within the range of metaphysical thinking."[51] Heidegger now iden-

tifies all philosophy with metaphysics, with that which has forgotten Being but can never get away from it. "Philosophy does not concentrate on its ground. It always leaves its ground—leaves it by metaphysics. And yet it never escapes its ground [i.e., the light or truth of Being]."[52]

In response to this predicament, Heidegger now calls for an "end" (*Vollendung*) to philosophy and a turn to the "task of thinking."[53] This "end" is not merely the termination of philosophy. Rather, it is both a goal and a dissolution. Philosophy has dissolved into the special sciences, and the "lighting," or "clearing" (*Lichtung*) of Being has therefore been veiled. This too, however, is a dispensation of Being, an inevitable part of the history of Being. "Each epoch of philosophy has its own necessity. We simply have to acknowledge the fact that a philosophy is the way it is."[54] As he writes in "Overcoming Metaphysics," "The decline of the truth of beings occurs necessarily, and indeed as the completion of metaphysics."[55] Heidegger wonders if another kind of thinking, one that is not merely pragmatic or calculative, is even possible today, as we stand at the end of metaphysics and philosophy. Ours is an age of technology, in which consumer and calculative thinking dominates the earth and makes impossible the letting-be of Being. Therefore, "before Being can occur in its primal truth, Being as the will must be broken, the world must be forced to collapse and the earth must be driven to desolation, and man to mere labor. . . . The decline has already taken place. The consequences of this occurrence are the events of world history in this century."[56]

Heidegger was highly critical of the "enframing" of beings in mere technological thinking. An instrumental and merely practical ordering of all beings is dangerous, for the earth and for Dasein. The true danger does not come solely from the lethal machines and instruments of death and destruction. It also comes from Dasein forgetting its true self in mere practical concerns. "The rule of Enframing threatens man with the possibility that it could be denied to him to enter into a more original revealing and hence to experience the call of a more primal truth."[57] Where can human Being (Dasein) best hear the call to this more primal truth? Heidegger points us in two directions: art (especially poetry), and an uncovering of the ground of metaphysics through a deconstruction of the history of metaphysics. By seeking the true origin of the experience of Being in Western philosophy, dating back to the pre-Socratics, Heidegger hopes to overcome metaphysics. But this can also be done in art, and especially poetry.

In his "Letter on Humanism" (1947), an important reply to Jean-Paul Sartre (who we will cover in the next chapter), Heidegger turns to language as a clearing for Being. "Language is the lighting-concealing advent of Being itself."[58] Notice how, for the later Heidegger, Being is always and everywhere both revealed and concealed in the same event: this reminds one of Luther's notion of the hiddenness of God even in his revelation. This revelation or unconcealment occurs in language, and especially in poetry. "Language is the house of Being. In its home man dwells."[59] Yet while language is the house of the truth of Being, it can become merely technical, mere chatter and noise, an "instrument of domination over beings." Poetry revives the true character of language as the house of Being, as the concealing-revealing event of Being. "The thinker utters Being. The poet names what is holy."[60] In his important lecture, "On the Origin of the Work of Art" (1935) he claims that "all art, as the letting happen of the advent of the truth of being, is as such, in essence, poetry. . . . Poetry is the saying of the unconcealedness of beings."[61] The poet speaks the truth of Being far better, thinks Heidegger, than the professional philosopher.

To recapture the true ground of thinking, the clearing of Being, we need a nonmetaphysical way of thinking about it. In its own manner, poetry shows us this way. Heidegger struggled to bring to language a manner of thought which did justice to his rejection of "systems" and of traditional philosophy. "The system is a system only as an absolute system" he wrote in some late notes on metaphysics.[62] Whether the system is Plato, Aquinas, Kant or Nietzsche, metaphysical thinking cannot get us back to the ground of thinking about Being. "We want to say something about Being without regard to its being grounded in terms of beings."[63] But how can this be said, and using what language? How can we recover "thinking" (which is his new term to replace philosophy or metaphysics)? Heidegger experimented with different ways of bringing into language the event of the unconcealment of Being.

In his essay *The Question of Being,* Heidegger experimented with putting an X through the word *Being,* in order to indicate the now nonmetaphysical use of the word (Being). He did not follow this practice for long.

Yet other than denying that Being can be thought of by means of beings, Heidegger has very little positive to say about it. Being is presence, which is why Being and time must go together. But there is little else apart from quasi-poetic sayings about Being. Being is not even an "it," not a thing at all (no-thing), but also not nothing! In the end, Heidegger had to turn away from the word "being" with its metaphysical overtones and create his own language. He began to speak of Being and time in terms of "the event of appropriation" *(Ereignis)*. The terms *Ereignis* means simply "event" in ordinary German, but Heidegger brings out the connection with "own" *(eigen)*. Recent translators, then, have created a new word, *Enowning*, to translate Heidegger. By whatever terminology, Heidegger began to reflect upon this "event" as early as 1936, but this set of notes and studies on Enowning has only recently come to light as his *Contributions to Philosophy*.[64]

Enowning, or Appropriation, is an event which allows us to think about Being from within Being, rather than from an abstract metaphysical standpoint. Enowning happens in two areas of particular import: in the coming together of Being and time (and so in our thinking these together), and in the light of the relationship between Dasein and Being. In other words, Enowning has become for the later Heidegger the key concept—which has no conceptual essence!—that he was seeking in *Being and Time*. For this reason, Enowning becomes the key idea in his late lecture, "Time and Being" (1962). Enowning is an absence or self-withdrawal which bestows a kind of presence, and in this way sends or gives both Being and time. "The history of Being is at an end for thinking in Appropriation [enowning]. . . . Thinking then stands in and before That which has sent the various forms of epochal Being."[65] In the end, then, Heidegger has to move away from talking about Being in order to better clear a path for the truth of Being in the light of Enowning. No example or conceptual description of the event of Enowning can be given. Rather, it must give itself. It is an experience with Presence, with the absence which is also a gift of Being, that one must encounter oneself.

In light of Heidegger. The philosophy of Heidegger influenced the way of Western thought in the development of existentialism and in the later growth of postmodern philosophy. Both of these movements deserve their own place in our story, which we will later supply. But while Heidegger's work was influential, few thinkers have followed upon the path which he marked out in his later writings. Like Frege, Heidegger seems to have failed in the central quest of his philosophy. He ends up saying almost nothing in answer to the question of Being. He pointed out many problems with traditional philosophy, but his own mysticism of Being or Enowning has not fared well as positive alternative. But also like Frege, Heidegger's was a magnificent defeat. He developed tools and terminology which greatly assisted other thinkers and scholars in the task set before them. In these terms his greatness and influence are lasting contributions to philosophy.

A final word must be said about Heidegger and Christian theology. Much of his intellectual development could be described as seeking to ask the key questions of scholastic philosophy, and yet to do so free from the constraints of traditional metaphysics. He appropriated several of the moves of negative theology, using them to speak of what cannot be described (Being, Enowning). At the same time, Heidegger believed that one who had a faith in God could not really think, for thinking could only be real in the face of the question of Being. Theists, he held, already know the answer to this question. Furthermore, Heidegger characterized the essential theological quest as reflection upon faith, rather than a knowledge of God.[66] In both of these moves, Heidegger is no friend to good theology. Theology, too, can think about deep questions, even questions of God and Being, without necessarily having to drag along traditional answers! The whole history of liberal theology proves Heidegger wrong on this point. I would also protest, against Heidegger, that the true goal of theology is to know God. Therefore, the key issues of theology are about God, not about "faith." This is not to deny a proper role for faith, but rather to point to the central question of theology, "Who is God?" (not "what is the meaning of Christian faith?").

Heidegger's importance, then, is not found in his own religious thought. Yet he had an enormous generative influence upon other religious thinkers. For Heidegger himself it was the quest to describe the reality of human being, and then of Being, which proved to be important. In seeking a nontraditional, nonmetaphysical analysis of human being, and then of Being itself, Heidegger provided an attitude, a vocabulary and a direction to Western thought which proved to be astoundingly influential and enduring.

Existentialism in German: Buber and Jaspers

While Heidegger himself rejected the term *existentialism,* this philosophical movement which he helped to shape was dominant in Western thought for most of the middle of the twentieth century. We will discuss existentialism more fully in the next chapter. For now, we should note that existentialism is more of a style than a true school of thought. The famous existentialists were French and very much in debt to Heidegger; but two other philosophers who wrote in German deserve to be mentioned here, if only in brief outline. They are Martin Buber and Karl Jaspers.

What is existentialism? Considering these three philosophers together (Heidegger, Buber and Jaspers) can help us see the difficulty of this simple question. These three were roughly contemporary, educated in much the same central European, German-speaking culture, and all wrote philosophy in the German tongue. Yet their philosophies are different in so many ways. How can we put them together in the same movement? There are few common doctrines among Jaspers, Heidegger and Buber. While Jaspers tells us that a "philosophy of existence" is something he took from Kierkegaard, all three rejected the label "existentialist" as a description of their work. The term became associated with French thought, but these Germans were the source of much of it. We can identify several common elements that justify our understanding of them all as existential thinkers—after all, scholars do not always get treated as they wish by history! These include a rejection of traditional philosophy (especially grand systems of thought and fixed conceptual frameworks); a priority given to life and the human situation; the uniqueness of each individual life; and the insistence that life (existence) is prior to and more basic than philosophy, method or metaphysics. Their work was typically marked by the quest for the characteristic elements of authentic human existence, especially such things as freedom, anxiety and dread. At the same time they rejected the notion of a fixed human essence. Existential thinkers were not only philosophers, but almost always had larger cultural interests in art, literature, drama and psychology. Among the three Germans we are discussing, Buber had the widest interests.

While Heidegger had the greatest influence upon existentialism, Buber was an important voice in his own right. His major work, *I and Thou* (1922), is one of the classics of twentieth-century philosophy.[67] He was the most important and influential religious existentialist of the century. For these reasons, we cannot here do justice to the sweep of his thought, which included works on Jewish religion, Bible translation, education, psychology, literature and philosophy.[68] Our focus will be on his main work as a philosopher, including his philosophy of religion.[69]

Buber. Martin Buber (1878-1965) was a Jewish philosopher, born in Vienna but raised by his grandfather who was a rabbinic scholar (Solomon Buber) in what is now Poland.[70] The young Martin was not particularly interested in religion, but became interested in the Zionist movement and Jewish culture after studying philosophy at several universities. In 1904 he graduated with a Ph.D. thesis on two Christian mystics from the middle ages and soon became interested in Jewish mysticism, especially the Hasidim of Eastern Europe. In his encounter with the Hasidic movement, which he made famous with his lively retelling of their legends, Buber moved from an individual mysticism to a more interpersonal understanding.[71] He was no longer interested so much in God and the soul as in the authentic interhuman encounter. Already in the preface to one of his collections of Hasidic stories, he briefly mentions some key ideas about God, human encounter and the world that would be central to his classic text, *I and Thou.*[72] Buber's existentialism is deeply rooted in his Jewish faith, including his reflections upon Hasidism.

Buber begins his most famous book with a reflection upon two primary words: I-You and I-It.[73] "Word" here is not a mere puff of air or marks on the page, but is based upon a more biblical understanding of the term. Primary words *(Grundworte)* are the central principles of existence (compare the fact that God created humanity and all things by speaking in Genesis). The most basic "words" of our lives we speak with our very lives: "being spoken they establish a mode of existence. Primary words are spoken with one's being."[74]

The two basic ways of being-together with others constitute the central theme of I and Thou. We can relate to other people or things as objects (he, she, it). This objective relationship—the I-It relationship—is mediated, practical and part of our everyday existence. We cannot live in the world without I-It. But there are also personal encounters, real meetings, with people or things, which call forth the fullness of my personal being. Buber identified this with the primary word, I-You. It is the world of relations and meetings that gives life its power and depth. Living only in objective relationships is finally dehumanizing, because every "I" is only an "I" because of the I-You relations in our lives. That is why Buber can say, "In the beginning is the relation."[75] At end the first part of his book, he likewise claims: "And in all seriousness of truth, you, hear this: without It humans cannot live. But the one who lives with It alone is not human."[76]

The third part of this work deals with God, the Eternal You. In Buber's philosophy of religion, God is immanent within personal relations. We cannot and should not create vast systems of theology; however, we can experience and speak to God as the eternal You who is implicit in all real personal encounters. He begins the third part of *I and Thou* this way: "The extended lines of relations meet in the eternal You. Every particular You is a glimpse through to the eternal You." Thus, authentic human life is a dialogue, an I-You encounter with the world which is at the same time a dialogue with the Eternal You. He explains these ideas more fully in his essays on the Hasidim. Drawing from his Jewish roots, Buber argues that we are responsible for bringing the presence of God into history. It is through us—through human beings—that God's presence will be made manifest. Buber quotes a Hasidic saying, "God dwells where one lets him in," with this commentary: "The hallowing of the world will be this letting in. But grace wants to help the world to hallow itself."[77] God's presence in history waits upon those who live authentic lives. "We have realized that just the same You that goes from person to person is the You that descends from the divine to us and ascends from us to the divine."[78] This authenticity depends upon attending to this world, that is, to genuine I-You encounters.

Jaspers. While Buber was one of the most important and influential religious existentialists of the century, there were other philosophical voices which brought together a concern for genuine human existence with a philosophical notion of God. Early among these was the German philosopher Karl Jaspers (1883-1969), whose lectures on the *Philosophy of*

Existence (1937) helped to make the term *existentialism* popular.[79] While
Jaspers has been overshadowed by his more famous contemporaries,
Heidegger and Buber, his voice was an important one in the development of existential philosophy.[80] Concerning Jaspers's influence on German intellectuals of his time, the noted physicist and philosopher Carl
Friedrich von Weizäcker once wrote: "For fifty years educated Germans
have paid attention to the voice of Karl Jaspers. As they listened, agreed
or disagreed, they found that his words touched the questions of their life
as a community."[81]

    Jaspers's intellectual development parallels in some ways the Ameri-
can philosopher William James. He first studied law, then medicine,
graduating with his doctorate from Heidelberg in 1909. After working in
psychology, like James he became interested in philosophy. His second
major book was published under the title *Psychology of Worldviews* (1919),
and while the title contains the word psychology, in fact this is a philosophical text. In this rambling volume, Jaspers exhibited a central theme
of his philosophy which would come to characterize existentialism as a
movement: "I thought about nothing else than authentic human
being."[82] Three years later Heidelberg allowed him to move to a chair in
philosophy. Unlike Heidegger, Jaspers stood against the rising tide of
National Socialism. As a result, he was not allowed to lecture and was
finally ejected from his position at Heidelberg by the Nazis. However,
before being completely silenced by the Nazis, Jaspers was able to publish a significant three-volume work, *Philosophy* (1932), which sets forth
the main themes of his thought. His widely read book, *Man in the Modern
Age* (1930), was written for the general public and is a summary of his philosophy at the time. Soon afterward he gave an influential lecture series
later published as *Philosophy of Existence* (1937). Then Jaspers's voice fell
silent. While living through WWII, unable to lecture, teach or publish,
Jaspers worked on a massive book, *On Truth*, which he was finally able to
publish after the war.[83] Jaspers was reinstated as philosophy professor in
1945, when he began to urge a national repentance for the horrors of
National Socialism. He lectured on *The Question of German Guilt* (published in 1946), but was disappointed by the response he received from
the University and from the nation.[84]

    Jaspers then moved to the chair of philosophy in Basel, Switzerland, which he occupied for the rest of his career. He turned his mind to issues of politics, religion and history in relationship to philosophy. He published his major work in philosophy of religion, *Philosophical Faith and Revelation*, during this period, and began his massive history of world philosophy (*The Great Philosophers*, 3 vols.). He died in Basel in 1969, one of the most celebrated philosophers in central Europe.

Jaspers was a major influence upon German philosophy and the development of existentialism.[85] He preferred the term "*Existenz*-philosophy" as a label for his thought, which he defined as "the way of thought by means of which man seeks to become himself; it makes use of expert knowledge while at the same time going beyond it. This way of thought does not congnise objects, but elucidates and makes actual the being of the thinker."[86] Jaspers respected science but also wrote eloquently about its limits. Deeply influenced by Kant and Kierkegaard, he argued that the whole of reality is beyond the grasp of any empirical science, although reality gives itself to us in the objects of our experience. Likewise, human beings can be studied empirically by medicine and psychology, and human reason is subject to philosophical and logical analysis; but human *Existenz* develops in a dimension of spirit which is beyond science. Human *Existenz* is the genuine ground of human freedom and meaning, but it is non-objectifiable and so cannot be subject to rational analysis. We live our *Existenz* in authentic or inauthentic ways; we cannot study it.

Human reason seeks to know the world as a whole, to know the self and the Transcendent (or God), but Jaspers argued that none of these things can properly be an object of knowledge. For him, theology per se is impossible, as is traditional metaphysics. In keeping with his existentialist approach, Jaspers held that there are "ciphers" which point us toward the Transcendent, but contain no objective knowledge of it. These open symbols are grasped by the subject seeking truth and self-knowledge in many different aspects of life. Jaspers specifically lists as "ciphers" such things as religion, music, great art, myth, metaphysical systems and nature. Likewise there are limit-situations in life (such as death) which cause us to reflect upon the very meaning of our existence. We reach out toward that which is beyond our experience and knowledge. That which surrounds us and all being, without which there could be no being or truth, Jaspers called "the Encompassing." This is his word for

God, Transcendence or Being-Itself. Jaspers came to see all philosophy as a form of reasoning about the Encompassing, and the many dimensions of truth and rationality as differing modes of thinking about it within various domains (politics, art, religion, science and the like). On these grounds, Jaspers sought to replace religious faith with philosophical faith: a faith in human freedom, reason, *Existenz* and the open-ended quest for truth in the various modes of the Encompassing. This is authentic human existence.

Jaspers, Heidegger and Buber represent three quite different philosophical perspectives. What they have in common is a passion for philosophical reflection on human existence, and the contexts, issues and elements which make it free and meaningful—or shallow and inauthentic. Existentialist philosophy will live and grow in the shadow of world war and depression, becoming a major movement in Western thought. We investigate this development in the next chapter, as we journey from Heidelberg to Paris.

4. BEING AT PARIS: FRENCH EXISTENTIALISM

F rench existentialism carries over from its German counterpart many of the same concerns that we found in the previous chapter. Both react strongly against the optimism of the nineteenth century and reject its confidence in corporate humanity. Indeed, existentialism represents a clear rebellion against every philosophy that turns the individual into an abstract entity. Similarly, both German and French existentialism sharply question systems that advocate any neutral and objective approach to philosophy. Not only is a detached scientific approach impossible, they argue, but it is also inadequate for understanding the subjectivity of personal existence.

While we find continuity in the themes developed in these two forms of existentialism, distinct differences in tone are also discernible. One significant difference is that the French thinkers tended to reject the lengthy systems and tightly argued philosophical treatises often found in the German existentialists and instead chose such literary vehicles as novels, plays, brief essays and journals to communicate their ideas. As a result, existentialism in the French world tended to be more directly absorbed by the general population, while German existentialist thought seeped into the popular mind primarily through theology. Another distinction is that German existentialists sought to recover the meaning of human existence in a world that had sacrificed relationships under the lure of the impersonal, calculable, scientific and rational. While the French thinkers want to retain the personal facet of human existence, they often see relationships as just another attempt to escape from an absurd world, another path to inauthenticity. This is especially true of Sartre and Camus, who view "the Other" as problematic rather than salvific. Thus, more often than not, French existentialism offers a picture of the alienated person, radically alone in the universe. Finally, in existentialism's French expression, philosophy moves away from understanding the human being as a thinking individual. It is the acting individual that inhabits French existentialism.

It should be acknowledged at the outset that our designation of the four thinkers in this chapter as existentialists is open to debate. Only Sartre openly accepted this label, and even he later sought to be free of it. Marcel declares himself a dialectical thinker, Camus describes himself as an absurdist, and Weil is probably most accurately classified as a mystic. This is further complicated by the fact that the figures surveyed here embrace radically different conclusions. For example, Marcel and Weil are Christian theists while Sartre and Camus are atheistic. Camus ultimately rejected the idea that all acts are morally equivalent, leading to a split with Sartre who remained steadfast in his rejection of objective moral standards. Sartre proclaims that "hell is other people," while Marcel argues that we only become authentic in the context of relationships. Additional tensions between these thinkers will be noted in the course of the chapter, but it is only proper to admit from the beginning that we are dealing with a diverse group. However, there is sufficient unity both in what they reject as well as the types of themes that rise to the surface in their work that we find some justification in bringing them together in this chapter.

Gabriel Marcel

In one sense, Gabriel Marcel (1889-1973) was an existentialist before existentialism.[1] Prior to discovering the works of Kierkegaard or Heidegger and predating Sartre's work by several years, he developed a philosophy that mirrors the major themes of existentialism. Marcel usually avoided referring to his philosophy as existentialist, preferring to call himself a "concrete philosopher" or a "Christian Socratic." This hesitancy has some justification because Sartre, whose thought eventually exerted such immense influence on perceptions about French existentialism, always views the Other (whether divine or human) as a threat and hindrance to authentic humanity. Marcel, in stark contrast, argues that we only experience personal existence in relation to the other, especially the divine Other.

Despite clear differences between himself and Sartre, many of Marcel's philosophical themes are nevertheless characteristic of existentialism. Perhaps most notably, he is concerned about the threat that modern society presents to human freedom. Under the sway of confidence in scientific "technic," as he calls it, we are tempted to turn the world, and eventually ourselves, into a set of problems to be solved. This technical method requires a diagnostic detachment from the mechanism we are attempting to analyze and fix, but with this supposed neutrality comes also a loss of mystery. Marcel's response is that if we are to recover our humanity, we must instead approach the universe as a mystery in which we participate through faith, hope and love.

Marcel's personal background provides hints of the philosophy he would develop only by way of contrast. His father, a French government official and, for a brief period, ambassador to Sweden, embodied the spirit of the age in his belief that the social and natural sciences would point the way to a brighter world. Though nominally Catholic, he viewed faith as antiquated and threw himself into his political duties. Marcel's mother died when he was four, and he was raised by an aunt who was Jewish by birth but had adopted a moralistic form of Protestantism. In his childhood, Marcel sought escape from a home atmosphere he describes as "arid" through his imagination, creating fanciful companions and stories. Marcel was a particularly gifted student, and he wrote his thesis on the metaphysics of Coleridge and Schelling at the age of eighteen. However, he found that the abstractions of the German idealism that dominated his education only paralleled sterility of his upbringing. His growing impatience with attempts to reduce philosophy to an overarching system can be found in both the ideas and form of his *Metaphysical Journal*.

The *Journal*, which he started writing in 1914, consists of occasional diary entries that register his objections to any philosophy that removes the individual from concrete situations and turns persons into abstractions. While his intention was to systematize these ideas for publication, he ultimately published them as written. As he states in the preface, "I became aware that I would be being unfaithful to myself if I tried to set out in a systematic form what had occurred to me in quite a different way."[2] With the exception of his Gifford Lectures (1949-1950, published as *Mystery and Being*), which come closest to outlining his thought in a systematic manner, his other philosophical works are diaries or collections of lectures and essays.

Marcel's service with the Red Cross during World War I, where one of his duties was to search for missing soldiers and communicate with their families, only reinforced his distaste for systems that reduced people to numbers. It also forced him to think through the questions of religious faith, and these issues figured prominently in his writing even before his conversion to Christianity. In 1928, Marcel had presented a defense of faith's validity (although not specifically Christian faith) with such force that he later received a letter from a Catholic thinker, François Mauriac, who asked why Marcel had not cast his lot with them. Marcel interpreted this as a divine call, and shortly after, became a convert. Thus on March 5, 1929 he wrote in his journal (later published as *Being and Having*), "I have no more doubts. This morning's happiness is miraculous. For the first time I have clearly experienced grace. A terrible thing to say, but so it is. I am hemmed in at last by Christianity—in, fathoms deep. Happy to be so!"[3] Marcel is unusual among philosophers in that he spent most of his life not as a university professor but as an independent writer, critic and dramatist (more than thirty of his plays were staged). However, he did briefly lecture in several academic settings, including the University of Aberdeen (1951-1952) and Harvard (1961-1962).

First reflection: The universe as problem. Marcel's philosophy is primarily concerned with metaphysics and, as is characteristic of existentialism, his focus is directed toward human existence. However, he specifies that "it is not enough to say that it [his philosophy] is a metaphysic of being; it is a metaphysic of *we are* as opposed to a metaphysic of *I think*."[4] With this, he signals his belief that philosophy had taken a wrong turn by following Descartes's lead. Descartes understands human beings as pure intellects (*res cogitans,* or thinking things) who are capable of gaining knowledge by detaching themselves from the concrete circumstances of life. For Marcel, this obscures the fact that we do not exist autonomously and abstractly. Instead, human existence is situated in the midst of suffering, limitations imposed by physical obstacles and social relationships, unanticipated events, the possibilities offered by love and hope and above all, the presence of God.

For Marcel, freedom is never freedom from the concrete situations and relationships imposed by life. Our relationship to others, which always comes with the awareness that the Other is an indication of our finitude, is the presupposition of freedom. However, this freedom is not automatic; we are constantly confronted with decisions about how we will respond to our situation. We must choose between intersubjective participation and neutral observation. When we embrace our limits and uniqueness and participate in others, we can become whole. The alternative is the temptation to take the route provided by Descartes, in which we attempt to assume a neutral position and treat everything external to us as object.

The Cartesian model, which Marcel refers to as "first reflection," finds expression in scientific modes of thinking. In science, the world is viewed as a series of problems waiting to be solved. To resolve a problem, the dispassionate scientist analyzes and quantifies objects in an attempt to control the outcomes. "The world is treated as a machine whose functioning leaves much to be desired. Man is luckily at hand to correct some of the faults; but for the moment, unfortunately, the whole is not in his control."[5] Once we have objectified the world, the next step, the examination of our own existence as purely objective, follows naturally. Since, in first reflection, we are only an aspect of a depersonalized cosmos, the human being also "is quite prepared to see in himself certain defects of working, which must be curable by taking various measures, and applying various kinds of individual or social therapeutic action."[6]

Of course, the inescapable difficulty with the scientific approach's attempt to solve all our problems by "technic" is that there are elements, both in the cosmos and in human nature, that remain ungovernable. When confronted with these untamable problems, we have the opportunity to acknowledge mystery. However, "first reflection" takes a different course. If a problem does not yield to the methods of science, it is arbitrarily declared a nonissue and we move on. Marcel argues that this capitulation to scientific method, in which we allow a particular technique to define the issues, has devastating consequences that only become clear later. Over time, what was originally viewed as a means by which we investigate and solve our problems ultimately has profound implications for our treatment of human beings. Once persons are reduced to the category of problematic objects rather than mysterious beings, the logical conclusion is that we have no reason to treat humans as though they have a privileged place among other problematic objects. All intellectual roadblocks against dehumanizing the human being are removed by a method which is, by its very nature, detached and depersonalized. Marcel understands this as the philosophical and cultural background to the tragic events that engulfed Europe, and indeed the entire world, in the first half of the twentieth century.

Second reflection: The universe as mystery. Despite deep concerns about the dangers of "first reflection," Marcel does not propose a return to a prescientific world. "It [science] is a legitimate mode of representation and even one that can be called indispensable. It only becomes vicious when it is erected into a metaphysical construction."[7] The danger of turning technic into a "metaphysical construction" can be avoided when "first reflection" is transcended (but not ignored) in "second reflection." In the latter, what was previously approached as a problem is now entered into as a mystery. The door that leads to mystery swings open when we "begin by working out the distinction, at the spiritual level, between what we call an *object* and what we call a *presence*."[8]

Thoughtful engagement with the world ought properly give rise to the recognition that ultimately, we cannot divorce thinking from being. While "first reflection" begins by looking at the world as a mechanism that is separate from us, it can never legitimately end at this position, because we are always beings in a world. Our existence is never general or abstract being. Instead, we live in concrete situations, intimately related with the objects of our thought. We can never simply think about the world, God, evil, death or our bodies. We are always enveloped by them; they are constantly present to us as we participate in them. This "presence" is the very precondition of thought, because it would never occur to us to reflect on that which does not concern and encompass us.

Marcel uses the issue of evil to illustrate this point. When we approach evil as a problem, we treat it as a mechanical breakdown or functional failure of some sort. But this is not the way we actually encounter evil in the world. "Evil reveals itself to me as, on the contrary, a mystery when I have recognized that I cannot treat myself as something external to evil, as simply having to observe evil from the outside and map out its contours, but that on the contrary I am implicated in evil—just as one is implicated, for instance, in some crime. Evil is not only in front of my eyes, it is within me: even more than this, in such a realm the distinction between what is within me and what lies outside me becomes meaningless."[9]

The Cartesian model of knowledge as the objective investigation of "problems," then, betrays our very existence because true knowing always engages the person who can never stand outside of what she knows. Therefore, the more personal and existential our knowledge, the greater its reality. This interpenetration of knowing and being is what Marcel calls the ontological mystery. We discover the realm of mystery when we push scientific thought far enough to recognize that our existential questions can never be answered by science, or first reflection, alone. At this point, we are confronted with a crucial question: will we reduce the realm of thought to the mechanical and, in the process, lose our identity as persons, or make the decision to enter the mystery? Viewed from this perspective, then, we can see why Marcel does not dismiss first reflection completely. First reflection, properly employed, draws us into the existential question. As he states it, "A mystery is a problem which encroaches upon its own data and invades them, and so is transcended *qua* problem."[10] Scientific thought plays its proper role when awareness of its limitations opens us up to the ontological mystery.

Being and having. The temptation that drives so many toward the naturalistic perspective implicit in first reflection is pride, which Marcel speaks of as "having." If we can master the universe through technic, it becomes our possession: we become, in Descartes's words, "the lords and possessors of nature."[11] We make something ours by employing our energies to fix problematic mechanisms. The more we appear to have fixed the problems, the more completely we own it. However, Marcel argues that the danger in these attempts toward "having" is that what we possess ultimately consumes us. "In exact proportion as I am attached to these things, they are seen to exercise a power over me which my attachment confers upon them, and which grows as the attachment grows."[12]

The view that we "have" a body is where we experience most acutely the paradox of being owned by objects we possess. Marcel writes,

> The tyranny it [our body] exercises over me depends, by no means completely, but to a considerable degree, upon the attachment I have for it. But . . . I seem, in the last resort, to be annihilating myself in this attachment, by sinking myself in this body to which I cling. It seems that my body literally devours me, and it is the same with all the other possessions which are somehow attached or hung upon my body. So that in the last analysis . . . having as such seems to have a tendency to destroy and lose itself in the very thing it began by possessing.[13]

The quote above helps put Marcel's strong opposition to Descartes's dualism of body and soul in context. Under the Cartesian model, the thinking aspect of the human being (the soul or mind) *has* a body that can be understood as a mechanism, and that has no intrinsic connection to essential human being. This means that the body, with its imperfections, appetites and limitations, is a problem that must be solved by detachment and analysis. Marcel, however, argues that our body is essential to our existence in the world, and thus he argues for an "incarnational" view.

Under an incarnational approach, the body is no longer a problem but a mystery. "I *am* my body only in so far as for me the body is an essentially mysterious type of reality, irreducible to those determinate formulae (no matter how interestingly complex they might be) to which it would be reducible if it could be considered merely as an object."[14] Our own incarnate existence in the world is the basis for our understanding of God as mystery, a mystery which becomes manifest in the incarnation of Christ. In his humanity, Christ experiences the tensions and limitations of bodily life. At the same time, the divinity of Christ corresponds with our own intuitions of transcendence and our yearning to be united with God. For Marcel, then, the incarnation of Christ is not a difficult logical puzzle to be solved, but a mystery in which we are participants.

If our bodily existence and our relationship to God are thought of as problems, the presupposition is that these are temporary obstacles to be overcome with the right type of methods. By contrast, Marcel says, mysteries remain open-ended. Thus, he says that religion "constitutes a realm where the subject is confronted with something over which he can

obtain no hold at all. If the word transcendence describes anything whatever, it must be this—the absolute, impassable gulf which opens between
the soul and Being whenever Being refuses us a hold."[15] In other words,
mystery eliminates the possibility of "having." It is something in which we
participate, and to the extent that we participate, it is open to us.

The fact that we can never get to the bottom of a mystery throws light
on Marcel's rather eccentric form of writing. If mysteries have no defin-
able limits, a systematic expression of metaphysics is impossible. In fact,
he states that "it is probable, indeed, that the philosophical activity has
no other boundaries than those of its own dissatisfaction with any results
it can achieve. Where that dissatisfaction disappears, and instead we have
a sense of somehow being snugly settled, the philosophical activity has
disappeared, too."[16]

Faith, love and hope. Because we only enter the realm of mystery
through intersubjective relationship, according to Marcel, God should
not be thought of as "he" or "it." "When I speak of someone in the *third
person*, I treat him as independent—as absent—as separate; or, more
exactly, I define him implicitly as external to a dialogue that is taking
place, which may be a dialogue with myself. Religious life begins as soon
as this relation is transformed."[17] This transformation requires that we
encounter God as "Thou." In such an encounter, relationship is already
assumed, and this assumption renders traditional proofs of God's existence invalid. To attempt speculative proofs of God's existence is to trans-
form God into a problem, so that whatever results are drawn from our
intellectual quest will be something we "have." Yet any god we possess is
merely an idol. Therefore, Marcel argues, "If a man has experienced the
presence of God, not only has he no need of proofs, he may even go so
far as to consider the idea of a demonstration as a slur on what is for him
a sacred evidence."[18]

True belief in God always transcends knowledge; belief in God
involves faith from the beginning. As Marcel understands it, faith is
never an abstract term, but one that involves concrete participation.
"Hence to think faith is to think faith in God. When I say that faith bears
on God I add nothing to the idea of it."[19] Thus, faith is impossible for
speculative reasoning because it reduces God to an object or the third
person. To have faith is to know God as a "Thou," one with whom we are

already related. In a similar way, "My soul is always a *thou* for God; for God it is always confounded with the subject who invokes him. And this can only occur for a subject in the measure in which the subject, through love, imitates what must be called the divine attitude."[20] Marcel reminds us that faith, which is ultimately an affirmation, is inextricably linked with love. To fail to love God is to remove oneself from faith. However, as we have noted above, we never exhaust a mystery. In this life, we are always on a pilgrimage that takes us toward the future. Thus, the virtue of hope is always present where free beings in relationship with a free God live out this relationship in concrete situations. Therefore, faith, love and hope are not just ideals we strive for—let alone virtues we can attain through adherence to a problem-solving regimen—but are part of the ontological structure of mystery.

Reflecting on Marcel. In an age when many had built their optimism around the possibilities of technology and scientific method, bolstered by philosophers such as Dewey, political ideologies such as Marxism, or the powerful impact of capitalist economics, Marcel is one of the first dissenting voices. Each of these forces offers itself as a savior from the threats presented by the external world. Marcel's response to such visions of scientific salvation is twofold. First, he maintains a strong pessimism about our pretensions for control and conquest. Secondly, he argues that these attempts to conquer natural and social forces come at the cost of our personhood.

Marcel's prescription for preserving our status as persons is to recognize what we all intuitively know: that we do not exist abstractly and apart from others. To attempt to grasp the world objectively and neutrally is to fail to recognize the world as it is. As we will also find in the other thinkers covered in this chapter, Marcel recognizes that our freedom is at risk as soon as we identify ourselves with roles imposed on us by society. However, he marks a radical departure from Sartre, and Camus to a lesser extent, in rejecting the idea that others inevitably threaten a realization of our true identity. Instead, he lines up more closely with German existentialism in his argument that our salvation is found by acknowledging our individual finitude and immersing ourselves in mystery through the medium of interrelatedness.

Finally, we find strong similarities between Marcel and the other French thinkers in this chapter in his rejection of science, or what he calls "first reflection," as the means of accurately understanding the universe. Like them, he argues that allowing the methods of science to define all of reality inevitably objectifies human existence and makes freedom impossible. Despite the parallels in his conclusions, however, Marcel has a more positive view of the role of first reflection. We must first know the inadequacies of treating the universe as a problem before the world, the self and God are revealed as mysteries.

Marcel is well aware that the open-ended nature of his metaphysics will leave him vulnerable to accusations of irrationality. His ready response is that such a verdict assumes the standards of rationality imposed by first reflection and that such rationality ultimately forces human existence into an untenable abstraction. He thus counters that mystery imposes upon concrete, existing beings a chastened rationality that assumes we will never reach the bottom of mystery, and instead finds its own verification through our absorption into the life of the Other.

Albert Camus

When Paris was liberated in August 1944, it quickly became known that Albert Camus (1913-1960) was the editor of *Combat*, an underground paper that had nourished the French spirit during the German occupation of their country. [21] Only thirty-one at the time, Camus already had fame within France for his novel *The Stranger* (1942), and the collection of essays titled *The Myth of Sisyphus* (1942); however, this newest revelation brought him to the attention of the whole world. His celebrity, which he found a burden throughout his life, was a sharp contrast to his childhood. Camus was born in Mondovi, Algeria, in 1913, on the eve of World War I. His father was killed in the war when Camus was only one year old. Camus's mother, illiterate, nearly deaf and newly widowed, moved Albert and an older brother to Algiers, where they shared a small apartment with his paralyzed uncle and his grandmother, who suffered from cancer.

Although sickness and poverty surrounded the young Camus, his childhood was relatively happy, with intellectual pursuits and sports—he was an accomplished soccer player in his university years—providing important outlets. His intelligence was recognized by an elementary school teacher, Louis Germain, who helped him prepare for the lycée and to whom he later dedicated his Nobel Prize in Literature. Following the lycèe, Camus entered the University of Algiers as a philosophy student. During doctoral studies in 1930, however, he contracted a severe case of tuberculosis, which was to be a recurring obstacle for him (another difficult attack slowed his work between 1937-1942). Not only did this illness curtail his beloved athletic activities, it also made him ineligible for teaching since he could not pass the required medical examination. Many commentators see his health struggles, acting in conjunction with the circumstances of his childhood, as formative for the ideas of absurdity, oppression and illness which arise as consistent themes in his works.

Following his university years, Camus worked as a journalist, writing frequently about the plight of the impoverished Arabs in Algeria, and he briefly aligned himself with the Communist Party. He was forced to leave Algeria in 1940 because of his leftist political activities, although he had by then severed all ties with Communism, and ended up in France. He completed *The Stranger* and *The Myth of Sisyphus* during the early years of the Second World War, and became the editor for the clandestine resistance newspaper *Combat*. During this time he also forged an important alliance with Jean-Paul Sartre and Simone de Beauvoir, and came to share their views about God's absence, the absurdity of life and the need to embrace freedom as a rebellion against the irrationality of the world. This relationship, however, would later be severed by a rancorous disagreement that remained unresolved at Camus's death.[22]

After the war, Camus remained occupied with his writing and working as an editor for his own publisher, Gallimard. In 1957, he was honored with the Nobel Prize in Literature, the second youngest person ever to receive this prestigious award. Tragically, his life ended at the age of forty-six, in a 1960 car crash. Camus, who hated automobiles, had been convinced by his publisher, Michel Gallimard, to ride back to Paris with him instead of taking the train. The unused portion of an already purchased train ticket was found in Camus's pocket and a manuscript of an unfinished semi-autobiographical work tracing his childhood in Algeria was found scattered around the crash site. The latter was finally published in 1995 as *The First Man*.

A philosophy of the absurd. The twin themes that permeate Camus's writing are absurdity and rebellion. However, it would be a mistake to interpret these ideas in a one-dimensional manner across his brief career. The atrocities of World War II compelled a significant evolution in Camus's thought that is not often recognized by those familiar only with his two important early works, *The Stranger* and *The Myth of Sisyphus*. While these writings do introduce Camus's motif of revolt against the absurdity of the world, we will need to examine later works in their chronological order to show how this concept develops over the course of his life.

Camus's early attempt to come to grips with the absurdity of existence is reflected in the opening words of *The Myth of Sisyphus*: "There is but one truly serious philosophical problem, and that is suicide. Judging whether life is or is not worth living amounts to answering the fundamental question of philosophy. All the rest . . . comes afterwards."[23] This stark premise grew out of the French experience in the first half of the twentieth century, with the conquest and German occupation during World War II coming so closely on the heels of the massive destruction they had suffered in the earlier Great War. Many had abandoned any hope of finding meaning in either political or spiritual sources. Thus, when Camus poses the possibility of suicide, a French audience could immediately identify with the deep pessimism that turns life itself into a question.

Camus recognizes that people are quite willing to die for ideas that are supposed to give meaning to life. However, he thinks these reasons for existence are illusory or, as we will see below, simply a different form of suicide. The real question is whether one should choose to live in a world that is absurd. Camus acknowledges that the default position for human beings is life, since "we get into the habit of living before acquiring the habit of thinking."[24] However, for those who truly think about life, it cannot be taken for granted that the "habit of living" should be maintained.

For Camus, the world taken by itself is not absurd; it is merely irrational. Absurdity is what results when this irrational world is inhabited by humans who attempt to subject it to rational thought. Our reason strives for understanding and unity, and the world thwarts this desire. The inability to bring an illogical world into conformity with the logical categories of our minds renders human beings forever exiles, or strangers, in the world they must occupy. Thus, when Camus turns to the fate of Sisyphus, he finds the universal story of human existence. Condemned by the gods to the unending punishment of pushing a boulder up a hill only to let it roll again to the bottom, Sisyphus is a tragic figure, but only because he is conscious. Any thinking human who remains conscious of reason's inability to penetrate an irrational world shares Sisyphus's fate.

Physical suicide, therefore, appears to be a viable resolution for those who recognize life's absurdity. To end one's life amounts to a renunciation of the absurd, since death is the end of our consciousness. However, to renounce absurdity is very different from resolving it. Thus, Camus sees physical suicide as the coward's way out. Similarly, our attempt to end absurdity by finding some meaning for existence is what he calls philosophical suicide. If we seek hope in an irrational world, this denies the reality the world itself presents to us. This is, in the end, Camus's reason for rejecting any theistic solutions. To speak of God in the context of a world of suffering is to close one's eyes to everything that surrounds us. In short, then, physical suicide attempts to destroy the absurd by ending consciousness while philosophical suicide tries to circumvent it through denial of the world. Both are dishonest.

As an alternative to either form of suicide, Camus argues that we should squarely face the unmerciful trinity of irrational world, intelligence and the resulting absurdity with an attitude of revolution. "Revolt gives life its value. Spread out over the whole length of a life, it restores its majesty to that life. To a man devoid of blinders, there is no finer sight than that of the intelligence at grips with a reality that transcends it."[25] Instead of renouncing consciousness or the world, we give up all hope of conquering the transcendent reality of this world, embrace meaninglessness and rebel against it. Thus, for Camus, absurdity does not mean that life is dismal. Once one recognizes that there are no limits created by false hopes, one discovers freedom. By rebelling, we are no longer chained to a past and, because we have given up hope for the future, one is liberated to the present. Each potential action in the present is free because every possibility open to us is equivalent.

This type of freedom is illustrated by Meursault's indifference in *The Stranger*. Throughout the book, he repeats the refrain that no one choice is superior to any other. He is indifferent about his conviction for rather randomly murdering an Arab, a conviction which results more from his apathy toward his mother's death, which was completely unrelated to the murder, than the murder itself. He sees no need to explain himself to the jurors and he believes that no attitude toward the death of his mother (or even his own death) is better than any other. There is no spectrum of values ranging from good to evil; everything is equal.

Ironically, Meursault's full grasp of his freedom comes just prior to his execution by guillotine. A priest comes to Meursault's cell to urge him to set his spiritual affairs in order. When the priest insists that the condemned man needs to find reconciliation, Meursault explodes in anger. To seek reconciliation would be to assume the spectrum of values that he rejects, along with the notion of a higher harmony or order in the world to which he is responsible. When the priest finally leaves in sorrow, the book ends with Meursault saying, "It was as if that great rush of anger had washed me clean, emptied me of hope, and, gazing up at the dark sky spangled with its signs and stars, for the first time, the first, I laid my heart open to the benign indifference of the universe. To feel it so like myself, indeed, so brotherly, made me realize that I'd been happy, and that I was happy still."[26]

The idea that meaning emerges from rebellion against the absurdity of an indifferent world is echoed in *The Myth of Sisyphus.* Sisyphus is keenly aware that his eternal task is futile, and it is this awareness that fascinates Camus. Without this consciousness of his fate, there is no punishment. At the same time, "The lucidity that was to constitute his [Sisyphus's] torture at the same time crowns his victory. There is no fate that cannot be surmounted by scorn."[27] The gods that control the world can sentence Sisyphus to the absurd task of shoving the rock up the hill, but they can do nothing about his defiance. He knows his condemnation is final, but he can revolt against it, and the gods are powerless to do anything about that. Sisyphus is free; "He is stronger than his rock."[28] Thus, Camus's rebellion in the face of absurdity is not a sad resignation. The freedom and happiness of a Sisyphus or Meursault is the ultimate form of defiance.

Everything is not equal. The same series of events during the Second World War that made it so clear to Camus that absurdity accurately described human existence also caused him to abandon his early claim that no qualitative difference exists between various values. One signal of this shift is found in the movement from suicide as the primary philosophical question, as in *The Myth of Sisyphus*, to the problem of murder, which becomes the focus in *The Rebel* (1951). "Awareness of the absurd, when we first claim to deduce a rule of behavior from it, makes murder seem a matter of indifference, to say the least, and hence possible. If we believe in nothing, if nothing had any meaning and if we can affirm no values whatsoever, then everything is possible and nothing has any importance. There is no pro or con: the murder is neither right nor wrong. We are free to stoke the crematory fires or to devote ourselves to the care of lepers. Evil and virtue are mere chance or caprice."[29]

As his thought evolves, Camus steadfastly holds to the absurdity of the world, but now focuses his attention on ideologies such as Nazism or Communism, which claim to save humanity while "stoking the crematory fires." All attempts to find salvation, whether on earth or in heaven, ultimately bring about the murderous circumstances that have marked history throughout its course, since they falsely promise order and explanation in an irrational world. For Camus, neutrality toward murderous systems is no longer an option; we must choose sides against all ideologies. In the face of unrelenting murder and death, Camus argues that rebellion requires justice and solidarity with our fellow human beings. Despite the fact that we never defeat the death-grip of these ideologies, we should revolt against them by affirming the human drive for life.

Camus's new understanding of revolt is best illustrated in his novel *The Plague*, in which an entire city has been placed under quarantine because of a mysterious disease that is decimating the population. This brutal plague is a metaphor for life's absurdity under murderous ideologies, and the novel uses certain characters to lay bare the various responses one might take toward them. Some simply endure the plague by getting lost in the routines; others use upheaval as an occasion for financial gain. Camus finds a more reflective approach to the plague in Christianity, represented by a highly educated priest named Paneloux. At the beginning of the novel, Paneloux interprets the plague as a sign of God's condemnation, but as the story moves on he becomes more deeply and directly involved with working to alleviate the suffering of those afflicted with the disease. This progression reaches its climax in a funeral oration for a young child who endured an agonizing death. Father Paneloux tells of a plague in which only four of eighty-one monks in a monastery survived. Three of the survivors lived by fleeing, only one stayed behind. His exhortation to the mourners was, "My brothers, each of us must be the one who stays behind."[30] Toward the end of the story, Paneloux, who remains to help those suffering, succumbs to the disease.

As two people leaving the boy's funeral contemplate the change in Paneloux's understanding of the plague, one mourner reminisces about a priest during World War II who had renounced his faith upon witnessing a young soldier whose eyes had been shot out. His friend responds by stating, "Paneloux is right . . . When an innocent youth can have his eyes destroyed, a Christian should either lose his faith or consent to having his eyes destroyed."[31] While this statement demonstrates a greater appreciation for a sacrificial Christianity than we find in Camus's earlier works, his own approach is different.[32] Camus believes that rebels should do both: lose our faith and have our eyes destroyed. This is reflected in the words of the main protagonist in the book, Dr. Rieux. At one point in *The Plague*, an outsider named Tarrou, who has joined with Dr. Rieux in the futile task of saving those stricken by the disease, asks the doctor why he keeps up the struggle. Rieux responds:

> "Since the order of the world is shaped by death, mightn't it be better for God if we refuse to believe in Him and struggle with all our might against death, without raising our eyes toward the heaven where He sits in silence?"
>
> Tarrou nodded.
>
> "Yes. But your victories will never be lasting; that's all."
>
> Rieux's face darkened.
>
> "Yes, I know that. But it's no reason for giving up the struggle."
>
> "No reason, I agree. Only, I now can picture what this plague must mean for you."
>
> "Yes. A never ending defeat."
>
> Tarrou . . . , who was staring at the floor, suddenly said:
>
> "Who taught you all this, Doctor?"
>
> The reply came promptly:
>
> "Suffering."[33]

For Camus, the absurdity and the rebellion are still there from his early writings, but a new feature is the idea of suffering in solidarity with fellow human beings. As he puts it later in *The Plague*, "there's no question of heroism in all this. It's a matter of common decency."[34]

The individual penitent. At the end of *The Plague*, the scourge subsides as mysteriously as it began. As Tarrou prepares to leave the city, his parting conversation with Dr. Rieux introduces an idea that will characterize Camus's latest writings. Up to this point in the novel, the killing condition has been represented as a scourge created by others. However, toward the end, Tarrou implicates himself directly:

> For many years I've been ashamed, mortally ashamed, of having been, even with the best intentions, even at many removes, a murderer in my turn. As time went on I merely learned that even those who were better than the rest could not keep themselves nowadays from killing or letting others kill, because such is the logic by which they live; and that we can't stir a finger in this world without the risk of bringing death to somebody. . . . I know positively . . . that each of us has the plague within him; no one, no one on earth is free from it. And I know, too, that we must keep endless watch on ourselves lest in a careless moment we breathe in somebody's face and fasten the infection on him.[35]

The turn toward individual responsibility and penance for the plagues that unleash absurdity in human life is clear in Camus's last full-length novel, *The Fall* (1956). This book is composed entirely of the narrative of Jean-Baptiste Clemence, a formerly prominent lawyer who is now the self-appointed "judge-penitent" for patrons of *Mexico City*, a seedy bar in Amsterdam. With this book, Camus addresses religious issues more directly, as evidenced by the title of the book itself and the clear reference to John the Baptist, the one who calls people to repentance, in the name of the narrator. The *Mexico City* is located at center of six circles of canals in Amsterdam, symbolic of Dante's circles of hell.

Beyond the symbolism of the names and geography of the book, however, is the theme of individual guilt, which marks a new trajectory in Camus's thought. In his early career as lawyer, Clemence believes himself superior to all because he has taken up the cause of justice in the courts. However, one rainy night, a woman standing on a bridge over the

Seine leaps into the water immediately after he passes her by. When he hears the splash, he makes no attempt to save her and avoids reading the newspapers for several days in hopes that his ignorance about her fate will relieve his guilt. This proves fruitless, and he becomes plagued by inner sounds of laughter that will not let him forget his inaction.

After failing to escape the damning laughter by several other avenues, Clemence find his way to the bar in Amsterdam and becomes the judge-penitent of self-selected "clients" at *Mexico City*. He is the penitent because he seeks expiation for his own sin by confessing, not just his unwillingness to attempt to save the suicidal woman in Paris, but also by revealing his own impure motives for what he tried to conceal under cover of justice while working as a lawyer. However, this penitent is also judge by calling his conversation partners to become authentic about their own fallenness. "Inasmuch as every judge some day ends up as a penitent, one had to travel the road in the opposite direction and practice the profession of penitent to be able to end up as a judge."[36] Thus he says about the rightful attitude of the judge-penitent, "No excuses ever, for anyone; that's my principle at the outset. I deny the good intention, the respectable mistake, the indiscretion, the extenuating circumstances. With me there is no giving of absolution or blessing."[37] With brutal honesty, Camus reveals the fallenness of all and the deep impulse toward redemption.

Camus in transition. The transition from the solitary Meursault, who finds happiness in his private rebellion against an indifferent world, to Dr. Rieux's revolt, grounded in a stubborn solidarity through human nature, is profound. In Camus's late works, we move from Dr. Rieux, who ministers to the needs of the oppressed while stating that "Salvation's much too big a word for me,"[38] to Clemence, who seeks salvation from the damning laughter that fills his head. The trajectory of Camus's work during his brief career leads him toward specifically Christian themes as he explored the problem of personal redemption. Where this might have eventually taken him had his life not been cut short has led to much speculation, but unfortunately it can be little more than that.[39] In the end, what is so compelling about the direction of Camus's thought is that it mirrors the story of so many who sought an appropriate response to the apparent absurdity that characterized this period in history.

Jean-Paul Sartre

Although Camus garnered significant attention within French intellectual circles, after World War II he was quickly overshadowed by Jean-Paul Sartre (1905-1980), who popularized existentialism and provided a more systematic expression of its ideas.[40] While Camus tended to assume the absence of God, Sartre was much more intentional in his atheism. For Sartre, the very structure of human existence demands atheism. If we are free and conscious beings, God's existence is rendered impossible or, at minimum, superfluous. Thus, Sartre states that "existentialism is nothing else than an attempt to draw all the consequences of a coherent atheistic position."[41] If human beings are alone in a universe without God (and Sartre will also say that we are utterly alone in a world full of other human beings), every question of existence, value and purpose must be thrown open to reevaluation.

It is risky business to draw too many conclusions about the connections between an individual's biography and his subsequent ideas, but Sartre's own insistence that we cannot divorce philosophy from concrete existence makes it impossible to ignore the parallels. When Sartre was born in 1905, his father, a naval officer, had already died. His mother, who had married just a year earlier, was forced to move back to her parents' home.[42] The young Jean-Paul was cross-eyed, small, sickly and, by all accounts, rather homely. As he puts it later, "Things would have been fine if my body and I had got on well together. But the fact is that we were an odd couple."[43] In his autobiographical work, *The Words* (1963), he recounts how his mother would take him to the park in hopes of finding playmates. After countless rebuffs from other children ("we would go from tree to tree and from group to group, always entreating, always excluded"),[44] they would return to their apartment where Sartre would find refuge in "words," creating his own world through reading and writing.

Though socially isolated, his intellect allowed him entrance into some of France's finest schools. Following his preparatory education, he was accepted into the École Normale Supérieure where he became acquainted with such future intellectual luminaries as Simone Weil, Maurice Merleau-Ponty and Claude Lévi-Strauss. However, the most significant relationship developed during this time was with Simone de Beauvoir.[45] In 1928, Sartre, through careless preparation, had finished last in his class on his agrégation (which is a form of comprehensive examination). The two met while Sartre was awaiting the next opportunity to take these examinations, and he quickly recognized Beauvior's intellectual talents. The two began to study together for the agrégation, with Sartre and Beauvoir ultimately finishing first and second respectively on the examination. Throughout the remainder of their lives, the two were both romantic and professional partners. However, like almost everything else in their lives, their relationship was highly unconventional. They never married or, for that matter, lived together, and each had various lovers with the full knowledge of the other. However, at her death in 1986, Beauvoir's ashes were buried beside Sartre's.

Upon his graduation, Sartre was conscripted into the French military for eighteen months, after which he taught at several lycées. He took a year away from his teaching duties to study under Heidegger and Husserl in Berlin during 1933-1934. In 1938, he produced his first widely received novel, *Nausea*, which outlined a number of the themes he would develop in his later works. However, Sartre's teaching and literary activities came to an abrupt halt with World War II. In 1939, at the age of thirty-four, he was once again drafted into the French military and was captured by the German army the following year. He was released by the Germans in 1941, and it is unclear whether his freedom was granted because they did not believe that Sartre, blind in one eye at this time, was ever actually a soldier or they simply did not consider him a threat.

After his release, Sartre became a member of the French Resistance and wrote for underground newspapers, working under the cover of his teaching duties. He also turned his attention back to writing, producing plays titled *The Flies* (1943), which was a thinly veiled attack on Nazism, and *No Exit* (1944), as well as completing his most famous philosophical work, *Being and Nothingness* (1943). The enthusiastic acceptance of *Being and Nothingness* allowed Sartre to give up teaching and devote his time to writing, editing and lecturing. In 1945, he became editor of *Les Temps Modernes (Modern Times)*, through which he continued to disseminate his ideas.

In Sartre's later career, he seemed to move away from his interest in existential philosophy to focus more on Marxist politics. Although he prided himself on the fact that he never joined the Communist party and was often highly critical of Soviet practices, he wrote *The Critique of Dialectical Reason* (1960) in defense of Marxist philosophy. However, he became progressively more disillusioned with Marxist systems after the Soviets sent their tanks into Hungary in 1956 and never completed the second volume of his *Critique*. Instead, he turned his attention to his multivolume study of Flaubert *(The Idiot of the Family)* which occupied almost the whole of his energies during the 1960s. In 1964, he was awarded the Nobel Prize for Literature, but refused to accept the award. Because of poor health brought on by heavy smoking, drinking and amphetamine use, his writing production dropped off sharply in the last decade of his life. At his death in 1980, thousands of people lined the streets for his funeral procession.

The problem of existence. Five years prior to the publication of *Being and Nothingness*, Sartre had already outlined his foundational ideas on the question of existence in his novel *Nausea*. This book takes the form of a diary kept by a historian named Antoine Roquentin and found among his personal effects following his death. The diary records Roquentin's attempt to understand Marquis de Rollebon, a political figure who had long passed from existence. As he tries to grasp the meaning of another person's existence, he comes face to face with the question of what it means to exist. The more Roquentin becomes absorbed in the life of de Rollebon, the more he realizes that his own existence is reduced. As he puts it:

> M. de Rollebon was my partner; he needed me in order to exist and I needed him so as not to feel my existence. I furnished the raw material, the material I had to re-sell, which I didn't know what to do with: existence, my existence. . . . I was only a means of making him live, he was my reason for living, he had delivered me from myself. What shall I do now?[46]

The question of Roquentin's existence is sharpened by another character in *Nausea*, the "Self-Taught Man." The Self-Taught Man frequents the library used by Roquentin for his research and is reading through the collection alphabetically in an endeavor to learn everything knowable. Thus, Sartre says, "He has read everything; he has stored up in his head most of what anyone knows about parthenogenesis, and half the arguments against vivisection. There is a universe behind and before him. And the day is approaching when closing the last book on the last shelf on the far left: he will say to himself, 'Now what?'"[47] Indeed, the Self-Taught Man confides to Roquentin that he longed to complete this task of gaining knowledge so that he could have "an adventure." For Sartre, the Self-Taught Man represents the futile attempt to know objectively. This approach to knowing, characteristic of most philosophy, makes existence impossible, because it pulls us away from concrete reality.

What Roquentin discovers as he progressively retreats from his absorption with de Rollebon is that he is confronted by an uncaring, unconscious, inert and absurd world of things. These objective realities induce "nausea" because they are so unlike himself, a conscious and free being, yet they seek to impose themselves on his existence. Thus, he says, "Objects should not touch because they are not alive. You use them, put them back in place, you live among them: they are useful, nothing more. But they touch me, it is unbearable. I am afraid of being in contact with them as though they were living beasts."[48]

Sartre argues that we try to overcome nausea by one of two means. Either we allow contingent objects to give meaning to our life, which is impossible because meaning cannot be deduced from things that have only instrumental purposes, or we fabricate a necessary, causal being—a God—as the giver of our significance. However, Sartre insists that "no necessary being can explain existence; contingency is not a delusion, a probability which can be dissipated; it is the absolute, consequently, the perfect free gift."[49] In the end, there is no escape from contingency: "Every existing thing is born without reason, prolongs itself out of weakness and dies by chance."[50]

Being-in-itself/being-for-itself. The themes first explored in *Nausea*—the radical disjunction between objective and subjective existence, the absurdity in finding meaning outside ourselves, the problem of "the Other" for authentic existence—are all developed by Sartre in his later writings. The first of these themes, however, provides the foundation for his formulation of the other concepts. In a rebellion against the modern scientific ethos that attempts to reduce reality to mechanical explanations, Sartre argues that that the sort of existence that pertains to objects must be radically distinguished from the mode of existence experienced by human beings. He thus refers to the existence of material artifacts as being-in-itself, while conscious beings possess being-for-itself.

Being-in-itself is an existence in which the essence of the object comes before the actual creation of the object. Sartre uses the example of a paper cutter, which "is an object which has been made by an artisan whose inspiration came from a concept."[51] The concept (or essence), which includes both the design and the purpose of the paper cutter, must be present in the mind of the artifact's creator before the actual object can be brought into existence. This understanding of artifacts as dependent on the mind of an artisan reflects Husserl's influence, who argues that it is the nature of consciousness to posit an object. In keeping with this tradition, Sartre argues that being-in-itself does not exist apart from consciousness.

The artisan's role in granting design and purpose to a thing is particularly significant in the light of Sartre's atheism. While we may assign reasons, design and purpose to the objects we create, if the physical world we inhabit has no creator (the logical result of atheism), then being-in-itself has no reason for its existence. Moreover, no object is capable of providing any meaning, explanation or justification for our existence. Things just are. The pure contingency and meaninglessness of the objective universe is what creates Roquentin's nausea.

It is the role of consciousness, what Sartre calls being-for-itself, in creating the essence of objects and assigning meaning to them that raises the question of the existence of consciousness itself. Again, Sartre's atheism forces a departure from the conventional approach to the nature of consciousness. When we conceive of human beings as the product of a divine creation, "the concept of man in the mind of God is comparable to the concept of a paper-cutter in the mind of the manufacturer, and, following certain techniques and a conception, God produces man, just as the artisans, following a definition and a technique, makes a paper-cutter."[52] Without God, however, there can be no preexisting concept of a human being. To put it in Sartre's terminology, our existence precedes our essence. We are born with no prescribed nature or purpose.

> Man is nothing else but what he makes of himself. . . . For we mean
> that man first exists, that is, that man first of all is the being who hurls
> himself toward a future and who is conscious of imagining himself as
> being in the future. Man is at the start a plan which is aware of itself,

rather than a patch of moss, a piece of garbage, or a cauliflower; nothing exists prior to this plan; there is nothing in heaven; man will be what he will have planned to be.[53]

The assertion that human beings are "a plan" points to the key distinction between being-for-itself and being-in-itself. Objects are what they are. Their existence is contained in their essence. In contrast, being-for-itself—human existence—is free. Since being-for-itself has no prescribed essence, an infinite range of possibilities is available to us. The demand of freedom, then, is that we choose our identity. This choice is not a once-for-all event, but a never-ending process in which new possibilities continue to emerge, along with the demand that we continue to choose from among them.

The key concept that describes what makes freedom possible is "nothingness." Being-for-itself—consciousness—is not simply conscious; it is always conscious *of* something. Consciousness requires an object of which to be conscious. Thus, human consciousness is aware of objects such as paper-cutters, and the paper-cutter cannot be understood apart from my consciousness of it. However, we are also conscious of what an object is not. When we hold the paper cutter, we are also conscious of what is not in our hand (e.g., a book or pencil). Consciousness of what is absent (nothingness) is the source of our freedom because it creates awareness of my alternatives. I could put down the paper cutter and pick up the book or pencil. I can move to another city, change religions, feed the poor or start forest fires. What I do now does not determine what I will do in the future. In other words, we know that our identity is never fixed because countless alternatives present themselves to us.

Another aspect of nothingness is that it reveals a truth that crystallizes the problem of human existence. Consciousness of nothingness makes clear to us that we are incomplete. When I choose to pursue a profession such as teaching, this is also a choice not to be engaged in other professions. Thus, I am simultaneously aware of being a teacher and of not being a scuba instructor, an airline pilot or the Secretary of State. The latter roles all represent possibilities, even if distant, that are not actualized. This awareness of nothingness, of unrealized possibilities, evokes a desire for transcendence within us. We have an impulse, not just to be more than we are, but to be everything. In other words, we perpetually strive to overcome nothingness by our choices. Yet because our choices always take place within finitude, this is a self-defeating endeavor. With each new choice, I wall off others and thereby increase my consciousness of what I am not.

It is this desire to eliminate nothingness and escape contingency that, according to Sartre, generates our idea of God. God is conceived as a being that lacks contingency, a being in which no reality is unactualized. It should be noted that this is precisely the pursuit we engage in when we desire an unchanging perfection. Thus, Sartre says, "man is a being whose project is to be God."[54] Stated otherwise, Sartre says that our goal is to be being-in-itself-for-itself. We want to be both free (for-itself) and complete (in-itself). However, this project puts us in an impossible situation. The only type of existence that is complete is being-in-itself. To the extent that a paper cutter fulfills its purpose as a paper cutter, its existence is identical with its essence. By contrast, being-for-itself is, by definition, incomplete, because only in consciousness of nothingness is freedom possible. As long as we are conscious, our essence remains open.

We cannot have it both ways. Nor, for that matter, can God. On the one hand, completeness requires that we forfeit consciousness, which is always confronted by nothingness. Objects that are complete lack awareness of their plentitude, which, for conscious beings, defeats the intent of eliminating nothingness. On the other hand, to be aware is to be conscious of division, contingency and imperfection, the very conditions of human freedom. Thus, the desire to attain perfection is incompatible with freedom. Such is the impossible predicament of human existence. The impossibility of any resolution to this predicament also stands at the root of Sartre's rejection of God's existence.

Condemned to be free. As we have seen, freedom makes the perfection we long for impossible. Since we cannot shake ourselves free of the desire for transcendence, it remains in tension with our freedom. The incompatibility of these two forces then clarifies Sartre's assertion that freedom is a burden. Caught between our desire to become God and the impossibility of attaining perfection, humans face the temptation to divest themselves of their freedom.

There are many avenues by which we can attempt to deny the very

freedom that defines our existence as being-for-itself. We can claim that
we are subject to laws of physical necessity, are under obligation to some
sort of transcendent standard or norm, or are driven by supernatural
determinism. However, one of the most common attempts at avoiding
freedom is to allow ourselves to be defined from without by a role. Sartre
speaks of this in his well-known example of the waiter he observes while
sitting in a café:

> His movement is quick and forward, a little too precise, a little too
> rapid. He comes toward the patrons with a step a little too quick. He
> bends forward a little too eagerly; his voice, his eyes express an inter-
> est a little too solicitous for the order of the customer. Finally there he
> returns, trying to imitate in his walk the inflexible stiffness of some
> kind of automaton while carrying his tray with the recklessness of a
> tight-rope-walker by putting it in a perpetually unstable, perpetually
> broken equilibrium which he perpetually reestablishes by a light
> movement of the arm and hand. All his behavior seems to us a game.[55]

The game the waiter plays is "*being* a waiter in a café."[56] In one sense,
he is a waiter. However, this role can never be the whole story for a
waiter. The function of "waiter" falls into the category of being-in-itself, it
is the type of thing that is given a definition that assumes an external
standard by which it is judged. To the extent that a waiter is a waiter, he
can never be anything else. But this is obviously not true of the *human
being* who is a waiter, because a human being is also a free and conscious
being. Thus, Sartre says that this man's attempt to be nothing more than
a waiter obscures the fact that the waiter chooses this role from an infinite array of options. Being a waiter does not provide any ultimate definition for his existence, because he could choose to do something else.
And even if the waiter convinces himself that this is not the case, the very
fact that he would have to convince himself indicates his awareness that
he has a choice.

Anguish and bad faith. Why does this waiter attempt to define himself in
terms of his role? Sartre says that his role removes the anguish of freedom. While the waiter knows clearly all the options available to him and
is aware that he is free to select from a myriad of alternatives, he is also
aware that he would be expected to provide some justification for his
choice. This evokes anguish (fear of freedom) because he now becomes

responsible for a decision that transcends what he will do as an occupation. His choices shape his entire identity. Thus, when the question of
identity is placed in juxtaposition with our desire to become God, our
choices take on infinite proportion. If we grasp this, we realize that we
have nothing to appeal to beyond ourselves to explain or justify our
choice. As Sartre puts it:

> In the bright realm of values, we have no excuse behind us, nor justifi-
> cation before us. We are alone, with no excuses. That is the idea I shall
> try to convey when I say that man is condemned to be free. Con-
> demned, because he did create himself, yet, and in other respects is
> free; because, once thrown into the world, he is responsible for every-
> thing he does.[57]

The fact that our freedom assumes such immense responsibility
explains why the waiter tells himself he must get up and be a waiter when
the alarm clock goes off in the morning. This is, of course, a lie, because
he could turn the alarm off and go back to sleep, wake up and go to the
bookstore and apply for a job there, or buy a new book, take it to the café
and sit there sipping coffee rather than waiting tables. Sartre analyzes the
waiter's desire to lose himself in his role as an attempt to seek refuge in
being-in-itself. He wants an essence that is chosen by others, just as the
essence of a paper cutter (being-in-itself) is determined by another. He
does this because being-in-itself is exempt from responsibility; it does not
have to justify itself. Thus, to the extent that the waiter allows himself to
be determined by his role, he is being-in-itself and does not have to validate his identity. However, this attempt to relieve the anguish of freedom
amounts to the waiter's denial of his existence as being-for-itself. Being-
for-itself does not simply have freedom, it *is* freedom. Therefore, to forfeit freedom is to lose the self.

Sartre calls the attempt to avoid anguish by denying our freedom *bad
faith*. Bad faith is a lie because it is dishonesty about our freedom, but it is
a unique type of lie. In bad faith, we lie to ourselves. For our waiter, the
lie is that he can define himself as an objective reality obligated to a set of
external standards that defines his essence. However, bad faith is not just
a matter of lying to ourselves. As Sartre points out, "The essence of the lie
implies in fact that the liar actually is in complete possession of the truth
which he is hiding."[58] Thus, bad faith consists in knowing the truth about

ourselves while at the same time we attempt to deceive ourselves. In bad faith, then, we freely tell ourselves that we are not free—that we are obligated to conform to objective standards, that we cannot escape our history or are determined by forces beyond ourselves. Thus, we are divided within ourselves, or as Sartre frequently expresses it, we are inauthentic.

The Other. Being-for-itself demands that we embrace our radical freedom within a silent world where neither God nor others can rescue us. In fact, the presence of others is the greatest threat to authenticity. Sartre sets up the situation in this manner:

> I am in a public park. Not far away there is a lawn and along the edge of that lawn there are benches. A man passes by those benches. I see this man; I apprehend him as an object and at the same time as a man. What does this signify? What do I mean when I assert that this object *is a man?*[59]

If this person is understood as an object, we can think of him as an object among other objects, indifferently related to the things so that his disappearance from the park does not change the relationship between the other objects in the park.

However, to understand an individual as an object is not to apprehend him as a conscious being. The man we observe in the park also observes the park, not indifferently, but as a subject. He touches various objects in the park, uses them and assigns significance to them. Moreover, he is also capable of observing me as a physical, objective presence in relationship to other objects in the park. As Sartre puts it, then, we are aware of the man's existence as a subject because "I cannot be an object for an object."[60] Thus, when we observe our man in the park as an object, we do not treat him as a conscious and free being and do not know him as being-for-itself. However, it is fruitless for us to claim that we know him as a subject. His consciousness is interior, beyond our knowledge and control.

While I encounter difficulty in any attempt to truly know another conscious being, it is "the Other's" ability to see me that represents the problem for my own existence. As long as I am the observer, watching and making evaluations of another human being, I remain safe because everything is viewed from my perspective. However, if the man turns and stares at me, even though everything in the park remains objectively the same, the situation has taken a decisive shift. There is now a second consciousness in the equation. My perspective is not the only one present. The unity that previously characterized my world, and my control over it, disappears because another consciousness also apprehends the world, but is completely free to apprehend it in a manner radically different from mine. Moreover, the perspective of the Other includes me. This alien viewpoint is now part of my world and it therefore must be included in how I see the world. At the same time, the Other's viewpoint is beyond me since it is interior to another consciousness.

Behind all this lies Sartre's phenomenological approach to ontology. My awareness of the existence of other consciousnesses is not the result of a detached knowledge. My observations of others put them only in the realm of objects. Instead, I know the Other as a conscious being by the responses they evoke in me, such as shame, fear or moral superiority. In my endeavor to come to some conclusion about what I am—the fixed and pure existence that constitutes our desire for perfection—I depend on the evaluation of others. This is the origin of the overwhelming desire to see ourselves as the Other sees us. Ultimately, however, this represents bad faith since the Other always views us as an object. In other words, when we try to view ourselves via the consciousness of another, we view ourselves as being-in-itself. The temptation is always to seek the safety of conformity to the evaluation of others. However, this endeavor fails at two points. First, we cannot enter the consciousness of the Other to know what her evaluation is, so our attempts to be what others have judged us to be are doomed from the outset. Moreover, since the only way another can know us is as object, whenever we attempt to construct our existence according to the gaze of the Other, we cease to be what we really are: conscious, free beings.

Sartre's understanding of our relationship to the Other becomes even more complex when we recall that our project is to become God. Not only do we need the perspective of free and conscious beings who can tell us who we are, we want them to validate our belief that we are complete. However, we cannot control the perspective of a free consciousness to assure the picture we desire. If we could determine their verdict, they would cease to be the type of being who could pass the judgment we crave. And even if we did receive the evaluation we long for, it is useless:

the determinations of another cannot sustain the freedom we want to preserve as well. Our relationship to the Other, then, is destined for futility. As a result, our own project of becoming perfect while retaining our freedom is similarly futile.

Sartre illustrates this conundrum in his famous play *No Exit*. In the play, three recently deceased individuals find themselves in Hell and are fated to spend eternity together in the same room. Each must rely on another character to validate his or her own identity, but this pursuit is frustrated by the simultaneous expectation of the Other to find the same justification. Given this, each character recognizes that the Other intends to use them as an instrument or object rather than acknowledging that he or she is a free individual. At the end of the play, then, Garcin, one of the characters, comes to an insight about their situation. "So this is hell. I'd never have believed it. You remember all we were told about the torture-chambers, the fire and brimstone, the 'burning marl.' Old wives' tales! There's no need for red-hot pokers. Hell is—other people!"[61]

Sartre's evaluation that "hell is other people" is deeply indebted to Hegel's idea of the master-slave dialectic, a struggle in which our social relationships are marked by attempts to gain recognition from the Other. However, while Hegel is confident that interpersonal conflict can be resolved into mutual recognition, Sartre does not envision a transcendence of this tension. Instead, the impulse that drives us toward both the frozen facticity of perfection and the freedom of conscious existence is an impossible pursuit—an impossibility that is unavoidably revealed in our encounters with others. Moreover, we do not avoid the problem by conceiving of God rather than human beings as the Other. If God is a conscious being, we are still only an object to God. On the other hand, if God is not a subject, "he can only experience it [the self] without knowing it."[62] Thus, Sartre can proclaim that "existentialism isn't so atheistic that it wears itself out showing that God doesn't exist. Rather, it declares that even if God did exist, that would change nothing."[63]

As was the case with Camus, Sartre concludes that human existence is absurd, but for different reasons. For Camus, the irrational world lacks unity. Sartre, in contrast, says that life's absurdity arises when our unified world is disturbed by our need to find our identity in the Other—from objects, other human beings or God. But Sartre says that each fails to sup-

ply what we seek because they cannot take our freedom into account.
The only authentic response to these things is indifference, but that does
nothing to satisfy our impulse for transcendence. In view of this absurd
situation, Sartre concludes that "man is a useless passion. We have no
reason to be here and no hope of achieving the finality we seek in our
identity, but our impulse for transcendence continues to drive us toward
its pursuit."[64]

Evaluating Sartre. Sartre has been properly lauded for a number of
important insights, not least of which is the reappraisal of the question of
freedom. The tendency among philosophers, particularly in the century
prior to Sartre's life, was to view human freedom as a pure good and
inherently desirable. Sartre, with keen psychological insight, demonstrates what a fearful thing freedom can be, especially when it is unteth-
ered from traditional metaphysical moorings. His examination of our
denial of freedom through the mechanisms of bad faith has more than
just a hint of truth to it. In his consideration of bad faith, the reader recognizes how seductive it is to define ourselves according to the roles created by the expectations of those around us. Thus, if we view Sartre from
the perspective of the agenda he sets out—"to draw all the consequences
of a coherent atheistic position"—his philosophy represents an honest
and serious attempt to do just that.

Despite these valuable elements in Sartre's thought, serious gaps
remain in some fundamental areas. One such gap is a noticeable vague-
ness is Sartre's explanations about the origin of the objective world. He
locates its source in consciousness, but makes no serious attempt to
explain why the means by which we are conscious of an external realm
must also be viewed as the originator of this world. Moreover, he simply
passes over the question of how consciousness itself comes into being.
Given his commitment to phenomenological ontology, it is clear that
questions about origin will be problematic. However, it seems arbitrary to
decide from the start that we will not ask such questions, particularly
since conclusions about origins would appear to have considerable bear-
ing on the very topics that interest him the most, such as our impulse for
transcendence or our need to find validation in the Other.

Sartre's analysis of Being provides the foundation for his atheism.
However, one cannot help but notice that when he arbitrarily limits the

categories of existence to being-in-itself and being-for-itself, it is inevitable that he will conclude that God does not exist. After all, no one wants to argue that God is an unconscious object (being-in-itself) or a conscious being whose pursuit of self is dependent on the Other (being-for-itself), as even Sartre recognizes. Instead, he asserts that our concept of God arises from fusing the two concepts, so that God, in our conception, is being-in-itself-for-itself, a perfect and conscious being. He then attempts to show that such a view is incoherent. This argument comes off as a straw man, however, since I am not aware of any serious theist whose concept of God is limited to some hybrid of ontological structures found in time and space.

In the end, Sartre's ontology leaves some of the most basic philosophical questions unasked. If we are existing, transcendent, free beings who naturally ask questions about origin, purpose and the good, how do we come to exist as such in a world in which our existence, transcendence and freedom have no discernible origin or *telos*, as Sartre believes? In a world that does at times seem absurd and purposeless, Sartre's conclusions will have resonance with some. However, it seems too easy to arrive at those answers without asking the types of questions that lead many to very different conclusions.[65]

Simone Weil

The very short life of Simone Weil (1909-1943) is full of the odd features and eccentricities that make her an irresistible subject for biographers and arouse curiosity in the rest of us.[66] She was born to agnostic Jewish parents, was an outspoken atheist through her early years and eventually became a Christian mystic. After her conversion, Weil had a deep appreciation for Catholicism but refused baptism on several occasions, including just prior to her death. Her amazing intellect was evident early in life; she mastered several languages in her youth and finished in first place at the École Normale Supérieure. Yet she always felt intellectually inferior in the shadow of her brother, Andre, a mathematical prodigy who eventually taught at Princeton.[67]

Weil's university years, and those immediately following, were framed by passionate commitment to Marxism, pacifism and political activism. By the end of her life, however, she had renounced the first two allegiances, and her political activism was absorbed into her Christian mysticism. Although respected for her intellect, she was dismissed from several teaching positions because of her unorthodox teaching methods and involvement with workers' union politics. At several points in Weil's life, she took on factory jobs or peasant work in the countryside to express her solidarity with the lower classes. However, she never stayed at any of these jobs for more than three months, leaving either because of illness or because she was sacked for incompetence. Adding to her embarrassment at being unable to sustain these associations with society's forgotten was the fact that her wealthy parents frequently had to rescue her from these misadventures.

Because of her Jewish lineage, Weil was denied a teaching position when the Germans occupied France, and her family fled to the United States in early 1942 out of fear for their safety. However, Weil, once secure in America, was racked by guilt by her awareness of the suffering of her fellow French citizens (although she rarely referred to any sense of identity with the plight of her fellow Jews). Unable to tolerate this guilt, she left America for England after a few months and volunteered to do clerical work for DeGaulle's Free France in London. To identify with those suffering in occupied France, she lived in a small, unheated apartment and restricted her diet to what she supposed were the rations allowed to her fellow French citizens. After less than a year from her arrival in England, she contracted tuberculosis and was sent to the Grosvenor Sanatorium. While there, she refused to eat and died soon after in 1943, at the age of thirty-four.

A final irony of Weil's life is that in its brief duration, she published very little, mainly political essays and articles in trade union papers. However, before she left for America, she had entrusted her notebooks to the French lay theologian, Gustave Thibon. These, in combination with additional manuscripts that had been carefully preserved by her parents, would result in a collection of works that surprised her admirers by their magnitude.[68] Perhaps even more startling to these early readers was the subject matter. She had published few Christian writings prior to her death and most of her acquaintances had little indication of the direction her life had taken in the final five years.

As shocking as her conversion was to acquaintances and readers however, it seems to have been no less unexpected to Weil herself. During one of her ill-fated adventures, having gone to show solidarity with the anarchists in the Spanish Civil War (where she refused to take up arms because of her pacifism), she stumbled over a pot of boiling oil and burned herself badly. Her parents took her to Portugal to recover, and from there she found her way to a monastery at Solesmes. During her stay, she writes of her experience upon hearing the Gregorian chants of the monks,

> I was suffering from splitting headaches; each sound hurt me like a blow; by an extreme effort of concentration I was able to rise above this wretched flesh, to leave it to suffer by itself, heaped up in a corner, and to find a pure and perfect joy in the unimaginable beauty of the chanting and the words. This experience enabled me by analogy to get a better understanding of the possibility of loving divine love in the midst of affliction. It goes without saying that in the course of these services the thought of the Passion of Christ entered into my being once and for all.[69]

Shortly after, one of the monks introduced her to the seventeenth-century British metaphysical poets, and from there she began to devour the works of Christian mystics. Looking back on this discovery, Weil says, "God in his mercy had prevented me [before this time] from reading the mystics, so that it should be evident to me that I had not invented this absolutely unexpected contact."[70]

Creation as divine self-limitation. The idea that God comes to us unexpectedly is seen throughout Weil's work, which, though unsystematic, is characterized by recurring themes such as looking, slavery and decreation. Each of these motifs finds a crucial link in her understanding of God's creative act. While most theologians view creation as a manifestation of God's power, Weil sees it quite differently. "On God's part creation is not an act of self-expansion but of restraint and renunciation. God and all his creatures are less than God alone. God accepted this diminution. He emptied a part of his being from himself. . . . God permitted the existence of things distinct from himself and worth infinitely less than himself. By this creative act he denied himself, as Christ has told us to deny ourselves. God denied himself for our sakes in order to give us the possibility of denying ourselves for him."[71] The manner in which we experience this withdrawal of God from creation is in the fact that he has given the world over to necessity, or the force that Weil consistently refers to as gravity. God removes himself in order that the laws that govern the universe might function.

As the passage above indicates, God's creative act reflects his loving nature since his absence allows us to choose him freely. Paradoxically, creation is also the same act that allows for the evil and suffering of this life. In the structures that God has set in place, all created things are ruled by a necessity that sometimes brings benefit, but just as often crushes us. The indifference of the universe to our suffering signals God's desire that we love him freely and as he is. If God rewarded good actions in this life, we would be drawn to him for merely instrumental reasons. But such reasons do not meet the standard of love, which must be given without condition. In this sense, then, the good we experience in this world is not something different from evil. What we perceive as evil is the result of looking at the world as absent of God. At the same time we experience God's absence, however, God is present in weakness.

While the gravity of necessity is an inescapable aspect of creation and exerts a downward pull on us, God's presence is apparent through beauty. This beauty, according to Weil, is found within the same universe that can be the scene of so much suffering. Reflecting the influence of Plato, who she greatly admires, she sees both danger and possibility in our recognition of the beautiful in creation. The beauty in the objects and order of the universe originates in God and is designed by God to draw us to him. However, as partial and distorted copies of God's beauty, the beauty found in creation is secondary. As Weil puts it, "Our immediate universe is like the scenery in a theater."[72] Therefore, "All these secondary kinds of beauty are of infinite value as openings to universal beauty. But, if we stop short at them, they are, on the contrary, veils; then they corrupt."[73]

The choice beauty confronts us with, then, is a choice between gravity and grace. If we invest the beauty of this world with the power to save us, our souls are pulled back to earth by the forces of gravity. However, if we understand that worldly beauty is reflected (or is a means rather than an end), grace allows us to transcend gravity and enlivens our longing for God. More precisely, "The longing to love the beauty of the world in a human being is essentially the longing for the incarnation. It is mistaken if it thinks it is anything else. The incarnation alone can satisfy it."[74] God's beauty is found primarily in his self-denial, manifest both in creation and in God's unity with humanity.

Thus, in the paradoxical style that marks Weil's thought, the created order that obscures also reveals. The universe whose laws impose on us an indifferent necessity also reveal God as the loving, incarnate sufferer. While "the soul's natural inclination to love beauty is the trap God most frequently uses in order to win it and open it to the breath from on high,"[75] this love of beauty also threatens to chain us to this world of necessity. Weil sums up this paradox by an analogy. "Two prisoners whose cells adjoin communicate with each other by knocking on the wall. The wall is the thing which separates them but it is also their means of communication. It is the same with us and God. Every separation is a link."[76]

Looking and eating. One of the characteristic ways in which Weil expresses the difference between our separation and our linkage with God is through the contrast between eating and looking. Eating grows out of our craving to take or possess. It is a willful activity (or muscular activity, to put it in Weil's customary vocabulary) that seeks to satisfy a need. The problem with the will, according to Weil, is that eating destroys what it consumes. We see what is good and beautiful in creation and attempt to seize it as a final reality rather than understanding it as a means. Our will to possess, however, operates within a limited domain and cannot ultimately attain what it desires.

> The will only controls a few movements of a few muscles. And these movements are associated with the idea of the change of position of nearby objects. I can will putting my hand flat on the table. If inner purity, inspiration or truth of thought were necessarily associated with attitudes of this kind, they might be the object of will. As this is not the case, we can only beg for them.[77]

Nevertheless, while the will is not sufficient in itself for salvation:

> The right use of the will is a condition of salvation, necessary no doubt but remote, inferior, very subordinate and purely negative. The weeds are pulled up by the muscular effort of the peasant, but only sun and water can make the corn grow. The will cannot produce any good in the soul.[78]

The muscular effort she refers to is that we acknowledge our striving for control and force (our hunger) and remain hungry. It is this willingness to hunger and thirst that she understands as repentance.

For Weil, the efforts of the intellect fall into the same category as those of the will. Thus, she says that it is wrong-headed to speak of seeking for God. Seeking reduces God to a problem that can be resolved by data. "It does not rest with the soul to believe in the reality of God if God does not reveal this reality. In trying to do so it either labels something else with the name of God, and that is idolatry, or else its belief in God remains abstract and verbal."[79] From this, then, it is apparent that Weil does not conceive of gravity as a force that acts exclusively on physical objects. Indeed, it applies primarily to the highest of our soul's natural abilities—our volition and our intellect. All uses of these native powers of the soul, then, compel us toward worshiping something other than the real God.

For Weil, the opposite of willing or eating is expressed by words like waiting, desire and looking. "One of the principal truths of Christianity, a truth that goes almost unrecognized today, is that looking is what saves us."[80] While eating represents our attempt to grasp salvation, looking and waiting represent our receptiveness to *God's* salvation. To find this openness, we have to accept the reality that creation does not possess goodness or purpose in and of itself and, through grace, to receive from God a desire for him, because "it is desire that saves."[81] Thus, while our impulse is to seek salvation by our own actions, Weil says that

> the attitude that brings about salvation is not like any form of activity. The Greek word which expresses it is *hypomenē,* and *patientia* is rather an inadequate translation of it. It is the waiting or attentive and faithful immobility that lasts indefinitely and cannot be shaken. The slave, who waits near the door so as to open it immediately when the master knocks, is the best image of it. He must be ready to die of hunger and exhaustion rather than change his attitude. It must be possible for his companions to call him, talk to him, hit him, without even turning his head.[82]

Slavery and decreation. Through such things as the beauty of creation, the love of neighbor or the rituals of the church, God seeks to make us receptive to divine love. Since the divine love is a self-emptying love on God's part, however, we can only gain it through denial of ourselves. Weil speaks of this self-denial as becoming a slave, a self-identity she had assumed during her incursions into manual labor.

As I worked in the factory, indistinguishable to all eyes, including my own, from the anonymous mass, the affliction of others entered into my flesh and my soul. Nothing separated me from it, for I had really forgotten my past and I looked forward to no future, finding it difficult to imagine the possibility of surviving all the fatigue. . . . There I received forever the mark of a slave, like the branding of the red-hot iron the Romans put on the foreheads of their most despised slaves. Since then I have always regarded myself as a slave.[83]

It was only later, while working in the vineyards just prior to her conversion, that she made the connection between Christianity and her identification with the underclass. "There the conviction was suddenly borne in upon me that Christianity is pre-eminently the religion of slaves, that slaves cannot help belonging to it, and I among others."[84]

The repetitiveness and anonymity of manual labor offer the most concrete recognition of this life's absurdity and our obligation to the unbending mechanical necessity of nature's laws. Here we see most clearly the futility of attempting to assert our will and make ourselves something. Thus, the slave, who has given up hope of possessing in this world, is already in a position to understand God's self-denial. When we can forsake our desire for justice and embrace our powerlessness, we create the condition under which God can remake us in his image.

Among men, a slave does not become like his master by obeying him. On the contrary, the more he obeys the greater is the distance between them. It is otherwise between man and God. If a reasonable creature is absolutely obedient, he becomes a perfect image of the Almighty as far as this is possible for him.[85]

Those who have been stripped of possessions find it easier to have no attachment on earth. This attitude of detachment explains Weil's unwillingness to receive baptism and become part of the Roman Catholic Church.

What frightens me is the Church as a social structure. Not only on account of its blemishes, but from the very fact that it is something social. It is not that I am of a very individualistic temperament. I am afraid for the opposite reason. I am aware of very strong gregarious tendencies in myself. My natural disposition is to be very easily influenced, too much influenced, and above all by anything collective.[86]

Her concern is that if she identifies with any group that possesses social standing or power of any type, she would fall into a "Church patriotism," a sense of being at home in some earthly institution. Moreover, because the feelings of social inclusion are so similar to those that arise from religious experience, she fears that she might confuse the two. Thus, while she did not condemn baptism or church membership for anyone else, Weil understood her call to be such that, "it is necessary and ordained that I should be alone, a stranger and an exile in relation to every human circle without exception."[87]

Another way in which Weil speaks of the Christian renunciation of power is as "decreation." When God creates us, he does so by limiting his own power. Therefore, in order that God may once again be all in all, we must consent to become nothing, to decreate ourselves. "Our existence is made up only of his waiting for our acceptance not to exist. He is perpetually begging from us that existence which he gives. He gives it to us in order to beg it from us."[88] The idea Weil wishes to communicate in decreation is not that we should cease to be, but that we cease to be apart from God. Once again, the paradigms by which the Christian understands decreation are creation and incarnation. Since God relinquishes power in the creation of the universe, "we participate in the creation of the world by decreating ourselves."[89] The power of freedom God gives human beings in creation can then be clearly understood alongside the incarnation. "An imaginary divinity has been given to man [in creation] so that he may strip himself of it as Christ did of his real divinity."[90]

Conclusion

Just as Weil's thought defies systematization, it also resists simple classification. In a very real sense, her tendencies toward mysticism make her an uneasy fit in a chapter on existentialism. On the other hand, it is not difficult to see the parallels with others in this chapter. For example, all four thinkers have a strong sense of life's absurdity, which exists alongside an individual drive for transcendence. Our response to futility, then, requires a decision that cannot be informed by the social structures or ideologies of the age since they are the fuel of absurdity. Camus and Sartre seek this transcendence by taking the role of the knowing outsider. To avoid being sucked into the machinery, we must remain aloof.

In contrast, Weil parallels Marcel's thought in her conclusion that we find transcendence through relationship with God and that this relationship can only be understood in terms of mystery. The element that sends Weil's understanding of the divine-human relationship along a different trajectory is the centrality of creation as a divine self-limitation. While Marcel speaks of the importance of inter-subjectivity in our quest to become fully human, he is concerned that contact with the unconscious masses is something to be avoided lest we get dragged into a depersonalizing anonymity. Weil, however, says that it is in our anonymity among the slave class that we are most likely to find the self-denying God, and through this, to gain our true identity. It is precisely within God's hiddenness and absence that we see God most clearly. Thus, the more we are hidden and perceived absent from the forces that govern this world, the more Godlike we become.

5. EXISTENCE AND THE WORD OF GOD: DIALECTICAL THEOLOGY AND NEO-ORTHODOXY

I t is an oft-repeated statement that Karl Barth's Romans (Römerbrief), first published in 1919, "fell like a bomb on the playground of the theologians."[1] Those who study the history of theology agree that a decisively new theological movement was initiated with its appearance. This is where the agreement ends. In fact, one finds tremendous debate over such mundane matters as what this new movement should be called, though it is not for any lack of suggestions.

An early designation affixed to this new theological trend was "crisis theology" (or theology of crisis), which alludes not only to the deep cultural and theological crisis that confronted Europe, and indeed the whole world, at the end of World War I but also to the idea that God's Word challenges humanity with its call to decision. Some have preferred the label "kerygmatic theology," in view of this school's renewed commitment to the church's proclamation of God's revelatory act in history. Others, noting the attempt to recover themes from the theology of the Reformers have called it "neo-Reformation theology."

A more common form of reference to this new theological approach has been neo-orthodoxy. Even though this name has had greater longevity than most others, it was coined by opponents of this new style of theology. For this reason, the theologians most likely to be identified as neo-orthodox are also the least likely to identify themselves as such. A key

reason for this is that these "neo-orthodox" theologians were highly critical of the theological school identified at that time as "orthodoxy," and
wanted a greater level of distinction from "orthodox" theology than the
prefix *neo-* provided. Although we will occasionally refer to this group as
"neo-orthodox," the label we prefer is "dialectical theology."[2] While the
term *dialectical* is rather ambiguous, this ambiguity reflects the continuing
debate about the boundaries on this theological approach. Despite controversy on the finer points of what constitutes dialectical theology, it is
possible to identify various features that are generally characteristic of
the movement.

For one thing, dialectical theology registers its discontent with theological systems that attempt to reduce Christianity to a series of timeless,
logical truths about God. Instead, when we speak of a God who is wholly
Other, we are confronted with paradoxes that cannot be neatly unrav-
eled by discursive reason. Jesus Christ, who is both fully human and
divine, is the means by which the eternal intersects history. While reason
itself cannot neatly explain the incarnation or the means by which the
eternal enters the temporal realm, these paradoxes (and others) lie at the
heart of the Christian message. Thus, dialectical theology is a protest
against rationalistic religion in whatever form it occurs, whether the natural theology of Thomism, a theological liberalism shaped by idealist
philosophy or a conservative orthodoxy that reduces theology to logically
systematized propositions.

Closely connected with dialectical theology's negative attitude toward
rationalistic attempts to ground theology and its positive embrace of paradox are two additional tendencies: a rejection of any philosophical system as normative for theology and a substructure, either implied or
explicit, informed by existentialism. To some, these two tendencies seem
to be in tension because existentialism is in fact a philosophical system of
sorts. However, with the notable exception of Tillich (and Bultmann to
some extent), dialectical theology relies on existentialism as a method
rather than a metaphysical system. Thus, dialectical theologians follow
the lead of Kierkegaard by arguing that we cannot approach theology as
neutral observers who rationally discern objective truths about God.
Instead, existentialist methodology argues that God is known only in and
through faith. God's Word is never God's Word in isolation from per-

sonal decision. It is always God's Word "for us." This means that all of the dialectical theologians, though to different degrees, depart from liberal theology by making a clear distinction between religion in general and Christian theology. While religion can be studied from a position of objectivity, theology is always and only the task of the community of faith: the church.

Dialectical theology's rejection of the belief that theological claims must be grounded in or justified by philosophy or history is intrinsically connected to its renewed emphasis on revelation. Liberalism, with its emphasis on God's immanence, stressed the continuity between theology and other forms of human science. In contrast, dialectical theology argues that our knowledge of God is not something that can be discovered in and through the natural course of events. Instead, God, as wholly Other, transcends the created order and stands in judgment over all human efforts. Knowledge of God is a unique category that has no analogy in any other type of knowledge. Thus, revelation must not be subordinated to anything comprehended by rational investigation. This means that the theologian is driven back to Scripture's witness in order that God can be known. However, while the dialectical theologians view Scripture as the vehicle of revelation, they do not equate Scripture with revelation itself. Instead, the Bible becomes revelatory as we encounter God's Word through the mediation of Jesus Christ.

An additional characteristic of dialectical theology to be noted is its renewed emphasis on human sinfulness. The message of Christianity is not simply that our understanding of God is limited by finite human capacities, but that our sinfulness places us at odds with God. In the light of this, salvation is not a process by which we incrementally outgrow our ignorance or polish out our moral blemishes. Theological liberalism's optimism gives way to dialectical theology's unambiguous pessimism about the extent of human ability for salvation. Thus, dialectical theology speaks of salvation in terms of divine grace, not moral improvement or educational and political reform.

While, as we have mentioned above, the neo-orthodox theologians attempted to distance themselves from the conservative orthodoxy of the early twentieth century, their most strident criticisms were directed toward theological liberalism. They were particularly critical of liberalism's almost exclusive emphasis on God's immanence, their reliance on reason as the gatekeeper for interpreting Scripture and their confidence in human capacities to turn back the power of sin. The reasons behind their harsh condemnations can be found in their biographies. Each of the theologians in this chapter was educated in the liberal tradition and came through his educational process deeply influenced by this school of thought. However, events that transpired in the early part of the twentieth century led them all to the conclusion that liberalism had betrayed Christianity. Thus, while they defend dialectical theology on a number of fronts, their response to liberalism is especially pointed.

Our final introductory word concerns the problem of determining who should be included as representatives of dialectical theology. Our choice to group together Karl Barth, Emil Brunner, Rudolf Bultmann, Reinhold Niebuhr and Paul Tillich is, without doubt, subject to disagreement. However, this combination is not arbitrary, since each exemplifies the general tendencies noted above to some degree. If nothing else, it can be said that they are largely unified by agreement in their rejection of the liberal tradition in which each had been educated as well as by their unwillingness to return to reactionary orthodoxy. Yet we will admit that this grouping is problematic for a number of reasons, not least of which is the fact that some of their most severe criticisms were reserved for each other. Nevertheless, it is also the case that those who are the closest neighbors have the loudest arguments, and the fact that their words are often rancorous betrays their own awareness of certain commonalities, which also made them more keenly conscious of their divergences.

Karl Barth

Karl Barth (1886-1968) is arguably the most influential theologian of the twentieth century, and history will certainly place him among the greatest theological minds in church history.[3] Regardless of whether one agrees or disagrees with his ideas, no serious theologian today dares ignore his thought. However, attempts to engage Barth's theology run up against challenging factors. First, his writing style is less than accessible. Second, Barth's monumental (but ultimately unfinished) *Church Dogmatics* is twice the length of Aquinas's *Summa Theologiae*. When you add to this the considerable number of other significant writings from his hand, the sheer volume of material is overwhelming. Moreover, because his work covered a broad span of time, debates continue about whether and where his ideas changed over time. Wading into such deep waters is indeed a daunting undertaking, and several decades after Barth's death, scholars are still sorting out the details of his theology. Given our limited space and intent, we will focus our attention on just a few pivotal areas in Barth's thought, drawing mostly from the early work that was so foundational to the movement known as neo-orthodoxy.

Barth grew up in a scholarly atmosphere. His father was a lecturer at a Reformed preachers college in Basel, Switzerland, and two of Karl's brothers also entered academia. Thus, it was not surprising that the younger Barth determined that he would become a theologian during his preparation for confirmation. His formal theological instruction began at the age of eighteen at Bern. While there he first encountered Kant's philosophy and decided to transfer to Marburg so he could study with Wilhelm Herrmann, Germany's leading proponent of Kantian-influenced theology. Barth's more conservative father, concerned about Herrmann's liberalism, convinced him to attend Berlin instead. However, this attempt to shield Karl from liberal theology backfired when he came into contact with Adolf von Harnack, the liberal church historian at Berlin. Barth then transferred to Tübingen for a brief period, but his studies with Harnack had only increased his interest in Marburg. He finally enrolled at Marburg in 1908 and studied under Herrmann for three semesters.

After graduation and ordination in 1911, Barth took a pastorate in Safenwil, fully expecting to return to the university to complete doctoral studies after a few years. Barth never did begin doctoral studies, but the unanticipated events that followed made this gap in his education very insignificant. The fateful chain began as Barth attempted to prepare sermons from the texts specified in the lectionary. In this process, he became aware of a vast distance between God's Word and the human attempts to speak of God he encountered in his liberal educational background. This compelled him to investigate Scripture anew, and years later he says that this introduced him to "the strange new world within the Bible."[4] In 1914, his disenchantment with classical liberalism grew more pronounced when ninety-three of Germany's leading intellectuals, including several of Barth's former professors, signed a document in support of the Kaiser and his war aims.

Now convinced of the bankruptcy of a liberal theology that would so easily sell out Christianity to nationalism, Barth sought avenues to respond to what he rightly foresaw as an impending crisis. The most visible result of these endeavors was the publication of *Der Römerbrief (The Epistle to the Romans)* in 1919, which was followed by a greatly revised version three years later. This second edition, which breaks more decisively with philosophical frameworks as an adjunct to theology, generated tremendous attention to Barth's thought. While some saw the commentary as a retreat into reactionary orthodoxy, many found Barth's approach as a promising way forward in the disillusionment with theological liberalism that followed World War I.

In the same year that the second edition of *Der Römerbrief* was published, Barth and several friends (Georg Merz, Eduard Thurneysen and Friedrich Gogarten) began publishing a journal titled *Zwischen den Zeiten (Between the Times)*. It quickly became an important vehicle for disseminating the views of what many now referred to as dialectical theology. This core group was soon joined by others who would become the luminaries of the movement: Rudolf Bultmann, Emil Brunner and Paul Tillich. Many of the tensions we will survey later in the chapter created splits between this inner circle and eventually brought about the demise of the journal in 1933. However, the basic direction had been set for a radical shift in the theological world.

Mainly on the strength of his Romans commentary, Barth was offered a professorship at the University of Göttingen. He later moved to Munster, then to Bonn, where he became a pivotal force in the Confessing church, which was a response to the "German Christians" and their alliance with Hitler. In 1934 he was the main drafter of the Barmen Declaration, which contained an unambiguous rebuke to the growing German nationalist movement. The next year he was removed from his university position and expelled from the country when he refused to take an oath of allegiance to Hitler.

As a result of his exile, Barth returned to the city of his birth in 1935 and was offered a theology professorship at the University of Basel.

Three years earlier, he had completed the first of what would grow to be thirteen volumes in his massive *Church Dogmatics,* the publication of which would span more than three decades (1932-1967). Although much of his energy was directed toward this project during the next two decades, he was also deeply involved in efforts to bring reconciliation to postwar Europe. In 1946 he returned to his old position in Bonn as a visiting lecturer in theology to help reestablish theological studies there. These lectures were published as *Dogmatics in Outline.* By the 1950s, Barth's work had generated such great acclaim that students traveled to Basel from all over the world to study under him. He retired from Basel in 1962 at the age of seventy-five and shortly thereafter embarked on a lecture tour to the United States, his only visit to this country. His academic endeavors were limited in his final years by failing health, but he managed to publish one last section of the fourth volume of *Church Dogmatics* in 1967, although this volume remained unfinished (his projected final volume on eschatology was never started). Barth died the following year.

Barth's theological revolution. While debates continue over almost every aspect of Barth's theological work, it is clear that his theology cannot be viewed as an attempt to "fix" the problems in the liberal tradition by means of modification. Barth's point of departure is diametrically opposed to that of his liberal teachers, and perhaps no way of expressing this difference crystallizes the issue as clearly as his views on religion and, by extension, philosophy and natural theology. The tendency in liberalism was to examine the nature of religion and demonstrate that Christianity satisfies human religious functions and aims in a superior way. In this approach, Christianity becomes the highest expression of our spiritual yearnings and hopes. Barth, instead of placing Christianity on a continuum with other religions, sets revelation over against religion. His uncompromising view of the chasm between the two is clear: "We begin by stating that religion is unbelief. It is a concern, indeed, we must say that it is the one great concern, of godless man."[5]

To many, this gives the appearance of a flight back to the conservative orthodoxy of his time. However, while Barth agrees with the orthodox party concerning the exclusivity of Christian claims, his understanding of the relationship between Christianity and religion is more nuanced than often supposed. First, he reminds his readers that, to the extent that Christianity is externalized as religion, it falls under the same condemnation and critique as any other religion: one based not on Christianity but the Word of God. The second point is that Barth, although he never states it with the same volume as he does his negative assessment of religion in general, agrees with his liberal forebears that the religious impulse is the highest expression of human existence. He even goes so far as to state that, "The revelation of God is actually the presence of God and therefore the hiddenness of God in the world of human religion."[6]

Despite such occasional affirmative statements about religion, Barth is uncompromising in his view that religion, and the philosophical, historical and scientific investigations upon which it is constructed, holds no soteriological value. The problem is twofold. First, sin stands as an insurmountable obstacle to any theology of religions that possesses soteriological significance. So while Barth allows that our human religious capacities make it *possible* for us to know God, he is also adamant that, "Between 'he could' and 'he can' there lies the absolutely decisive 'he cannot,' which can be removed and turned into its opposite by revelation."[7] While dependence on religious impulses exalts human capacities, only revelation exposes our sinful condition, and that which is sinful can never be the *source* of our knowledge of God.

The problem sin presents to human striving for the knowledge of God is intensified by the second key element: the otherness of God. While we are trapped within our finitude and temporality, God transcends every category that defines human existence. There is an infinite qualitative difference between God and the creaturely realm. In other words, Barth rejects the idea that any *analogia entis* (analogy of being) exists to facilitate our relationship with God. God's otherness dictates that he cannot be revealed by anything in the natural realm, including our rational or spiritual capacities. Seen against this background, we can understand Barth's radical rejection of natural theology and the use of philosophical systems in theology.[8]

Revelation as the basis of theology. While Barth dismisses the idea that God is knowable from our side by analogy to anything in the created order, he does not believe that God is unknowable, or for that matter, that no analogy exists as a means of knowing God. Instead of an *analogia*

entis, there is an *analogia fidei* (analogy of faith) that constitutes the revelation of God to humanity. However, this is never established on the
human side. Instead, God in his eternity comes into our temporal situation through Jesus Christ, his Word, in self-disclosure. The centrality of
Jesus Christ to Barth's doctrine of revelation is apparent in the oft-stated
dictum that his theology is essentially an extended christology. The Word
of God, although it confronts us in various forms, never stands apart
from the revelation of God in Christ. "Revelation in fact does not differ
from the person of Jesus Christ nor from the reconciliation accomplished in Him. To say revelation is to say 'The Word became flesh.'"[9]

The fact that Barth brings the person of Jesus Christ together with reconciliation in his understanding of revelation is a point that cannot be
stressed enough. Revelation is always an event, an act initiated by God
that draws us into the redemptive story. To put it otherwise, revelation
involves both that to which we respond as well as our response itself.
Thus, though theology must speak of each of these two aspects of revelation separately, we should never forget that revelation is not revelation
unless it reveals *something* that happens *to us*. To the extent that it is
"something" revealed, we speak of the objective revelation of God in
Jesus Christ. On the other hand, when it is revealed *to us* and effects our
reconciliation, we speak of the Holy Spirit's subjective work within us to
mediate God's Word through Scripture and proclamation.

Since Barth argues that we never know God in a merely objective way,
but always as Redeemer, theology faces danger if it abstracts these two
elements of revelation. Nevertheless, theology must begin from the
objective pole of God's Word in Jesus because it reminds us that God the
Father confronts us as a reality that precedes the possibility of our reconciliation with him through the Holy Spirit. In Jesus, God the Father is
revealed as the wholly Other. This self-revelation of the Father in the
Son makes clear that Christian theology can never have an anthropological starting point. Only after the gift of revelation in Jesus Christ is established can we speak of the Holy Spirit's work in us through Scripture and
the church's proclamation. Thus, Barth can state that Jesus *is* the Word of
God while Scripture and proclamation are forms of the Word of God
which are events, that is, the "happening" of God's Word through
redemptive reception in the Holy Spirit. By drawing together Christ,

Scripture and proclamation in this manner, we can see how Barth unfolds his idea of the threefold Word of God.

The event-character of the Word of God in Scripture, as Barth understood it, created a significant amount of controversy across the theological spectrum. In Barth's view, orthodoxy's attempt to equate Scripture per se with revelation turns revelation into a static set of propositions that divides what is revealed from its work in us. Instead, Barth speaks of Scripture as a "primary witness to the Word of God." To the extent that the Bible's witness is appropriated in faith, it is God's Word. Thus, while keeping in mind that faith is always part of God's revelation, Barth argues that "the statement that the Bible is God's Word is a confession of faith, a statement of the faith which hears God Himself speak through the biblical word of man."[10] This position, in turn, brings charges of a simplistic fideism from the liberal side of the theological spectrum. However, Barth's response is that no basis other than God should be sought for the authority of Scripture. "It must either be understood as grounded in itself and preceding all other statements or it cannot be understood at all. The Bible must be known as the Word of *God* if it is to be *known* as the Word of God."[11] The moment we appeal to anything other than God as the basis for Scripture's authority, we have subordinated God to human standards.

While Barth clearly affirms the divine Word in Scripture, he argues that we should not do so in a manner that obscures the fact that the Bible is also fully human. "In the Bible we meet with human words written in human speech, and in these words, and therefore by means of them, we hear of the lordship of the triune God."[12] Since the words of Scripture are human, they bear true witness to the Word. However, through the Holy Spirit, this witness becomes revelation. Thus, "If we want to think of the Bible as a real witness of divine revelation, then clearly we have to keep two things constantly before us and give them their due weight: the limitation and the positive element, its distinctiveness from revelation, in so far as it is only a human word about it, and its unity with it, in so far as revelation is the basis, object and content of this word."[13]

The final mode of the threefold Word of God is preaching, or proclamation. Barth describes proclamation as "human speech in and by which God Himself speaks like a king through the mouth of his herald, and which is meant to be heard and accepted as speech in and by which God Himself speaks, and therefore heard and accepted in faith as divine decision."[14] As is the case in Scripture, the humanity of proclamation remains intact, and there is nothing in our speech itself that causes it to become God's Word. God adds his own Word to human speech in such a way that this divine Word does not "cease to be itself when it allows itself to be served by human utterance. But as it allows itself to be served by it, it is itself this human utterance, and as this human utterance serves it, it itself is God's own Word."[15]

While Barth maintains the logical priority of Jesus Christ as God's Word throughout his *Dogmatics,* he is quick to add that "there is no distinction of degree or value between the three forms."[16] These are different *forms* of the Word, not three different Words. Moreover, none of the forms exist apart from the others. He summarizes the mutual relationship of these three modes by stating that

the revealed Word of God we know only from the Scripture adopted by Church proclamation or the proclamation of the Church based on Scripture. The written Word of God we know only through the revelation which fulfills proclamation or through the proclamation fulfilled by revelation. The preached Word of God we know only through the revelation attested in Scripture or the Scripture which attests revelation.[17]

It is not by accident that Barth's description of the internal relationship between the modes of the Word of God mirror classical trinitarian language.

The doctrine of the Word of God is itself the only analogy to the doctrine which will be our fundamental concern as we develop the concept of revelation. This is the doctrine of the triunity of God. In the fact that we can substitute for revelation, Scripture and Proclamation the names of the divine persons Father, Son and Holy Spirit and *vice versa,* that in the one case as in the other we shall encounter the same basic determination and mutual relationships, and that the decisive difficulty and also the decisive clarity is the same in both—in all this one may see specific support for the inner necessity and correctness of our present exposition of the Word of God.[18]

While Barth affirms a rather traditional understanding of Trinity, like every other aspect of his theology, he gives this doctrine a unique christo-logical twist. For Barth, the Christ event is at the heart of our confession of God as Trinity.

> It is believed that the original Christian confession consisted of the three words, "Jesus Christ (is) Lord," to which were only later added the first ["I believe in God the Father . . .] and third ["I believe in the Holy Spirit"] articles. This historical event was not arbitrary. It is also materially significant to know that historically the second article is the source of the whole. A Christian is one who makes confession of Christ. And Christian confession is confession of Jesus Christ the Lord.[19]

Thus, Barth states that while the Trinity is not found explicitly in Scripture, it is apparent in the logic of God's self-revelation in Christ.

Election. Because the Christian concept of God is God as Trinity, it is only after this doctrine has been established that Barth proceeds to speak of God in his specific "ways of being"—as Father, Son and Holy Spirit. In volume two of the *Church Dogmatics (The Doctrine of God),* he outlines the attributes of God, and here he focuses attention on two divine perfec-tions—God's freedom and God's love. These will set the stage for his exposition of reconciliation in volume three. The christocentric approach is evident once again at the beginning of his development of the section of divine love:

> God's being is His loving. He is all that He is as the One who loves. All His perfections are the perfections of His love. Since our knowledge of God is grounded in His revelation in Jesus Christ and remains bound up with it, we cannot begin elsewhere . . . than with the consid-eration of His love.[20]

However, when Barth moves to the perfections of the divine freedom in the following chapter, he makes clear that these two attributes, although they must be separated in our theology, are never abstracted from each other in God. There is a dialectic in which God's love always points to his freedom, and *vice versa.* Thus, we cannot subordinate one to the other. "God's freedom is no less divine than His love. God freedom is divine as the freedom in which God expresses His love."[21] It is in this divine combi-nation of love and freedom that God moves outside himself to reconcile the world to himself. Thus, Barth moves to the doctrine of election.

As in all other areas of Barth's theology, God's love and freedom is known christologically: "in our consideration of the divine perfections everything became clear and orderly when He, Jesus Christ, emerged as the perfect One, the fullness of the love and freedom of God Himself, the love and freedom of God in which all the divine perfections are neither more nor less than God Himself."[22] However, Barth argues that we cannot simply stop with a definition of who God is in himself, otherwise we turn God into an intellectual abstraction. The picture is only complete when we know God as free and loving *for us,* and as is the case in all knowledge of God, this reconciling work is effected in the Christ event. It is in Jesus that the divine and the human meet.

> Without the Son sitting at the right hand of the Father, God would not be God. But the Son is not only very God. He is also called Jesus of Nazareth. He is also very man, and as such He is the Representative of the people which in Him and through Him is united as He is with God, being with Him the object of the divine movement.[23]

When he puts all these elements together, Barth finds himself compelled to formulate a revolutionary statement of election. In the chapter titled "The Election of Jesus Christ," Barth's summary of the doctrine states:

> The election of grace is the eternal beginning of all the ways and works of God in Jesus Christ. In Jesus Christ God in His free grace determines Himself for sinful man and sinful man for Himself. He therefore takes upon Himself the rejection of man with all its consequences, and elects man to participation in His own glory."[24]

First, Jesus Christ, in his unity with God, is the God who elects. In his divine freedom and love, God in Jesus Christ chooses to predestine us from all eternity. Second, as the representative of all humanity, Jesus is the object of God's election. "From the very beginning (from eternity itself), as elected man He does not stand alongside the rest of the elect, but before and above them as the One who is originally and properly the Elect."[25] In this understanding of election, then, it is not a specific segment of humankind that is chosen for reprobation. Instead, Jesus alone becomes the condemned and rejected one—and the elected and glorified one. Because God has freely elected us in Jesus Christ from eternity, however, all are included in him as our representative. Thus, the doctrine of election does not directly address the question of the eternal fate of each individual human being. It becomes our election because God has graciously chosen us in Christ. Obviously, this position raises questions about universalism, and it is difficult to see how it leads to any other conclusion. On this matter, however, Barth refused to give a direct answer.

Evaluation. Barth's theology can be analyzed in a number of ways, but perhaps one of the most helpful perspectives is to view it as Barth himself understood it: as a renewal of the Reformation's themes. Liberalism had placed great emphasis on divine immanence. According to this view, God's activities and purposes are discernible by rational scrutiny of natural processes. In contrast, Barth recovers the Reformation's focus on the transcendence of the wholly other God. While he does not sever God from the movements within the creaturely world, Barth resolutely insists that the wholly other God remains hidden within these processes. God's transcendence is also evident in the prominence Barth gives to revelation, which is another retrieval of Reformation themes. Because God is not discovered in philosophical or historical investigation, he is knowable only in his gracious self-disclosure in the Christ event. This understanding of Jesus Christ as God's Word stands in sharp relief to liberalism's portrayal of Jesus as spiritual teacher and moral guide. Accordingly, Barth's discussion shifts from the Gospels to the writings of Paul, marked by greater attention to Reformation themes such as grace, faith and human sinfulness.

While Barth anchors his theology in Reformation motifs, we are mistaken if we view it as a mere recapitulation of the older theology. Although he returns Scripture to a place of centrality by making it the means by which Christ is made known and the ground of the church's proclamation, his unwillingness to equate Scripture itself with revelation and his embrace of the critical methods indicate that he is not simply casting the Reformation's theology in new language. In a similar manner, Barth recovers the Reformers' emphasis on God's election, but in a radically unique way. While the Trinity was an afterthought for liberalism, Barth moves his exposition of the Trinity to the beginning of his *Dogmatics*. Thus, while he affirms the Reformers' adherence to trinitarian theology, the placement of this doctrine in theological prolegomenon is distinctive, as is the christological structure of his formulation.

Barth's restoration of these themes from the Reformers resonated with a generation of theologians who were compelled to reevaluate liberalism's confidence in human capacities and possibilities in the wake of two horrific world wars. However, questions have been raised about whether his renewed stress on God's transcendence and human finitude created an equal but opposite imbalance. One common criticism on this count has been that, in his emphasis on God's transcendence, Barth has made human activity irrelevant. This point arises frequently in the context of his doctrine of election, in which every human rejection of God's grace is overridden by God's election of the entire human race in Jesus Christ. The universalism implicit in this view makes it difficult to see how human response to God's call has any significance. In short, Barth's understanding of predestination tends to make Jesus the only human of any importance since all other human activities are swallowed up in his election. This difficulty spills over into other areas of Barth's theology as well. If our election is secured in eternity in Christ, it appears to negate Barth's emphasis on proclamation as the Word of God by which the Holy Spirit brings reconciliation. Similarly, if the role of the Christian in society is limited to witness to what has already been wholly accomplished, it is difficult to see how this can be integrated into an ethics of social transformation.

The question of whether Barth's theology offers resources for social engagement also raises the question of how and whether Christians can enter into discussion with those outside the faith. The radical disjunction between revelation and reason appears to eliminate any common ground on which Christians might join the debate, leaving little choice but to either withdraw from such discussions or simply assert Christian claims against all others. This concern about the lack of any foundation for apologetics is behind the frequent charge that Barth's theology is fideistic, an accusation that is also directed toward Barth's view of Scripture. Since he allows no standard for accepting the veracity of Scripture beyond what is witnessed to in Scripture, there is a circularity (which Barth defends as a necessary circularity) in the claim that Scripture is God's Word. Moreover, Barth is attacked from both sides for what appears to be an inconsistency between his theology of Scripture and his use of it. On the one hand, he denies the verbal inspiration of Scripture or that the Bible is revelation in an unqualified manner. On the other hand, he treats Scripture as if it is verbally inspired, refusing to allow critical methods to pass judgment on its content.

Every new theological approach must clearly distinguish itself from those systems against which it is framed, and it cannot be doubted that Barth's theology is characterized by clear delineations between his views and liberalism. Many have accepted the boundaries as drawn by Barth. However, others have adopted the broad outlines of dialectical theology while simultaneously arguing that his specific doctrinal formulations are a necessary overreaction to what precedes it. While they agree that an overreaction was needed to point out the shortcomings of previous theologies and to change the theological agenda, they maintain that modification is now required for a more nuanced theology that addresses the potential problems we have seen. It is against this backdrop that we might understand the other theologians in this chapter. To some degree (and perhaps in some it is a very small degree), they are sympathetic to the theological direction established by dialectical theology. At the same time, they want to recover what they view as a more balanced theology. In doing so, they offer alternatives to Barth's views on election, reason and apologetics, Scripture, ethics and revelation. This led to tensions between the other theologians surveyed in this chapter and Barth, who saw their modifications as destructive of the heart of dialectical theology.

Emil Brunner

Emil Brunner (1889-1966) had the ambiguous fortune of being closely connected with Barth theologically, chronologically and locally.[26] Because of this circumstance, a theologian who might well have been considered the preeminent figure of his generation in the field remained in Barth's shadow. Some measure of justice might be found in this situation, however. Brunner's more accessible style and his more frequent contacts with the English-speaking world often provided a larger audience than Barth's more cryptic style, leading to a common complaint from Barth's disciples that the theologian from Basel is often interpreted through the lens of Brunner.

Like Barth, Brunner was born into the Swiss Reformed tradition and educated in the liberal theology that dominated the German-speaking universities of the day. In 1913, he received his doctorate from the University of Zurich and began his career in the pastorate. He returned to Zurich to teach theology in 1924 and remained there until 1955, when he retired. During these decades, he traveled and lectured frequently in both England and the United States, and at the end of his career, taught for two years at the Christian University of Tokyo.

Brunner's own three-volume *Dogmatics* (English translations 1950-1962) seems somewhat modest when compared to Barth's massive *Church Dogmatics*. However, his prolific writings cover a broader span of subjects than Barth's and include such significant works as *Revelation and Reason* (1941), *The Divine Imperative* (1932), *The Divine-Human Encounter, Justice and the Social Order* (1943) and *Man in Revolt* (1937). We might view this wider scope of interest as a paradigm for what separates Brunner from Barth since many of the works noted above combine the latter's focus on God's transcendence with the more personalistic approach that Brunner advocates. Thus, while theological history has zeroed in on their rather rancorous debate concerning natural theology (which we will briefly survey below), this disagreement is best viewed as part of a larger divergence about the scope of human response and action.

Throughout his career, Brunner consistently rejects theological liberalism's attempt to gain access to divine truth by human means. In his view, liberalism had replaced revelation with reason and philosophy. Because of an emphasis on God's immanence, liberalism focused on the similarities between divine reason and human morality rather than the discontinuities. Given this starting point, liberal theologians determined that a critical approach to Scripture and history would yield a purified picture of Christianity once it understood who Jesus "really was." Brunner sees the substitution of reason for revelation as an illegitimate attempt to declare independence from God and views the result as disastrous for our understanding of Jesus. As he puts it, "Theological liberalism is an arrogant attempt to see 'Jesus Himself,' without being led to this view by the Apostles."[27] The contiguities between God and humanity are superimposed on the picture of Jesus to the extent that "liberal theology represents the view that Jesus is not the Christ, the Son of God, nor is He the Saviour of the world; He is merely one outstanding religious personality among many others, a *primus inter pares.*"[28]

Even though the orthodox scholars of his time joined with Brunner in rejecting liberalism's reliance on reason and critical methodology to determine the nature and role of Jesus Christ, he is equally critical of them:

> In orthodox theology, however, the question [of why we should accept Jesus as the revelation of God] . . . is never raised, because it already presupposes a positive answer, on the basis of the testimony of the New Testament. We believe in Jesus Christ because the Bible teaches that He is the Christ.[29]

The problem with the conservative orthodoxy is that it does not address the questions that naturally arise for modern human beings. Theology cannot go back to a fideistic past in an increasingly secularized society because the message will seem obscure and provincial. Instead, "Christian theology owes it to the world to show that we do not believe in revelation because we ignore the protests of the world, but that we believe in spite of the fact that we know these objections, and have indeed wrestled with them seriously."[30] Thus, while Brunner agrees with orthodoxy's rejection of the attempt to construct theology on a philosophical basis, he conversely argues that it cannot ignore philosophy and the results of critical methods. A third way must be found for theology to go forward in a post-critical world.

Eristic theology. Although the theological approach Brunner suggests has elements that are similar to apologetics in the sense that it attempts to address the non-Christian world, his rejection of any philosophical system as a basis for theology will not allow him to employ this term. Instead, he uses the term "eristics" as a term to describe the "explicit 'discussion' between the Christian and non-Christian knowledge of God and of the Good."[31] Brunner's qualification of this "discussion" means that Christian theology does not come to the table with just another answer to the dilemma of human existence. Eristic theology

> is also a polemical, radically critical denial of man's natural view of his own nature. The message of Christ is a declaration of war on his present, supposed "knowledge"; indeed, its very existence depends on the fact that it triumphs over the previous view. Faith always also exists as conflict with the earlier view, and indeed it only becomes real faith

"when it clearly perceives its previous error."[32]

As with apologetics, Brunner's eristic theology addresses the demands of reason, but it can only do this by first reducing arrogant rationalism to an awareness of sin that can only be revealed through an encounter with God in Christ. Thus, "In the realm of theory it [eristics] does what every true sermon does in its practical application to the individual hearer: it shows man, who cannot avoid desiring to understand himself when he understands himself in the light of faith in the Creator revealed in Christ."[33] The proper self-understanding to which this should bring us is simple: "God, not man, is the centre."[34] However, Brunner goes on to say that

> this truth must be expressed not only in theory but in practice. Hence this message is not concerned with "God in Himself," but with "God for us," the God who manifests His nature and His will in the Son of Man, in order that in man this centre may once more become the true centre.[35]

Personalistic theology. Brunner makes a clear distinction between knowing "God in Himself" and "God for us" as a means of expressing what he calls "Personalism." On the Godward side of divine communication, he stresses the fact that "Jesus Christ Himself is more than all words about Him; the 'Word' of God, the decisive self-communication of God, is a Person, a human."[36] Moreover, the recipients of this revelation are never more nor less than fully human in their faith. Thus, what God reveals about himself should never be reduced to objective knowledge, nor should it descend into mere subjective experience. It is always personal knowledge.

The personal character Brunner ascribes to revelation is indebted to the existentialist thought of Martin Buber and an early advocate of dialogical personalism, Ferdinand Ebner. Following their lead, Brunner says that we must be careful not to confuse truths about an "it" with truths about a "Thou." I-it knowledge is derived through neutral observation and thought, and is a fitting route for comprehending objects because it allows us to use nature in advantageous ways. However, to cut science free from faith and "understand it as the final truth, as truth absolutely, is to degrade persons to things, and, theologically speaking, to make science a superstition hostile to personal being."[37] This is the basis for

Brunner's opposition to natural theology. To use philosophy as the beginning point for knowledge about God makes our reason autonomous and reduces God to an object whose existence and nature will always be in question.

In contrast to I-it knowledge, the I-Thou relation is never abstract, neutral and detached. When God encounters us as subjects, we are put in a position where response is required. Thus, Brunner frequently refers to our encounter with God as conversation. "Genuine theology must be dialectical. It is always a conversation between God and man, in which the human partner in the conversation is not ignored, but, even though he is entirely receptive, he is apprehended with his whole nature."[38] Brunner hastens to add that because the human being is viewed by God as a responsible subject, "revelation does not extinguish the human reason, but claims it wholly for this process of reception."[39]

Before revelation can lay hold of our reason, however, we must understand how sin affects rationality. Brunner argues that our "objective" knowledge of nature, history and culture is largely unhindered by sin. However, this is not the case with the personal aspects of our existence. "The more closely a subject is related to man's inward life, the more natural human knowledge is 'infected' by sin."[40] Sin damages our self-knowledge to the extent that we cannot be honest about our true spiritual state. Only in our encounter with God through Jesus Christ does self-understanding find redemption. "Hence it is part of the genuine Christian experience that only the man who has been influenced by the truth of Christ is honest with himself, because he alone dares to look the naked truth in the face."[41] When we have been confronted by God's Word, our rational powers can take the proper, complementary role to theology that God intends.

> From the standpoint of the Christian, not philosophy, but *theology* is the first and most important, because by drawing from the Word of God in the Bible it throws light upon his existence as a Christian. But from the standpoint of being and thought in general, Christian *philosophy* is the first and most fundamental thing, because it thinks systematically the principles of being and of thought, freed from the false axiom of autonomy.[42]

The nature and grace debate. While Brunner decisively places rationality under the authority of revelation, even the minimal role that he allows for reason to serve as a point of contact between humanity and God brought strong criticism from Barth. Disagreement between the two theologians on this matter had been simmering for several years, and it finally boiled over in 1934 when Brunner wrote "Nature and Grace." Barth responded immediately with an essay, tersely titled "Nein!" (No!).

As we have seen above, Brunner is in complete agreement with Barth that natural theology cannot lead us to faith in the God of Scripture. However, for Brunner, Barth's view that the Fall destroys any natural point of contact between God and humanity amounts to a denial that we retain the image of God even in our fallenness. In order to maintain the tension between these two ideas, Brunner distinguishes between the formal idea of the *imago Dei*—the imprint God has placed on us that makes us responsible beings, in contrast to the rest of creation—and the material sense of the image. "Formally the imago is not in the least touched—whether sinful or not, man is a subject and is responsible. Materially the imago is completely lost, man is a sinner through and through and there is nothing in him which is not defiled by sin."[43] Since God communicates God's self through creation, and this communication remains formally intact, natural theology contains authentic revelation. Nevertheless, it cannot be the criterion for faith.

In contrast, Barth will not allow a place for even this limited view of general revelation. "Every attempt to assert a general revelation has to be rejected. There is no grace of creation and preservation. There are no recognizable ordinances of preservation. There is no point of contact for the redeeming action of God. The new creation is in no sense the perfection of the old but rather the replacement of the old man by the new."[44] At the center of his objection is the belief that Brunner's position is incompatible with the principles of *sola scriptura* (by Scripture alone) and *sola gratia* (by grace alone) and that any so-called natural knowledge of God is an idolatry that leads away from faith rather than functioning as preparation for it. Therefore, Barth concludes his essay by stating that natural theology in any variation is such that "only the theology and the church of the antichrist can profit from it. The Evangelical Church and Evangelical theology would only sicken and die of it."[45]

Election. A second area of contention between Barth and Brunner was the doctrine of election. In a rather harsh evaluation of Barth's position, Brunner says that, "No special proof is required to show that the Bible contains no such doctrine, nor that no theory of this kind has ever been formulated by any theologian."[46] If all are elect in the preexistent Son, two devastating problems result. The first is that the incarnation is stripped of its significance as an event within our history. The second problem is the universalism implied in Barth's formulation. Brunner's dislike of Barth's view of election was matched by his dislike of the traditional doctrine of the Double Decree, which he called "the most ruthless determinism that can be imagined."[47] While Brunner avers that the doctrine of double predestination is "logically satisfying . . . it sacrifices the reality of human decision to determinism."[48] Freedom is the presupposition of I-Thou relationships, and this is what is missing in predestination.

The influence of Brunner's Personalism is evident in his statement that

> the doctrine of Election is therefore not intelligible in theory, but only in the decision of faith, not as a doctrine—"about", but only as an address to the "Thou", as the Word of God, which in Jesus Christ, through the Holy Spirit, addresses us in such a way that we ought to believe, we are able to believe, and we must believe.[49]

The aspect of election that is expressed in predestination is that truth that God's Word of love "goes 'before' my existence." However, "my decision . . . [is] that which makes it [election] possible."[50]

Brunner on Scripture. At the beginning of our exposition of Brunner's thought, we noted that he sought a middle path between the fundamentalism and the liberalism of his day. Perhaps no area of doctrine exemplifies this attempt to find a different avenue than his view of Scripture. He disliked fundamentalism's view of verbal inspiration, arguing that "it deifies the 'letter' of the Bible, as if the Spirit of God were imprisoned within the covers of the written word."[51] Although he agreed with the conservative theologians that the testimony of Scripture is the indispensable means of revelation, Brunner believed that they had incorrectly concluded that a high view of Scripture foreclosed the use of critical methodology to study Scripture. On the other hand, while he concedes that liberalism is justified in its use of such methods, he likewise takes it to task for using historical criticism to "purify" Scripture in order to determine the true content of revelation. Brunner concludes that, "Even the most intensive historical criticism leaves 'more than enough' of the Gospel story and its picture of the central Person to enkindle and to support faith. Indeed, we may put it still more strongly, and say that the total result of historical criticism of the tradition concerning Jesus, so far as its central truth is concerned, is nil."[52]

For Brunner, the proper approach to Scripture had to be modeled on the incarnation: "The Bible shares in the glory of the divinity of Christ and in the lowliness of His humanity."[53] The Bible is produced under the Spirit's control, but this does not eliminate human reflection or frailty. Thus, Brunner maintains that Scripture is not the *basis* of our belief in Christ, but is instead the *means*. "We cannot believe in Jesus the Christ without the Bible; but we should not believe in Jesus the Son of God because the Bible says so."[54] In a manner similar to Barth, Brunner says that the apostolic witness in Scripture, "becomes to me the word of God through the fact that God, through His Spirit, permits it to dawn on me as the word of His truth."[55] To the extent that God chooses, Scripture is God's word in that it reveals his saving intent in Jesus. This view of revelation corresponds closely with Brunner's personalistic approach. Knowledge of God is not dependent on our efforts or susceptible to rational proof or disproof. "It is knowledge in the dimension of personal encounter: God Himself discloses Himself to me."[56]

By placing knowledge of God within the realm of personal encounter rather than subjecting it to the judgment of reason, Brunner shifts the focus from the unity of doctrine within Scripture to what he calls a unity of revelation. By attempting to present the Bible as a text that provides a unified vision of doctrine, Protestant orthodoxy turned theology into an abstract idea. Moreover, he argues, the doctrinal differences within Scripture are so great that "anyone who tried to make a scientific unity of view out of all these different and contradictory elements would only knock his head against a wall."[57] The unity of Scripture is known only in faith when it goes behind doctrine to find Jesus Christ, to whom doctrine is witness.

This leads Brunner to a view that troubles many on the more conservative side of the theological spectrum because it requires that he develop something of a "canon within the canon" of Scripture. In his view, not all parts of Scripture bear God's Word to the same degree. As the early church had to determine what was apostolic, so too the church in every age has the responsibility to put dogma to the test and revise it if necessary. To bolster his case, Brunner cites Luther's doubts about the apostolic character of James and Revelation. The historical nature of Scripture means that we must continue to view the canon as "an entity with undefined frontiers."[58]

Evaluation. At the heart of Brunner's differences with Barth is his belief that human longing and questioning provides the human-divine point of contact that Barth is so fearful of acknowledging. While he maintains, with Barth, that revelation is always initiated from God's side through Jesus Christ, Brunner's personalistic approach makes the human being a participant, a conversation partner, in the process. The question remains, however, whether the distance between the two theologians on this matter is a distinction without a difference since even our retention of the formal aspect of the *imago Dei* is of no significance to faith. In the end, Brunner refuses to place whatever can be known apart from revelation anywhere on a continuum with the revealed truth of Christianity. Thus, as with Barth, revelation and faith come down to an "all or nothing" matter.

Moreover, it has often been argued that Brunner's personalistic approach moves him back toward the very subjectivism that he views as so destructive in liberalism. When the accent is placed on the primacy of the I-Thou nature of revelation, it is not clear how we move from this to a doctrinal expression of the relationship. If the difference between I-It claims and I-Thou truths is so clear-cut and the line that separates them so impenetrable, it is difficult to see how we avoid a relapse into the anthropologically-based theology Brunner dislikes so intensely. This problem comes to the surface most vividly in Brunner's view of Scripture. On the one hand, he criticizes those who allow historical critical methods determine the content of revelation. On the other hand, he argues that the boundaries of the apostolic witness are still open to discussion and, potentially, modification. This creates a rather messy problem of how theology is to rely on encounter with God's Word in revelation when the borders of the divine message remain undefined. It does not seem that we have any means to exempt theology from philosophical assumptions and reliance on human rationality if biblical criticism cannot be pried from these fatal faults.

Rudolf Bultmann

Like so many of the German intellectuals of the nineteenth and early twentieth centuries, Rudolf Bultmann (1884-1976) was a son of the Lutheran parsonage.[59] His educational process took him through Germany's leading universities of the day: Tübingen, Berlin and finally Marburg, from which he received his degree in 1910. He spent a year teaching in the *Gymnasium* in his hometown of Oldenburg and later lectured at Marburg from 1912-16. In 1916, he received a professorship at Breslau and was then called to succeed Bousset at Giessen in 1920. However, after only a year there, the invitation came to return to Marburg as professor of New Testament, and Bultmann remained there until his retirement in 1951.

The list of Bultmann's teachers reads like the "Who's Who" of German scholarship, including famous professors like Gunkel, Harnack, Jülicher, Weiss and Herrmann. As was true of the others who became identified with dialectical theology, Bultmann broke sharply with the conclusions of his liberal professors, especially Gunkel and Weiss, whose "History-of-Religions" approach seemed to define Christianity in purely historical and psychological terms. However, while he developed his theology in a different direction, the critical methodologies of his liberal predecessors remained influential for Bultmann.

The publication of *The History of the Synoptic Tradition* in 1921 established Bultmann as a key figure in form-critical analysis of the Gospels. On its surface, it appeared to place him squarely in the tradition of his liberal teachers, and this was certainly Barth's impression at the time. However, the next year, Bultmann commented very favorably on Barth's *Römerbrief*, which was highly critical of liberal theology. Barth's perplexity about where Bultmann fit in the theological constellation was not unusual. Given his neo-orthodox criticisms of liberalism, Bultmann was clearly not completely at home in the theological world in which he had been educated. At the same time, his ready acceptance of critical methodologies, the skepticism that marked his conclusions concerning the historicity of Scripture, and his program of demythologizing the New

Testament guaranteed vocal criticism from those on the more conservative side of the theological spectrum. Moreover, unlike the other advocates of dialectical theology surveyed in this chapter, Bultmann was a
New Testament scholar, not a theologian in the traditional sense. However, the manner in which he blurred the line between biblical exegesis
and systematic theology created a paradigm that concerned scholars of
every stripe.

   An existentialist theology. Perhaps the one thing that most distinguished
Bultmann from his theological contemporaries was his open embrace of
existentialist philosophy. While it is difficult to deny the influence of existential thought on all of the neoorthodox thinkers, Bultmann was much
more explicit in acknowledging his reliance on this school. He reveals
his awareness of the rift this reliance on existentialism caused between
himself and Barth in his observation that "in my efforts to make philosophy fruitful for theology, I have more and more come into opposition to
Karl Barth. Nevertheless, I remain grateful to him for the decisive things
I have learned from him; and I am convinced that a final clarification of
our relationship . . . has not as yet been reached."[60] The roots of Bultmann's existentialist loyalties should be traced to Herrmann, who distinguished between the external data that could be gleaned from historical
or sociological investigation and the internal life of the individual person. It is the latter that is of spiritual relevance, and Herrmann's influence is clear in Bultmann's attempt to redirect attention away from a
sterile analysis of the events of Jesus' life to the existential meaning of
Christ and the cross.

   While Herrmann's thought provided the foundation for Bultmann's
existentialist approach, it was Martin Heidegger who provided the framework.[61] The two men were colleagues at Marburg from 1923-28, and they
remained close until the mid-1930s when Heidegger threw his support
behind the Nazi regime. While a personal reconciliation between the two
would not come until after World War II, Bultmann remained unwaver-
ing in his appreciation of Heidegger's philosophy throughout his career.
Heidegger objected to any metaphysical system that viewed the human
being as an object. Objects, which are "extant," can be described in
universal and causal categories. Human beings, in contrast, possess
"existence" *(Existenz),* and cannot be defined by objective data and mea-

surement. Existence is determined instead by the decisions and commitments we make in concrete historical situations. Bultmann linked these concepts to the idea of faith. Those who understand themselves in terms of their "objectivized" existence and are not receptive to the future are in retreat from faith. To be in faith means that we forsake our attempts to ground our security in physical entities and open ourselves to possibilities that transcend material relationships.

Along with metaphysical systems that view the human being as a describable "object," Bultmann rejects an underlying assumption of liberal Protestant theology, which along with other rationalists believed scholars and interpreters can and should remain neutral in relation to their subject matter. In opposition to this, Bultmann states that, "your own relation to the subject matter prompts the question you bring to the text and elicits the answers you obtain from the text."[62] Every interpreter brings personal interests to the table when he or she engages in exegesis. Moreover, we bring with our concerns and fears a tradition that always presupposes some philosophy. Thus, whether consciously or not, the liberal tradition had superimposed its own idealistic philosophy on Christianity. Bultmann, on the other hand, rejects any philosophical approach that arrives with a predefined set of conclusions, as was the case with idealism. "We must realize that there will never be a right philosophy in the sense of an absolutely perfect system, a philosophy which could give answers to all questions and clear up all riddles of human existence."[63] Existentialist philosophy is different, however, because, "while it gives no answer to the question of my personal existence, [it] makes personal existence my own personal responsibility, and by doing so it helps to make me open to the word of the Bible."[64] Precisely because existentialism does not begin with a set of universal principles and general truths, it allows God to confront us with his revelation and makes this Word the judge of our conclusions. In short, existentialism infuses us with the proper attitude for doing theology.

Our openness to divine encounter is the place where Bultmann has his most decisive split with Heidegger, who depicts authentic Being as a goal that we can potentially achieve on our own. Bultmann says that all people are aware of the alienation present within their existence, an alienation Christians speak of in terms of the Fall. Existentialists such as

Heidegger believe that if we recognize our situation, we can escape it. However, Bultmann states that all attempts to do this by self-assertion fall apart when we recognize that the opposing forces in the world over-whelm our abilities. Thus, Bultmann concludes, "the only reasonable attitude for man to adopt apart from Christ is one of despair, to despair of the possibility of his ever achieving authentic Being."[65] Ironically, the desire to find God through natural theology grows from the same impulse that we find in philosophical self-assertion. In natural theology,

> Man speaks of God because he knows himself beset by his own desires and fears, because he knows himself helpless before the unknown, before the enigma. He hypostasizes his dream-wishes and his fears into a being who can bring fulfillment or annihilation to his life. This supreme being is certainly not the God of whom faith speaks.[66]

In other words, natural theology, like the liberal theology of the nineteenth century, imposes philosophically-derived concepts of God on its conclusions. Bultmann argues that an existentialist approach—an approach that confronts us with our own existence as it is, not as systematizing reason dreams it might be—allows the true God to address us on God's terms. Only then can our despair be defeated.[67]

Because existentialism does not require that we approach Scripture with our doctrines and beliefs already in place, we can remain open to faith. But our decision to exercise faith places the person of today in a paradoxical situation.

> I need to see the worldly events as linked by cause and effect not only as a scientific observer, but also in my daily living. In doing so there remains no room for God's working. This is the paradox of faith, that faith "nevertheless" understands as God's action here and now an event which is completely intelligible in the natural or historical connection of events. This "nevertheless" is inseparable from faith.[68]

We find the same paradox in the New Testament's language about the opposition of Christ and the world. The lure of being in the world comes from the illusion that we can master its processes. However, Bultmann states, "By means of science men try to take possession of the world, but in fact the world gets possession of men."[69] When the latter occurs, we descend once again into despair because a merely scientific understanding of human nature is incomplete. To be "in Christ" means that our possibilities are not limited by the causal nexus that governs the physical world. Without the soteriological element that faith in Christ brings, we will never see ourselves fully or find resolution to our despair.

Historie *and* Geschichte. Since the question of existence holds out the prospect that we will encounter God, this drives us to examine the Word and its demand for decision. However, Bultmann is keenly interested in an issue that must be addressed prior to our consideration of God's revelation. Scripture, which communicates the divine self-disclosure, is a historical document. The question that arises, then, is how a historical document, and history itself, should be understood in the light of an existentialist approach. Bultmann's response is that "the ultimate purpose in the study of history is to realize consciously the possibilities it affords for the understanding of human existence."[70] This necessitates an important distinction in Bultmann's theology between *Historie*, which designates the events and facts of the past, and *Geschichte*, which refers to the relevance of those events for me.[71]

Bultmann quickly clarifies that his distinction between *Historie* and *Geschichte* is not an arbitrary choice on his part, but one embedded in the New Testament itself. He points out that the Synoptics (Matthew, Mark and Luke) demonstrate almost no concern about the specifics of Jesus' life. "There is no historical-biographical interest in the Gospels, and that is why they have nothing to say about Jesus' human personality, his appearance and character, his origin, education and development."[72] While the Synoptic Gospels do contain stories that appear to record events in Jesus' life, even a cursory reading reveals that personal details and sequence are secondary to the teaching itself. Once Bultmann has taken these accounts through the demythologizing process (described in more detail below), little historical basis remains for the events and chronology of Jesus' life. And once we leave the Synoptics, we are struck with an almost complete absence of any information about the historical person of Jesus.[73]

The New Testament's relative lack of interest in the facts of Jesus' biography dovetails with Bultmann's existentialist approach. Historical (*historisch*) research always pays homage to a closed system of cause and effect in order to get at a detached, factual evaluation of events. The information gleaned from such investigations is of only academic interest. However, when we bring this information into relation with our exist-ence, we can speak of the historic *(geschichtlich)* significance. This is exactly what Bultmann discovers in the New Testament documents. They bear none of the marks of a detached historical approach. Instead, the New Testament authors speak of the relevance of Jesus for his followers, not historical data and detail. The theological significance of Jesus will never be apparent to the neutral observer; it is known only to faith. Thus, as Bultmann frames it, it is not the "Jesus of history," but the "Christ of faith" that we discover in the New Testament.[74] In this way, Bultmann can argue that the relative absence of historical information about Jesus is not an obstacle to faith, but an opportunity. The New Testament docu-ments themselves signal interest in the theological significance of Christ crucified and resurrected, not the activities or personality of the historical Jesus.

Myth and demythologizing. According to Bultmann, it is this "Christ of faith" that we find at the center of the early church's kerygma (preach-ing). The kerygma reflects the redemptive significance the early believers experienced in their encounters with Jesus. However, this redemptive message is couched in mythological language, which must be interpreted in order that we can discover it for ourselves today. This need for inter-pretation brings us to Bultmann's famous program of demythologizing the New Testament. While he is notoriously inconsistent in his definition of myth, Bultmann describes myth's function as

> an expression of man's conviction that the origin and purpose of the world in which he lives are to be sought not within it but beyond it— that is, beyond the realm of known and tangible reality and that this realm is perpetually dominated and menaced by those mysterious powers which are its source and limit.[75]

When the New Testament authors speak of their convictions about Christ's transcendence of the tangible, they communicate in the lan-guage of myth. Thus, Bultmann opens his famous lecture, "New Testa-ment and Mythology" (1941):

> The cosmology of the New Testament is essentially mythical in charac-ter. The world is viewed as a three-storied structure, with the earth in the centre, heaven above, and the underworld beneath. Heaven is the abode of God and of celestial beings—the angels. The underworld is

hell, the place of torment. Even the earth is more than the scene of natural, everyday events, of the trivial round and common task. It is the scene of the supernatural activity of God and his angels on the one hand, and of Satan and his daemons on the other.[76]

In Bultmann's evaluation, the cosmology of the New Testament is not itself the message. Instead, we are to draw from this metaphorical representation an understanding of God's transcendence, his activity in the earthly sphere, and the reality of corrupting forces at work in the world. Similarly, he finds the salvific work of Jesus wrapped in the imagery and vocabulary of Jewish apocalyptic and Gnostic redemption myths. In order to get at the theological message, we must distinguish between the mythological forms surrounding the kerygma and the kerygma itself.

Bultmann acknowledges the value of historical-critical methodology in allowing the exegete to recognize the mythological elements in the New Testament, and for this he expresses a debt to his liberal predecessors. However, he comes to a very different conclusion about our response to myth. Liberal theologians believed that once they stripped away the mythological "husk," they would find the eternal kernel of Jesus' teaching that would yield universal principles (generally understood as ethical truths) that could then be used to recover Christianity. Bultmann believed that such an approach was thoroughly wrongheaded. First, it assumes that we could arrive at biblical truths by assuming the neutral perspective of the historian (a view that is diametrically opposed to Bultmann's existentialist assumptions) and that the truths derived were static factual entities (in contrast to Bultmann's idea that existential truth always confronts us personally). Secondly, the liberal "questers" had searched for Jesus' significance in his teaching. However, Bultmann argues that "the message of Jesus is a presupposition for the theology of the New Testament rather than a part of that theology itself."[77] For Bultmann the kerygma is not the good news about a coming reign or kingdom of God but the proclamation of Jesus Christ as crucified and risen. "Thus, theological thinking—the theology of the New Testament—begins with the kerygma of the earliest Church and not before."[78] Finally, he rejects liberalism's conclusion that once the mythological components were isolated and the kerygmatic kernel extracted, we could simply discard the myth. According to Bultmann, the "aim [of demythologizing] is not to eliminate the mythological statements but to interpret them. It is a method of hermeneutics."[79] When liberal interpreters eliminated myth, they also eradicated the kerygma. Instead, because myths give this-worldly objectivity to other-worldly truths, the theologian's task is to transcend myth's "objectifying" aspects by identifying the underlying existential significance.

This brings us to Bultmann's rationale for demythologizing the New Testament. The presence of mythological ideas in Scripture such as the three-storied cosmology noted above stands as an obstacle to modern readers. He says that any expectation that modern people would accept such a cosmology

> would be both senseless and impossible. It would be senseless, because there is nothing specifically Christian in the mythical view of the world as such. It is simply the cosmology of a pre-scientific age. Again, it would be impossible, because no man can adopt a view of the world by his own volition—it is already determined for him by his place in history.[80]

Requiring modern people to sacrifice their intellect so they can accept the Christian message results in spiritual insincerity. In addition to the intellectual hurdles myth places before people of a scientific world, any demand that we accept the New Testament's cosmology or any other mythological feature threatens to distort the message itself. "The importance of the New Testament mythology lies not in its imagery but in the understanding of existence which it enshrines. The real question is whether this understanding of existence is true. Faith claims that it is, and faith ought not to be tied down to the imagery of New Testament mythology."[81] With this strong emphasis on faith, Bultmann is being true to his Lutheran heritage. Still, he recognizes how inflammatory his idea of demythologizing is, and so Bultmann continually stresses that the point of demythologizing is not to reject Scripture but the obsolete worldview that is wrapped around the kerygma. Unless we demythologize that, we communicate the imagery itself as part of the message, making acceptance impossible without what Bultmann calls intellectual schizophrenia. Thus, he states that, "the task of de-mythologizing has no other purpose but to make clear the call of the Word of God."[82]

Bultmann's demythologizing of the New Testament's spatial concepts leads him to the much more controversial attempt to demythologize its temporal language as well, particularly its eschatology. He agrees with Schweitzer and other "questers" that both Jesus and the earliest believers expected an almost immediate return of Christ as the Son of Man. In view of this expectation, Bultmann says, "The mythical eschatology is untenable for the simple reason that the parousia of Christ never took place as the New Testament expected. History did not come to an end, and, as every schoolboy knows, it will continue to run its course."[83] The fact that the early church was factually wrong about Jesus' imminent return is supported by historical investigation. However, Bultmann reminds us, the results of historical inquiry are not determinative for theology. Theological significance is found only when we reinterpret the New Testament's eschatological language to reveal its message for today. The deeper meaning of the eschatological message of Jesus is, then,

> to be open to God's future which is really imminent for every one of us; to be prepared for this future which can come as a thief in the night when we do not expect it; to be prepared, because this future will be a Judgment on all men who have bound themselves to this world and are not free, not open to God's future.[84]

Understood in this way, the New Testament is thoroughly eschatological, not in the sense that it provides information about future events that bring history to an end, but because it reveals God's future for us in the here and now.

Bultmann defends his demythologizing of kerygma by arguing that the New Testament writers, specifically Paul and John, have already taken this step. While the early church looked for the imminent return of the triumphant Son of Man, Paul and John are already beginning to distance themselves from the earlier eschatology in their writings and instead speak of salvation as a present reality for those who have faith. For Paul, Bultmann says, "Christ's death and resurrection . . . are cosmic occurrences, not incidents that took place once upon a time in the past. By them the old aeon along with its powers has been basically stripped of power."[85] As Paul gives theological expression to the meaning of Christ, then, the redemption of the universe is no longer a future expectation, but a call to a decision of faith that brings the possibility of transcending temporal and physical limitations.

In addition to employing critical methods to identify and reinterpret the mythology in Scripture, Bultmann says that criticism is necessary to correct the theological content *(Sache)* of the New Testament. The New Testament writers' proclamation of the kerygma is limited and incomplete because they include concepts of God, the world or self that are not fully shaped by faith. Thus, theologians must employ *Sachkritik*, or theological criticism, to determine where the New Testament writers failed to provide a complete articulation of the kerygmatic message. Such a critical process is justified because, in Bultmann's view, even the theological propositions of the New Testament "can never be the *object* of faith; they can only be the *explication* of the understanding which is inherent in faith itself."[86] Thus, just as Luther employed a theological criticism of Scripture by raising questions about the Epistle of James, Bultmann argues that theologians today must use *Sachkritik* to distill the kerygma as it appears in the New Testament.

Bultmann argues that the focal point of the kerygma is the cross. While he accepts the historicity of Jesus' crucifixion, it is only when the cross transcends historical facticity and acquires cosmic dimensions that it takes on significance for faith.[87] In its cosmic scope, "The abiding significance of the cross is that it is the judgement of the world, the judgement and the deliverance of man. So far as this is so, Christ is crucified 'for us.'"[88] However, the message of the cross is not complete without the resurrection. On the one hand, "An historical fact which involves a resurrection from the dead is utterly inconceivable!"[89] The idea that a dead person would be resuscitated (which is how Bultmann understands resurrection) is foolishness to the modern mind and must be rejected as a historical fact. Instead, Bultmann interprets resurrection to mean that Christ abolishes death and brings immortality to those who believe. In this way, then, "Cross and resurrection form a single, indivisible cosmic event which brings judgement to the world and opens up for men the possibility of authentic life."[90] Therefore, we should abandon mythological and "primitive" concepts that involve a forensic process whereby a sinless Christ assumes the guilt of sinful people. Understood existentially, atonement and forgiveness mean that we are free from sin to obey; that is, forgiveness means that we are free for faith and can open ourselves completely to the future. Thus, by demythologizing the concepts of cross, resurrection and atonement, Bultmann believes that we are in a position to grasp the eschatological message of the New Testament. As we appropriate the work of Christ "for us," death loses its grasp on us and we are liberated to experience the immortality of the present.

In summary, Bultmann's aim is to avoid the reduction of the Christian message to a list of eternal truths that we attempt to weave into a fabric of interconnected theological propositions. While such systems are attractive because they seem to correspond with the idea of a God who remains the same yesterday, today and tomorrow, Bultmann says that such a hope is illusory for two closely related reasons. First, since the criteria by which we determine what ideas fit into the category of "timeless truth" are constantly in flux, this makes the content of revelation dependent on human decisions. Second, we can make an intellectual decision about timeless truths and still remain existentially neutral. However, Bultmann argues that faith does not envision such a possibility. "On the contrary, to hear the Scriptures as the Word of God means to hear them as a word which is addressed to me, as kerygma, as a proclamation. Then my understanding is not a neutral one, but rather my response to a call."[91]

Evaluation. While a more complete examination of Bultmann's legacy as an exegete will be left to biblical scholars, a few observations are in order. His work in form-criticism marked a key development in biblical scholarship, and his basic methodology is still widely employed today in biblical exegesis. At the same time, many of the conclusions Bultmann derived through these critical methods are widely discounted. There is broad agreement that his skepticism about the historical veracity of the Gospel accounts was too radical, that he reads back into the New Testament texts a level of Gnosticism that was not present in the early church, and that he drives too deep a wedge between early Christianity and Judaism.

Bultmann's existentialist approach provided a good corrective to his liberal teachers' highly rationalized formulations, which moved faith and commitment to the margins. His observation that neutrality in the interpretation of texts is never completely possible and that our existential concerns should come into play in exegesis provided an important counterbalance to the reigning assumptions about historical method. Moreover, his attempt to frame a theology that gave attention to a scientific worldview without becoming reductionistic is commendable. However, Bultmann is also susceptible to criticism for the radical existential turn he made in his interpretation of Scripture. Although Bultmann has some basis for stating that existentialism differs from idealism in that the former has no defining set of beliefs, it is less clear that existentialism is neutral in determining our understanding of what constitutes revelation. For example, guided by his existentialist assumptions to sharply distinguish between the truths of existence and external or historical facts, Bultmann removes all revelatory significance from history and directs it toward an other-worldly sphere. The divorce is so complete that, on the one hand, we must accept scientific evaluations that God's activity cannot puncture the nexus of cause and effect to effect miracles (such as Jesus' resurrection) but, on the other hand, we should accept by faith that God is able to transcend the causal structures to open new existential possibilities for the believer. Because the latter cannot in any way be supported by reason, it is difficult to see how Bultmann can avoid the charge of fideism. Moreover, it is a fideism that appears to be shaped more by his existentialist presuppositions than Scripture, creating problems for his claim that existentialism does not impose itself on revelation, but remains open to it.

Another manifestation of Bultmann's commitment to an existentialist "pre-understanding" of theology is an implicit individualism. Macquarrie has noted that the term *koinonia* does not appear at any point in the rather extensive index of Greek terms in Bultmann's two-volume *Theology of the New Testament*.[92] It would make a rather flimsy case to base this evaluation on a single example, but it seems symptomatic of a system that places all the weight of faith on the individual's decision and experience of the divine. Thus, even though he speaks frequently of the kerygma as the proclamation of the church, the prominent role given individual decision makes the corporate aspect of Christianity unclear. The teaching and disciplinary functions of the Christian community or a Christian social ethic (to name just two examples) would be difficult to frame in view of the individualistic direction of Bultmann's existential theology.

Reinhold Niebuhr

Reinhold Niebuhr (1892-1971) was the most influential American proponent of dialectical theology.[93] However, his thought assumed a decisively different tone than that found in his continental counterparts. One reason for this may be that the disillusionment experienced by European theologians in the wake of the world wars was not felt as deeply and directly on the American scene. Whatever the actual explanation, it is clear that Niebuhr was not as wary of divine immanence as Barth or Brunner. He claims more common ground for conversation between the Christian and the non-Christian, and, as a result, his gaze is turned toward communicating and relating Christianity to secular society. This attempt to reach beyond the church made Niebuhr one of the most visible theological figures in mid-twentieth-century America. At the same time, he shares neo-orthodoxy's dislike of the rationalism, optimism and one-sided immanence that characterize liberal theology. Thus, despite his strong objections to Barth's theology,[94] these points of contact have caused him to be grouped with those in this theological stream.

Niebuhr's theological roots were in the Evangelical Synod, which grew out of the merger between the Prussian Reformed and Lutheran traditions. After undergraduate study at Elmhurst College, he went to Eden Seminary and then completed his theological education at Yale, receiving an M.A. in 1915. Following his father's footsteps, Niebuhr took a pastoral position. While Niebuhr's education in the liberal tradition sent him into the pastorate fully convinced that humanity could be purified, his tenure with a blue-collar congregation in Detroit was a decisive turning point for him. The devastating impact of industrialization on the working class deeply shook his optimism that the innate goodness of human beings would unfold inevitably in an earthly kingdom of God. Several decades later, as Niebuhr reflected on this experience in his "Intellectual Autobiography," he states, "In my parish duties I found that the simple idealism into which the classical faith had evaporated was as irrelevant to the crises of personal life as it was to the complex social issues of an industrial city."[95] His response, like that of the earlier figures examined in this chapter, was to seek an alternative that reclaimed the vitality and relevance of orthodox faith while not ignoring the insights and questions raised by liberalism.

Niebuhr's new theological outlook led to an amazing growth in his small church. This, and the attention drawn by his early writings, led to an appointment to teach ethics at Union Theological Seminary (New

York). At this time, Union was arguably the most prominent theological school in the United States, so many were surprised to see this position go to an academic newcomer, especially one without a doctorate. The sharp upward spiral of his career was capped by the invitation to deliver the Gifford Lectures in 1939. This set of lectures formed the basis for Niebuhr's two-volume *The Nature and Destiny of Man*, which is his best-known work.

Much of Niebuhr's writing was in the field of social ethics, and he complemented his concerns about the role of the Christian in society with deep political involvement. He made several attempts to gain public office running as a Socialist, but eventually became highly disillusioned with Communism. Later in life he lent his efforts to the Liberal party in New York. Though involvement with minority political parties meant that he would never wield direct influence through holding public office, his writing provided a platform that made him one of the most visible theologians in American society. Niebuhr's vast accomplishments are especially noteworthy given the ill health he endured for the last twenty years of his life, beginning with a heart attack in 1952. Though forced to retire from Union in 1960 because of the toll exacted by his various maladies, he remained active in speaking and writing until a series of strokes in his last five years sharply curtailed his abilities. Niebuhr died in 1971.

Niebuhr's theological context. Niebuhr was reluctant to refer to himself as a theologian, and it is true that his work assumes a different format and tone than what we find in Barth or Brunner. Nevertheless, his social ethics and apologetics address the realities of a world in which optimistic assumptions and hopes had been shattered. Thus, despite his objections, Niebuhr is an indispensable theological resource. His attempt to look beyond the walls of the church and find common ground with those outside the faith reflects the influence of his liberal roots. Like his liberal ancestors, he uses the theological resources made possible by God's immanence. However, he believes that classical liberalism came to the wrong conclusions about the implications of divine immanence. It had viewed humanity as perfectible and history as a process that pushes inevitably toward the better. By contrast, Niebuhr says that we must view both human beings and their history as more ambiguous. While we should work diligently toward recognizing and overcoming both the individual and corporate effects of sin on the world, it is prideful to think that human society will be purified by discovering immutable ethical principles or rationally deciphering the metaphysics of God. Rationalistic optimism, which he saw as an essential characteristic of liberal theology, detaches truth from actual life and represents an attempt to bypass the truth of revelation in Christ. Niebuhr's response to liberal rationalism is that "the truth in Christ cannot be speculatively established. It is established only as men encounter God, individually and collectively, after the pattern set by Christ's mediation."[96]

Many on the conservative side of the theological spectrum were thrilled with Niebuhr's desire to restore the centrality of the transcendent Christ of Scripture. However, he was equally critical of the fundamentalistic orthodoxy of the day, arguing that it espoused a theology that was just as rationalistic as liberalism, albeit in a different form. Through its literalistic interpretation of biblical myths, fundamentalism had reduced revelation to a series of interconnected and logically constructed logical propositions. Niebuhr finds two equally disturbing results in this approach. A literalistic interpretation of Scripture places revelation in an irreconcilable tension with science and forces an unnecessary either-or decision. Either one must reject science outright when it appears to conflict with Scripture, or science is distorted in order to square it with one's interpretation of Scripture. In either case, we are left without any way to speak of how God and nature are related.

Human nature and sin. Niebuhr's analysis of human nature is at the heart of his attempt to develop a theology that speaks to an increasingly secular world in a way that liberalism and fundamentalist orthodoxy could not. In the early pages of *The Nature and Destiny of Man*, he outlines a dialectic that he views as essential in order to properly understand the human constitution. "The obvious fact is that man is a child of nature, subject to its vicissitudes, compelled by its necessities, driven by its impulses, and confined within the brevity of the years which nature permits its varied organic form, allowing them some, but not too much, latitude. The other less obvious fact is that man is a spirit who stands outside of nature, life, himself, his reason, and the world."[97] In short, we are both animal and spirit. While our status as spiritual beings may be "less obvious," the very fact that we raise questions about the purpose and value of our existence is evidence that we are not limited exclusively to our animal nature. Instead, we have transcendent capacities that permit us to evaluate our aims and actions, and thus stand both within and outside the processes of nature.

Our hybrid nature as both spirit and animal provides the basis of Niebuhr's analysis of sin, one of the most influential aspects of his theology. Our transcendence, represented in our morality, rationality and ability to project ourselves into the future through hope, is always threatened by the dependence and mortality of our animal nature. We spiritually aspire to so much more than we can attain because of our finitude. This results in anxiety, which Niebuhr, following Kierkegaard, describes as "the dizziness of freedom."[98]

While freedom offers the possibility to attach meaning to our life, the contingencies of our existence threaten this meaning. The resulting anxiety compels us to latch on to something that we believe will protect us from the dangers that confront us in nature. This leads us inevitably into sin, which assumes two dimensions that correspond to the two poles of our nature. Either we will ignore our spiritual character and descend to a life of animal sensuality, or we will disregard our finitude and pridefully claim autonomy. The first, the sin of sensuality, denies our freedom and thus our spiritual nature. The second, the sin of pride, absolutizes our freedom and independence from God. In either case, Niebuhr says, our inability to negotiate "the dizziness of freedom" leads us inevitably, but not necessarily, into sin.[99]

For Niebuhr, the sin of sensuality is not essentially a life of unrestrained gluttony, sexual license or some other form of physical excess, although it may assume these manifestations. At its core, "sensuality represents an effort to escape from the freedom and the infinite possibilities of spirit by becoming lost in the detailed processes, activities and interests of existence, an effort which results inevitably in unlimited devotion to limited values. Sensuality is man 'turning inordinately to mutable good' (Aquinas)."[100] While sins of sensuality have been more readily condemned by the church than those of pride, Niebuhr views the sin of pride as more pervasive and dangerous. At its base, it is a denial of our finitude and dependence on God. While this is the basic characteristic, Niebuhr abstracts three types of pride for the sake of analysis. Pride of power blinds itself to the provisional and limited nature of our resources. The pride of knowledge is inherent in claims that human reason can autonomously discover ultimate truth about ourselves and the universe. Pride of virtue is self-righteousness, which constantly falls prey to the temptation to judge ourselves and others by our own arbitrary standards.

Social ethics. For all the dangers of individual pride, Niebuhr believes that the social dimension of human existence magnifies the depth of this sin. Thus, his thesis at the beginning of *Moral Man and Immoral Society* is "that a sharp distinction must be drawn between the moral and social behavior of individuals and of social groups, national, racial, and economic; and that this distinction justifies and necessitates political policies which a purely individualistic ethic must always find embarrassing."[101] In social groups, our egoistic impulses are less likely to be curbed by our transcendence, reason or sympathy than in our individual relationships. While our identification with groups provides opportunities to overcome egoism by working for a greater good, this corporate identity also offers "possibilities of self-aggrandizement beside which mere individual pretensions are implausible and incredible."[102]

Corporate pride has its roots in the same anxiety that gives rise to individual pride. The difference is that we seek protection from life's contingencies not by individually asserting ourselves against God but by seeking refuge in that which transcends the individual—the group. The most obvious vehicle for collective pride is the nation, which has powerful resources at its disposal. Claims of technological, military or moral superiority can sweep the individual into the illusion of safety against life's ambiguities. Given this, Niebuhr's writings encourage vigilance against the pride of nationalism. However, he warns that the church also "can become the vehicle of collective egotism. Every truth can be made the servant of sinful arrogance, including the prophetic truth that all men fall short of the truth. This particular truth can come to mean that, since all men fall short of the truth and since the church is a repository of a revelation which transcends the finiteness and sinfulness of men, it therefore has the absolute truth which other men lack."[103]

In view of the ambiguities of collective life and the inevitability of sin, Niebuhr contends that we should temper our expectations concerning attempts to correct social injustices. We can make steps toward improvement, but even positive movements will result in new evils. Thus, the Christian must walk a delicate balance. We are compelled by Christian responsibility to work toward social change. At the same time, we should not confuse any human structure with Christianity itself and must survey all social commitments with a critical eye. This combination of activism and realism is clearly present in the most readily recognizable of Niebuhr's quotations, the so-called Serenity Prayer: "God, give us grace to accept with serenity the things that cannot be changed, courage to change the things that should be changed, and the wisdom to distinguish the one from the other."[104]

Sin and revelation. Niebuhr identifies pride as the culprit behind the pervasive perception that Christianity is irrelevant to modern human beings. As a result of our self-divinization, he says, "modern man has an essentially easy conscience; and nothing gives the diverse and discordant notes of modern culture so much harmony as the unanimous opposition of modern man to Christian conceptions of the sinfulness of man."[105] Liberalism had abetted this "easy conscience" by finding the biblical account of the Fall to be myth, and thus discounting it. Based on its commitment to rationalism, then, liberalism reinterprets sin in terms of irrationality, which can then be eradicated by education. In other words, liberalism makes sin peripheral to our essence.

While Niebuhr has no interest in recovering a literal account of the Fall, he is adamant that only a biblical view fully recognizes the gravity of sin. As he puts it, "The Christian estimate of human evil is so serious precisely because it places evil at the very centre of human personality: in the will."[106] And while he rejects any rationalistic apologetic to establish the reality of human sinfulness, he does not resort to a fideistic view either. Instead, he maintains that the doctrine of human sinfulness "is supported by overwhelming evidence taken both from a sober observation of human behavior and from introspective analysis."[107] Therefore, Niebuhr's experiential understanding of sin parallels his view of faith. Liberalism's mistake, he argues, is that it identifies sin as a flaw or lack of development in our rational capacities, and thus relocates salvation to the realm of reason. Niebuhr, by contrast, views sin as a problem of the will, which makes it a failure of faith. If sin is therefore a misuse of freedom in that it rejects our dependence on God, faith is the acknowledgment of our reliance on divine aid.

Niebuhr's view of the will as the locus of sin and faith allows him the latitude to allow a greater role to general revelation than Barth or Brunner and, simultaneously, avoid a descent back to liberal rationalism. He outlines his position by stating, "The revelation of God to man is always a twofold one, a personal, individual revelation, and a revelation in the context of social-historical experience. Without the public and historical revelation the private experience of God would remain poorly defined and subject to caprice. Without the private revelation of God, the public and historical revelation would not gain credence."[108] The symbiotic relationship between the two forms of revelation is significant. As Niebuhr understands it, general revelation is the presupposition of special revelation. Without rational consciousness and its ability to see beyond the temporal and partial, God's eternal Word in Scripture would have no resonance with us. In addition to providing a point of contact between the conscious individual and Scripture, reason can validate the adequacy, even the superiority, of special revelation. On the other hand, reason alone cannot discover the distinctive and central truths of Christianity, nor can it provide logical proofs for faith. Indeed, Niebuhr argues that, "The truth that the Word was made flesh outrages all the canons by which truth is usually judged."[109] In short, while he rejects a propositional view of general revelation, in which it functions according to the rules of discursive reason, he does allow a central role for general revelation if it is understood in an experiential, or existential, manner.

Myth and Scripture. Niebuhr's existential approach to general revelation, coupled with his desire to maintain the dialectic between the spiritual and the natural in human nature, is reflected in his insistence on interpreting the major doctrines of Christianity as myth. Myth, he argues, is the necessary vehicle of revelation because purely rationalistic interpretations miss an important facet of human existence: rationality, with its ability to comprehend the partial and temporary, draws its conclusions based on sequences found in history. "But these sequences reveal nothing of the internal unity in all organic growth. For this reason scientific descriptions of reality always tend to a mechanistic interpretation of it."[110] Myth transcends purely rational interpretations because it includes the eternal dimension and the unity this offers to our life. Thus, while myth

places the central truths of faith in the context of history, the meaning
conveyed in the myth is not exhausted in the historical. Instead, the
mythical form indicates that it points toward a dimension that includes
the partial and transitory, but transcends it. "Whenever typically modern
men become conscious of this dimension and seek for an interpretation
of life which will do justice to this dimension, they elaborate a mystical
doctrine in addition to their rationalistic one."[111]

Since revelation involves interplay between the eternal and the temporal, Niebuhr argues that "it is important to take Biblical symbols seriously but not literally."[112] If we fail to take symbols seriously, then we do
not see how history finds its consummation in the eternal. If, on the
other hand, symbols embedded in myth are interpreted literally, the eternal dimension simply becomes an alternative form of history. Thus, Niebuhr argues that if we interpret the myth of the Fall in a literal manner,
we will be forced to choose between the inevitability of sin or our responsibility for sin. However, Niebuhr states that a symbolic view helps us
maintain both sides of this paradox, both of which are grounded in our
experience. While in our freedom we are not shackled to natural necessity and can therefore either choose faith or sin, the anxiety that results
from our uncertainty and transcendence leads all into sin. Thus, "the
final paradox [of the Fall] is that the discovery of the inevitability of sin is
man's highest assertion of his freedom."[113]

In a similar manner, Niebuhr resists the attempt to define Christ's two
natures or to separate the temporal and eternal in the incarnation, arguing that this ends in logical absurdities. Nor should be resurrection of the
body be considered literally true. All ideas of ultimate fulfillment "use
symbols of our present existence to express conceptions of a completion
of life which transcends our present existence."[114] The doctrine of judgment reminds us that our sin, and not our finitude, is confronted by the
ideal possibility of human existence. Thus, in encounters with biblical
symbols of judgment and ultimate salvation, "it is unwise for Christians to
claim any knowledge of either the furniture of heaven or the tempera-
ture of hell; or to be too certain about any details of the Kingdom of
God."[115]

Evaluation. As we have seen, Niebuhr's theological anthropology is at
the heart of his thought. To understand human nature as perfectible in

this life, as liberalism did, requires that we overlook the spiritual ambiguities embedded in our existence and so starkly exposed in the historical events of his early life. Instead, human beings exist in a constant tension between the contingencies and demands of the material pole of our being and our inner awareness of a deeper spiritual reality. Since it is in this tension that God's word confronts us, Niebuhr views any theology that lifts us out of our historical context and addresses us in abstract and ideal categories as a perversion of the gospel. Therefore, his social ethics recognizes that despite the potential for good in human institutions, the historical reality is that even the best social structures are inevitably tinged with a God-displacing pride. Likewise, his apologetics argues that while reason can serve the revelation of God in Scripture, we are never completely free from the temptation to distort it into a gatekeeper that dictates what we will hear and accept as revelation.

Given Niebuhr's insistence that we not view human beings in an ahistorical manner, many find his understanding of myth as very inconsistent. The dilemma is how the gospel can address the person in the midst of historical ambiguities if the symbols that communicate the central truths of the gospel have no roots in historical events. Thus, for example, if the incarnation is not really about the two natures of Jesus, but symbolizes that the fulfillment of our possibilities can be found beyond our present situation, it is difficult to see how this can avoid the charge of subjectivism. With no grounding in history, the myths then appear to have no foundation other than our existential awareness of a reality that transcends the partial and material realm. Niebuhr's response is that the divine reality behind these symbols is clear to those with faith. However, while Barth may have been happy to leave matters at this point, such a conclusion has much more serious consequences for Niebuhr, whose thought is built around the belief that Christians have common ground with those outside faith and that this provides a basis for conversation that does not lapse into subjectivism.

Paul Tillich

Paul Tillich (1886-1965) was the son of a Lutheran pastor, and a major Lutheran theologian of his day.[116] He was born in a small town near Berlin, and the family later moved to Berlin when his father received a position there. His interest in philosophy and theology developed early, and in his autobiographical reflections he speaks of philosophical discussions with his father as a bright spot in what was an otherwise rather strained relationship. Tillich's studies took him to the universities of Berlin, Tübingen and Halle, and he completed his doctorate at the University of Breslau in 1910 with a dissertation on the nineteenth-century Romanticist Friedrich Schelling.

Following his education, he received ordination in the Lutheran state church and, starting in 1914, served as a military chaplain until the end of World War I. First-hand experience with the horrors of war challenged the conservative political views of his upbringing, led to two nervous breakdowns and threw him into deep doubt about his faith. Like so many others during this period, his optimism about culture evaporated and he became deeply involved in efforts to restructure the government of postwar Germany. In the fifteen years following World War I, Tillich taught at a number of Germany's leading universities—Berlin, Marburg, the Dresden Institute for Technology and Frankfurt. Only at Marburg was he part of the theology faculty, and that was a less than happy time for him. The fact that the other three appointments were not theology positions brought him great satisfaction because it symbolized the idea behind his "method of correlation"—the belief that true theology functions at the point where the questions of contemporary society touch the teaching of faith.

Tillich's strident criticism of the growing Nazi movement caused him to be branded an enemy of the state, and he was later forced to flee Germany when Hitler came to power in 1933. With the assistance of Reinhold Niebuhr, he was offered a professorship at Union Theological Seminary in New York. Thus, at the age of forty-seven and with no fluency in English, Tillich began the American phase of his career. Although the transition to American life was sometimes difficult, his professional life at Union was very gratifying, and he recalled that "during eighteen years at Union Seminary I had not had a single disagreeable experience with my American colleagues."[117] In 1948, he was catapulted into the public eye by a rather unlikely event. A collection of sermons he had delivered in Union's chapel, titled *The Shaking of the Foundations*, was published and became an immediate bestseller. This was followed three years later by publication of the first volume of his *Systematic Theology*, which generated tremendous attention in the academic world. He was appointed as University Professor at Harvard when he retired from Union in 1955, and then took an appointment as theologian in residence at the Divinity School at the University of Chicago in 1962. When he died in 1965, he was arguably the best-known theologian in America.

The paradoxical quality of Tillich's theology is paralleled by a rather paradoxical life. Much of his writing is obscure even to the best-educated readers and his thick accent made his lectures extremely difficult to understand. In spite of this, his books sold widely, even to lay audiences, and he was an immensely popular lecturer and preacher. He was a very gifted preacher and his theology is centered on the church, yet he almost never attended church when not preaching. While he spoke frequently of the centrality of ethics in the Christian faith, his womanizing was legendary. In view of such paradoxes, it will not be surprising that it is very difficult to know where to put Tillich theologically. Continental interpreters tended to put him in the liberal camp, and his full-fledged acceptance of biblical criticism and the explicit reliance of his theology on philosophy can be cited in support of this positioning. On the other hand, he is often grouped with the dialectical theologians by American readers, who point toward his cultural pessimism and insistence on Jesus as the ultimate revelation of the divine. Perhaps the best route is to focus on why his ideas brought him such prominence and leave the task of categorization to others.

The method of correlation. At the beginning of his *Systematic Theology*, Tillich states:

> Theology, as a function of the Christian church, must serve the needs of the church. A theological system is supposed to satisfy two basic needs: the statement of the truth of the Christian message and the interpretation of this truth for every new generation. Theology moves back and forth between two poles, the eternal truth of its foundation and the temporal situation in which the eternal truth must be received.[118]

This bipolar movement is what he refers to as the "method of correlation." "In using the method of correlation, systematic theology proceeds in the following way: it performs an analysis of the human situation out of which existential questions arise, and it demonstrates that the symbols used in the Christian message provide the answers to these questions."[119] Tillich's pairing of "questions" and "answers" provides the framework for his three-volume *Systematic Theology*. The five questions in these volumes express our existential concerns about truth, non-being, alienation and sin, moral and cultural finitude and the significance of history. These questions are met with the response of the Christian faith, which are expressed in the symbols of Logos, God the Creator, Jesus the Christ, Spirit and the kingdom of God.

While Tillich believes that these five questions are constants in human nature, they receive different and new expression in each generation. If theologians hope to explain to a skeptical world how the enduring symbols of Christianity are relevant and revelatory, they must engage the surrounding culture in conversation. To put it differently, theology must always be apologetical or it becomes obsolete. On this matter, Tillich represents a sharp break with Barth, who accused Tillich of retreating too far back toward liberalism in his dialogue with contemporary culture. However, both are in agreement that the concerns raised in the analysis of our existential situation are not the source of our answers. Tillich is emphatic that only God answers the questions derived from our analysis of existence. However, contrary to Barth, he says, "It is equally wrong to derive the question implied in human existence from the revelatory answer. This is impossible because the revelatory answer is meaningless if there is no question to which it is the answer."[120]

Our questions and existential concerns must always precede God's revelatory answer because "Only those who have experienced the shock of transitoriness, the anxiety in which they are aware of their finitude, the threat of nonbeing, can understand what the notion of God means."[121] This concern about our finite existence provides the context for understanding Tillich's emphasis on ontology. We are philosophers by nature because we cannot but ask the question of being. Indeed, the very act of asking provides a key preparatory insight: "It is man in his finitude who asks the question of being. He who is infinite does not ask the question of being, for, as infinite, he has the complete power of being. He is identical with it; he is God."[122] We become aware of our nonbeing in the process of philosophical questioning, and this sense of emptiness prepares us to receive revelation.

Theology also asks the question of being, but in a decisively different way. "Philosophy deals with the structure of being in itself; theology deals with the meaning of being for us."[123] The question of "being for us" means that the theologian cannot approach being in a detached manner, but must engage it with an existential attitude of passion and involvement. Thus, for Tillich, while there is no essential conflict between philosophy and theology, neither should we seek a synthesis of the two. Philosophy reveals the ontological problem, and thus generates in us initial concern about ultimate being. However, theology alone has the resources to tell the story of Being itself in a way that satisfies our deepest anxieties.

Faith and ultimate concern. When we raise the question of nonbeing, we enter what Tillich calls a "boundary situation." We recognize the finitude of our resources and, simultaneously, the fact that these limitations represent a threat to our being. We must then make a decision about how we will face the threat of nonbeing, and this decision goes to the heart of all we are. It reveals what Tillich refers to as our "ultimate concern." "Our ultimate concern is that which determines our being or non-being."[124] This ultimate concern is the object of theology because whatever concerns us in an ultimate way becomes our god—a point that goes all the way back to Luther. But not every "god" is God. When our concern falls to the conditioned, partial and finite, we descend into idolatry. However, no idol has the power to decisively confront nonbeing because it also participates in finitude. For Tillich, then, sin is "the elevation of preliminary concerns to the rank of ultimate concern."[125] In contrast, faith "is the state of being grasped by an ultimate concern."[126]

By shifting the definition of faith to refer to that which expresses our ultimate concern, Tillich significantly broadens the concept of religion. For example, he wrote frequently about how art and architecture reveal our deepest concerns. Given this understanding, Tillich argues that even an atheist committed to the quest for truth was living a life of faith, although unconsciously. Tillich argues that everything has the potential for mediating revelation, and whenever the finite world raises matters of ultimate concern that are embraced, faith is present.

God, being and existence. Because our ultimate concern should be only

that which is unconditional and unlimited, Tillich finds the traditional
language of God and God's existence lacking. In fact, he argues paradoxically that it is as atheistic to affirm that God exists as it is to deny God's
existence. The problem is created by the terms *existence* and *being:*

> The being of God cannot be understood as the existence of a being
> alongside others or above others. If God is a being, he is subject to the
> categories of finitude, especially to space and substance. Even if he is
> called the "highest being" in the sense of the "most perfect" and the
> "most powerful" being, this situation is not changed. When applied to
> God, superlatives become diminutives. They place him on the level of
> other beings while elevating him above all of them.[127]

In place of language about God's existence, then, Tillich suggests that
we speak of God as "being-itself," or the "ground of being." As the
ground of being, God is the source of the power of being that enables
everything to exist. In a similar manner, Tillich is concerned that language about the personality of God can be misleading. Properly understood, the statement that God is personal, "means that God is the ground
of everything personal and that he carries within himself the ontological
power of personality. He is not a person, but he is not less than personal."[128]

Tillich argues that our understanding of Christianity's symbols follows
from the idea of God as the ground of being or personality. For example,
"The doctrine of creation is not the story of an event which took place
'once upon a time.' It is the basic description of the relation between God
and the world. It is the correlate to the analysis of man's finitude. It
answers the question implied in man's finitude and infinitude generally."[129] Similarly, the Fall should not be interpreted as historical event,
but as a symbol describing the universal human situation. "The symbol
'Adam before the Fall' must be understood as the dreaming innocence of
undecided potentialities."[130] Creation in its essence is good. However,
when creation is actualized, the inevitable result of freedom is universal
alienation because, "the state of existence is the state of estrangement."[131]
The Fall is the symbol that expresses the breach between essence (or
Being itself) and actual existence, which is inevitably conditional and sinful. Thus, Tillich assumes the paradoxical position of stating that the Fall
was not an ontological necessity while simultaneously arguing that

human freedom cannot be a reality without sin as the result.

Further, Tillich argues that the symbol of the incarnation must undergo severe reinterpretation in view of this distinction between Being and existence. The uniqueness of Jesus has nothing to do with the divine being incarnate in a human being, an idea Tillich refers to as "transmutation." Jesus of Nazareth cannot be both in the state of existence, conditioned by finitude, and in a state of pure Being. Instead, "all reports and interpretations of the New Testament concerning Jesus as the Christ possess two outstanding characteristics: his maintenance of unity with God and his sacrifice of everything he could have gained for himself from this unity."[132] Jesus is the model of what it means to be completely open to the unconditional and to sacrifice all to it. However, if Jesus becomes the object of our worship, this is an idolatrous "jesusology" and Christianity is no more than just another religion. Instead, Jesus sacrifices himself to the Christ, which means that he does not attempt to impose himself, a finite being, on other finite beings. Jesus the person is not the revelation, but the medium of revelation as he points to the Christ.

Tillich's view that Jesus is the mediator rather than the object of revelation explains his almost complete lack of interest in the historical Jesus. He goes so far as to argue that if historical investigation should make it probable that Jesus of Nazareth had never existed, it would not matter. The faith of the church is faith in Christ, and by its participation in the Christ, a new reality is proclaimed: that essential being can arise even when subject to the conditions of existence. This unity of Being and existence is what Tillich refers to as the New Being; this is why Christ is the final revelation. All prior forms of revelation raised the hope that estrangement could be overcome by providing a glimpse of the unconditional through finite things. The proclamation of Christ as the New Being means that, in him, alienation is overcome, not by abolishing finite existence, but through his unification of existence with the ground of being. The Logos became flesh. Christ's followers participate in this by means of the resurrection. While history cannot offer any positive support for or negative evidence against our conclusions about the resurrection, faith gives certainty "to the victory of the Christ over the ultimate consequence of the existential estrangement to which he subjected himself. And faith can give this certainty because it is itself based on it. Faith is based on the experience of being grasped by the power of the New Being through which the destructive consequences of estrangement are conquered."[133]

The participation of the church in New Being is decisive for Tillich's understanding of Scripture. Following his method of correlation, he argues that we should reject neo-orthodoxy's claim of the Bible as the only source of theology. "The biblical message cannot be understood and could not have been received had there been no preparation for it in human religion and culture. And the biblical message would not have become a message for anyone, including the theologian himself, without the experiencing participation of the church and of every Christian."[134] Without receptivity, there is no revelation. The standard for theology always involves an encounter between the Bible and the church. Thus, "The Bible is a document both of the divine self-manifestation and of the way in which human beings have received it."[135] Scripture, for Tillich, is not God's Word. It only becomes God's Word when we embrace it with openness to the New Being, because the attitude of receptivity cannot be divorced from the message of Scripture itself.

Evaluation. In its basic configuration, Tillich's process of correlation appears to provide a necessary corrective in its willingness to hear how questions about value, meaning, and truth are raised in contemporary society. However, reading Tillich's work raises suspicion that the questions he refers to are not directly derived from culture, but are heavily filtered through existentialist metaphysics before they get to the reader. While it is true that all of the theologians examined in this chapter rely on existentialism to some degree, the others are more inclined to use it as a method. Tillich, however, is much more heavily invested in existentialist ontology. Therefore, because the ultimate concerns he identifies come to us in ways that are determined beforehand by his ontological categories, the answers that seem most appropriate require formulations stated in categories that often appear to be imposed on theology rather than derived from it.

One of the clearest examples of the problems his understanding of existence creates lies in his analysis of sin. In Tillich's ontology, to exist is to be in a state of estrangement. Given this, it is hard to see how sin is avoidable or humans redeemable. Even though he asserts that he does not view sin as an ontological necessity, his concept of existence dictates that he cannot speak of God as existing and personal. Instead, God is Being itself and the ground of personality. However, this stress on God's utter transcendence sits uneasily (if at all) alongside his rather radical view of God's immanence, which, at minimum, borders on panentheism. Finally, his ontological paradigm requires up front that the historical Jesus can hold no relevance for theology. When he defines our fundamental problem as the need to reconcile existence and essence, the Jesus who exists in history can be of no help to us since he also is caught up in all the vicissitudes of fallen and alienated existence.

The Influence of Dialectical Theology

While you will still find many theologians today whose orientation is strongly informed by dialectical theology, in some sense it is proper to see dialectical theology as a movement that began to wither in the 1930s when *Zwischen den Zeiten* was discontinued. The internal tensions within the core of this movement pushed all of the key players toward different trajectories. Nevertheless, it was also the case that this core group of young scholars who brought dialectical theology into existence remained active and played prominent roles in their fields for several decades. As a result, these men have educated and molded many of today's most influential theologians, and many of the themes that characterized dialectical theology are still discernible, even if they also bear the distinctive marks of the particular theologian through whom they were developed. Thus, while few today will identify themselves as neo-orthodox or dialectical theologians, we still hear the echoes of this school in the major theological voices at the end of the twentieth century.

6. PRAGMATISM AND PROCESS: AMERICAN ADVENTURES IN IDEAS

*H*aving considered one of the great chapters in the story of theology, we now turn back to philosophy and to the United States. Again our interest is in the age following World War I, when two major voices sought to make serious revisions in the intellectual tradition they inherited. Like the early Wittgenstein and the logical positivists, each of these men wanted to reconstruct philosophy and bring it into line with science, though each developed a different philosophical vision. They are John Dewey (1859-1952) and Alfred North Whitehead (1861-1947). From the time Whitehead moved to Harvard until his death, these two men were America's foremost living philosophers. Each of them worked in the empiricist tradition, each valued science and its import for philosophy, and each developed some of the ideas of William James. Yet their philosophies remained distinct. Of the two, John Dewey was the better known in his day. His faith in progress and the power of technology best represents the spirit of American intellectual life during the 1930s; we begin with him.

Dewey

John Dewey was born in New England and followed in the footsteps of C. S. Peirce and William James. His is the third great pragmatic voice in American philosophy.[1] As philosophical education became more technical and professional in the States, Dewey remained a public intellectual. He wrote and spoke on a number of general topics, including politics, education and morality.[2] He was often involved in organizations seeking social improvement at home and abroad. His greatest continuing influence remains in the philosophy of education, where he successfully argued for a more practical conception of intelligence. He was a prolific author and lecturer, writing forty books and over seven hundred articles in his long career.[3]

Dewey began his academic career modestly enough, as a high school teacher in Vermont. At this very early stage, he was attracted to Scottish common sense philosophy. Encouraged by a friend to seek further study, Dewey attended the newly organized Johns Hopkins University, where C. S. Peirce was then teaching philosophy. At this point in his development, however, Dewey became interested in Hegel and idealism, only later moving to a pragmatic stance. One might say that in his person Dewey recapitulates the history of American philosophy, starting from common sense realism, then moving to idealism, and finally to pragmatism.

Soon after graduating from Johns Hopkins, the young Dewey showed interest in psychology and early on published some essays in psychology from an idealist perspective which eventually resulted in his first book, *Psychology* (1887).[4] A growing interest in experimental psychology (he studied with G. S. Hall at Johns Hopkins) drew the young philosopher toward a more scientific understanding of philosophical method and back to the ideas of Peirce and James. The classic text by James, *The Principles of Psychology* (1890), exercised a heavy influence on Dewey's philosophical development. During this early period, he moved between several universities, teaching at Michigan, Minnesota and Chicago. At Chicago he helped to found the "laboratory school" later known as the Dewey school, and he developed a significant interest in education. Indeed, the philosophy of education may be the area where, above all others, Dewey has enjoyed the greatest influence. In 1904, Dewey left the Midwest to take up a position in philosophy at Columbia University in New York, where he taught until 1930 and developed his mature philosophy. When he retired in 1930, he did not retire from philosophy, for Dewey was a life-long public intellectual. He lectured all over the world and received numerous honorary doctorates from prestigious universities. He regularly wrote about the political and social issues of the day, not in technical journals but in magazines of public opinion. At the age of seventy-eight he traveled to Mexico where he chaired the Commission of Inquiry into Leon Trotsky, who was accused by Stalin of treason against the USSR; Dewey and the Commission found Trotsky not guilty. Dewey likewise was an early critic of Stalin's government (he visited Russia in 1928). At this time many Western intellectuals were still infatuated with Stalin and critical of Dewey for this reason.[5] It is typical of Dewey that he welcomed open criticism of his ideas and free inquiry into moral and social problems; later he would defend the right of Communists to teach at American universities during the McCarthy era. Dewey published a number of lectures and books into his eighties and nineties. While his influence on philosophy did not last far beyond World War II, at his death in 1952 at the age of ninety he remained one of the best known philosophers in the world.[6]

Dewey's mature philosophy combined the pragmatism of James and Peirce with a strong attachment to science and the scientific method. Dewey was adamant that only by adopting a scientific mode of thinking could culture evolve and philosophy advance. In his studies in logic and his philosophy of education, he emphasized the practical and problem-solving character of reason (or inquiry). Dewey preferred to call his philosophy "instrumentalism" because of his emphasis on philosophy as an instrument for solving problems. Since the best way to solve problems is the scientific method, he insisted that morality and social science must adopt this method if culture was to evolve, and these disciplines were to make any headway. Furthermore, Dewey sought to ground logic and meaning in a view of language close to existence and life several years before Wittgenstein made this move.[7] For Dewey, knowledge begins and ends with experience and existence, and for this reason philosophy must be experimental.

> Knowing, for the experimental sciences, means a certain kind of intelligently conducted doing; it ceases to be contemplative and becomes in a true sense practical. Now this implies that philosophy, unless it is to undergo a complete break with the authorized spirit of science, must also alter its nature. It must assume a practical nature; it must become operative and experimental.[8]

Notice how, in this passage, the force of the "must" for philosophy comes from the "spirit of science." Dewey adopted a kind of scientism, as did much of America during this period.[9] In other words, for Dewey science was the exemplary method for approaching knowledge and truth, and the basis of our hope in the future for "industrialized society."

When he came to the University of Edinburgh to deliver his Gifford lectures, Dewey expanded upon the implications of his experimental approach for philosophy. He began by rejecting what he saw in the Western intellectual tradition as *The Quest for Certainty* (1929). Grouping together the Greek philosophers, Spinoza, Descartes, Kant and Hegel under the rubric of "the classical tradition," Dewey then attacked this tradition's search for a reality that was above the flux of history and a solid foundation of knowledge that was certain and absolute. Philosophy ought to follow science, he maintained; it ought to be more down to earth and more open to revision in light of experience. In many ways this book is, like much of Dewey's philosophy, a "consideration of the significance of the method of science for formation of the theory of knowledge and of mind."[10]

As a philosopher with lasting interest in psychology, Dewey's conception of mind was a central aspect of his thought. Following the influence of Hume and James, Dewey conceived of the human mind as a series of habits that grows over time in crucial connection with its environment. He rejected any thought of a separate substance for the soul and was consistently critical of mind-body dualism (á la Descartes) as unscientific. In fact Dewey carried over from his Hegelian youth a distinct penchant for seeing things in a whole system; he was a trenchant critic of all forms of dualism. Furthermore, what goes for the mind and human body is equally true of reality as a whole. In his most ambitious metaphysical book, *Experience and Nature* (1925), Dewey places the life of the mind firmly within the natural world. "Experience is *of* as well as *in* nature."[11] Like the mind itself, nature is constantly evolving. "Every existence is an event. . . . The conjunction of problematic and determinate characters in nature renders every existence, as well as every idea and human act, an experiment in fact."[12] Since nature is constantly in process (with its structure stable but not fixed and eternal) any living organism must therefore adapt to fit with a changing environment. This is just as true of the mental life of a human being, from childhood to death, as it is of the smallest biological organism. Influenced by Hegel and Darwin, but moving beyond them both, Dewey views reality as an organic and dynamic whole, in which the life of the mind is placed firmly within the larger biosphere of which humans are a natural part.

Dewey believed that reality was constantly evolving, and therefore our ideas and values must evolve with it. Unlike many who embraced scientism, Dewey held that human values were particularly important for civilization and thus for philosophy. But how can we know what is truly of value? For Dewey, the ultimate moral end is growth itself. There are no eternal or a priori goods, rather, the good is a human construct arising out of our experience with nature. The only ultimate goal which is in keeping with modern science is growth: not perfection, but improvement, progress, evolution is the ultimate moral end.[13] As a public intellectual, Dewey defended democracy on these pragmatic grounds. In an age of rising communism, fascism and anti-democratic political forces (not only in Europe but also in North America) it is no small thing that Dewey consistently defended democratic ideas. He argued that democracy was not just a political system: democracy is a way of life, one in keeping with the need to be open to new realities and new challenges as society grows and develops.[14] Dewey also applied his conception of value, society and open inquiry to religion in his short work, *A Common Faith* (1934).

While Dewey followed Peirce and James on many matters, he rejected their belief in God. For Dewey, God was nothing more than a symbol for the unity of our higher values. In other words, God does not actually exist, but the word "god" can be accepted as a kind of cipher for the best within human culture and value. "It denotes the unity of all ideal ends arousing us to desire and action."[15] Needless to say, such a use for the word *god* is highly idiosyncratic, even misleading. His faith in science and his philosophical naturalism, combined with his insistence that there is no supernatural, eternal or ideal realm beyond nature: all of these combined to create an evolutionary form of humanism that served as Dewey's philosophy of religion.

Dewey was a popular philosopher and a public intellectual who captured the spirit of his time and culture. While his unshakable faith in science and progress looks naive today, this is only after a century of experience with the problems that our technology brings, and the complexities of understanding the diverse nature of the sciences. There are still valuable lessons to be learned from his philosophy. For example, we certainly do need a better understanding of the mind, one more in keeping with modern science than the mind-body dualism of the past. Dewey is surely right that, whatever else we may be, humans are a part of the natural world. But Dewey's brand of social Darwinism, scientism and solid faith in "growth" would not survive the rigors of World War II. During those years of worldwide conflict, humans used their scientific knowledge to horrible ends. Technology allowed humanity to destroy itself with greater efficiency than ever before.

A related problem is internal to Dewey's moral philosophy. By electing to make science the foundational method for all philosophical problems, including ethics, Dewey makes it impossible to rationally justify the values which science is based upon. The high value Dewey places on science cannot be justified by scientific methods, but only by conceptual and rational argument which avoids circularity only by abstaining from any appeal to science and its methods. We can no longer assume that scientific methods always lead to the common good and the general welfare, as Dewey did. Finally, Dewey's brand of constructing a total philosophical system was soon out of fashion. The rise of logical positivism made his philosophy of science out of date. Ironically for a philosopher so attached to science, Dewey's philosophy of science is problematic for today. After the struggles with logical positivism, the philosophy of science has advanced well beyond Dewey's simplified scheme. If the pragmatic tradition Dewey represented was to live on, it would have to be among more technical (and less popular!) philosophers trained in the new symbolic logic and the rigors of analytic philosophy. This is in fact exactly what happened. Even during Dewey's lifetime there arose an important school of logical pragmatism, with W. V. O. Quine being the chief representative. But before we move on to Quine in the next chapter, we must consider the other important voice in American philosophy during the period between the wars.

Whitehead

Despite their many differences, Whitehead and Dewey shared much in common. Both were active and influential philosophers in the northeast corner of America during the same period of time. Both were interested in education as well as the larger role of philosophy in culture. Both saw the importance of value and the moral dimension in systematic philosophy. Both were influenced by William James and by idealism, yet logic was central to their philosophical development. They both stood in the tradition of British empiricism insofar as they insisted that philosophy must begin with experience, but they also maintained that it cannot end there. Both came to see, with some reluctance, that their projects required a systematic approach to metaphysics; furthermore, both developed a metaphysics in which reality is a dynamic process of change, movement and structure.[16] The similarities are there—but equally obvious are the differences. Whitehead represents the idealist tradition in his interpretation of nature and science, while Dewey represents the naturalistic side of American philosophy. Indeed, in his Harvard period Whitehead developed the last great metaphysical system in English (at least so far).

We have noted that Whitehead develops the idealist tradition, but he does so in a creative and realistic way that has come to be known as process philosophy, an approach with a long history in Western thought.[17] The essence of process philosophy lies in its emphasis upon change and the dynamic character of reality. Hegel and Henri Bergson are thus important representatives of process philosophy, even though they did not use those terms. In their more metaphysical works, both James and Dewey could also be considered process philosophers in this broad sense. But the work of Whitehead and his followers has come to dominate this tradition to such an extent that, in the narrow sense of the term, process philosophy is identified with the work Whitehead and his followers. The focus on Whitehead has meant that the work of his fellow Englishman in the process tradition, Samuel Alexander (1859-1938), may be overlooked.

Samuel Alexander was a Jewish philosopher who was born in Australia but spent much of his career as a teacher in Oxford.[18] He was in fact the first professing Jew to hold a Fellowship (or teaching position) at either Oxford or Cambridge. Alexander was interested in Darwin and Hegel, and his first works were in morality understood along natural scientific grounds (not unlike Dewey). His greatest contribution to philosophy, however, was his Gifford lectures on *Space, Time and Deity* (1920).[19] Alexander derives his notion of space-time from Einstein's work, and he develops a process conception of space-time as the basic stuff of reality. Complexity and intelligence emerge out of the process of material change and becoming. God or deity is at the top of this new chain of being-in-becoming. But God does not exist fully for Alexander. "God as actually possessing deity does not exist, but is an ideal, is always becoming."[20] Deity for him refers to the ideal unity of all reality, something not far from the God of Spinoza. In modern process philosophers like Alexander and Whitehead, science (and the process of scientific discovery) must be understood within a larger metaphysical system. Accordingly, both men emphasize the dynamic character of reality, and the role of deity in that larger whole.[21]

Whitehead is the most important process philosopher of the twentieth century; but he did not start life as a philosopher. He first became interested in philosophy through his study of mathematics, logic and modern physics. As befits a process thinker, Whitehead's philosophy grew and developed over time.[22] He began his academic career in mathematics. In 1884 he became a fellow of Trinity College, where he taught mathematics to Bertrand Russell and J. M. Keynes, among others. His earliest work was in algebra and geometry, but Whitehead's enduring contribution is to mathematical logic. His joint work with Russell, *Principia Mathematica* (1910-1913), is one of the most important texts in the history of Western logic.[23] Whitehead joined Russell in the quest for a mathematical form of deductive logic, in order to found all mathematical truth in logic. At this time Whitehead moved to London and began to study new areas of physics, especially Einstein's theories. He became a professor of applied mathematics in 1914 and began to write a series of papers on educational reform, and in the philosophy of science.[24] This London period is essential to understanding his growing interest in metaphysics. He published three early works on physics and its philosophical interpretation, especially the concept of nature which is essential to modern science.[25] Given as lectures in Cambridge, *The Concept of Nature* (1920) is one of his first philosophical works addressed to the general reader. In it he spells out the philosophical conception of nature that he believes is necessary for modern physics, a conception which he also develops in the other, more technical books.

In this early period, Whitehead struggled with the philosophical interpretation of space. He rejected on scientific and philosophical grounds the concept of nature inherited from the Greeks to Newton, especially the view that there is a metaphysical substratum behind or below the world we experience. Instead, Whitehead defined nature as "that which we observe in perception through the senses."[26] At the same time, Whitehead insisted on the objectivity of science. The data of natural science, which are observed in sense-impressions, must be "self-contained as against thought."[27] Experience of nature is always experience of something, not merely inner subjective events. Yet Whitehead strongly objects to the bifurcation of nature into phenomena that are perceived and the supposed underlying causes in a material "nature" that is not perceived. Instead, he seeks a coherent, relational conception of nature, in which perception takes a natural part.

The ultimate data for the natural sciences, Whitehead states, are events. He defines an event in this early period as "the specific character of a place through a period of time."[28] There is no going behind events to a container notion of space, to a material substrate or to physical objects. Rather, for modern science the events themselves become nature's fundamental reality. Abiding structures like Cleopatra's Needle in London are simply enduring structures of events and are not the ultimate constituents of nature. Even in these early works, we can see Whitehead anticipating his later process understanding of reality, which he would call a philosophy of organism. So like Bradley and Royce, Whitehead saw reality as a kind of fusion of mind and nature (as ordinarily understood). But while these idealists focused on an Absolute One that was the unifying principle of reality, Whitehead takes this Absolute and breaks it into a plurality of ultimate events. His mature conception of reality is that of a vast plurality of streams of experience, interactive through a complex web of relationships, each event having elements of the mental and the physical (as ordinarily understood).

As he neared retirement in England, Whitehead was offered a chair in philosophy at Harvard. He moved there in 1924 and soon produced another trilogy of philosophical books, this time moving more clearly into metaphysics and religion.[29] For Whitehead, the philosophical interpretation of modern science was impossible apart from metaphysics. He set himself firmly against the materialistic and atheistic conception of science prevalent in philosophers like Dewey, even going so far as to argue for a place for God in his larger system of philosophy.[30] But Whitehead's major work in metaphysics was his Gifford lectures of 1927-1928, *Process and Reality*, which presents his mature metaphysical system.[31] In this comprehensive work, he sets for himself the ambitious task of constructing a "complete cosmology," that is "a system of ideas which brings the aesthetic, moral and religious interests into relation with those concepts of the world which have their origin in natural science."[32]

Whitehead's *Process and Reality* is a classic example of Western metaphysics in the grand style.[33] Much of the work can be understood as his mature philosophical analysis of being as becoming, of reality in all its manifest dimensions including the moral and aesthetic. The hero of this work is the "actual entity" or "actual occasion," Whitehead's word for the most basic and real elements of the world. In order to understand what he means by an actual entity, we must peer briefly into the heart of this challenging philosophical work.

Whitehead's approach to metaphysics followed his earlier work in geometry, mathematics and symbolic logic. His tendency is to set up basic axioms or principles and then to develop an entire system based upon these core doctrines. Whitehead's specialized vocabulary results from this approach. Just as in mathematics a function can be defined in any manner we please, as long as it is consistent with and serves a function in the larger system, so Whitehead felt free to use words in totally new ways, as well as to create totally new words, investing them with specialized meaning that only made sense within his philosophical system. He did not usually bother to defend his terminology or his core doctrines in a positive manner, except as they fit together in a consistent and comprehensive way. He does typically criticize other approaches, putting forth his system as a better alternative. As he puts it, "the true method of philosophical construction is to frame a scheme of ideas, the best that one can, and unflinchingly to explore the interpretation of experience in terms of that scheme."[34] He goes on to claim that his core doctrines or "fundamental ideas, in terms of which the scheme is developed, presuppose each other so that in isolation they are meaningless."[35] This is nothing less than a geometrical approach to metaphysics, reminding the reader of Spinoza's attempt to do ethics *more geometrico*. At the very the beginning of *Process and Reality* he explains his larger understanding of the goals of such a "speculative philosophy."

Whitehead tells us that the goal of speculative philosophy, and hence of his book, is nothing less than "a coherent, logical, necessary system of general ideas in terms of which every element of our experience can be interpreted."[36] This really is philosophy in the grand manner. Metaphysics thus understood is a great system of ideas into which the whole of reality, and all of our humanity, can be interpreted and rightly understood. Such a metaphysical system is based upon reason and experience. It needs to be logical and coherent on the rational side, but also "applicable" and "adequate" to our experience. However grand his ideal of speculative philosophy, Whitehead is certainly aware of the need to be open to criticism, revision and intellectual development. "In philosophical discussion, the merest hint of dogmatic certainty as to finality of statement is an exhibition of folly."[37] Still, the reach of these lofty goals is certainly breathtaking.

At the core of Whitehead's system is the actual entity, which he simply defines as "the final real things of which the world is made up."[38] Actual entities are not the ordinary objects of our common life, however. Rather they are very tiny, brief events (in keeping with his event-based understanding of nature developed earlier). For this reason they can also be called actual occasions. The objects of our everyday life are "societies" of these tiny, brief events. Relationships between actual occasions form the nexus or web of reality, the dynamic and changing procession of time and the cosmos. According to Whitehead, every actual entity "prehends" (is related to) all previous actual occasions in either a positive or a negative way. In this way, each actual occasion brings unity to all of reality: in its very act of coming to be, the actual entity connects all of reality in its brief moment of life. What is more, each and every actual occasion is an experiencing subject. Freedom is not limited to humans in Whitehead's view: every actual entity is free is some degree, however small. Creativity and novelty are very important to his understanding of reality, and they are part of all real things, however small. Real self-consciousness, however, is more rare and limited. Whitehead does use the language of our mental life (feeling, anticipation, satisfaction and the like) to describe all actual occasions, and to some extent his philosophy can be called "panpsychism" (literally, "all is soul"). But he does not attribute consciousness to rocks and trees. Rather, he makes realistic and atomistic the tradition of British idealism, which insisted that nature is finally mental in character. What we experience as the material world is at bottom a constant flux of subjective, experience-based events or occasions, which band together to create to objects we experience. Whitehead's tiny atoms of reality, the fundamental stuff of cosmic process, are "drops of experience"—a phrase Whitehead borrows from James.[39]

Whitehead's philosophy of organism emphasizes relationality just as much as it does process. Each subjective occasion of experience can only be what it is in terms of it relationship with (or prehension of) all prior actual entities, as well its grasp of form and possibility given by the "eternal objects." The eternal objects play the role of Plato's Forms in Whitehead's thought. Each atom of reality, each subjective occasion of experience out of which the whole cosmos is formed, is made up of relationships. Any actual occasion is thus the self-creative coming together of its relationships to all other prior occasions, and to some eternal objects: a coming-to-be which for each occasion is a creative act of novelty. Each actual occasion is thus in some ways the unification of all reality: but only in God is this fully the case. Yes, God is also an actual entity (but not an actual occasion). Whitehead sees the actual entity, therefore, as being self-caused in some sense. It satisfies Spinoza's definition of substance as that which is *causa sui*, i.e., that it causes itself to be. Just to give the reader a flavor for Whitehead's technical jargon, we continue the quotation:

> To be *causa sui* means that the process of concrescence is its own reason for the decision in respect to the qualitative clothing of feelings. It is finally responsible for the decision by which any lure for feeling is admitted to efficiency. The freedom inherent in the universe is constituted by this element of self-causation.[40]

If you can understand these sentences, you will have come a long way toward understanding *Process and Reality!*

Unlike Dewey (but like Peirce, James and Royce), Whitehead's metaphysics holds an important place for God.[41] Philosophers who believed in God were understandably attracted to Whitehead as an alternative to Dewey's naturalism. God plays several key roles in the philosophy of organism. His "primordial nature" (which is eternal) contains all of the eternal objects, which are the source of form and possibility in the world. In his "consequent nature" which is temporal, God experiences and remembers the whole of reality, organizing it all into God's own process of becoming and God's larger understanding of the whole. For this reason, Whitehead's doctrine of God is called "dipolar theism," for God as a finite actual entity has both a primordial nature and a consequent nature.

After publishing his Gifford lectures, Whitehead continued to lecture, write and explain his philosophy. As a famous philosopher in his day, he received many honorary doctorates from prestigious universities. Whitehead also enjoyed giving lectures, and his last book, *Modes of Thought* (1938), contains the published version of lectures to a broad audience of college students at several institutions. During this period, he also wrote his historical overview of key ideas important to human civilizations, *Adventures of Ideas* (which still makes for a good introduction to Whitehead's thinking on a variety of subjects).[42] He died in 1947 at the age of eighty-six; his ashes were scattered in the graveyard of Harvard's Memorial Church.

Evaluation. Attempting to evaluate Whitehead is a daunting task. Simply getting his ideas clear in the first place can be long and arduous labor, let alone reflecting on them in depth. There is a large body of secondary literature that discusses and evaluates his philosophy;[43] here we can only indicate a few brief areas of concern. The notion of an actual entity, first of all, can be quite difficult to accept. Of course we believe there are real things (actual entities in the normal sense of the term). The problems lie in Whitehead's definition of them. Can there be simple events that exist of themselves, unify all reality, include both mental and physical, provide the basic stuff of all reality and yet come to be in a single instant? Whitehead is surely right that we need to rethink the concept of substance or entity, what Aristotle called *ousia*. But we have little reason to accept his complicated and speculative definition.[44] As for his methods, the project of developing a vast system of speculative philosophy, based upon core doctrines which only make sense in the context of a larger system, has not proved to be a happy one. Here I believe Dewey's approach to metaphysics is superior to that of Whitehead's.[45] Metaphysics certainly needs revision, as Whitehead insisted, in conversation with natural science. But the harmony of our basic conceptual notions should be sought at the end of our metaphysical work, not imposed from the beginning. Our core doctrines may need to be more experimental, developed at the outset in isolation from the rest, and be open to common experience and reason as a starting point.[46]

Despite problems in his system and approach, Whitehead has much to teach us philosophically.[47] He is certainly right that natural science does not interpret itself, but needs philosophical explication and interpretation. Surely any contemporary metaphysics needs to keep in close contact with what modern science is teaching us about nature. But one must say that reading Whitehead is an acquired taste, and not for everyone. His popularity among philosophers has never been great.

The exception to this rule has been a number of philosophers of religion who found in Whitehead an important means of rethinking the nature of God and defending the existence of God on rational grounds. These thinkers are generally classed under the rubric of "process theologians," though not all of them are in fact followers of Whitehead. This rich and complex tradition in philosophy of religion cannot be fully explored; so we must limit ourselves to the most important two figures apart from Whitehead. These are Charles Hartshorne (1897-2000) and Pierre Teilhard de Chardin (1881-1955).

Process Theology

The French philosopher, theologian and scientist Pierre Teilhard de Chardin is best remembered for his combination of evolutionary science and Christian theology.[48] Representative of the French school of process thought, he was influenced by Bergson rather than Whitehead. Teilhard joined the Society of Jesus as a young man (1899) and excelled in the academic study of science.[49] His years of teaching in the Jesuit secondary school at Cairo, Egypt (1906-08), awoke his interest in prehistoric archeology and anthropology. This scientific interest deepened during his theological studies in England. Returning to France for advanced scientific research, his love of philosophy brought him into contact with Professor Eduard Le Roy, a student of Bergson, and the two came to share many of the same ideas. He pursued doctoral studies in geology and paleoarcheology at the Sorbonne, but was interrupted by World War I where he served in the medical corps (after the war he was decorated for bravery). He graduated in 1922, and was appointed to the famous Institut Catholique as professor of geology.

By this time his theological and philosophical conceptions were becoming famous in Paris, even though he had published very few of them. His concern to interpret Catholic teachings in the light of evolutionary biology was not looked upon with favor by conservative Catholic officials at the Vatican. Teilhard was devoted to St. Ignatius and his order; because of his religious vows, he could be directed by Rome through the Jesuit superior general. He was removed from his post at the Institut Catholique in 1925, then asked to leave Paris. The Catholic authorities blocked Teilhard's efforts to publish his theology all of his life and even forbade him to take a chair at the College de France. At this point in his career, he decided to return to China, where he was free to do further scientific research.

Teilhard's work in China had already commenced in 1923, and focused on paleoanthropology. He excelled in this field. Indeed, at one point he was considered one of the greatest experts in the world on human prehistory in China, having helped discover the famous "Peking Man" in 1929. During this time of scientific advance, his more speculative and mystical side was not idle. Teilhard wrote the beautiful *Mass on the World* (1923), a spiritual reflection upon the Eucharist in cosmic terms.[50] He also wrote his theological masterpiece, *The Divine Milieu* (1927), setting forth his version of Christian evolutionary panentheism. It was in China, too, that he finished a first draft of his most important work, *The Phenomenon of Man*.

Teilhard remained in China during the difficult, dangerous years of World War II and the Japanese occupation. After the war, he returned to France but once again found that his ideas were not accepted by the church theologians. He spent his last years in America, lecturing, writing and consolidating his writings. He died in 1955, having made plans for the publications of his books. *The Phenomenon of Man* soon became an international bestseller, and still exerts influence on those interested in the relationship between religion and science.

Teilhard viewed the world in both evolutionary and mystical terms. He sought unity in his complex philosophy, rejecting dualism of any kind. Rather than a tight division between matter and consciousness, Teilhard thought that the phenomenon of human consciousness could only be understood scientifically if it was the highest point of an evolving universe, the whole of which was in some degree conscious. Thus for him, all things have both a "within" of subjectivity, and a "without" of objective reality. The history of the universe is an evolutionary one, with key "critical points" which mark major new innovations in reality's ongoing complexity and evolution. Three main critical points in this history are the development of matter on planets, the origin of life and the evolution of consciousness. He used the term *sphere* to describe the many layers of the cosmos, including a geosphere, biosphere and noosphere. He invented this last term, *noosphere,* to describe the layer of complex, self-reflective mind which has evolved on earth in humanity. Evolution he thought of as being directed toward greater complexity, and greater forms of consciousness, by spiritual energies at work in all things. Spiritually Teilhard also affirmed a "christosphere" of all those on earth advancing the kingdom of God. God is intimately involved in the process of evolution (both biological and spiritual), and indeed Christ is incarnate in all the matter of the universe. Teilhard's mystical vision was directed toward "this one basic vision of the union between yourself [Lord Christ] and the universe."[51]

The love-energy of God directs the whole of the cosmos toward a spiritual union and perfection, which Teilhard calls the omega point. "In the perspective of a noogenesis, time and space become truly humanized— or rather, superhumanized. . . . The Future-Universal could not be anything else but the Hyperpersonal—at the Omega Point."[52] The future of the universe, for him, is not impersonal matter, dark and dead; but the culmination of consciousness, the super-personal union of all things in God. The incarnation of God in Jesus was a foretaste of this omega point within time. The whole universe is a eucharist, a transubstantiation of Christ into matter, and in the process of evolution, all matter into Christ. This is the omega point, which is the end of evolution. Teilhard was a firm believer in not only biological and spiritual evolution, but also evolution within God himself. Jesus was and is the decisive advance in evolution which heralds the union of all things in God.

Teilhard's philosophy was a combination of evolution, panpsychism and Catholic teaching. While he thought of unity and synthesis as powerful virtues, his critics point out that his interpretation of science and Christian doctrine are dubious just because he brings them too closely into a grand system. His view of biological evolution is too directed, too much like the discredited theories of Jean Baptiste de Lamarck; while his Christian theology is too pantheistic, and not grounded enough in Biblical revelation and orthodox tradition.[53] These problems seem to arise from over-interpreting both theology and science, failing to do justice to each discipline in its own terms. Yet his attractive vision of cosmic purpose and spiritual unity, and the lyrical character of his mystical writings, will continue to be attractive. He rightly insisted that Christian theology must take evolution seriously, and so his work is still read with appreciation by those interested in the dialogue between science and religion.

Like Teilhard, the American philosopher Charles Hartshorne (1897-2000) was not primarily a theologian, yet together with Whitehead they represent the most influential representatives of process theology in the twentieth century. Indeed, in many ways Hartshorne made process popular among the theologians in ways that Whitehead never did. During the central decades of the twentieth century, Hartshorne was America's most distinguished philosopher of religion, and his many students made process theology an important movement.[54]

Hartshorne was born in Pennsylvania, and showed academic promise at a young age.[55] He was educated at Haverford College, but left for a few years to serve as an orderly in France during the first World War. He returned to Harvard, earning his A.B., M.A. and Ph.D. in record time in the philosophy department (1923). He studied philosophy in Germany for two years, attending the lectures of Edmund Husserl and Martin Heidegger; yet their work did little to influence him. Whitehead and his other teachers at Harvard exercised far greater influence, as did a four-year research project editing the works of C. S. Peirce for publication. Hartshorne then entered the philosophy faculty of the University of Chicago (1938-1955), where he also lectured in the federated theology faculty of that city. He quickly developed a reputation in philosophy of religion, as well as in the field of metaphysics, becoming the chief exponent of process philosophy. He moved to Emory University in 1955, and then to the University of Texas in 1962. While Hartshorne was very influential among theologians, his entire career was spent in philosophy, and he thought of himself primarily as a philosopher. He lived a long and productive life, dying at the advanced age of 103.

Hartshorne accepted Whitehead's grand metaphysical system, including the commitment to experience-events (actual occasions) being the most fundamental reality. He insisted that philosophy could only be complete when it included metaphysics, ethics, aesthetics and religion in a complete vision of reality. Systematic philosophy was, for him, the heart of the discipline, and he described his own worldview as "neoclassical metaphysics." Becoming and creativity are key concepts in his metaphysical system; Hartshorne was very critical of philosophies that ignored or undervalued the importance of change and becoming. Here he felt more at home with Buddhist philosophy than with aspects of the Greek metaphysical tradition. God is no exception to this underlying process, and he embraced Whitehead's panentheism, calling it neoclassical theism.

Neoclassical theism, Hartshorne taught, avoids the errors of classical pantheism (e.g., Spinoza) as well as those of classical theism (e.g., Aquinas). Rather than holding to a finite God of pantheism or a God of absolute perfection and infinite Being à la classical theism, Hartshorne argued for a God who was absolutely perfect in some respects, and *relatively* perfect in others. God's relative perfections are those in which the Deity is unsurpassable by any particular, other being. An example of this is divine power: for Hartshorne, God is only relatively perfect in power, having more power than any other being (but not infinite, omnipotent power). Hartshorne conceives of God as a growing, developing being-in-becoming, whose power and knowledge is unsurpassable by anyone other than himself. As a philosopher, he commended panentheism on philosophical grounds alone: Hartshorne was rationalist in the philosophy of religion and did not base his views of God on special revelation.

While a student and defender of Whitehead, Hartshorne was not a slavish follower. He brought many new ideas and arguments to the tradition of process theology and focused a great deal more on God and the philosophy of religion than did Whitehead. In particular, Hartshorne developed and defended Anselm's definition of God as the unsurpassable One, and also developed a modern version of Anselm's ontological argument.[56] Unlike Whitehead, he argued that God is not a single actual entity, but rather a series of actual entities, developing over time. Yet in many respects Hartshorne's philosophical theology is very similar to, and a clear development of, Whitehead's own. Hartshorne also called his view "dipolar theism," not unlike the theology of his teacher at Harvard. He called these two poles "abstract essence" and "concrete states." Hartshorne thought of God more as a living person, that is, a personal-oriented "society" of actual occasions extended over time. God is that which unifies all of reality, and for this reason he insisted that God was dipolar in many ways. He even developed what he called a "principle of polarity," in which nothing real (and certainly not the reality of God in all of his fullness) can be described "by the wholly one-sided assertion of simplicity, being, actuality, and the like." Philosophers must also pay close attention to the opposite pole, to "complexity, becoming, potentiality, and related contraries."[57] It was a main contention of his that Western philosophers had overlooked these latter elements in their understanding of God, and thereby created a one-sided and incoherent theology.

Hartshorne developed a relational and complex understanding of God, based upon metaphysical reasoning. He found both atheistic humanism and classical Christian theism intellectually unsound. Highly critical of the classical attributes of God, he developed revised notions of God's eternity, aseity, omnipotence, omniscience and omnipresence. At the same time, he defended a rational belief in God during a dark period for philosophy of religion in the middle decades of the century. Theology students found his lectures and books attractive just because he was able to give a solid philosophical argument for theism in the face of its many critics and detractors.

His most famous students were Daniel Day Williams (1910-1973), Shubert Ogden (b. 1928) and John B. Cobb Jr. (b. 1925).[58] Each of these theologians taught at major seminaries and helped to promote process theology in North America. Each scholar developed process theology in different ways, and they should not be lumped together as though they represented a single perspective. Nevertheless, enough similarities of thought and worldview remain to see them as a coherent school of thought. We cannot here do justice this theological movement, but mention these scholars as important examples of Hartshorne's influence on American theology.

There are major problem with process theology for theologians grounded in a biblical and Christian worldview. The school as a whole is an excellent example of what happens when we tie Christian doctrine too closely to an all-explanatory philosophical system. As the school begins to unravel and die out due to increased criticism (and the whims of human fashion in philosophy), the doctrine suffers a similar fate.[59] More importantly from the position of evangelical thought, such an approach does not give a central enough place to the gospel and to Jesus Christ in defining who the triune God is.[60] Key doctrines such as the full deity of Christ and creation out of nothing are given up by those who embrace this perspective. Nevertheless, process theology has provided an important service. It has called into question traditional notions of God that are more philosophical than they are biblical. Theologians who engage process thought come away as better theologians, just because of the clarity and rigor of the argument. Process theology has thus created a space in which more traditional theologians have reconsidered and revised some of the attributes of God, to the benefit of both sides of the debate.[61]

Process philosophers defended the existence of God in a philosophical climate that was quite hostile to theism as a worldview. This is one reason the school has been so attractive to believing intellectuals. Yet the emphasis on systematic metaphysics was wholly out of step with the rest of Anglo-American philosophy. We now turn to that more mainstream development, returning to England and the work of Wittgenstein.

7. MEANING AND ANALYSIS: DEVELOPMENTS IN ANALYTIC PHILOSOPHY

I n this chapter we return to British philosophy and Ludwig Wittgenstein, tracing more recent developments within analytic philosophy as well. Necessarily this will entail hearing from a variety of voices only loosely joined in song, with no claim to overall harmony. There is a great deal of diversity in the analytic tradition, including what has been going on in philosophy of religion.

As you may recall, we left Wittgenstein in Austria, having solved the main problems of logic and philosophy (or so he thought at one point), now doing "real" work as a school teacher.[1] This was, however, a task for which he was wholly unsuited, and he ended it by 1926. He then spent some time back in Vienna, doing odd jobs such as building a home for his sister. Slowly he began to feel there was more philosophical work for him to do. His journey back into philosophy was greatly assisted by Mortiz Schlick, the leader of the Vienna Circle. By 1927 he was meeting regularly with the group, which discussed his *Tractatus*. In 1929 he was sufficiently interested in new philosophical problems to return to Cambridge, where he lectured from 1930 until 1936. After traveling in Norway and Ireland, he was appointed professor at Cambridge in 1939. This was an important transition or middle period, during which he did not publish any major works but lectured intensely with a few students in his rooms, struggling to give birth to a completely new approach to philosophy.

The Later Wittgenstein

It is difficult to characterize in a few paragraphs the shift in philosophical method that Wittgenstein struggled for several decades to express.[2] Unsatisfied with several attempts and notebooks, he did not publish another book during his lifetime. His reputation for genius, however, sparked a great deal of interest. His ideas became known in the 1930s and 1940s only through lecture notes, most notably a couple of hand-copied booklets prepared by a select group of his students for distribution to the rest (known by the color of their covers as the *Blue and Brown Books*).[3] Once again Wittgenstein was interested in the relationship between language and the world, seeking an approach that would clarify the many problems of philosophy. But now he completely abandoned the "pseudo-propositions" of the *Tractatus*. Instead of logic, the new focus was on "grammar," a term Wittgenstein filled with new meaning for philosophers. Once again, he believed that he had found a method to solve the problems of philosophy. This time, however, he saw the work of the philosopher as *therapy* rather than solution. The only real task of the philosopher is to show how the traditional problems of philosophy arise as deep misunderstanding of our language and ideas. As he says in *The Blue Book:*

> Philosophers constantly see the method of science before their eyes, and are irresistibly tempted to ask and answer questions in the way science does. This tendency is the real source of metaphysics, and leads the philosopher into complete darkness.[4]

After attempting several times to write a book that set forth his new method, Wittgenstein eventually resigned from his chair in philosophy in 1947. He spent the war years doing "useful" work in two English hospitals. After leaving Cambridge, he spent time with some of his former students and friends, living in various places (mostly Ireland), and visiting America for a brief time. He began to have health trouble (mostly with his stomach) and often found he could do no further work on his new book, which would later be published as *Philosophical Investigations*. He made plans with his students to publish the work after his death.

During this last decade of his life, Wittgenstein began a series of remarks and notebooks applying his new philosophical approach to various issues in philosophy. These works were later published by the editors of his *Nachlass* (posthumous writings), among the more important of which are *On Certainty, Culture and Value, Remarks on Colour, Remarks on the Foundations of Mathematics,* and *Remarks on the Philosophy of Psychology.*[5] Because he is dealing with a specific problem in each text, such as certainty in epistemology, these works are often more positive in tone than the *Investigations* (which is highly critical of other philosophies). Toward the end of his life, he stayed in Cambridge with one of his students, G. H. von Wright. Wittgenstein visited the family physician, Dr. Edward Bevans, who examined him and diagnosed his illness as cancer of the prostate. Since he did not wish to die in an institutional hospital, the Bevans family welcomed Wittgenstein into their home for the last few months of his life. He died in 1951, and his second great masterpiece, the *Philosophical Investigations,* was published in 1955.[6]

Investigations

The *Philosophical Investigations* is quite different in style and tone from his earlier work. In fact, with this text, Wittgenstein invents a whole new style and direction for the analytic tradition; in so doing, he moves philosophy closer to ordinary life and everyday language. As part of this move, his style becomes far less abstract and propositional. Instead, we are given stories, aphorisms, parallels, analogies and parables. There is no unified coherent argument around which the *Investigations* is organized. Rather, Wittgenstein moves around and about his themes, dancing back and forth between several topics, turning and returning to his subject. As such the book is extremely difficult to summarize. While Wittgenstein is still concerned about the nature of thought and epistemic justification, and the relationship between language and world, his whole approach to philosophy has made a shift toward the particular and the everyday.

Wittgenstein's editors have divided the *Investigations* into two parts. The first part consists of 693 numbered paragraphs, worked over by Wittgenstein for publication. The second part has been placed there by the editors, without paragraph numbers (cited by page number instead); this portion illustrates the new method with special reference to the philosophy of mind and language. At the heart of this new approach is life and action. In seeking the "meaning" of any expression, we must no longer consider the sentence in isolation (as some logical positivists were wont to do). Rather, Wittgenstein now wants us to look at the way the sentence is used, its context in a living language and a set of connected behaviors associated with that way of life, or "form of life" as he puts it. The meaning of a sentence is not found in logical analysis of its abstract character, but rather by looking at the way it is used in a "language game," that is, in a holistic pattern of language and behavior that is communal and everyday. That is why he can now say that "for a *large* class of cases . . . the meaning of a word is its use in the language."[7] Wittgenstein is still interested in the general structure of meaning in language, but his approach has changed quite radically from the *Tractatus*.

Wittgenstein came to believe that the history of philosophy was filled with wrong turns and dead ends. In this he resembles Heidegger. What Heidegger had to say about the history of ontology is not unlike Wittgenstein's problem with meaning in philosophy. What led philosophers astray in the past (including himself and his teachers) is something deeply embedded in our language. Our language contains words which look like they must refer to some kind of essence: being, truth, beauty, knowledge and the like. Philosophers have ignored the place of such language in our everyday world, in the "game" of speech (or language game).

> When philosophers use a word—"knowledge," "being," "object," "I," "proposition," "name"—and try to grasp the *essence* of the thing, one must always ask oneself: is the word ever actually used in this way in the language-game which is its original home? What *we* do is to bring words back from their metaphysical to their everyday use.[8]

Wittgenstein is rejecting a logical, abstract approach to meaning and analysis. In the beginning of the *Investigations,* he compares language to a game. Games come in many types, and may or may not have written rules. Games exist as a part of our ordinary life, and they have no abstract essence or structure. No strict definition covers them all. They do, however, have certain things in common; they are related to each other in a variety of ways which often differ between different games. Vastly different games can still resemble one another in some respects. In this way Wittgenstein thinks that language is much more like a game than a fixed structure. Compare playing cards to swinging on a rope into a lake or playing golf, for example. These are completely different activities, but they share certain features: each is done for amusement, each requires that one obey certain rules for optimal success, and so on. Language is much more like a game than a mathematical formula or logical structure, which have fixed essences. "These phenomena have no one thing in common which makes us use the same word for all."[9] Instead what we find is a kind of "family resemblance" between the uses of the same word in different language games. Just as we can see similarities in the face, walk or voice of family members without being able to specify the precise character of the family resemblance, so words and games can be similar in different words without having an abstract *essence*. "*Look and see* if there is anything common to all."[10]

For this reason, Wittgenstein can say of the right kind of analysis: "What *we* do is to bring words back from their metaphysical to their everyday use." Wittgenstein is not abandoning analysis of language. Rather, he wants us to embark upon a very *different kind* of analysis, one that is grounded in the forms of life in which our everyday language games occur. He called this analysis "grammatical."

Our investigation is therefore a grammatical one. Such an investigation sheds light on our problem by clearing misunderstanding away. Misunderstandings concerning the use of words, caused, among other things, by certain analogies between forms of expression in different regions of language.[11]

The result of this kind of grammatical analysis is the clearing away of misunderstandings, and the gaining of clarity into the everyday, living meaning of our words. "For the clarity we are aiming at is indeed *complete* clarity. But this simply means that the philosophical problems should *completely* disappear."[12]

The study of our language games and the forms of life in which they are embedded provides a new approach to understanding meaning. This kind of grammatical analysis helps us see when we are using language with sense and when we are speaking nonsense. Wittgenstein kept something like the old division between meaningful language use and nonsense, but the focus is no longer on verification or logic but on a proper understanding of the grammar (in his special sense) of our language. Nonsense arises when we take a word out of its natural place in a form of life and language game. It is easy to get fooled by surface similarities; we get captured in a picture or root metaphor which misleads us. This mis-understanding leads to a quest for metaphysical claims which have no justification in our communal, practical language use. We get fooled by a picture and misunderstand the multiplicity of meanings any word can have in different settings in life within a community of speakers. In other words, the exterior form of some key terms fools us into thinking that more is at work in a word than the use it plays in one of our everyday language games. "We remain unconscious of the prodigious diversity of all the everyday language-games because the clothing of our language makes everything alike."[13]

At this point we need a good example of his approach. Let us take the word *understanding*. Some philosophers might argue that to understand something is to grasp its philosophical essence. But Wittgenstein would look at the various ways in which a community of speakers uses the term *understand* in a great variety of situations in life. Joe understands how to drive a car; Sue understands the criminal justice system in her state; John understands his wife's grief; and the like. A whole variety of language games lie behind the term *understand* as it is actually used: driving cars, going to court, comforting a person in grief and so on. In the first two examples, "understanding" is a kind of goal-directed activity. One sees how to navigate the roadways in an automobile or the legal paths of the court system. In the last case, however, the word is very different: to understand a person's grief is to act or speak in a particular way toward them, one filled with sympathy and compassion. Yet it is still a kind of behavior: John doesn't meditate upon the abstract essence of his wife's grief, if he is a decent husband, he comforts her! Understanding, then, is not (according to this rather simple grammatical analysis) an inner mental list of propositional truths which describe the metaphysical essence of something. *Understanding* is used in various language games to describe behaviors of a certain type. The abstract philosophical notion of "understanding" is thus a misunderstanding.

The above is a brief and rather simple example of his approach. Take an even simpler one: the game of solitaire. It would seem that the very idea of "solitaire" logically must mean a card game one plays by oneself. Then one learns about *double* solitaire! Once again, the dynamic use of a term in life confounds the carefully stated logical analysis. With a variety of cases, examples, and analogies, Wittgenstein pressed this new way of seeing meaning and disclosing nonsense. Most of traditional philosophy, it turns out, is nonsense—or so he thought. Nonsense or confusion is often the result of language being pressed beyond its everyday sense and then misunderstood in the new context. Many believers still think that God our heavenly Father is something like a grey-haired old man in the sky, for example—a confusion surrounding the word heaven *and* the word father.

It is a tragedy that Wittgenstein was unable to develop his later philosophy to any further extent. The notes, remarks and lectures we have are, all of them, incomplete and sketchy. Yet this may indeed be just what he wanted. By using jokes, parables, dialogues and anecdotes, Wittgenstein exemplified a certain unsystematic approach to traditional philosophical problems. He may well have left us no system, no theory of language or of mind, on purpose. Rather, his later philosophy is an exercise in how to go on in the same manner, without any philosophical foundations or systems at all. The philosopher has no business constructing elaborate theories, systems of metaphysics or essential analysis. Wittgenstein rejected metaphysics as nonsense. Rather, the job of good philosophy is a kind of enlightenment, a clearing away of the need for such things. "Where does our investigation get its importance from, since it seems only to destroy everything interesting, that is, all that is great and important? . . . What we are destroying is nothing but houses of cards, and we are clearing up the ground of language on which they stand."[14]

Wittgenstein's philosophy is a helpful corrective to the abstraction, logicism and speculative system-building often found in earlier philosophy (including his own). His rejection of these approaches helped to herald a postmodern turn in philosophy, especially in the analytic tradition. We will discuss the notion of the postmodern in philosophy later in this work; for now we simply remark that Wittgenstein's later philosophy is a step in that direction. His criticism of rationalistic, abstract and essentialist methods is a trenchant critique of modernity in some of its forms. It is also helpful in clarifying the meaning of religious language.

Wittgenstein and religion. As we noted earlier, the question of the meaning and verification of religious language was a central part of the philosophy of religion after the rise of logical positivism. One of the benefits of following Wittgenstein's later philosophy is that religious language is no longer subject to an artificial criterion of verification in order to be exonerated of the charge of being nonsense.[15] Rather, Wittgenstein and his followers rightly insist that the meaning of religious terms is found in a whole way of life—discipleship, worship, prayer, ethics, religious practices and spirituality—which grounds their use. As he noted in *Culture and Value* (which includes a number of reflections on religious faith): "The *words* you utter or what you think as you utter them are not what matters, so much as the difference they make at various points in your life. How do I know that two people mean the same when each says he believes in God? . . . *Practice* gives the words their sense."[16] Wittgenstein's approach allows religious language, like any and all human language, to be found meaningful according to the use such speech takes within a particular community, in a particular time and place; he eschews the attempt to discern meaning from artificial and abstract criteria, which may not fit religion or life at all.

Wittgenstein's later philosophy provides an important corrective to many of the excesses in the analytic tradition. Yet his new approach has its flaws and problems too. It is too easy for followers (sometimes called "Neo-Wittgensteinians") to make the everyday use of words the only possible meaning. Language-games may become a kind of straitjacket that limits further philosophical investigation. This is particularly true when we begin to ask after the *truth* of our sentences, rather than their meaning. While Wittgenstein does give us a useful beginning point for looking at the meaning of terms, which are often diverse and interesting, his later approach is of very little help when we want to know whether (in some cases and for some sentences) what the sentence means is true. To take a religious example, the meaning of the question, "Where does all of this come from?" does have an important place to play in the way we live our life as a whole. It is certainly not a simple natural scientific hypothesis, whose answer we could seek in a lab or out in space. Wittgenstein is right when he insists that, for the believer, God is the answer to this question. When she gives this answer, the believer understands herself as "expressing an attitude towards all explanations." The manifestation of this answer in the believer's life is key to the meaning of the sentence, "God made all that we see."[17]

Suppose, however, that we wish to ask after the *truth* of the sentence, "God made all that we see." It would certainly be wrong to seek the truth of this sentence *just like* we seek to verify a scientific hypothesis or a mathematical equation. So far we can and should agree. But there may be some similarities as well. Sentences like "God is love" and "God made everything that exists" cannot be *only* grammatical remarks, as D. Z. Phillips (1934-2006) and other Wittgensteinians claim. When Phillips writes, "The claim 'God is love' may mislead us into thinking that it is a descriptive statement rather than a rule for the use of the word 'God,'" he makes two mistakes.[18] The first is the claim that "God is love" is not a descriptive statement for Christian theology: it most certainly is. It is not a description of ordinary objects in our world, but it is descriptive nevertheless. However, the claim that "God is love" is *only* a grammatical remark about how to use the word God is a misunderstanding of what ordinary believers mean by their language. While Phillips is right that "God is love" is a grammatical remark—a remark about the way certain religious communities use the word "God"—that is merely the beginning, not the end, of our quest to know if it is true. The question of the truth of this sentence is open even after we know that it is embedded in a whole way of life, i.e., that it is a grammatical remark for some religious communities. After all, a form of life can embed important empirical and metaphysical assumptions, which nevertheless remain open to question. The form of life surrounding the practice of voting in a modern democracy, for example, assumes that the votes of all citizens (including one's own) will be fairly counted—but in some cases this assumption may be false. Thus his second mistake is assuming that a *sound* grammatical remark is free of the question of truth. Phillips is quite ready to turn away unsound religious beliefs and expressions, rejecting them as superstition or "grammatic" confusion. But he does not believe that the philosophical task includes that of judging the truth of well-formed religious expressions.[19] Now we will certainly have to be sensitive to the different ways in which we can seek to know whether such claims are true or not. But the fact that humans find them meaningful in practice does not automatically mean they are correct. So we should reject his early and programmatic claim that "the criteria of the meaningfulness of religious concepts are to be found in religion itself."[20]

The typical Wittgensteinian response to such criticisms would be something along these lines: "You are still confused. You are confusing religion and science, or you are turning God into an ordinary object." "God is love" is not a descriptive statement because any quest for its verification is absurd, they will assert. But this response assumes that only science is capable of answering the question of truth, or that we can only verify the existence of ordinary objects. Seeking truth in religion takes us beyond the practices of religious communities into questions regarding revelation, religious experience and the character of religious truth. It is not a scientific quest, but it also leaves behind the Wittgensteinian prejudice that philosophy and theology have no truths to discover, only nonsense to clear away. Wittgenstein once remarked, "If Christianity is the truth then all the philosophy that is written about it is false."[21] This sentence itself is an example of the problem with his later philosophy: it sometimes stops inquiry rather than stimulating it. As a corrective to the excesses of the Enlightenment, Wittgenstein is valuable. His later philosophy provides us with a sound approach to finding meaning in human languages. But when it comes to the question of truth, his approach can limit philosophical investigation.

Ordinary Language Philosophy

Wittgenstein's philosophical journey was tremendously influential, especially in the analytic tradition. Along with the work of Moore, Wittgenstein's turn to everyday language use stimulated a whole generation of English philosophers to seek meaning in the stream of human life rather than in a purely abstract logical analysis. Of course, logical positivism in many forms was still very powerful, but the new "ordinary language" school of linguistic analysis was growing in influence. J. L. Austin (1911-1960), Gilbert Ryle (1900-1976) and Peter F. Strawson (1919-2006) formed the core of this school. While each retained a distinctive approach and their published works differ in many respects, the similarities are also clear. As they were all at Oxford together in the period after World War II, this movement was also called Oxford philosophy.

Austin. J. L. Austin was an influential professor at Oxford during the middle decades of the twentieth century.[22] His work exemplifies the careful, almost painstaking analysis of everyday usage which became associated with ordinary language analysis. His approach assumed that our everyday language, when carefully attended to, gives us important guidance in the world, especially in practical matters. He would spend a great deal of time and effort looking at the many and various ways one can use a word like "if" or "promise." His approach came to be known as speech-act theory, because of his insistence that speaking is a kind of doing. His most famous book is *How to Do Things with Words* (1962), which is based on lectures he gave many years earlier at Oxford and Harvard. Unlike Wittgenstein, Austin continued to develop theories about meaning. He held that a sentence is also a kind of action, and his speech-act theory allowed for three types of such action: the locutionary, the illocutionary and the perlocutionary. Not every sentence embodies all of these types, but many do. Take for example the sentence, "I promise to pay you tomorrow." On the one hand, there is the informational content of the sentence, which Austin called *locutionary*. The sentence tells the hearer something, it gives some information. Yet there is more than information in this sentence. By uttering it, I am also *making a promise*, which is not the same act as the conveying of information. The *illocutionary* force of such a sentence is its performative character, that is, the social and public force of the speaker's utterance beyond mere information. Related to this, Austin also considered the rhetorical or persuasive influence of the sentence upon the hearers or audience, which he called the *perlocutionary* force of the speech-act. In the case of our example, all three of these forces are present: I convey the information that tomorrow I will pay back the money I owe (locutionary); I actually make a promise by uttering that sentence (illocutionary); and I cause my friend to cease worrying about her money and rest assured that she will have it back tomorrow (perlocutionary). This division enables Austin to make an interesting epistemological move. When applied to a statement like "I know" or "I believe," he suggests these sentences have an illocutionary force rather than locutionary—they announce the way we will live and act rather than report the inner mental state of the speaker.

Austin's theory of meaning is clearly different from that of logical positivists like A. J. Ayer, and he also differs from Wittgenstein. Unlike Wittgenstein, he put forth a theory of meaning (or at least part of one). His speech-act theory is more open to the analysis of meaning in religious language than positivism. It has been used to good effect in examining the language of prayer, of religious rituals and of sacred Scripture.[23] Of course, Austin himself would be the first to say his approach provides us only with a beginning for analysis. Like many other linguistic analysts, his focus was more on meaning than on the truth of utterances.

Ryle. Professor Gilbert Ryle was widely seen as the coleader of the Oxford school in the 1950s.[24] He was friends with Wittgenstein in the 1930s, but this relationship did not last long. Ryle took up the theme of clarifying philosophical errors through linguistic analysis, but did not show much interest in developing theories of his own. In an early paper, "Systematically Misleading Expressions" (1932), he argued that careful attention to ordinary language can clarify our thinking and lead to better philosophical analysis.[25] He is famous for introducing the notion of a "category mistake" into philosophy and for a trenchant attack on mind-body dualism in *The Concept of Mind* (1949). Ryle argued that we need greater category sensitivity in philosophy; i.e., a sense of the proper use of our ordinary concepts, how they are related and ordered. Category mistakes arise when we put our concepts to improper use. An example would be a mistaken notion of types of things: imagine a child seeing all the floats, animals and bands in a parade, but then wondering where the parade itself was. A simpler mistake would be to wonder what color the number three is in reality, after seeing it written in many different colored crayons. These category mistakes display a lack of sensitivity to the concept of a parade and of a number. In *The Concept of Mind* Ryle called for greater sensitivity to our use of language about mental states. As he put it, "The philosophical arguments which constitute this book are intended not to increase what we know about minds, but to rectify the logical geography of the knowledge which we already possess."[26] He rejected as mistaken our common notion of an inner soul or mind which is somehow the real "me" while at the same time pointing out the problems in a purely materialistic concept of mind. Likewise, he rejected the idea of a "ghost in the machine" as hopelessly confused: "mind" is our word for a range of activities and practices that the whole person does. It is not some occult inner spirit. Those who think of the mind as some kind of thing are making a category mistake. To be sure, Ryle also rejected the other common view, physicalism or behaviorism, which holds that our minds simply reduce to the physical workings of our brain. After clearing away all of these misconceptions, however, Ryle had very little positive contribution to make toward a new philosophy of mind. His focus was on proper method and clarifying mistakes, not on building new theories.

Strawson. Peter F. Strawson was the youngest member of our three exemplary professors in the Oxford school, and he was also the most prolific.[27] He was Austin's student and took up his chair in 1968; he also developed the tradition of ordinary language philosophy in conversation with the new logic. Austin and Ryle were not adept in the new symbolic logic which was taking philosophy by storm at this time. Strawson's contribution, therefore, was to continue the tradition of ordinary language analysis in dialogue with symbolic logic, including the work of Bertrand Russell. He also engaged in an important dialogue with Austin on the nature of truth. Strawson first became famous in 1950 when he published a critical response to Russell on the logical meaning of denotation (definite description). His paper defends the view that ordinary language has no exact logic and that Russell failed to find the "real" meaning of ordinary referring sentences with his translation into symbolic propositions.[28] He furthered this approach in his first major book, *Introduction to Logical Theory* (1952). Strawson understood formal logic to be a powerful tool and a system of entailments; but it is also an abstraction, and cannot completely describe the complex meanings of ordinary human language. He then applied this approach to metaphysics in his most famous work: *Individuals* (1959). Strawson defended metaphysics against those who would reject this field of philosophy, but in doing so he made an important distinction between descriptive and revisionist metaphysics. Descriptive metaphysics seeks to clarify and organize the common, ordinary conceptual scheme by which humans make their way in the world. This is the "massive central core of human thinking which has no history . . . categories and concepts which, in their most fundamental character, change not at all."[29] Our everyday language provides us with key insights into this scheme, which needs clarification but not revision. Revisionist metaphysics, that is, the project of improving upon our ordinary world-picture through proposing new concepts, he set aside. Like Ryle, Strawson was critical of Cartesian dualism. He argued for a notion of the person as central to our ordinary conceptual framework, a "primitive concept" which is basic to the central core of human thought. Strawson held that skeptical arguments about our everyday conceptual scheme are "idle" in the face of the "original, natural, inescapable commitments which we neither choose nor give up."[30] One of his last books, *Scepticism and Naturalism*, defends this position over against a number of contemporary philosophical approaches.

Both the later Wittgenstein and the Oxford school sought to ground meaning in our everyday world and in human action. Because ordinary language philosophers like Strawson held to a groundwork of basic concepts common to humans in general, their approach did not long endure. There were too many questions about this philosophical faith, too much emphasis upon diversity, plurality and particularity during the latter part of the century for this "universal" perspective to long endure among students of philosophy. They did give important impetus to a new kind of linguistic analysis, however. Furthermore, just because Wittgenstein's later works are so fragmentary and free of any system or theory, his philosophy has grown in influence over the decades. In the meantime, however, a very different type of logical analysis was being developed across the water in New England, which interacted with the British tradition in new and creative ways.

Quine and Logical Pragmatism

In the last half of the twentieth century, in and around Harvard University, there developed an important and influential group of philosophers in the pragmatist tradition. The first of these was Clarence Irving Lewis (1883-1964), a student of Royce with strong interest in logic, epistemology and value theory. His students at Harvard included Nelson Goodman (1906-1998) and W. V. Quine (1908-2000). At the height of his powers, Quine was America's foremost philosopher, and his books and essays set the agenda for many issues in philosophy at midcentury. He was deeply influenced by the Vienna Circle and Russell as well as pragmatism.

C. I. Lewis continued and furthered Pierce and Royce's interest in the philosophy of logic.[31] Royce introduced Lewis to the *Principia Mathematica* of Russell and Whitehead, which stimulated his own interest in symbolic logic. He wrote the most influential textbook of its time on logic in the United States, *Symbolic Logic* (1932), which included the first systematic discussion of the logic of necessity (modal logic). While arguing for the importance of a priori truths for the ordering of our experience, he developed a more flexible conception of the a priori in keeping with the pragmatist tradition. His most widely discussed work, *An Analysis of Knowledge and Valuation* (1946), was an important American work on epistemology in the post-war period. As a pragmatist, he held that knowledge, action and values are essentially connected. Empirical knowledge (the standard kind of knowing) is connected to action. It summarizes our interaction with the world, and it guides our actions in the future. Logical truths, on the other hand, are purely analytical and apply to any possible experience. Unlike the logical positivists, however, Lewis held that values have empirical meaning. Our values are predictions of goodness or badness which will be experienced under certain circumstances. For him questions of value are empirical questions.

This powerful combination of pragmatism, empiricism and modern logic was quite influential in American philosophy. But Lewis's work was eclipsed by his most famous student, Willard Van Orman Quine.[32] Quine studied mathematics as an undergraduate and made a significant contribution to symbolic logic and the philosophy of mathematics, as well as issues in the philosophy of language, epistemology and ontology.[33] He rejected pragmatism for the most part, adopting in its place a radical form of empiricism and naturalism. Although he studied with Whitehead at Harvard, it was Russell (who lectured at Harvard) who made a lasting impression upon him. He also traveled to Vienna, to listen in on the Vienna Circle. He met Rudolf Carnap, and the two became lifelong philosophical friends.[34] He also studied mathematical logic at Warsaw and Prague, where he met the logician Alfred Tarski. In some ways Quine's philosophy continued the tradition of logical positivism and Russell's logicism, but his radical relativism, holism and scientism put him in a unique philosophical position.[35] In the end what is important about Quine is the criticism he made of standard views and assumptions in the analytic tradition. His key arguments seem to have generated a hundred echoes in the literature of philosophy. He took up Lewis' chair in philosophy at Harvard following World War II (in which he served as a naval officer). Generally understood to be America's most distinguished philosopher, he received the first Shock Prize in Philosophy and Logic in 1993 (like the Nobel Prize, it is given by the Royal Swedish Academy of Sciences) and was awarded the Kyoto Prize in 1996. His death on Christmas day, 2000, was noted in major papers and journals around the world.[36]

Quine was committed both to the rigors of mathematical logic and empiricism. He always sought the least number of axioms and assumptions necessary to get the job done. His lifelong faith in science, especially physics, is a good example of scientism in philosophy. For him natural science, especially physics, supplies us with the only reliable source of knowledge; philosophy has no real domain of knowledge all its own. Central to his philosophy is the axiom that there is no first philosophy that can ground the sciences in something more basic. The sciences do not need philosophy in order to do their work.

On the other hand, the results of the sciences (especially natural science) are determinative for philosophy. According to him, the sciences advocate a physicalist ontology and an empiricist epistemology. Philosophy must fall in line with natural science and so must be radically revised in order to make it part of nature; it must become a discipline that is as much like physics as possible. He called this the attempt to "naturalize" philosophy. For Quine physics requires two, and only two, ontological commitments: natural objects and mathematics. Quine thus set about "naturalizing" ontology by reducing our understanding of reality (beings) to these, and in fact reduced them even further. Natural objects are, for epistemological purposes, nothing more than biological sensations in our bodily organs. Which ontology we then adopt to make sense of these is, he argued, purely a matter of internal coherence and fit with observational sentences in a particular language. In this last move we can see the influence of pragmatism on his thought. He once put his position this way:

> I am a physical object sitting in a physical world. Some of the forces of this physical world impinge on my surface. Light rays strike my retinas; molecules bombard my eardrums and fingertips. I strike back, emanating concentric air waves. These waves form a torrent of discourse about tables, people, . . . joy and sorrow, good and evil.[37]

But what about mathematics? Traditionally the foundations of mathematical reasoning were understood to be metaempirical. For Quine the objects of mathematics could be reduced to sets, functions and definitions—he was a Platonist when it came to the philosophy of mathematics, since sets were real abstract objects. But he was a realist about very little else. According to his radical program of scientism and naturalism, both epistemology and ontology should be naturalized, reduced to what physics (or natural science) requires and made to fit a purely natural worldview. In this way philosophy could follow in the steps of the best theory we have of the world, the one given by natural science.

As part of his radical agenda for rethinking all of philosophy, Quine was a severe critic of any theory of *meaning* as a basis for discovering the truth. He was convinced that Russell's theory of names (in which the logical "meaning" of a name is reduced to a definite description of the object named) gives us a logical model which can do away with "meaning" altogether. His most famous paper was a critique of a key part of most theories of meaning, namely, the distinction between analytic and synthetic sentences. An analytic sentence, according to this viewpoint, is one whose truth can be known by the meaning of the words in the sentence. His attack upon this "dogma" of the analytic traditions (in "Two Dogmas of Empiricism") soon became a classic of twentieth-century analytic philosophy.[38]

According to Quine the two dogmas inherited from Russell and the Vienna Circle are reductionism and the analytic/synthetic distinction. In effect, his attack on these dogmas also served as an attack upon the verificationist theory of meaning for individual sentences, because Quine challenged a key element of verificationism. Truths of logic and mathematics, according to the logical positivists, can be "verified" or known to be true by the meaning of the terms alone. In other words, such propositions express logically necessary truths. An example of such a supposed necessary truth is "All bachelors are unmarried."

Quine finds all such theories of logical verification too circular to be acceptable. The supposed synonyms *(bachelor, unmarried)* could be rejected by some speakers of the language who use these terms in idiosyncratic ways. After all, the lexicographer merely reports on current usage by a majority of speakers—not on the logical necessity inhering in such terms. Quine does allow, however, for a stipulative definition of a new technical term or symbol to be an analytic truth, but this does not help the theory of meaning or the analytic/synthetic distinction as a general principle.

Quine also takes aim at what he calls "radical reductionism" in which individual sentences are the unit of analysis. This move is central to the verificationist program, so that meaningful sentences can be analyzed one by one into their empirical content. In place of this kind of reductionism (which is based upon the analytic/synthetic distinction he rejects) Quine puts forward a tentative and pragmatic *holism*. Sentences in a particular language-system (call it *L*) have meaning only in virtue of their relationship with other sentences in *L*, i.e., the role that a sentence plays in the system of *L*. Such a philosophy of language implies a radical *indeterminacy of translation*, which is one of Quine's more famous doctrines. Since meanings are not fixed and depend crucially upon whole systems of a given language, touching upon empirical fact only at the edges, any particular translation of a text into another language is bound to be open to question and radically underdetermined by the data.

Moving from meaning to truth, if we think of the totality of our beliefs as a kind of loose system or web, it is only on occasion that a particular sentence will interact with direct sensations. Even very well-confirmed theories in natural science or the basic truths of logic and mathematics are, for Quine, up for grabs and open to revision just because the whole system only touches upon empirical reality "at the edges." In a famous quotation, Quine concluded: "The totality of our so-called knowledge or beliefs, from the most casual matters of geography and history to the profoundest laws of atomic physics or even of pure mathematics and logic, is a man-made fabric which impinges on experience only along the edges."[39] The data of sensation radically underdetermine the full-blown worldviews that humans carry with them. We accept theories and philosophies on pragmatic or even aesthetic grounds, not just on the basis of pure logic and direct sensations (the latter can be made coherent with a potentially infinite number of theories, Quine argued). Only Quine's scientism helps him avoid a thoroughgoing relativism at this point. He consistently maintained that natural science gives us the very best epistemology and ontology, and so he remained a firm naturalist in his philosophy. Some of his students and followers, however, were not as impressed by the natural sciences as he was. As we will discover in another chapter, analytic philosophy after Quine could take a decisive postmodern turn, as it did in the thought of Nelson Goodman and Richard Rorty.

After Quine: Davidson and Kripke

To conclude our story of developments in recent analytic philosophy for now, we will consider two important philosophers whose work extends, transforms and/or undermines Quine. Few philosophers in fact followed Quine completely—his influence came from the clarity and rigor of his approach and the problems he found in other philosophies. In this section we will canvass the views of two American philosophers, Donald Davidson (1917-2003) and Saul Kripke (1940-), looking briefly at the way their philosophical work shapes the analytic tradition after Quine. The postmodern turn in analytic thought will be the subject of a later chapter. Davidson and Kripke are two of the most important philosophers in this broad tradition at the end of the century—two voices in a large chorus. They should give us a good sense of analytic philosophy at century's end.

Davidson. Donald Davidson was a student of Quine, following Quine's conclusions and assumptions at some key points, while striking out in quite new ways on many fronts. Davidson was a brilliant essayist, and his major books are in fact collections of his papers and lectures.[40] His essays have been highly influential, and at the end of the century Davidson was one of the world's most important and respected philosophers. He continued to reflect on the problems of truth, meaning and interpretation after Quine, adopting Alfred Tarski's (1901-1983) definition of truth for symbolic languages in order to propose a theory of meaning for natural languages.[41]

A theory of meaning, Davidson argued, just is a theory of truth constructed along Tarskian lines: s is true in L if and only if p (where s is a sentence in the language being analyzed, and p is a sentence in which the theory is being stated). He came to call this a "T-sentence," and a typical one is: "Snow is white" if and only if *snow is white*. Like Quine, Davidson rejected the idea that "meanings" are somehow entities, and likewise rejected any appeal to internal intentions as a basis for the analysis of meaning. His approach to meaning as a theory of truth allowed him to

equate a theory of *meaning* with a theory of *truth* for a specific language.[42]
He could thus claim that "Tarski-type truth definitions, modified to fit natural languages, describe the basic semantic structure that informs the
human language ability."[43] This move then allowed for the meaning of a
sentence in a language to be based upon (in principle, at least) observation of behaviors and sounds, rather than internal dispositions or intentions of speakers; a theory of meaning for a language can be built up
from such empirical data. Davidson came to call this viewpoint "radical
interpretation." A radical interpreter needs to observe the behaviors of a
speaker of a language, and also know which of two sentences in that language the speaker believes to be true in a given circumstance. From this
the radical interpreter can build up a theory of truth, and so of meaning,
for any given language—again, in principle—without any further appeal
to the internal, psychological states of human speakers. Davidson is committed to the idea that the meaning of the sentence "It is raining" is connected to the fact that speakers of English report it to be true when it is in
fact raining.

In order for this to work, however, truth, meaning and situation have
to be tightly connected for all human speakers of a natural language.
Davidson drew just this conclusion in his paper "On the Very Idea of a
Conceptual Scheme." A "scheme" here is broadly the conceptual part of
a worldview, that is, a "system of categories that give form to the data of
sensations; they are points of view from which individuals, cultures, or
periods survey the passing scene."[44] Although different humans may
have different points of view, *knowing about* those differences suggests
there must be a common, very general scheme which humans share. So
to Quine's two dogmas of empiricism (which they both rejected) Davidson adds a third: the dogma of a dualism of scheme and world. Scheme,
world and language all come together for speakers in a holistic way. He
concludes, "In giving up the dualism of scheme and world, we do not
give up the world, but reestablish unmediated touch with the familiar
objects whose antics make our sentences and opinions true or false."[45]
Radical interpretation requires a principle of charity in which we interpret a speaker's language such that it is true (or as true as we can make
it)—one person's individual beliefs are supported by numerous other
beliefs which, taken together and as a whole, must tend toward truth.

Because truth, meaning, scheme and belief are so interconnected for speakers, Davidson argued that our beliefs are, on the whole, "intrinsically veridical."[46]

Davidson made significant contributions to philosophical reflection upon action, mind, value and subjectivity as well as issues of truth and meaning. Enough has been presented here to indicate how his philosophy continued some of Quine's interests in remarkable new directions. The younger philosopher Saul Kripke provides an alternative example of the vitality of analytic philosophy after Quine, in this case moving against certain fundamental points of Quinian dogma, as we shall see.

Kripke. Saul Kripke was one of America's most influential philosophers in the last quarter of the century. He first made his mark in mathematical logic, especially modal logic (which is the logic of necessity and possibility). Quine had called the concept of necessity into question, but Kripke's work undercuts Quine's conclusions at several key points.

Born in 1940 in New York, Kripke showed prodigious early promise in mathematics, creating a system of formal modal logic while still in high school, and publishing his first paper in *Journal of Symbolic Logic* at eighteen.[47] He earned a B.A. from Harvard in mathematics, where he studied with Quine, and was soon elected a junior member of the Harvard Society of Fellows and began to lecture at MIT. Kripke did not learn much from college (he tells us) and did not bother to earn any further degrees. He became a professor at Princeton in 1977 and retired in 1998, after earning many honors, including the award of the Shock Prize for logic and philosophy in 2001. After publishing his several papers on the semantics of formal modal logic (as well as other works in logic) the larger question still remained: what do these symbols mean in a larger philosophical context? As Kripke himself once remarked, "There is no mathematical substitute for philosophy."[48]

Kripke gave his answers to this question in an influential set of lectures, *Naming and Necessity* (1972). The book has become a classic of analytic philosophy in the twentieth century. Kripke begins by arguing against the Frege-Russell theory of names, or "descriptivism" (which provided the inspiration for Quine's theory of reference).[49] Giving counter-examples and appealing to common sense and our ordinary intuitions, Kripke argued that a name does not reduce logically to a set of descriptions (as both Frege and Russell maintained). For example, Aristotle might have died at age two, and all of our descriptions of him would have been false—yet he would still have been Aristotle, and his name would still have designated that person. In place of a descriptive theory of names, Kripke proposed a causal theory of names, appealing to his intuition that names are "rigid designators" which identify their objects under any future possible circumstance. The first user of a proper name ("initial baptist") may or may not fix its reference by some description, but it becomes a rigid designator for other, later users who learn of the name's reference through a historical or causal chain. For example, school children may learn the name "Richard Nixon" as the thirty-seventh president of the United States, but that name refers to that man even if he had lost the election. Indeed, for Kripke, a name applies to its referent regardless of circumstances, or in terms of modal logic, across all possible worlds. But a name is not an analytic truth, nor is it known a priori. "We have concluded that an identity statement between names, when true at all, is necessarily true, even though one may not know it *a priori*."[50] If names are rigid designators, then even when we discover an empirical fact (not a logical truth) about someone's name—say that Mark Twain is Samuel Clemens—that empirical fact is still true in all possible worlds. In other words, in any possible world where "Mark Twain" is used as a name in the way it is in our world, it will always point to Samuel Clemens. In possible worlds where "Mark Twain" points to someone else, it will be a *different name*.

By such arguments, Kripke opened the door to different kinds of necessity that are not dependent upon analytic or logical truths. Like Quine, Kripke accepted the idea that *stipulative definitions* are analytic truths and a type of "epistemological necessity" (*de dicto* necessity); but his theory of names needs another kind of necessity, *metaphysical* necessity, which attaches to the nature of things (*de re* necessity). Besides names, other examples of metaphysical necessity would be natural kind terms like water or gold: "water is H_2O" is not an a priori truth, nor an analytic statement, yet it is necessary and holds (Kripke thinks) across all possible worlds. Kripke claimed that this kind of necessity is known a posteriori (while epistemological necessity is known a priori). Because of this appeal to the essential properties of things, Kripke's view is sometimes called essentialism.

The contrast with Quine is quite clear: Kripke rejected several of

Quine's conclusions including his theory of reference, linguistic holism and his rejection of the analytic/synthetic distinction. Kripke did this not so much through formal argument as he did by appeals to our common sense or intuition. In responding to Quine's argument against necessary truths, Kripke appealed to what an "ordinary man" who was not a philosopher would think about specific cases. One case he used to press his point is the name "Richard Nixon." If Nixon is described as the winner of the 1968 presidential election, then (Quine would argue) it will have to be a necessary truth that "Nixon was the winner in '68." Yet if we describe Nixon in another way, such as the man who lost to Kennedy in 1960, this sentence is not necessary. Thus logical necessity becomes a problematic concept. Against this argument, Kripke appeals to our intuitive grasp of what might have been the case. It just might have been that *this man* did not win the election in '68, so the "ordinary" person will think, and "the term 'Nixon' is just the name of *this man*."[51] It's striking that Kripke simply appeals to common sense and to intuitions, especially in light of common claims that concepts without rigorous definitions should not be used in philosophy. Like Peter Strawson and H. P. Grice (in the tradition of Wittgenstein) Kripke rejected Quine's complaint that our everyday notions are not rigorous enough for logic and so have to be replaced by better philosophical theories.[52] He appealed, instead, to our rational intuitions and the common sense of everyday people.

The philosophies of Kripke and Davidson are two influential examples of current work in analytic philosophy after Quine. They also exemplify two ways in which philosophers have responded to Quine: either rejecting his views at a fundamental level, while learning from him at key points; or accepting the broad outline of his philosophy while taking it in new directions. There is a third important journey taken by analytic philosophy (very broadly understood) after Quine, and that would be a postmodern turn. This journey, however, we will map in a later chapter. Now we turn to the surprising growth of work in philosophy of religion by scholars in the analytic tradition during the last half of the century, a development of special interest to Christian scholarship.

Analytic Philosophy of Religion
Starting around 1955, growing out of seeds sown in the decade before, a

real flowering of philosophy of religion took place in the analytic tradition. This growth might be surprising, given the origins of analytic philosophy in logical empiricism and the hostility to the meaningfulness of religious language that was characteristic of that school. Our task here is to indicate some of the richness of this growth, without any claim to cover the whole field.[53] Toward this end we will examine a few philosophers who have been important and influential. Their work represents some of the best in philosophy of religion during our century and will give us a good sense of this tradition.

In considering the philosophy of religion, we should note that some important figures have already been introduced in this book. We previously introduced Charles Hartshorne, who was one of America's best known philosophers of religion in the middle part of the century. In this chapter, too, we looked at philosopher of religion D. Z. Phillips, who responded to the challenge of logical empiricism along the lines of a Wittgensteinian philosophy. We are ready now to canvass philosophers of religion who are closer to the center of the analytic tradition than either of these two men.

One of the most famous early books in analytic philosophy of religion was a collection of essays considering the challenge of the new linguistic philosophy to religious statements. *New Essays in Philosophical Theology*, edited by Antony Flew (1923-) and Alasdair MacIntyre (1929-) soon became a standard work in the new approach.[54] Explaining what was "new" about this kind of philosophical theology, the editors wrote: "it is only in these last few years that attempts have been made to apply these latest philosophical techniques and insights to theological issues."[55] The "latest philosophical techniques" in this quotation were logical analysis, and the publication of *Language, Truth and Logic* by A. J. Ayer in 1936 is what started this conversation in the English-speaking world.[56] In a long section of the book that addressed "theism" Ayer argues that religious statements are meaningless, i.e., they are neither true nor false. For example, Ayer asserts, "the theist, like the moralist, may believe that his experiences are cognitive experiences, but, unless he can formulate his 'knowledge' in propositions that are empirically verifiable, we may be sure that he is deceiving himself."[57] Flew presses this same point in a different manner, following a falsification criterion for meaning: "anything

that would count against the assertion" is part of the *meaning* of the assertion.[58] This led him to question whether religious assertions are meaningful: "What would have to occur or to have occurred to constitute for
you a disproof of the love of, or the existence of, God?"[59]

Flew's pointed question is in fact an important one to reflect upon,
even for those theologians and philosophers of religion who hold to a
robust theism. There soon arose a large literature concerning the meaning of religious statements, with philosophers and theologians of various
types proposing different answers. We have already investigated the
response of several philosophers (like D. Z. Phillips) in an earlier chapter, and a previous part of this chapter. The main point here is that questions surrounding the logical analysis of religious language are the
ground on which analytic philosophy of religion grew and blossomed.

Several issues soon became central ones for this tradition. The question of the meaning of religious language remained important for several decades; other problems soon came along to join it. Even after the
connection between the *meaning* of a statement and the empirical evidence for its truth (or falsity) was loosened, the analytic tradition in general remained interested in *evidence*. The centrality of logic, analysis,
natural science and a kind of general empiricism pressed analytic philosophers to question the evidence for religious belief. This eventually led
to a broad and complex consideration of religious epistemology, that is,
the character, claims and limits of religious knowledge. New work on
arguments for and against the existence of God began to appear. The
problem of evil also came into prominence, with some philosophers
going so far as to say that traditional theism was logically incoherent,
given the fact of evil and suffering in the actual world. What is more,
these arguments raised the possibility that traditional theism might be
falsified by evil. There may be evidence against religious belief, or at least
belief of a certain kind. A fourth issue that arose for analytic philosophers was the logical status of *specific* religious beliefs or theological doctrines. The question here was still about the meaning of religious
concepts, and especially their logical coherence (or lack thereof). Each of
these issues, and more, were pursued by a growing number of analytic
philosophers around the globe who were developing a new movement in
philosophy of religion. Our goal now is to sample some of this conversa-

tion, hearing the voices of some of the best known practitioners of analytic philosophy of religion.

Hick. By any standard, John Hick (1920-) was one of the most important philosophers of religion in the twentieth century.[60] He contributed to every theme in the above paragraph in his numerous books and articles.[61] His long and distinguished career earned him many honors, including the invitation to give the Gifford lectures, published as *An Interpretation of Religion* (1989).

After graduating from Oxford University, Hick published his dissertation as *Faith and Knowledge* (1957). This work in religious epistemology considers questions of evidence for and against religious faith, as well as the meaning of religious statements. In it Hick came to several conclusions that would stay with him during several changes in his philosophical and religious perspective. He saw the world as religiously ambiguous, standing between faith and unbelief. Religious and nonreligious responses to reality can be equally rational, he argued. Hick borrowed from Wittgenstein's notion that we "see" certain ambiguous objects "as" such-and-such (I see the picture as a duck, you see it as a rabbit). Both views can be defended; both seem right from different perspectives. Hick developed this into his notion that religious belief is a kind of "experiencing-as" of the world.[62] One person experiences the world as (say) the creation of God, while another experiences the world as nothing but pitiless material particles whirling in space. Both views can be equally defended; both may be rational. This leaves a certain "epistemic distance" between God and rational creatures, which provides freedom for faith. As for the once-hot topic of verification, Hick put forward the controversial thesis that some religious statements are in principle empirically verified in the afterlife, a view he called "eschatological verification."[63]

As we noted above, the issue of evidence for or against religious belief continues even when "verification" in the strict sense falls by the wayside. This raises the question of whether suffering falsifies a robust theistic faith. While a member of the theology faculty at Cambridge University, Hick wrote a book which was to bring the young philosopher international recognition. *Evil and the God of Love* (1966) is Hick's response to the problem of evil, and many scholars continue to find it the best single volume on the subject. Hick places his argument firmly in the Christian theological tradition, rather than in a world-religions context. His theodicy "for today" is based upon three elements: Christian experience, Christian myths and Christian theology. Many of the biblical stories from Genesis to the Gospels Hick treats as myth, i.e., as great and enduring "imaginative pictures" by means of which the church has expressed itself over time.[64] The main question of his investigation is, "Can the presence of evil in the world be reconciled with the existence of a God who is unlimited both in goodness and in power?"[65]

After a substantial and influential survey of Christian thinking on this subject (which takes up about half of the volume), Hick presents a basic typology of theodicy: Augustinian or Irenaean. The Augustinian type sees creation as good, indeed Being is good in itself. Evil is the privation of good or of being in some way. On this view, human suffering is understood to be either sin or a punishment for sin. It tends to place a great deal of ontological importance upon a literal, historical Fall of humanity (Gen 3) as the origin of sin and death, even among nonhuman creatures. The other type Hick traces back to Irenaeus (although it finds its clearest expression in Schleiermacher). In an Irenaean theodicy, the Fall was real but not as significant. Adam and Eve are seen as immature rather than perfect, and the "death" which resulted from the Fall is primarily a spiritual death. "For him [Schleiermacher], the 'original perfection' of the creation is its suitability for accomplishing the purpose for which God created it."[66] Humans are created for fellowship with God, and salvation is understood as the gift of eternal life in Christ, which is eschatological. Sin and suffering are inevitable and also valuable as a context within which humans can freely grow and develop into loving, virtuous adults in community (or tragically reject this opportunity). Hick also called this view a "soul-making" theodicy, since our struggle with evil makes sense within this larger plan for salvation with its eschatological consummation. Hick did not argue that he had completely solved the mystery of evil in the world. Rather, his more modest conclusion was, "All we can say is that in spite of the antitheistic evidence the religious claim [of an all-good, almighty God] *may* nevertheless be true."[67]

Hick's theodicy was well received and widely discussed, bringing the author international fame as a philosopher of religion. He was soon offered an endowed chair in theology at the University of Birmingham. At the time, Birmingham was one of Europe's most multicultural cities. Hick found himself living and working in community and university events with Jews, Muslims, Sikhs, Hindus—a great variety of people holding many different kinds of faith or none at all. Hick tells us this experience, rather than any rational argument, caused him to rethink his theology and philosophy. "It was not so much new thoughts as new experiences that drew me, as a philosopher, into issues of religious pluralism, and as a Christian into inter-faith dialogue."[68] The result of this combination of thinking, interfaith dialogue and multicultural experience was his programmatic work on religious pluralism: *God and the Universe of Faiths* (1973). The implications of Hick's new "Copernican revolution" in philosophy of religion for traditional Christian thought became clear in a book he edited and contributed to: *The Myth of God Incarnate* (1977). This book caused something of a theological furor, even though most of the ideas in Hick's long chapter "Jesus and the World's Religions" could be found in his earlier publications. His main thesis is that Jesus as the incarnation of God is a "mythological idea" which served the church at one time, but in our age must be rejected at a literal level. In part this is because, he claimed, a literal God-human incarnation is logically incoherent. "For to say, without explanation, that the historical Jesus of Nazareth was also God is as devoid of meaning as to say that this circle drawn with a pencil on paper is also a square."[69] Hick could only accept the incarnation as a myth: a story of the closeness of God, a mythological truth which could be found in other great religions of the world expressed in different myths. He was seeking a global theology of "incarnation" for a multicultural age. "It seems clear that we are being called today to attain a global religious vision which is aware of the unity of all mankind before God and which at the same time makes sense of the diversity of God's ways within the various streams of religious life."[70]

In 1982 Hick was appointed to the Danforth chair in religion at Claremont Graduate School and moved to California. He delivered the Gifford lectures, published as *An Interpretation of Religion* in 1989: this text develops Hick's "pluralistic hypothesis" and provides the summary statement of his philosophy of religion. Drawing upon the Kantian distinction between the *noumena* (the things in themselves) and the phenomena (the experienced, everyday world), Hick argued that there is a Real (the Transcendent or Ultimate Reality) that cannot be known directly, but is experienced in various ways in all the great world religions. All the great world religions are basically on par with each other in their access to the Real, to moral goodness, and to religious truth. Religious doctrines will have to be interpreted as myth, however, in order for all the great variety of religious worldviews to be equally "true" in their grasp of the Real.[71] He defines mythological truth in religion as follows: "A statement or set of statements about X is mythologically true if it is not literally true but nevertheless tends to evoke an appropriate dispositional attitude toward X."[72] Literal truth about the Real is not, in any case, necessary for "religious salvation/liberation," which Hick interprets along moral lines as turning from self-orientation toward the Real (what he means by the "appropriate dispositional attitude" is this moral conversion). But this reduces religious truth to morality, as Kant himself often did.

Reflecting on Hick's long and distinguished career, it is ironic that a philosopher who first made his mark defending the meaningfulness and truth of religious belief against positivism and the problem of evil would end up with a final position in which all the great religions contain only myth in their truth-claims about the Real. Does only Hick's philosophy of religion or some similar abstraction yield literal truth about the religious Ultimate?

Plantinga. In Alvin Plantinga (1932-) we find a philosopher of religion who comes from a very different theological perspective. Plantinga is one of America's better known philosophers, and a major philosopher of religion.[73] After decades of teaching at Calvin College (Plantinga's perspective on religion and philosophy has deep roots in the Dutch Calvinist tradition) he moved to the University of Notre Dame, where he currently teaches. Much of his work has been in philosophy of religion, but he has made significant contributions to modal logic, epistemology and metaphysics.[74] At the heart of his work in philosophy of religion has been a defense of the rationality of classical Christian theology (or theism). This key theme of this work could be called "negative apologetics": the task of showing that intellectual criticisms of classic Christianity are not fully cogent, and so they provide no grounds for altering or giving up Christian faith. This was clear even from his first book, *God and Other Minds*

(1967). The key question of this book is this: Is belief in God *rational?* It begins with a thorough review of arguments for the existence of God, and Plantinga concludes that natural theology alone does not provide enough evidence to undermine the "natural atheologian" from her atheism. "And so it is hard to avoid the conclusion that natural theology does not provide a satisfactory answer to the question with which we began: Is it rational to believe in God?"[75] The heart of his argument is that even though natural theology may not provide enough evidence for the atheist to change her mind, neither does the argument from evil (a key weapon in the hands of natural atheologians) provide a reason for theists to change their minds. In passing, and in response to the challenge of verificationism, Plantinga provides a brilliant and rigorous critique of the verification criterion. Since the verification criterion cannot (he argued) be given a clear and convincing definition, theologians and everyday believers should simply insist that their language is meaningful after all, despite the claims of current philosophy (at that time). The burden of proof is on those who claim religious language is meaningless to prove their point, he asserts, and so far they have not been able to do so. The main thrust of the book is that belief in God is similar to the epistemological situation of belief in other minds: while there is no evidential proof for the belief that other seeming personal beings I experience have minds, neither is there a conclusive disproof. Belief in God, like belief in other minds, is rational even when conclusive evidence and arguments in their favor are not forthcoming.

As part of this overall strategy, Plantinga gives a convincing refutation of the *logical* problem of evil. Some analytic philosophers, including J. L. Mackie (1917-1981) of Oxford, argued that classical theism is *logically incoherent* given the problem of evil.[76] The existence of evil, they held, is inconsistent with belief in a God that is omnipotent, omniscient, omnipresent and wholly good. Plantinga provides a famous and influential defense against the argument. It should be carefully noted that this is a *defense,* not a theodicy. Plantinga in no way seeks to *justify* God in the face of evil and suffering, but rather takes up the humbler task of showing that theism is not logically incoherent. To show the logical consistency of theism, Plantinga developed his Free Will Defense, arguing that it is logically possible that God cannot actualize (i.e., create) a world in which free moral agents retain their freedom yet never do evil acts. It is broadly accepted by philosophers of religion today that Plantinga was successful in this limited aim, since his defense has only to be logically possible (and not actually *true*) to refute the logical problem of evil.

In his next major work, *The Nature of Necessity* (1974) Plantinga updated his earlier views on the ontological argument for the existence of God and the problem of evil. In this technical work in modal logic and its metaphysics, Plantinga utilized new developments in the logic of necessity and possibility (modal logic) to present a rigorous and much discussed version of the ontological argument for the existence of God. He also used modal logic to re-present his free-will defense. He expanded it to include issues of natural evil and the "probabilistic" argument from evil.[77] Still, much of this technical monograph is devoted to issues of logic and metaphysics in general terms, not just philosophy of religion. Taken together, *God and Other Minds* and *The Nature of Necessity* demonstrate that a robust, traditional theism could be explicated and defended according to the highest standards of academic philosophy. They helped to make philosophy of religion a respectable discipline again, even at a time when analytic philosophy was dominated by subtle and (and occasionally not-so-subtle) disdain for traditional theism.

Plantinga returned to themes in epistemology in an influential collection of papers on *Faith and Rationality* (1983) which he edited with his colleague and friend Nicholas Wolterstorff (1932-).[78] Plantinga and Wolterstorff both reject the rationalist program of *classical foundationalism*. Foundationalism in epistemology is, broadly, the view that our system of ideas has basic beliefs which are justified or warranted, but *not* on the basis of *other beliefs*. These basic beliefs provide the "foundations" of one's worldview. Classical foundationalist epistemology insisted that in order to be properly justified, such basic beliefs have to be certain, self-evident, beyond doubt or some similar epistemic virtue. Good historical examples of classical foundationalism would be Descartes and Locke. One of the few things that continental and analytic philosophers today agree upon, in general, is that this rationalist attempt to create a system of certain knowledge is a failure.[79] In *Faith and Rationality* Plantinga and Wolterstorff propose an alternative epistemology, which they jokingly called "Reformed epistemology." This name stuck and has now been widely discussed by philosophers and theologians (a cautionary example to others who would name their own philosophies!). The hallmarks of this position are (1) there is no good reason to reject belief in God (and other religious beliefs) as part of the properly basic set of beliefs which provide the (fallible) foundations of my worldview, and (2) the call by many philosophers to adjust our beliefs according to publicly available evidence should be rejected. Belief in God is properly basic even when it is not based upon evidence. However, the properly basic beliefs that ground my worldview remain fallible—Plantinga and Wolterstorff reject the classical foundationalist insistence on certainty—because *defeaters* to these beliefs may arise which need to be addressed. Nevertheless, simply because these defeaters may arise it does *not* follow that belief in God cannot be properly basic and must be based upon rational arguments or evidence in order to be reasonable. Still, Plantinga admits, "conditions can arise in which perhaps I am no longer justified in this [theistic] belief."[80]

Plantinga's work on religious epistemology culminates in his trilogy on warrant.[81] The first volume presents a critical overview of contemporary issues in epistemology, and the second volume sets forth his proposed solution to these issues. Plantinga develops a concept of *warrant* (whatever we add to true belief which makes it count as knowledge) which is external rather than internal and based upon the idea of *proper function*. Typically philosophers have spoken in terms of "justification" for our beliefs, and there is a strong tradition of internal justification for knowledge in Western thought, going back through Descartes to Plato. For the internalist, rational and critical reflection by the philosopher can discover whether or not we are justified in our beliefs. Plantinga is critical of this tradition and opposes it with a reliabilist and externalist theory of epistemic justification or warrant. In broad terms, he sees warrant in the following way: a person S knows a proposition p if and only if S believes that p, p is true, and S's belief that p is the product of faculties that are functioning properly in their appropriate environment, and these faculties aim at truth. These faculties need to be reliable, that is, they successfully yield truth for the most part. Having made these moves in general epistemology, Plantinga is ready to address the case of religious belief.

Warranted Christian Belief (2000), the third volume in this trilogy, is a major work in twentieth-century philosophy of religion. The book is an expanded and revised version of his first set of Gifford lectures in 1986-1987. A wide-ranging volume, the heart of his argument is that Christian belief is warranted if core Christian beliefs about God are true. To see why this is so, notice that in the definition of warrant above, *p* has to be true for *S* to have warranted knowledge that *p*. So Plantinga's case is only that Christian belief is *possibly* warranted, and key to that possibility is the condition that what is believed is true. For example, say that you believe the God of the Christian Bible is the true God. You are warranted in this belief, according to Plantinga, only if it is true. The "interesting conclusion" that Plantinga draws is that the question of the rationality of theistic belief (de jure objections, as he puts it) cannot be separated from the question of the *truth* of theism (de facto objections).[82] This means that natural atheologians cannot simply argue that theistic belief is epistemologically defective—they must argue that theism is false. "A successful atheological objection will have to be to the *truth* of theism, not to its rationality, justification, intellectual respectability" and so forth.[83] This book and its arguments have received worldwide attention and critique.[84] Plantinga's work has the virtue of being interesting, especially to other analytic philosophers. No one has contributed more to the revival of analytic philosophy of religion.

Swinburne. Richard Swinburne (1934-) is Nolloth Professor Emeritus of the Philosophy of the Christian Religion at Oxford and a prolific author. He has made contributions not only to philosophy of religion but also to philosophy of science, epistemology, philosophy of mind and metaphysics.[85] Among his many honors, he is a Fellow of the British Academy and a Gifford lecturer. One of the most distinguished philosophers of religion of his time, he is arguably the foremost natural theologian of the century. By natural theology in this case we mean a branch of philosophy (not religious doctrine or Christian theology) that examines arguments for and against the existence and attributes of God. Swinburne's early work was in the logic of probability and the philosophy of science. At an early stage he was still attracted to a version of verificationism. This view was soon to change, however. His study of the philosophy of science led him to reject even modest versions of the verification criterion for meaningful sentences. Also at this early stage of his career he published *The Concept of Miracle* (1971), a hint of later interest in philosophy of religion.

Swinburne was invited to give the Wilde lectures at Oxford (1975-1978), which he expanded into an influential trilogy of books in natural theology defending a generic theism. He used the philosophical insight and logical rigor developed over ten years of study in the philosophy of science to great effect in this new specialty. *The Coherence of Theism* (1977) begins with philosophy of language, clarifying and correcting the largely verificationist and falsificationist debate about religious language characteristic of British philosophy of religion for the previous twenty years. Rejecting each of these, Swinburne laid out his own more sophisticated criteria for coherence and meaning in religious language. It would be too much to claim that Swinburne solved the problem of religious language, but he did make significant progress. The same can also be said about the other two sections of this book, which deal with the coherence of the divine attributes and the various types of necessity with respect to the divine nature. While he rejected the ontological argument (which entails that God's existence is logically necessary) he accepted the necessity of God's existence in other senses of the term. He concluded that belief in a God who is "eternally an omnipresent spirit, who is perfectly free, creator of the Universe, omnipotent, omniscient, perfectly good, and a source of moral obligation" is coherent, but gave some revisionist interpretations of these attributes in order to make them so.[86] *The Coherence of Theism* was at the forefront of analytic philosophical investigation into the attributes of God, an area which now can boast a significant literature. His next volume in the series, *The Existence of God* (1979), was equally influential.

Having clarified the concept of God, Swinburne next applied the logic of probability to arguments for the existence of God. His argument for the existence of God was based upon modern scientific findings and a rigorous application of probability theory. Several important points are made in this work concerning philosophy in general, such as the discussion of various types of explanation, including personal explanation. Swinburne put the cosmological, teleological and moral arguments on a solid philosophical ground once again, after years of relative neglect or outright hostility. He also developed arguments from divine providence and human consciousness. He considered the problem of evil and its tendency to lower the probability of theism; but on the whole of the evidence, he concluded that theism is more probable than not. His general approach to natural theology, namely that the arguments are *inductive* and *cumulative*, has become commonplace in the field. It is not too much to say that *The Existence of God* gave new academic respectability to positive theistic arguments (as distinct from Plantinga's negative apologetics).[87]

After moving to Oxford, where he was professor from 1985-2002, and publishing his Gifford lectures on the philosophy of mind, Swinburne turned to Christian philosophical theology. In other words, he left the broad and general philosophical horizon of "theism" to investigate issues that arise within the particularities of Christian theology. He published a significant four-volume series of books on philosophical issues in Christian thought. In the first volume, *Responsibility and Atonement* (1989), he examined key concepts in moral philosophy and applied them to the doctrines of sin, redemption and personal eschatology. The volume *Revelation: From Metaphor to Analogy* (1992) revisits his earlier work on religious language and extends the discussion to cover creeds, Scripture and the church as an interpretive community. Swinburne held that some language for God is literal, while other sentences are metaphors or analogies. This work provides an illuminating clarity concerning the logic of religious language. In *The Christian God* (1994) he revisited the topic of coherence, this time with a special focus on Christianity. After a substantial first part dealing with general metaphysical issues like time, substance and necessity, Swinburne moves on to discuss philosophical issues in the nature of God, the doctrine of Trinity and the incarnation. This book re-presents coherent versions of the attributes of God, but now also argues for the coherence of the doctrine of the Trinity, and of the two-natures of Christ in the incarnation. For the most part, with notable exceptions concerning eternity and omniscience, Swinburne's God is that of classic Christian theology.

Swinburne was criticized by a number of philosophers and theologians for his rational approach to theodicy in his early book on the existence of God. In *Providence and the Problem of Evil* (1998) Swinburne developed his greater-good theodicy, this time drawing upon the more complex goods available to Christian faith, such as eternal life. In this work he responded to some of his critics, but maintains his generally rationalist approach to a full-orbed theodicy. Unlike Plantinga's "defense," Swinburne argues that rational Christian faith needs evidence and so theodicy in the strict sense is a necessary part of demonstrating the reasonableness of Christian belief. Yet Swinburne did caution that his theodicy is "not an account of God's actual reasons for allowing a bad state to occur, but an account of his possible reasons."[88] Even so, he attempts to give a "total theodicy," such that for each bad state that occurs, God has a (possible) moral reason to allow it.[89]

Rowe and Adams. As we close this brief listening session, it is only right that we consider some other voices in the choir of analytic philosophy of religion. To this end we will hear from William Rowe and Marilyn McCord Adams, two major philosophers whose work is distinct from the voices of Hick, Plantinga and Swinburne, yet remains part of the overall philosophical choir. A major theme in this fugue, as we have seen, is the problem of evil. How do Rowe and Adams develop this theme in their distinctive voices?

William Rowe (1931-) is an excellent example of a scholar who devotes his life to philosophy of religion yet is an avowed atheist. He has long been a professor of philosophy at Purdue University in Indiana (he retired in 2005). He wrote several important books in the philosophy of religion, including a widely used textbook.[90] In an oft-cited article, Rowe distinguishes three types of atheism.[91] The unfriendly atheist argues that theism is not a rational belief. The indifferent atheist is agnostic with respect to this question. The friendly atheist accepts the rationality of theistic beliefs, made coherent by philosophers like Plantinga and Swinburne, but not the *truth* of theism: Rowe understands himself to be such a "friendly atheist." At this point Rowe presents his famous "evidential" argument from evil.[92] He accepts Plantinga's Free Will Defense: by granting libertarian free will, Plantinga has shown the *logical* consistency of theism. However, even if theism is logically consistent, classical theism is falsified by the quality, extent and depth of the evil and suffering in the world. At the heart of his argument is the notion that the God of classical theism, who is wholly good, almighty and omniscient, would "prevent the occurrence of any intense suffering it could." Given the depth of suffering in the actual world, Rowe concludes, "There does not exist an omnipotent, omniscient, wholly good being."[93]

Marilyn Adams (1943-) is an American philosopher with strong interests in medieval philosophy, analytic philosophy and philosophy of religion. She has taught at UCLA and Yale, and works closely with her husband Robert Adams, an excellent philosopher in his own right.[94] An Episcopal priest, since 2004 she has been Regius Professor of Divinity at Oxford and a canon of Christ Church Cathedral. She is a good example of a recent movement which interprets the great medieval philosophers and theologians using the tools of analytic philosophy, as well as developing contemporary analytic philosophy in conversation with the middle ages. Adams may be best known for her outstanding two-volume interpretation of the philosophy of William of Ockham.[95] Yet her work on the problem of evil in contemporary philosophy is quite significant and is the focus of this discussion.[96] Adams is unhappy with the generic "theism" approach to the problem of human suffering that has been typical of analytic philosophy. God may, she holds, have good generic and general reasons for allowing evil and suffering, but in addition to this, God must (morally must) be *good to* individual humans as well.[97] In making a case for just how God is good to individuals, philosophers will need to draw more fully upon the particularities of specific religions. For her part, Adams turns to Christian tradition and theology, in particular the mystical theology of the middle ages (e.g., Julian of Norwich), including the notion of a "beatific vision" in the afterlife. In the beatitude of our relationship with the triune God in the next life, humans will come to retrospectively accept the horrendous evils they suffered, as part of their mystical identification with Christ. This viewpoint is developed as a full-blown Christology in her Gifford lectures, *Christ and Horrors* (2006). In this latest book, she considers what Christ must be in order to be the Savior of all humanity, one who redeems people from the meaning-destroying effects of horrendous evils. In many ways the book is a contemporary version of Anselm's project in *Cur Deus Homo? (Why Did God Become Human?)*. She defends on biblical and philosophical grounds a fully human, fully divine Jesus, and a genuine bodily resurrection, as part of thinking through the issues of God and human suffering. I believe that Adams's feminist theology has given her a greater concern for the real bodies of suffering women (and men), and may be a motivating factor in her different approach. Her work is a model of thinking about God and evil from the perspective of those who are undergoing genuine suffering.

Conclusion: Reflections on the Analytic Tradition

As we close the chapter on analytic philosophy (broadly understood), we look back upon a lively and flourishing tradition in the twentieth century. At the center of this dialogue stands the figure of Wittgenstein. His move from logical analysis in the *Tractatus* to "grammatical" analysis in the *Investigations* was of central and wide-ranging influence in this tradition. It also tells us something about the characteristics of analytic philosophy. Relying upon logic and the careful analysis of language (e.g., Russell and Moore), the analytic tradition as a whole has brought an exemplary clarity to twentieth-century philosophy. Reading analytic philosophers can be a breath of fresh air after the obfuscation that sometimes plagues the work of authors from other traditions. Yet the power of the analytic tradition may also be its weakness. By focusing on logical analysis and questions of truth or falsity, often following mathematics or the sciences as models, analytic philosophy can be too abstract and removed from real life. People get interested in philosophy for the "big questions" about life, meaning, beauty and truth. These are questions that the analytic tradition sometimes fails to deal with in an adequate manner. Second, because it tends to focus primarily on arguments and truth-claims, analytic philosophers can be overly abstract in their work on historical figures as well. The contextual richness of historical figures is too often skipped over, as if the meaning of their words was not colored by their sociocultural context. For these and other reasons, religion scholars often prefer to dialogue with the work of continental philosophers. This one-sidedness can be a form of sheer prejudice. There is much we can learn as theologians from the analytic tradition, and to ignore either side of the Western tradition is a blunder for scholars in religious studies. There are some signs that the divide between analytic and continental philosophy may become less stark in the twenty-first century.[98] One can hope that the biases and prejudice one sometimes finds in both camps toward the other side may be overcome, at the very least.

8. FAITH IN PHILOSOPHY: THOMISM, HERMENEUTICS AND CHRISTIAN PHILOSOPHY

I n this chapter we will cover some central philosophers whose work was influenced by their Christian faith. In some cases they incorporated their faith into the substance of their philosophical reflection, while in others faith was a dialogue partner in the philosophical journey. In particular we will survey philosophers who worked in the spirit of St. Thomas Aquinas (Thomistic philosophy) and we will revisit some of the analytic philosophers who embrace the name of "Christian philosophy." Both of these movements created a debate about whether there can or should be a specifically Christian philosophy. Still other philosophers were influenced by faith in less direct ways. The great hermeneutic philosophers Hans-Georg Gadamer and Paul Ricoeur will be our examples of this latter type. What is more, their work continues our emphasis on language and philosophy. These two continental scholars are central to the development of philosophical hermeneutics, including some issues related to biblical interpretation. They are thus included in this chapter on Christian faith and philosophy.

This chapter also looks forward to the next one, which covers the postmodern turn. Part of what we will discover is that any explicit appeal to a Christian philosophy is already an implicit rejection of modernity, at least in some of its aspects. How exactly to define the postmodern is an issue we will cover in the next chapter. Still, it seems fairly obvious that Enlightenment prejudice would exclude as impossible the very idea of a "Christian" philosophy, for such a value-laden and blatantly religious approach would undermine the rational, scientific and value-free character of academic philosophy (on the modernist account). In their own ways Gadamer and Ricoeur were also critical of Enlightenment rationalism and therefore qualify as postmodern to some degree, as we will see. We now turn our attention to the oldest of these three movements: Thomistic philosophy.

Philosophy in the Spirit of Aquinas

There is some disagreement among experts on just what counts as "Neo-Thomism" in twentieth-century philosophy. Broadly, the term designates the revival of philosophical work grounded in the thought of Thomas Aquinas, but updated to engage contemporary philosophy and theology.[1] Already in the nineteenth century the Catholic Church stimulated a revival of Thomism as a kind of antidote to modern philosophy and theology, much of which called into question Catholic dogma. For this reason Pope Leo XIII issued his famous encyclical *Aeterni Patris* (1879) recommending the further study of the philosophy and theology of St. Thomas, in order to "restore the golden wisdom of Thomas and to spread it far and wide for the defense and beauty of the Catholic faith, for the good of society, and for the advantage of all the sciences."[2] The Vatican did succeed in having Thomas taught more earnestly in Catholic seminaries, colleges and universities throughout the globe, in an effort to combat modernism in Catholic circles.[3] By all accounts the most famous and influential of these more traditional Thomists was Jacques Maritain (1882-1973). Yet because of this revival of Thomistic philosophy, another way of following in the spirit of St. Thomas soon developed.

After a careful study of Aquinas, some scholars wished to update the work of Thomas more fully by combining it with modern philosophy, for example with Kant. The root of this so-called transcendental Thomism lies in the philosophy of the Jesuit scholar Joseph Maréchal (1878-1944).[4] Maréchal sought to bring the Thomistic program and vision more fully into conversation with modern philosophy. He focused almost exclusively on Kant, seeing in his critical philosophy the root of much contemporary thought. Maréchal incorporated some of Kant's insights, though he remained particularly critical of Kant's views on metaphysics, the analogy of being and natural theology. His approach was highly controversial, especially among more traditional Thomists. Yet this version of Thomism, as we will see, turned out to be highly influential in the second half of the twentieth century. Given this variety in Thomism, there is a bit of confusion about how to use the term. We will use the word *Thomist* broadly, to apply to both schools of thought and others, thus allowing the term *Neo-Thomist* to designate the older and more traditional approach.

Maritain. In the life and thought of Jacques Maritain, Thomistic philosophy stepped on to the world stage.[5] Philosopher, statesman, literary critic and influential educator, Maritain was one of the two or three most influential and respected Catholic intellectuals of his time. Together with his colleague and fellow Thomist, the great medieval historian Étienne Gilson (1884-1978),[6] Maritain helped to spark an international and ecumenical respect for and interest in Aquinas. As a convert to Catholicism and then to the thought of St. Thomas, this was quite deliberate on Maritain's part. In the preface to an early work, *Antimoderne* (1922), he wrote: "It would be exceedingly naïve to enter upon modern thought and to sympathize with all the good that there is in it without first attempting to discern its spiritual principles."[7] Maritain embraced Thomism because he found other schools wanting on spiritual and philosophical grounds.

He studied philosophy at the Sorbonne and heard the lectures of Bergson at the Collège de France. Bergson pushed him in a new direction, for Maritain found the academic philosophy of the Sorbonne dry and narrow. Bergson excited his metaphysical and spiritual interests, but did not wholly satisfy. Maritain embraced the Catholic faith along with his wife, Raïssa, a Russian Jew whose family immigrated to France, and who was a poet, artist and philosopher in her own right. He soon began to study the philosophy of Thomas Aquinas, and in Thomism they both found a spiritual and philosophical home. Maritain had a distinguished career in philosophy both in France and in North America (they fled from the Nazis to Canada and America during World War II). He was the French ambassador to the Vatican after the war for three years, where he befriended the future Pope Paul VI (Giovanni Montini). Maritain also represented his government at the second UNESCO conference in Mexico City (1947) where he was president of the conference. Another high honor occurred when he was eighty-three. At the formal close of Vatican II, Pope Paul VI gave a special address to Catholic intellectuals, and Maritain was the person chosen to represent them at the ceremony. He spent the last years of his life in a monastic community with the Little Brothers of Jesus and was buried in 1973 by his beloved Raïssa in Kolbsheim, France (there is still a center devoted to their life and thought there, the Cercle d'Etudes Jacques et Raïssa Maritain). With such a distinguished international contribution to philosophy, culture, government and religion, it is easy to see why Maritain is considered one of the premier Catholic intellectuals of the twentieth century.

Maritain promoted Thomism not as a return to the past, but as a wisdom for the present and the future. As an intellectual movement and philosophy for today, Thomism needs to engage the philosophical and cultural issues of our age. He wanted "a *living Thomism*, a Thomism that will enter into the life of the age and work for the good of the world."[8] He did not want simply to return to the past, or to the rather dry Neo-Thomism of Catholic seminaries. Maritain saw in Aquinas the "apostle of modern times" who could reorient culture and philosophy to its true ground in reality, virtue, truth and beauty as these are themselves grounded in God. While philosophy thus conceived could not be separated from Catholic faith, it remained distinct from faith and dogmas, basing its investigations upon reason, nature and experience like any philosophical rationality. It was Maritain's vision that Aquinas, as the "common doctor" [or universal teacher] of the West, could unify and purify all the arts and sciences. "The Common Doctor would then become in all truth their common master; under his guidance they could work efficaciously for the restoration of the West and its unity."[9]

Maritain engaged the popular existentialism of his time with *Existence and the Existent* (1947). In this work, Maritain rejects the views of Sartre and others who argued that human existence is prior to any essence or nature, and that our radical freedom means there is no fixed human essence. Against such a position, Maritain argues that without metaphysics, true existentialism is impossible. Existence requires being, and Thomism provides the best analysis of being. He names Thomism as an "existentialist intellectualism," a philosophy which takes metaphysics, being and intellect seriously, as philosophy should.[10] From these points it

can be seen that Maritain was not afraid to swim against the intellectual
tides of his time. The impulse that drove his philosophical journey began
in an early work on metaphysics, knowledge and the supernatural: *Distinguish to Unite, or the Degrees of Knowledge* (1932).

Generally known by its subtitle, *Degrees of Knowledge*, this book is Maritain's major philosophical work. In it he unites his concerns for knowledge, his critique of scientism, and his focus on the metaphysics of being.
He works in the domain of philosophy, which, following Thomas, he
considers a separate discipline from theology. The philosopher works on
the basis of principles and reasoning that are open to and can be known
by anyone. Yet Maritain refused to separate philosophy from faith, for he
would thereby be separating it from the truth, indeed from the First
Truth.[11] He gives first priority to metaphysics, to the quest for reality and
being which lies at the heart of the human intellect. Thus metaphysics
"awakens a desire for supreme union, for spiritual possession complete
in the order of reality itself and not only in the concept. It cannot satisfy
this desire."[12] Given this spiritual understanding of reality, Maritain considers three domains of being, that is, three levels or degrees of knowing.
He begins with scientific knowledge: physico-mathematical, biological
and psychological knowing. These provide us with knowledge of sensible
nature, but are wholly dependent upon philosophy and first principles
which science cannot provide. Next he considers metaphysical knowledge, which is philosophy proper. He names his epistemology "critical
realism," but it is quite different from the use of this name in Anglo-American philosophy; its realism lies in its focus on being or reality, and
it is critical because of the reflective quality of the intellect in critical
analysis of the act of knowing. For Maritain, philosophy does not have to
demonstrate the existence of real things to the skeptic; rather, being and
knowing come together in the act of the intellect which constitutes
knowledge of the real. Consideration of the metaphysics of being soon
leads to a consideration of God as the ground of being. "Thus, the divine
perfections are attained by us in the perfection of created being, which
by the analogy of being makes us pass to uncreated Being, which no created mind can naturally attain in itself."[13]

This move from being to God leads to the third degree of knowledge,
which is mystical or "suprarational knowledge." Here Maritain turns to

Christian spirituality, especially John of the Cross. Great Christian spiritual writers provide models of how the human mind, assisted by divine grace, is able to reach the highest and most spiritual degree of knowledge. He defines mystical experience not in a loose or New Age way, but as the *"experimental knowledge* of the deep things of God."[14] Yet Maritain continues to insist that he is doing philosophy, not theology or religious studies. Metaphysics or natural theology, because of its basis in rational thought, can only demonstrate the existence of God; mystical knowledge is needed to complete the human quest to know the whole of reality, including the wisdom which lies above the natural order in God alone. Maritain's philosophy is clearly a form of Christian scholarship. Whether he continues to do *philosophy* properly so called in developing the spiritual and religious aspects of his thought was a major controversy surrounding his work in France.[15] But the question of the relationship between faith and philosophy continued to be raised by critics of Thomistic thought as it developed over the century.

Rahner. The most important Catholic theologian of the twentieth century may well have been Karl Rahner (1904-1984).[16] Owing to our focus on philosophy, we will consider his work as a philosopher, which indeed he was. Rahner's early works were philosophical, as was his early training. His thought is also a good example of transcendental Thomism, in contrast to Maritain's more traditional Thomism. Another good example of transcendental Thomism would be Canadian philosopher and Jesuit priest Bernard Lonergan (1904-1984), but we must limit our survey to just one example.[17] Although Rahner spent most of his life's work in theology, his work in philosophy is extensive and includes the first two of his published books. Philosophy plays an important part in his entire, extensive theological *oeuvre*.[18]

Rahner joined the Society of Jesus in 1922 and studied Thomistic philosophy. On his own he read the works of Maréchal. The order wished him to become a professor in the history of philosophy and sent him to Freiburg (near his family home) to work on his doctorate. While there, he attended lectures and seminars given by Heidegger. This proved decisive for the young Jesuit's intellectual development. Following Maréchal's model of integrating Thomism with more modern philosophy (i.e. transcendental Thomism), Rahner wished to bring Heidegger's question of being into conversation with Aquinas. After several years of work, his doctoral dissertation on Aquinas was rejected by his Thomistic supervisor because it was too influenced by Heidegger. Rahner left Freiburg for the University of Innsbruck, where he studied theology (earning his doctorate in that field) and became a member of the faculty. There he published his earlier philosophical dissertation as *Spirit in the World* (1939). Rahner's other early philosophical book is *Hearers of the Word* (1941), a book which sets forth his philosophical understanding of religion. The Nazis closed down the theology faculty at Innsbruck, but Rahner returned to it after the war. He soon became one of the most famous and prolific Catholic theologians in the world, in no small part because of his original and controversial engagement with Heidegger and Aquinas.

The philosophy he worked out in these early books, especially *Hearers of the Word*, created a kind of direction or framework for all of Rahner's subsequent work. This direction can already be seen in *Spirit in the World*, at least to some extent. This book is also important for answering the question of Rahner's relationship with the Thomistic tradition and his understanding of the relationship between philosophy and the Christian faith.

In structure *Spirit in the World* is an interpretation of one question in the *Summa theologiae,* in which Aquinas addresses empirical knowledge. Its focus is on the metaphysics of human knowing, including a reflection upon the human knower who asks the question of being. This text is not simply a historical and exegetical investigation of Aquinas, but a conversation and confrontation of Aquinas with Kant and Heidegger. Kant's critical philosophy and transcendental method provides a framework within which Thomas's epistemology is updated and reinterpreted for today. The book is filled with Heideggerian questions and terminology, and Rahner is rather obviously in debt to Heidegger's analysis of Dasein (human being). This complex book is a creative engagement of Thomistic issues with and in terms of modern philosophy. It is highly influential perhaps because it goes beyond the historical task of Thomistic exegesis to engage post-Kantian philosophy in the German tradition.

Rahner is interested in the analysis of human being as one that is open to being and, as such, is a questioning being that not only asks questions but questions the questioner. The title of the work uses the German term *Geist*, which can mean spirit or mind. "By spirit I mean a power which reaches about beyond the world and knows the metaphysical."[19] But in reaching out to the world, and also at the same time the metaphysical, the human mind/spirit also reflectively turns upon itself and questions its own being. Questioning is essential to human existence. "But this necessity can only be grounded in the fact that being is accessible to man [sic] at all only as something questionable, that he himself *is* insofar as *he asks about being*, that he himself exists as a question about being."[20]

Over against much of the Thomistic tradition, and Christian Platonism in general, Rahner insists that metaphysical knowledge does not come through some kind of rational intuition or vision. He agrees with Thomas that human knowledge of being is everywhere based upon sensations or "phantasms" (to use Thomistic language). But once we have made this rejection, we run up against Kant's problem: how then is metaphysical knowledge possible? Rahner's answer turns to the character of human being in the world. Human coexistence with being (or with the world) is itself *transcendental*. "When man becomes a metaphysician, he finds himself, by the fact that he is with individual existents here and now, already and always with being in its totality."[21] As a questioning being, the human reaches out not only to individual things, but to the totality of reality, to being as a whole. Existence in and with the world is a necessary precondition to human knowing and acting—in other words it is *transcendental* to human Being. Metaphysical knowledge is based upon a preconceptual, transcendental grasping after being as a whole, which Rahner calls a "pre-apprehension" (*Vorgriff*—a Heideggerian term). As a Catholic thinker, Rahner connects being as a whole to Absolute Being, that is, to God. Thus Rahner concludes that at the heart of any and all human existence is a preconceptual, unthematic consciousness of the Absolute, which provides the transcendental foundation for all developed theology and metaphysics.[22] These conclusions are decisive for Rahner's theological development. In the conclusion of *Spirit in the World* he wrote: "man encounters himself when he finds himself in the world and when he asks about God; and when he asks about his [Man's] essence, he always finds himself already in the world and on the way to

God."[23] In this way metaphysics is the "first and the last science" of human existence,[24] and provides a necessary foundation for theology.

These conclusions are developed more fully in a theological direction in Rahner's next book, *Hearers of the Word* (1941). In his first work, the young Rahner was struggling to interpret Thomas for a new age and using all the technical vocabulary of German philosophy to do so. In this second book, Rahner speaks more in his own voice. The book's topic is what Catholics call fundamental or foundational theology, that is, a Christian philosophy of religion understood as a preamble to Catholic doctrine. Although not a straightforward Thomist, Rahner's thought maintains many central themes from that perspective. For example, a classic point of Thomistic thought is that philosophy and theology can never come to know the true essence of God. Rahner follows this perspective in *Hearers of the Word:* "Metaphysics conceives God precisely as the absolute Unknown, as the One who cannot be unequivocally defined from below by human metaphysics."[25] Rahner's work as a whole has a strong anthropological orientation, as distinct from the Thomistic tradition. Thus *Hearers of the Word* is not a philosophical theology of God, but a philosophy of religion that examines human existence as it is open to being and to the Absolute, or to what Rahner will later call "Mystery." In this turn, Rahner develops a philosophical anthropology as a preamble to theology which is based upon divine revelation, that is, upon hearing the Word.

Rahner interprets human existence as a kind of being that is structured and situated with the potential to hear and obey God's word. He calls this the *potentia obedientalis*, the existential potential to hear a free word from God.[26] Every human being, as part of his or her very nature and existence as a human, has the capacity to hear the word of God. Human existence is, in part, a seeking after and listening to that Word. What is more, human being as a spiritual being is also historical and transcendent being. In our self-transcendence we are capable of relating to God, who is always everywhere present in human existence as the Mystery which surrounds human existence. The a priori transcendental conditions for the possibility of human subjectivity can be expressed in philosophy of religion as the innate capacity of human existence to hear the word of God. Yet our existence is also historical and communal, and therefore we listen for God in history. This questing after and listening for the voice of Mystery finds its fulfillment in that which is beyond philosophy, that is, in divine revelation in history and especially in Jesus Christ. Thus "listening to God is the condition of hearing the word of God, and this listening is the free act of man in his true existential self-understanding."[27] This conclusion is Rahner's contemporary way of putting the Thomistic point that God is the first cause of all being and ultimate end of human existence.

Rahner was certainly not a Thomist in the ordinary sense. But his version of transcendental Thomism picks up themes and principles from more traditional Thomistic views, and in this way we can situate Rahner within the larger Thomistic tradition and debate. What is clear is that Rahner's philosophy is a version of Christian philosophy in conversation with (and indebted to) Aquinas, Kant and Heidegger.

MacIntyre. The third major Thomistic voice we will consider here is the Anglo-American philosopher Alasdair MacIntyre (1929-). He is one of the best known moral philosophers in the world today, in no small part because of his trenchant critique of modern moral thinking and liberal political philosophy.[28] Yet MacIntyre is not exactly a conservative thinker either. This is the same MacIntyre, for example, who edited the *New Essays in Philosophical Theology* with Antony Flew (discussed earlier). Born in Scotland and educated in England, MacIntyre was involved in several philosophical transitions and approaches, including Marxism, Freudian analysis and grammatical analysis (á la Wittgenstein). In keeping with this varied intellectual journey, he taught at numerous universities over a long and successful career. Since 1970 he has lived and worked in the United States, where he currently is senior research professor at the University of Notre Dame.

The decisive shift in MacIntyre's philosophical journey came with the publication of *After Virtue* (1981), one of the most-discussed works in moral philosophy in our century. By 1970 MacIntyre had concluded that the various ideologies of modernity were not capable of sustaining moral inquiry or human flourishing.[29] *After Virtue* is a trenchant critique of "the Enlightenment project" of disembodied and supposedly neutral moral and political philosophy. What he argues for is a return to the Aristotelian tradition, which includes a virtue-based ethic and an understanding of rationality that is grounded in local communities and tradition. One of the problems with the Enlightenment project, he argues, is the rejection of tradition, as well as the illusion that philosophy can be done apart from communities, social location and value commitments.

In his next major book, which if anything was even more influential, MacIntyre offers Thomas Aquinas as his chief example of a practical rationality that develops over time, in debate with other options and traditions. In *Whose Justice, Which Rationality?* (1988) he finds in the long tradition of Thomism the best continuation of the ancient philosophy of Aristotle. What is more, Thomas provides an outstanding example of the way in which a particular tradition can be vindicated over time, even though human rationality is never neutral and universal. In other words, by focusing on human rationality grounded in practices, community and tradition, MacIntyre could be opening the door for relativism. His response to this is to argue that in some cases traditions can be shown to be rationally superior even in the light of what the other tradition would accept as good evidence and argument. Aquinas provides MacIntyre with his gold-standard example of this kind of rational vindication of a tradition.

> It is this contingent history of successive and successively more adequate formulations which needs to be understood as the history of practice of enquiry conducted within a tradition. . . . It is indeed precisely because and in so far as Thomist Aristotelianism enables us to achieve an adequate understanding both of our own history and of that of others in this way that it vindicates its claim to have identified the standards by appeal to which all practices and traditions are to be evaluated.[30]

This turn to Thomism was surprising to many followers of MacIntyre's work at the time. Yet if one takes seriously the arguments of *After Virtue* and begins to look for a community and a tradition that has over the centuries carried on the philosophy of Aristotle, Thomism is about your only option. Looked at retrospectively, MacIntyre's conversion to the Roman Catholic Church is perhaps not all that surprising.

MacIntyre embraces his own version of Thomism, recognizing that there are various strands within the tradition. He is skeptical of transcendental Thomism just because he is skeptical of the post-Kantian philosophical project. The following comment from his Aquinas lecture seems to be directed at Thomists like Maréchal, Lonergan and Rahner:

> Theory and idiom are to some significant degree inseparable. Insofar as I try to deny your theory, but continue to use your idiom, it may be that I shall be trapped into presupposing just what I aspire to deny.... So it has been to some significant degree with Thomism in its encounter with post-Cartesian philosophies.[31]

MacIntyre often goes his own way, but his version of Thomism seems to be more in line with that of Gilson and Maritain than with any attempt to rephrase the Thomistic tradition in the terms of post-Kantian philosophy. Yet MacIntyre is committed to developing the key philosophical positions of Aristotle and Thomas into the twenty-first century. This is clear from his Aquinas lecture and his later book *Dependent Rational Animals* (1999). In many ways this book continues the themes of *After Virtue*, especially with respect to virtue ethics today. In it, MacIntyre develops an argument from the biological character of embodied human nature to the necessity of virtues for human flourishing. The biological facts the book draws attention to include our animality, fragility and dependency. Using these notions MacIntyre extends the Aristotelian tradition of virtue ethics, developing a creative and powerful argument for a *natural* human moral end for individuals and societies. His work encourages generosity, practical rationality and the common good in a way that sees humans as animals who nevertheless move beyond animality to morality. In these and other ways MacIntyre continues to develop the Thomistic tradition in philosophy.[32]

Conclusion: Fides et Ratio. We have seen that Thomism provides a continuing, dynamic tradition of Christian philosophy. Maritain's call for a "living Thomism" was fulfilled in many ways. While some Thomists have been more willing to embrace modernism and post-Kantian philosophy, others like Maritain and MacIntyre have been critical of modernity. Yet because they take the Christian faith seriously as a beacon for philosophical inquiry and a guide to the truth wherever it may be found, Thomism as a philosophical tradition will always be critical of the pretensions of Enlightenment rationality, including any tendency toward the idolatry of reason in philosophy.

We started this section on philosophy in the spirit of Aquinas with the mention of a Papal encyclical; it is only right that we end in the same manner. The late Pope John Paul II (Karol Wojtyla, 1920-2005) was one of the most influential of modern popes, and also one of the most learned. He earned two doctorates, one in theology and one in philosophy, before becoming a professor of ethics. Near the end of his pontificate, he wrote a major encyclical on faith and reason, *Fides et Ratio* (1998).[33] Reflecting often upon the earlier encyclical of Leo XII *(Aeterni Patris),* this meditation on truth in philosophy and faith demonstrates the vitality of Thomism at the end of the century.

John Paul II embraces a broadly Thomistic approach, seeing the quest for truth among everyday people and among philosophers as directed spiritually toward God. He chastises philosophy when it has gone astray, especially when it sunders people from seeking an ultimate truth that finally transcends reason and the individual self (§5). Philosophy goes wrong when it takes our gaze away from truth and engenders agnosticism, relativism and skepticism. Since the church has received a truth through divine revelation in Christ, the best philosophical work will be done in dynamic relationship with Christian faith. John Paul II recognizes the distinct character of the vocation of philosophy and its use of reason to discover the truth about human beings and the world we inhabit. So philosophers have "their own terrain and their own purely rational method" but at the same time he calls philosophers to "extend their work to new aspects of truth" derived from Christian faith in the word of God (§76). While philosophy and Christian theology are distinct, the universal human quest for truth is best served when they collaborate in a dynamic reciprocity (§99). This approach is summed up in the metaphor which opens the encyclical:

> Faith and reason are like two wings on which the human spirit rises to the contemplation of truth; and God has placed in the human heart a desire to know the truth—in a word, to know himself—so that, by knowing and loving God, men and women may also come to the fullness of truth about themselves.

The Thomistic approach to reason, faith and philosophy was stimulated and made better known on a global scale by this encyclical, because of the worldwide influence and fame of the Roman Pontiff. This parade example shows how Thomistic thought has provided an important stimulus and home for Christian philosophy throughout the century. Yet for this very reason, critics of Thomistic philosophy have sharply raised the question of the validity of Christian philosophy.

The Question of Christian Philosophy

Two schools of thought on the continent, with roots in the nineteenth century, argued for the importance of a Christian philosophy. These are roughly Catholic (Thomistic) and evangelical (Dutch Reformed). Although something of a backwater in the larger history of Western philosophy, the nature of our task in this series on Christianity and Western thought brings this debate into sharper focus. Is Christian philosophy legitimate as an academic discipline? Is it really philosophy *per se* or more properly a type of theology? We will first return to the Thomistic discussion and then look more fully at the American evangelical conversation.

Thomistic Christian philosophy in France. We have already seen that Thomism is a vital tradition of Christian philosophy. The work of Gilson and Maritain, along with other Catholic scholars, sparked a large debate in French concerning the legitimacy of a Christian philosophy.[34] As Thomists, they both argued for the possibility and importance of Christian philosophy which in no way undermines philosophical inquiry, but rather strengthens it. The debate began in fact from the other side of the fence. The rationalist philosopher and historian from the Sorbonne, Émile Bréhier (1876-1952), published the first volume in his history of Western philosophy in 1927.[35] He called into question the very idea of a Christian philosophy. He understood Christian faith to be primarily a practical way of life, about such things as "brotherhood and mutual assistance."[36] The Christian religion does not add to theoretical knowledge or philosophy, and little but religious practice separates pagans and Christians when it came to philosophy. Indeed, he stated that Christian theology "represents the complete realization of that which Stoicism and the others schools [of pagan philosophy] were seeking."[37] The philosophy of Christian thinkers in the patristic and medieval period was an amalgam of Greek philosophy and not distinctive. For this reason he concluded "there is no Christian philosophy."[38] Bréhier held out for the independence and rational character of academic philosophy. To the extent that it bows the knee to Christian dogma, it is not philosophy, which must do its work on strictly rational grounds. Christian philosophy makes about as much sense as "Christian" mathematics or physics.[39]

Gilson was invited to debate Bréhier at the 1931 meeting of the French Society of Philosophy.[40] Gilson was fresh from delivering the first set of his Gifford lectures for 1931-1932, later published as *The Spirit of Medieval Philosophy*, the first two lectures of which expounded and defended the notion of a Christian philosophy.[41] He defended the notion that the Christian philosophy of the middle ages was a distinct development, not merely Greek philosophy redone for a church audience. A key difference between Greek philosophy and the Christian philosophy of the middle ages (especially that of Aquinas) is the intervention of God's Word. Christian philosophy is a genuine philosophy and therefore based upon the deliverance of reason. Yet it is engendered and guided by Christian truth which is divine in origin. "Thus I call Christian, every philosophy which, although keeping the two orders formally distinct, nevertheless considers the Christian revelation as an indispensable auxiliary to reason."[42] Gilson defended the distinctness of philosophy from faith, revelation and dogma: "A true philosophy, taken absolutely and in itself, owes all its truth to its rationality and to nothing other than its rationality."[43] So far so good. But Gilson tended to put too much emphasis on the subordination of Christian philosophy to "true" theology, as expressed in the Catholic dogmatic tradition and the work of St. Thomas. The Christian philosopher *qua* believer never critically examines the received doctrines of the faith. Instead, he asks himself "whether, among those propositions which by faith he believes to be true, there are not a certain number which reason may know to be true."[44] Gilson's position on this point became more entrenched as he continued to write about Christian philosophy, so that by 1960 Christian truth and the thought of Thomas Aquinas were almost identical for him.[45] Gilson claimed to respect the formal distinction between theology and philosophy in principle, but in fact came to advocate submission in practice of the "best" philosophy to the "right" theology.

Interestingly, some Thomists in the French debate agreed with Bréhier over Gilson, at least to some extent. Canon Professor Fernand Van Steenberghen was a central figure at the important Thomistic school in Louvain, Belgium. He was present at the 1933 meeting of the Thomistic

Society of France, where the debate was next taken up. Van Steenberghen made a distinction between philosophy in a general sense and
strict academic philosophy. The first view is a kind of philosophy of life
or a general worldview. Here Van Steenberghen agreed with Gilson
against Bréhier that a genuine Christian philosophy had existed historically and could indeed be both philosophy and Christian. Christian philosophy did manifest a number of new directions of inquiry and themes
by taking up ideas or presuppositions from Christian revelation. Yet the
Christian worldview or philosophy of life provided an enrichment or
guiding light; it was and is no substitute for academic philosophical argument. Academic philosophy in the strict sense, he maintained, could not
simply adopt the teachings of any religious faith. He spoke for the Louvain school when he sought "to show that the Christian thinker could
practice science and philosophy in the rigorous sense, as scientific methods; and consequently, to maintain common ground between Christian
and unbelieving thinkers."[46] How can a believing philosopher convince
other philosophers of the truth of their conclusions, unless they do so on
strictly general philosophical grounds? While philosophy as a science (in
the French sense of the term) must proceed on the basis of reason and
general human experience, at the same time revelation and faith are of
inestimable value to the Christian philosopher, as they are to any
believer. "Revealed truths, received by faith, enrich the Christian philosopher; they help him to produce an excellent philosophy."[47] But the critical independence of philosophy from theology and revelation must be
maintained by academic philosophy as a scientific community of rational
inquiry.

Because Maritain and Gilson were colleagues for many years, and are
often considered together, one might think they held the same view on
the nature of Christian philosophy. They often cite each other's work
with approval, helping to maintain this vision of unity. But in fact Maritain's view is not identical with Gilson's, and his defense of Christian
philosophy moves somewhere between Gilson and Van Steenberghen.
To explain his viewpoint, Maritain distinguished between philosophy as
a "nature" and a "state." By the nature of philosophy he meant what philosophy is in itself conceived in a normative or ideal manner. By the state
of philosophy he meant the state "in which it exists in real fact, histori-

cally, in the human subject, and which pertains to its concrete existence and exercise."[48] With respect to the nature of philosophy, Maritain argued that philosophy is the work of natural reason. Considered as a nature, Thomistic philosophy is "wholly rational; no reasoning issuing from faith finds its way into its inner fabric; it derives intrinsically from reason and rational criticism alone; and its soundness as a philosophy is based entirely on experimental or intellectual evidence and on logical proof."[49] Maritain cautions that we are here dealing with the nature of philosophy as an "abstract essence" rather than as really practiced by philosophers.

When he turns to philosophy as a practice, however, Maritain insists on the validity of the concept of Christian philosophy. The Christian state of philosophy occurs when the individual philosopher, who to philosophize must "put his whole soul into play, in much the same manner that to run he must use his heart and lungs," is elevated by faith, grace and revelation to "the supernatural plane," and thus has access to "things which unaided reason would be unable to grasp."[50] Yet as a philosopher, the Christian scholar does not receive the whole of divine revelation into her science, but only those aspects which deal with "elements of the natural order." Even then, the philosopher will "scrutinize them according to its own order."[51] Grace and faith also provide important subjective support for the philosopher (as for all believers), in no small part because "the wound of original sin" infects the life of the mind.[52] Maritain concludes that "Christian philosophy is philosophy itself in so far as it is situated in those utterly distinctive conditions of existence and exercise into which Christianity has ushered the thinking subject."[53] Although he constantly cited Gilson with approval, Maritain was less ready to allow that "in a Christian regime philosophy is subjugated to theology."[54]

The debate of the 1930s did not settle the question of what philosophical debate does. French philosophers soon moved on to other issues. Gilson and Maritain continued to defend and develop the notion of a Christian philosophy along Catholic lines for the rest of their long careers in the academy.

Analytic Christian philosophy in America: Going Dutch? We now turn to the question of Christian philosophy in the analytic school in America. In recent years, a specifically Christian school of philosophy has been developing in the analytic tradition. The roots of this school go back to the continent, especially to Dutch Calvinist thought in the work of Abraham Kuyper (1837-1920) and Herman Dooyeweerd (1894-1977);[55] however, since our focus is on the analytic school of philosophy we look to North American scholars in this tradition. As we will see, the debate in America mirrors in some degree the controversy in France we have just covered. In both debates the independence of philosophy and the relationship between faith and reason were key issues.

While the debate in America about the question of Christian philosophy has older roots, the larger conversation within the analytic tradition generally can be traced to the founding of the Society of Christian Philosophers (SCP) in 1978. Alvin Plantinga's inaugural lecture at Notre Dame ("Advice to Christian Philosophers," 1983) is a key early text in this debate. This lecture appeared in the first volume of the SCP journal, *Faith and Philosophy*.[56] It is no accident that Plantinga and his close friend and collaborator Nicholas Wolterstorff were both professors of philosophy at Calvin College and heirs to the tradition of Christian Philosophy in Holland. As we saw in a previous chapter, both were instrumental in developing "Reformed epistemology." They were also founding members of the SCP (Plantinga was its third president) along with a number of other scholars including several prominent Catholic thinkers.

In his "Advice" Plantinga paints a sharp distinction between a Christian worldview and other rivals. He encourages Christians who are philosophers to own their religious perspective in the very act or practice of doing good philosophy. While in the past this might not have been socially acceptable in academia, now there are more openly Christian philosophers. One's religious perspective as a thinker need not be hid under a bushel. Still, "the intellectual culture of our day is for the most part profoundly nontheistic and hence non-Christian—more than that, it is anti-theistic."[57] The main point Plantinga wants to make is that the Christian philosopher ought to stand firm on her Christian worldview or presuppositions, and this may well affect the practice of philosophy in some ways. Plantinga stands in the tradition of Dutch Reformed philosophy in which a system of thought grounded on biblical revelation is starkly contrasted with all other worldviews or philosophies.[58] The main point he makes in this lecture, however, is that antitheistic or unchristian assumptions ought to be called into question, and certain questions may need to be investigated philosophically in service to the church (rather than strictly in service to the profession). Plantinga's point is that the Christian philosopher will want to understand philosophical topics—even set theory—from a distinctively Christian or theistic point of view.

Because of his prominence as a well-known American philosopher, Plantinga's "Advice" was widely influential, especially among younger Christian scholars. Naturally it drew responses from a number of quarters. In the same issue of *Faith and Philosophy* there appeared a response by the Catholic philosopher and medieval scholar John Wippel. Wippel had studied at Louvain, and his response follows Van Steenberghen rather closely.[59] One helpful point Wippel makes is to distinguish between an "order of discovery" and an "order of proof" for academic philosophy. In the order of discovery there may well be a Christian philosophy, but in the order of proof, "nothing from religious belief or philosophy can enter in."[60] This distinction is roughly equivalent to Maritain's distinction between the nature and the state of philosophy.

We previously introduced D. Z. Phillips, and we now return to him on this question. Phillips was not slow to be critical of Plantinga, and in 1988 gave a lecture titled "Advice to Philosophers who are Christians."[61] Much of his critique is about the rhetoric Plantinga employed when speaking of Christianity being "on the move" in academic philosophical circles, and the like. Phillips felt the need to remark that "the critical character of philosophical enquiry is an essential feature of it," but only because Phillips misread Plantinga as advocating the exchange of one fashion (non-Christian) for another (Christian).[62] Phillips does better in pressing for a "mode of philosophical enquiry in which Christians and non-Christians can share."[63] Of course Phillips's preferred mode of philosophical inquiry is grammatical analysis á la Wittgenstein. He promotes Wittgenstein's later work as providing a method which Christians and non-Christians can engage in, one which investigates "the grammar of the various concepts involved in the language-games we play" in a religious form of life.[64] In this analysis the philosopher is not doing Christian philosophy or non-Christian philosophy: "he is simply doing philosophy."[65]

Phillips's position on this question can be found, *mutatis mutandis*, in the opinions of many a professional philosopher. While not all will follow Phillips in finding grammatical analysis the beginning and the end of philosophy, they will be sympathetic to the argument that "we are not doing non-Christian philosophy: we are just doing philosophy." But here Phillips and others who take this point of view fail to understand Plantinga in the larger tradition which he represents, a tradition going back to Augustine, Bonaventure, Calvin and Kuyper. Plantinga mentions these Christian thinkers in passing in his article, but Phillips seems to have misunderstood their importance. What is central here is to grasp the importance of *faith* for human reasoning and scholarship. In this tradition, faith is an ultimate and guiding concern, not a programmatic set of beliefs. Thus all philosophies of life or worldviews have some key faith at their center; this would include agnostic or atheistic worldviews. Faith— and we all have it in some form or other—is what is truly fundamental for life, including the life of the mind. Academic disciplines are not purely neutral in their religious or nonreligious presuppositions. This is especially true of philosophy, but would be equally true of all sciences and arts—yes, even mathematics and physics (*contra* Bréhier). This tradition of thought would completely reject the claim of Wittgenstein and Phillips to be doing philosophy in a manner that is neutral with respect to worldviews, philosophies of life or issues of our fundamental faith-perspective. No academic is without a worldview, and no worldview is without a fundamental faith-perspective which shapes and guides academic or scientific work. For these reasons, a position for or against Christ at this most fundamental level is *transcendental* to all academic inquiry. Such is the viewpoint of this tradition which goes under the name of Christian scholarship, and for lovers of wisdom, Christian philosophy.[66] Wittgenstein once remarked: "The philosopher is not a citizen of any community of ideas; that's what makes him a philosopher."[67] This remark will be rejected as naïve by advocates of Christian philosophy in this tradition.

In France or America, in the analytic or the continental tradition, the claim that there is a legitimate Christian philosophy seems to raise the same issues and engender similar positions. Philosophers are passionate about these issues because they touch on the nature of philosophy itself. Christian believers are interested in this question because it is a prime example of the larger issue of the relationship between faith and reason, and the role of faith in the life of the mind. By pressing the legitimacy of a Christian philosophy, believing scholars call into question some of the standard assumptions of Enlightenment rationality, including the religious neutrality of genuine academic inquiry and the value-free character of science (academic philosophy being one of the *sciences* [French] or *Wissenschaften* [German]). Thus any claim to legitimacy for Christian philosophy seems to take a step in the direction of a postmodern turn, to the degree that it rejects some of the pretensions of Enlightenment philosophy.

Faith and Philosophy in Dialogue: The Hermeneutic Philosophy of Gadamer and Ricoeur

There are several reasons for why we now turn to the work of Gadamer and Ricoeur in a chapter on faith in philosophy. The advocates of a Christian philosophy we have surveyed represent a conservative theology, whether Catholic or evangelical. They openly proclaim their Christian faith as a necessary element in their philosophy. Gadamer and Ricoeur represent a different approach. They are famous and widely respected philosophers in the continental tradition, and their work in hermeneutic philosophy is important for Christian theology just because of the importance of biblical hermeneutics. Any Christian philosopher should also be just as interested. Equally important for their place here, however, is their approach to faith and philosophy. Both rejected the idea of a "Christian philosophy." When one looks for evidence in Ricoeur's writings as a whole, his Christian faith is clear enough, but faith is not a starting point for philosophy in either man's view. Instead, we might say that both Gadamer and Ricoeur were philosophers who were friendly to faith and engaged in a serious dialogue with Christianity. They do not ignore Christian faith or Scripture, yet their approach to both is more religiously ambiguous, more open to other faiths or none at all. We might say that for Gadamer and Ricoeur, Christian belief provides a stimulus and illumination for some of their work, but is not allowed a place in the method or substance of their academic philosophy. They provide a model between Plantinga and Phillips or Gilson and Bréhier, one in which philosophy is in dialogue with and open to faith but is not based upon it. In Ricoeur and Gadamer the relationship between faith and reason is *dialogical,* so that faith and doctrine are open to questioning from philosophy and vice versa. As such they provide us with parade examples of yet another way in which faith enters into philosophy, a way more in keeping with the liberal-evangelical tradition.[68]

Gadamer. The three great hermeneutic philosophers of the twentieth century were Heidegger, Ricoeur and Hans-Georg Gadamer (1900-2002). Gadamer was a wide-ranging and highly influential philosopher; he was also a student and friend of Heidegger's.[69] At first little known, Gadamer grew to become the grand old man of German philosophy by the end of the century. For example, he was made a Knight of the Order of Merit in 1971, the highest academic honor awarded by the German government. Somewhat intimidated by his famous teacher, Gadamer could not bring himself to publish a book beyond his second doctorate (habilitation) until 1960, eight years before he retired from his chair at Heidelberg. Yet this one book made him world famous in academic circles. Hermeneutic philosophy touches upon many disciplines, since it studies human understanding as such, and this book changed the face of hermeneutics. Although he did write a number of other books, *Truth and Method* (1960) is Gadamer's magnum opus, the summary of his philosophical vision.[70] The linguistic turn so remarked upon in twentieth-century philosophy reaches a high water mark in *Truth and Method.* We may go beyond Gadamer, but we may not ignore his work.

In this text Gadamer sought to accomplish several goals. He wanted to write for a larger audience than Heidegger's "turn" had yet reached and thus to guide philosophers into the later work of his teacher and friend. This was especially true of the later Heidegger's work on art and truth.[71] He also wanted to reach back to the long tradition of hermeneutic reflection in classical Greek and Roman thought, biblical hermeneutics, legal hermeneutics and the philosophical hermeneutics of Schleiermacher and Dilthey. Gadamer also took up Dilthey's goal of setting forth the rationality of the human sciences. Like Dilthey and Schleiermacher, Gadamer moves hermeneutics away from a simple list of rules for exegesis toward a comprehensive epistemology and ontology of human understanding. Key to his approach is a rejection of the methods of the natural sciences for hermeneutics. Instead, Gadamer opts for a more dialogical approach, one much more like a conversation between friends than a set of rules or methods. For Gadamer, human understanding is a universal aspect of human existence. It is always situated in concrete experiences, always dialogical, always linguistic and always pointing toward the practical—in other words, understanding flows out of human Being in the world. "The problem of hermeneutics goes beyond the limits of the concept of method as set by modern science. . . . The understanding and the interpretation of texts . . . belongs to human experience of the world in general."[72] Gadamer grounds his hermeneutic philosophy of understanding in Heidegger's analysis of Dasein. In other words, Gadamer will ground the rationality of the human sciences in a phenomenological ontology of human being-in-the-world. Key to this is his view of language—but first he will spend a long section of the book on art.

The later Heidegger was particularly interested in thinking about the question of being in the experience of art and poetry. This is why Gadamer begins with aesthetic experience in his analysis of the character of human understanding. It also serves notice that scientific methods are limited, merely secondary compared to the primordial experience of understanding which is ontological rather than methodological. Methods may be helpful in their way, but science and technology will not help us grasp the character of human understanding at its most fundamental level. For that we need a phenomenology of human being. At the same time, Gadamer rejected the purely subjective understanding of aesthetic judgment—and its subsequent relativism—found in Kant and pretty much the whole of modern philosophy. Instead, the act of interpreting art and the truth which comes to us through art serve as preliminary examples for Gadamer of the kind of understanding found in the human sciences and the interpretation of texts. "If we want to know what truth is in the field of the human sciences, we will have to ask the philosophical question of the whole procedure of the human sciences in the same way that Heidegger asked it of metaphysics and we have asked it of aesthetic consciousness."[73]

Gadamer argued that art is a mode of the mediation of being and therefore about truth. It is not merely a subjective experience of aesthetic enjoyment. For this reason he spoke of the ontology of the work of art, a kind of encounter with a world within art in which time, play and experience are essential. Play is an important category for Gadamer and points to the antitechnological character of human understanding. Both play

and time are key to the experience of art; they are a part of great art's
capacity to create a world for us to experience. Truth is thus understood
in Heideggerian terms as "dis-covery," the unconcealment or clearing-
event which opens a space for being and thinking to come together.
When we are caught up in a great play, a musical performance or a moving film, we encounter the play of the artist in making a "world" for us to
experience; this is the manner through which art discloses the truth to
us. In the play between the world created by art and our world, we see
our life in a new way. The meaning of art, and so the truth that it medi-
ates, comes out of the dynamic play between art and spectator/audience.
For this reason, Gadamer can claim that play "is the mode of being of the
work of art itself,"[74] for in art the play of the artist is transformed into
structure.[75] Only by being transformed into structure can art mediate a
world to us, and thus only in this way can art mediate truth. One striking
example Gadamer gives of the ontology of the work of art comes from
religious art. The essence of God is beyond sight or speech; only in the
word or image can God be known. In religious art we grasp that art is not
merely a copy of something, "but is in ontological communion with what
is copied. . . . Word and image are not mere imitative illustrations, but
allow what they present to be for the first time fully what it is."[76]

In the second part of the book Gadamer reviews the history of hermeneutics, beginning with the theological interpretation of Scripture.
Schleiermacher and Dilthey are important figures in this story, as is Husserl: but it all leads up to the great Heidegger who makes the decisive
breakthroughs.[77] The concepts of time, self-projection, language and
understanding are all ontological (in the sense of Dasein) and all connected. This ontological turn means that "all such understanding is ultimately self-understanding."[78] To understand an expression is not only to
grasp what lies in the expression, but to have a world opened up and at
the same time to see one's own being in the world projected in time with
new possibilities. In less complicated language, understanding a text
opens up the world or "horizon" of the author; but this insight also
causes us to see our own history, our own world, our own horizon, with
new possibilities for the future.

From this ontological basis Gadamer drew several important conclusions which he developed in the last part of his book. (1) Understanding

is temporal. We come to the text with our presuppositions, situated in a long tradition of understanding. Gadamer developed a tradition-constituted rationality decades before MacIntyre. He also rehabilitates the importance of "pre-judgment" or prejudice against the rationalist dream of an unbiased and neutral rationality. (2) Human being (or "consciousness") is therefore effected by history, or in Gadamer's famous terms, our human being is "historically effected consciousness" *(wirkungsgeschichtliches Bewußtsein)*. Our connection to time is fundamental to our "Being-toward-the-text," so that the best model for hermeneutics is a dialogue of question and answer.[79] (3) All understanding is a "fusion of horizons," a coming together of the world of the text and the reader's world. Understanding another person or a text changes us too. For this reason all genuine understanding is always already practical. We look forward as well as back because we are temporal, hermeneutic beings. (4) Language and understanding happen together, so that "the fusion of horizons that takes place in understanding is actually the achievement of language."[80] This means that without language, being cannot mediate truth. "Being that can be understood is language."[81] Of course this echoes the famous line from Heidegger that language is the house of being. For Gadamer, language is a universal medium, the natural world for human consciousness in which we live, act and understand.

Gadamer's book was widely read and so bound to attract criticism. He was such a gracious and dialogical thinker that he always treated his philosophical critics with genuine openness and a willingness to learn. This resulted in his constantly updating his magnum opus, which eventually had multiple additions and appendices. Some of his most important critics, like Jürgen Habermas (1929-), argued that Gadamer's approach was too traditional, too "friendly" toward the text and the past. More room must be made for a critical distance, Habermas thought, and also for method as a rational part of that distancing critique of the textual "other." The danger in Gadamer's approach, argued Habermas, is an overly conservative, traditional political theory which supports the status quo.[82] Gadamer's response was both intellectual and practical; he responded to the criticism but also befriended the young Habermas. Gadamer was instrumental in bringing him to Heidelberg as a philosophy professor, and the two became friends. On the other hand, his debate with Derrida in Paris was something of a disaster, with the two famous students of Heidegger talking past one another.[83]

In a later essay, and in response to his critics, Gadamer explains that he is not against method per se, but only the pretensions of those pressing for scientific method in everything. His real goal is to bring together methodological success (rightly chastised of course) with the conditions of our social and practical life. To accomplish this "it was natural for me to return . . . to the tradition of the practical and political philosophy of Aristotle."[84] Gadamer, then, is also a follower of Aristotle, especially in his appropriation of *phronesis* or practical reason.

The third great hermeneutic philosopher of the century, Paul Ricoeur, was also influenced by and critical of Gadamer. Ricoeur's critique agreed in the main with Habermas and was colored by Ricoeur's appropriation of themes from French structuralism.[85] Ricoeur believed that Gadamer drove too great a wedge between truth and method, and thereby undermined the objectivity of the human sciences.[86] But we are getting ahead of ourselves; we must now pass from Heidelberg to Paris to meet this major French philosopher.

Ricoeur. One of the foremost French philosophers of the century, Ricoeur was involved in dialogue and conversation with every major philosophical movement in his long career.[87] This is no accident, for both in method and personality Ricoeur was a scholar interested in finding what is valuable in the thought of very diverse philosophers, past and present. Ricoeur was a dialectical thinker who constantly sought a mediation between seemingly opposed viewpoints. For example, as a major continental philosopher Ricoeur was famous for his extended engagement with the analytic tradition.

Ricoeur was born in 1913 to a French Protestant home and studied classics and philosophy as a young man. He eventually graduated from the Sorbonne, where he was tutored by Gabriel Marcel—an early mentor for Ricoeur. Ricoeur was always on the left politically and was a pacifist during the Second World War; he nevertheless served in the military and was captured in 1940. As an officer he was given certain liberties in the camp, and he studied German philosophy (German books being provided to him and other intellectuals in the camp), especially the existentialism of Karl Jaspers. Ricoeur's interest in existentialism thus stems from his early encounter with Marcel and Jaspers. After five years in the camps, Ricoeur was able to return to Paris and continue his studies. He published a French translation with commentary of Husserl's *Ideas I* and became an important interpreter of phenomenology and existentialism in Paris.

In 1948 Ricoeur took up the chair in the history of philosophy at Strasbourg. There he began a multivolume work on the phenomenology of the will. Ricoeur was always interested in human nature, as these early works illustrate. In the third volume of this series, *The Symbolism of Evil* (1960), Ricoeur began to move away from a strict phenomenological method. His implicit Christian faith came to the fore as he considered classical and biblical myths of human evil, including Adam and Eve. It is also in this work that Ricoeur began his interest in hermeneutic philosophy, for myth and symbol evoke careful philosophical interpretation. *The Symbolism of Evil* explores three primal symbols and their associated myths: defilement, sin and guilt. At this early period he defines hermeneutics as "a work of understanding that aims at deciphering symbols."[88] As we will see, his understanding of hermeneutics grows to include more elements, but this early work on the "double meaning" inherent in all symbols marks the beginning of his hermeneutic philosophy. This focus on the importance of symbol and myth led him to claim that "the symbol gives rise to thought."[89]

Ricoeur's fascination with human existence, our fallible nature and the interpretation of symbols soon brought him into contact with the social sciences. Of particular importance at this point were two movements in France: structuralism and Freudian psychology. In keeping with the spirit of his philosophy, Ricoeur entered into a fruitful dialogue with both movements, from which he took lasting insights as his philosophy developed. Like Ricoeur, both structuralism and Freudian psychology are interested in human nature and the interpretation of symbols, yet in very different ways. After reading through Freud's works in German and teaching classes on his thought, Ricoeur published his most influential early work: *Freud and Philosophy* (1965). He provided an interpretation of Freud's work that emphasizes its philosophical significance. Not the least of his philosophical points was the importance of the hermeneutics of symbols for Freud. By seeking to interpret (along Freudian lines, of

course) certain human utterances, mental events and actions in light of
the unconscious, psychoanalysis reveals itself to be a kind of hermeneutic of the self. At the same time, by implication, the psychological "self"
we all construct is revealed to be very much like a text or symbol. Ricoeur
even claimed that "every meaning that exists is a meaning caught up
within the body, a meaningful behavior," so that "every praxis involved
in meaning is a signifying or intention made flesh."[90] The allusion to the
incarnation of the Word is difficult to miss here. Although not unique to
Ricoeur, this transgression of the boundary between self/flesh and sign/
meaning has been a cornerstone of recent French philosophy.

   Structuralism. To understand Ricoeur's engagement with structuralism,
we will need to know a bit about it. Structuralism as a movement origi-
nated in the social sciences, especially linguistics. The key to structural
understanding of human language or any meaning-system is the idea of a
deep structure or *code:* an underlying structure which organizes the many
and various human symbolic products, whether language, narrative or cultural mores. The origin of structuralism lies in linguistics, and structural
linguistics in various schools is the dominant modern approach. The
Swiss linguist Ferdinand de Saussure (1857-1913) was particularly influential in French structuralism.[91] Saussure argued that particular acts of
human speech *(parole)* are based upon a larger system of signs which is
the language as a whole *(langue)*. Saussure understood language to be a
system of signs and distinguished importantly between the sign and the
sign-system (language), as well as between the signifier (sound) and the
signified (meaning). Also important for structuralism is the difference
between diachronic and synchronic analysis: structures can be studied as
they change over time (diachronic) or in abstraction as they exist over
time (synchronic). For structuralists, signs have meaning only within the
larger sign-system and can very often be analyzed by means of *binary oppositions* (a pair of opposites). Linguists, for example, have been able to organize all human sounds used in languages, often utilizing binary
opposition in describing the system of "phonemes" (meaningful sound-
units). It is then possible to study how phonemes change in meaning and
use over time (diachronic) as well as the system of phonemes in use in a
natural language at a particular time (synchronic).

   In French structuralism, this general approach was expanded to many of the human sciences broadly and also moved into philosophy. The anthropologist Claude Lévi-Strauss (1908-) was perhaps the best known and most influential in the French school of structuralism. He applies structural analysis to the "savage mind," seeking the deeper code behind tribal behaviors (such as the taboo) and primitive myths.[92] Beyond linguistics and anthropology there was a general movement which included sociology and psychology, and was at one time quite influential on French philosophy.[93] Structural analysis seeks to understand the conditions of meaning that lie in the code or deep structure of a cultural system, including such phenomena as language, myth and cultural mores, and Ricoeur's engagement with structuralism was typically dialectical. He was appreciative but also critical of the movement, taking away with him some enduring concepts and moves which are rooted in a structural methodology. He often set up a dialogue between two alternative perspectives in order to seek a mediation between them which was never a synthesis. In a published dialogue with Gadamer he once put it this way: "I don't think that it's the task of the philosopher merely to brood over this situation of conflict, but rather to try and bridge it. It is, I think, always the task of philosophical rationality to try to mediate, to work out a mediation, and to do so with passion."[94] He insisted against Gadamer and in line with structuralism that method and scientific perspectives, that is, "the linguistic model," remains important for hermeneutic philosophy.[95] He continued to hold a place in his philosophy of language for a structural linguistics, although he argued there was more to language and meaning than signs, codes and structures.

Ricoeur was elected to a chair in philosophy at the Sorbonne in 1957, but he chose to join the new experimental University of Paris at Nanterre in 1966. This was a radical time in Paris, and the leftist student movement was particularly strong at Nanterre. Ricoeur was embroiled in the political upheavals surrounding the so-called events of 1968 and other student-led mass protests. In 1970 Ricoeur resigned his post and took a three year leave of absence. He taught abroad at Louvain and Chicago, and was appointed as professor in the divinity school at the University of Chicago (a post he held until 1992). Ricoeur became more interested in Anglo-American philosophy of language, and in 1975 published a wide-ranging book *The Rule of Metaphor*. The book covers many topics, including ancient and modern theories of metaphor. The work demonstrates his development from a hermeneutics of symbol to a hermeneutic discourse and philosophy of language. The subtitle gives a much better sense of the work: "Multi-disciplinary studies of the creation of meaning in language." For Ricoeur, metaphors like symbols have a double meaning which must be explored to be understood. The living metaphor creates meaning in its work of resemblance; that is, it brings together dissimilar things. For this reason, at the literal level a metaphor creates a clash of symbols which is also a nonliteral, iconic evocation of new meaning. Ricoeur argues against the notion that a metaphor has no cognitive content. The last part of the work is a dialogue with philosophers such as Nietzsche, Heidegger and Derrida on the philosophical function of metaphor which argues, among other points, for the referential quality of metaphor and for a kind of metaphorical truth.

The issue of creativity in language led Ricoeur to a long study of narrative, again across disciplines and in dialogue with the long history of philosophy. Whether fictional or historical, narrative became the focus of his research and lecturing after the mid-1970s. Ricoeur retired from the University of Paris at Nanterre in 1980, having become one of the best known philosophers in the world. Beginning in 1983 he published his massive four-part study, *Time and Narrative*.[96] With this work French scholars rediscovered Ricoeur, and he again became a famous intellectual in Paris.

In *Time and Narrative*, Ricoeur continues to explore the "meaning-effects" produced by metaphor and narrative, which "belongs to the same basic phenomenon of semantic innovation."[97] In *The Rule of Metaphor* the focus was on the sentence, which is the minimum unit of meaning for a metaphor as opposed to a sign or symbol. In *Time and Narrative* the focus is on much larger units, texts as a whole. The study continues an interdisciplinary approach, combining phenomenology and the philosophy of time with the philosophy of history and literary theory to produce a major investigation of human temporality as mediated by and created in narrative language. Ricoeur argues for strong similarities in the constitution of both history and fiction as literary narratives. In both history and fiction, narrative texts structure time through "emplotment," the gathering together of characters, goals, causes and chance events into a narrative coherence that is necessarily temporal. Unlike some literary theorists, however, Ricoeur always included elements of human existence and being as part of his analysis; he did not seal literature off from life. The roots of narrative time reach to the "ultimate referent" of temporality, which is "that structure of existence that reaches language in narrativity."[98] For this reason the phenomenology of the human experience of time provided a starting point and guide for the study of narrative, a "common standard of measure" for the analysis of narrative in history and fiction.[99] Hence, a central theme in Ricoeur's argument is that the power of narrative time lies in the ability of the "poetics of narrative" [i.e., the creative power of narrative time in texts] in both history and fiction to respond to the "aporias of time brought to light by phenomenology."[100] In other words, narrative art in both history and fiction responds to the problems and issues that arise due to the temporality of human being in the world.

This major multivolume work was widely acclaimed on the continent and in North America, by scholars in many fields including history, literature and philosophy. Ricoeur recovered his position of philosophical influence and importance even in France. During this period of enhanced fame the University of Edinburgh invited him to give the Gifford Lectures for 1985. This gave Ricoeur the opportunity to explore some of the ethical issues raised in his notion of narrative identity for the self. These were eventually published as *Oneself as Another* (1990).

Narrative does not simply attribute character, identity and action to agents, but also moral obligation. His Gifford lectures are a long study in ethics and the hermeneutics of the self; in this study Ricoeur explores the concepts of narrative and personal identity, as well as the question of the self and its moral character in the light of practical wisdom. Seeking to mediate the moral philosophy of both Aristotle and Kant, Ricoeur distinguished between a goal-oriented notion of the virtuous person in a good community (Aristotle), which he labels "ethics," and the Kantian conception of moral obligation, which he calls "morality." Both are important for an understanding of the moral self in life, in community and in fellowship with the Other. Ricoeur argues for the primacy of the ethical (virtue in the good person) over the moral, but also for the necessity of the ethical goal to be guided by moral norms. Moral obligations inevitably conflict with each other, and so must be mediated by reference to our ethical goals. When ethics and morality are rightly mediated through self, other, community and narrativity, the result is a practical wisdom that is able to apply universal norms to real, concrete situations.

The Gifford lectures are traditionally devoted to natural theology, although in practice they have covered a vast array of topics. Still, one might think that these lectures would be a good place for Ricoeur to reflect more fully upon the Christian character of his philosophy. In the oral version given in Edinburgh, Ricoeur concluded with two lectures on the self in light of biblical hermeneutics, in which he had long shown an interest.[101] However, he chose to exclude them from the published version of the lectures, in keeping with his career-long choice to sharply distinguish between "an autonomous philosophical discourse" and his own religious faith.[102] Ricoeur acknowledges that this decision excludes any appeal to "biblical faith," and that the question of God is absent; indeed, it leads to "a suspension that could be called agnostic."[103] Ricoeur does not want theology to become philosophy, nor vice versa. His concern is to present arguments, addressed to human reason and arising out of general human experience, without a direct appeal to religious faith. In this context, Ricoeur makes the following interesting remark: "The dependence of the self [in biblical faith] on a word that strips it of its glory, all the while comforting its courage to be, delivers biblical faith from the temptation, which I am here calling cryptophilosophical, of taking over the henceforth vacant role of ultimate foundation."[104] By keeping clear the boundaries between theology and philosophy, Ricoeur believes that both disciplines are free to be what they ought to be.

Ricoeur settled outside of Paris in his retirement years and remained very active in philosophy. After his Gifford lectures he continued his interest in ethics and his dialogue with Aristotle in *The Just* (2000). This work, like Aristotle's *Politics* and Plato's *Republic*, considers the ethics of a just society. In a large study finished when he reached the age of ninety, Ricoeur again combined phenomenology, philosophy of history and ethics. In *Memory, History, Forgetting* (2004) Ricoeur develops a significant phenomenology of memory, connecting it with the epistemology of history and the ethics of forgiveness. His long and fruitful career came to an end in May 2005.

Conclusion

In this chapter we have introduced the philosophies of several scholars who might otherwise have little in common; yet all but one were Christian intellectuals whose faith more or less came to the fore in their publications and lectures. The philosophies of Ricoeur and Gadamer have provided us with example philosophy that is open to faith and so open to intellectual dialogue with theology. Ricoeur's cautions against making faith some kind of "ultimate foundation" for the work of philosophy are well placed and indicate the importance of a continued distinction between philosophy as an academic discipline (including Christian philosophy) and Christian theology. But as we have already seen, this concern for the independent rationality of philosophy was also voiced by Maritain. The difference appears not in the academic conception of the rigors of philosophy but in the degree to which God and Christian faith are acknowledged as a kind of light guiding the work of the philosopher. Ricoeur and Gadamer were scholars interested in Christian faith, but they insisted on the autonomy of philosophical reason from it. This autonomy is exactly what the proponents of Christian philosophy called into question.

All of the philosophers in this section worked against the prejudices of Enlightenment rationalism to some degree. Ricoeur in particular was a postmodern philosopher, along with his several compatriots in French thought. In the next chapter we will bring various threads of our story together, considering the ways in which both analytic and continental philosophies have made the postmodern turn.

9. JOURNEY TO POSTMODERNITY

Western philosophy in the twentieth century moved toward the postmodern in both of its main streams: analytic and continental. This movement was not inevitable. The story of this movement is not the working out of a goal or logic which somehow propelled philosophy to this particular end. Yet it is a matter of contingent historical fact that within the large, complex human story of Western thought this movement transpired.

Postmodernity is a difficult notion to grasp, not least because it covers so many areas of culture. If we could use a better or handier term we would. But for better or worse the word has become a term of art. Many aspects of society today are described as "postmodern" in some sense, including novels, film, architecture, psychology, religion and of course philosophy.[1] Our focus will be on philosophy in this chapter, but even here there is little agreement on what counts as postmodern. The term itself is just as conflicted as the movement it seeks to indicate.

We cannot agree with some analysts who have argued that the postmodern has not really happened, or that the so-called postmodern is nothing more than a degenerative form of late capitalism or hypermodernity.[2] Of course the postmodern carries on some of the themes of modernity, but there is a definite rejection and refusal as well. Postmodern thought is highly suspicious of the rationalism of the Enlightenment, the Romantic soul's quest for the transcendent and of certain rationalist themes in Western philosophy as a whole. While similarities exist, there is not enough in common among philosophers we might want to call postmodern for us to speak of postmodern-*ism* in the way we talk about Marxism or positivism. It is best to think of the postmodern as an attitude, a style and an approach which can only be because of modernity but which also refuses some of the central moves of modern philosophy. The philosophical duo of Agnes Heller and Ferenc Fehér make the point well:

> Postmodernity may be understood as the private-collective time and space, within the wider time and space of modernity, delineated by those who have problems with and queries addressed to modernity, by those who want to take it to task, and by those who make an inventory of modernity's achievements as well as its unresolved dilemmas. . . . Postmodernity thus can only define itself within this plurality, against those heterogeneous others.[3]

Broadly speaking, in philosophy the postmodern is a critical analysis and rejection of some of the key claims, practices, values and metaphors of Enlightenment reason or Romantic aesthetics, movements founded on the self or other transcendent ground. The postmodern also includes a celebration of a new way of being after modernity which nevertheless occurs in the midst of modern times.

The notions of a universal system of reason, a foundation of ethics and epistemology in a transcendental ego or absolute self, the Romantic insistence on the immediacy of the soul with beauty, or the quest to ground genuine knowledge in epistemic certainty are among the claims of modernism open to postmodern critique. Different postmodern thinkers have characteristic ways of naming this cluster of problems, but they tend to aim in the same general direction. The modernism they object to (and it is not a total rejection of everything modern or rational) is committed to the autonomous self and its freedom, as well as to the project of a self-critical and self-grounded rationality, along with claims about what is natural, universal and reasonable for any rational man.[4] Usually this ensemble of claims is likened to some end or goal which promises progress of some kind: enlightenment, liberty, scientific control, greater self-understanding or experience of transcendence. According to postmodern critics, modernism in philosophy tends toward an all-encompassing system of thought which runs roughshod over difference, particularity, locality and the flesh of our all-too-human existence. Whether we look at Descartes, Locke, Kant, Rousseau, Hegel, Husserl or Carnap, so the story goes, one finds various and sundry attempts to create such a modernism in philosophy.

Understood in this way, it becomes clear that Kierkegaard and Nietzsche are prophets of the postmodern already in the nineteenth century. Nietzsche's transvaluation of values and Kierkegaard's rejection of the Hegelian System have deep echoes in twentieth-century postmodern philosophy.[5] Kierkegaard's point (made under the pseudonym of Climacus) that for God the world may be a grand system—but never for us, never for mere mortals—sounds very much like the rejection of "totality" by postmoderns.[6] In fact it is the same gesture of rejection in a different mode.

The Postmodern Condition: Lyotard

It is difficult to make generalizations about postmodern philosophy which hold even a modicum of validity across diverse authors. We do better to speak of specific texts and specific voices as good examples of the postmodern in philosophy. A brief examination of the widely influential work by Jean-François Lyotard (1925-1998), *The Postmodern Condition,* will provide us with a concrete beginning as we seek to characterize the postmodern in philosophy.[7]

This controversial book was originally written as a report on the state of knowledge in the most advanced societies to the Quebec government's University Council. Published in 1979, it gained international notice as a kind of tract on French postmodern thought. With a strong interest in art and politics, Lyotard argues that the postmodern condition is first of all a larger cultural phenomenon. It is not limited to philosophy or science or politics. But the focus of the report is on knowledge, and Lyotard contrasts scientific knowledge (which is being transformed by a post-industrial, computerized society) with knowledge that is "narrative" in its form. He delimits two "grand narratives" of modernity, each of which concerns the legitimation of modern scientific knowledge, one being more political and the other more philosophical. The first involves a great story of emancipation, political liberty, democracy and the autonomy of the individual. The leitmotif of this narrative is justice. The second grand narrative—or metanarrative—seeks a rational unity between truth, science and spirit (his example is the founding of the University of Berlin). Here the focus is on truth. Both of these grand narratives seek rational legitimation through unity, control and the universal dominance of scientific knowledge. Each metanarrative is a "project of totalization" which seeks to bring society and the world into the purview of a single story.[8] Because scientific reason "questions the validity of narrative statements and concludes that they are never subject to argumentation or proof," the quest for rational legitimization in the great myths (grand narratives) of modernism leads inevitably to "cultural imperialism" in the West.[9]

In the postmodern culture he seeks to describe (or perhaps simply to promote) Lyotard states that such grand narratives have lost their legitimating power. "The grand narrative has lost its credibility, regardless of what mode of unification it uses, regardless of whether it is a speculative [philosophical] narrative or a narrative of emancipation."[10] These moves allow Lyotard, in the most famous sentence of his book, to give a simplified definition of postmodern thought: "Simplifying to the extreme, I define *postmodern* as incredulity toward metanarratives."[11] The claims of a universal reason or justice are exposed in postmodern critique as particular, local, mythological stories whose universal claims are power-moves by the status quo and thus such claims are brought into question by a postmodern "hermeneutics of suspicion" (Ricoeur).[12] Lyotard's arguments and attitudes give us a solid example of postmodern philosophy. In this chapter we will uncover a multiplicity of modes in which similar— but also quite distinct—postmodern moves are made.

Postmodern Themes in Analytic Philosophy

The postmodern exists always alongside the modern, using contemporary categories and language to point out the inherent ruptures in the discourse and practice of modernity. From a historical perspective, the most influential moves in postmodern philosophy were made by Wittgenstein and Heidegger. Both took a turn toward the study of language as a complex phenomenon (not merely a tool for communicating propositions), which interweaves meaning in rich and complex ways with human being in the world. This linguistic turn is key to postmodern philosophy in the twentieth century.

Many philosophers in the analytic tradition eschew the term *postmod-*

ern and are often critical of what they label postmodernism. Yet in the analytic tradition itself several postmodern moves or gestures have been made since Wittgenstein's *Philosophical Investigations.* One prominent example in moral philosophy would be Alasdair MacIntyre, whom we introduced earlier and will revisit later in this chapter. Another example would be the philosopher Alvin Plantinga, whose work in philosophy of religion we likewise already introduced. Plantinga is an open critic of postmodernism.[13] Yet at the same time, the "Reformed epistemology" championed by him and others is a postmodern move just because it rejects classical foundationalism. Of course it would be wrong to think of Plantinga as a postmodern philosopher, and MacIntyre does not accept the label of postmodern even though many commentators see him as such. My point is simply that particular moves they make philosophically are versions of a postmodern critique of Enlightenment rationalism.

Thomas Kuhn. After Wittgenstein himself, the most influential and widely discussed work which embodies a postmodern move in the analytic tradition is by Thomas Kuhn (1922-1996): *The Structure of Scientific Revolutions.*[14] Published in 1962 as part of a logical empiricist project titled "The International Encyclopedia of Unified Sciences," Kuhn's famous book soon came to undermine previous philosophy of science, especially in the mode of logical empiricism.

Borrowing broadly from Wittgenstein as well as newer works on the history of science, Kuhn rejected the older notion that scientific knowledge and progress was based upon logical analysis and empirical observation. Instead, Kuhn proposed a social and historical understanding of scientific knowledge, grounded in tradition and community. He used Wittgenstein's grammatical term "paradigm" for this cluster of previously accepted knowledge, theories and procedures of inquiry. Most of the time scientists operate in a context of a paradigm of "normal science" which he described as "research firmly based upon one or more past scientific achievements, achievements that some particular scientific community acknowledges for a time as supplying the foundation for its further practice."[15] Paradigms function to guide new research and provide a background against which questions can be asked and answered within a specific discipline at a particular time. Kuhn's revolutionary thesis was that at times of crisis within a scientific discipline, the way forward to new knowledge does not come merely from observation, logic and application of scientific methods but from a "paradigm shift" which is communal and value-laden. It is not as if scientists in times of revolution completely ignore reason, logic and observation, but these alone are not enough to explain the development of new paradigms in science. A classic example of a paradigm shift in the history of science, one that Kuhn returns to often, is the change from an earth-centered (Ptolemaic) to a sun-centered (Copernican) model of the solar system.

An important theme in Kuhn's philosophy of science is his notion of incommensurability. Comparing rival paradigms within a scientific tradition to different natural languages, Kuhn's thesis of paradigm incommensurability reveals the difficulties facing scientists from rival pre- and post-revolutionary "normal science" in understanding each other, including their key terms and forms of argument.[16] For example, the word *planet* means something different in a Ptolematic model of the cosmos compared to the one we all believe today, in which planets are small bodies that orbit a star and do not give off their own light. In an earth-centered model, the planets are heavenly bodies that wander about in the night sky, rather than follow a regular pattern of movement like the sun, moon and most of the stars. The English word *planet* in fact comes from the Greek word *planetos*, "one who wanders." Thus the debate between these two models of the cosmos already includes a debate about just what a planet really is. Yet unlike many of those who take up his ideas in more relativistic ways, Kuhn himself did not find this incommensurability to be complete. The translation problem between paradigms is difficult, but not impossible. "Since new paradigms are born from old ones, they ordinarily incorporate much of the vocabulary and apparatus, both conceptual and manipulative, that the traditional paradigm had previously employed. But they seldom employ these borrowed elements in quite the traditional way."[17] Kuhn argued on historical grounds that learning a science is not a set of rules, observations and techniques. It is more like learning a language according to Wittgenstein's philosophy: it is entering into a way of life. In his later philosophy (which was an ongoing struggle with his blockbuster of 1962), Kuhn continued to make this point in different ways. Noting that "the heavens of the Greeks were irreducibly different from ours" because of their different conceptual schemes, "that does not mean that one cannot, with sufficient patience and effort, discover the categories of another culture or of an earlier stage of one's own. But it does indicate that discovery is required and that hermeneutic interpretation . . . is how such discovering is done."[18] The move from a logic of science to a hermeneutics of science is a sign of the postmodern.

Kuhn's philosophy of science called into question the heart of modernity's metanarrative: the universal and trans-historical rationality of natural science. While he never embraced the term *postmodern* for himself, his exceedingly influential monograph provided a powerful impetus to postmodern thought. Some of those who followed Kuhn did not think he was radical enough and pushed his views in a more relativistic direction. One famous philosopher who did this, and who accepted the term postmodern for himself, is Richard Rorty.

Rorty. So far in our story of postmodern moments in analytic philosophy we have examined gestures, moves and traces of the postmodern. With Richard Rorty (1931-2007) analytic philosophy goes fully and clearly postmodern. He is not the only philosopher we could discuss under this rubric, but he is the most influential and important. Indeed, Rorty is America's most famous philosopher at the turn of the century, especially outside the professional guild.[19]

Rorty began his academic career studying analytic philosophy at Chicago and Yale. A distinct turn in his thinking was announced with the publication of his most programmatic work, *Philosophy and the Mirror of Nature* (1979), while he was a professor at Princeton. This work performs several rhetorical tasks. It is a survey of Western philosophy, pointing out a central problem in Philosophy (with a capital *P*) and Epistemology (capital *E*) which Rorty seeks to overcome. Putting the capital letters on these words, as Rorty sometimes does, is a way to indicate his special sense of the terms. He self-consciously follows Wittgenstein, Heidegger and especially John Dewey in seeking to overcome or dispense with philosophical activity altogether (as normally understood). Rorty embraces instead a pragmatist theory of truth and Quine's holistic philosophy of language, along with a relativist ("strong") reading of Kuhn's incommensurability thesis. The result is his unique form of neopragmatism which is not only postmodern but "post-philosophy."

In *Mirror of Nature,* Rorty traces the fundamental error of Philosophy back to Plato's quest for Truth (capital *T*) above and beyond the vicissitudes of flesh and language. The epistemological tradition of Western philosophy comes in for trenchant criticism, especially in the variety of ways in which epistemology (understood as a kind of "normal science" in Kuhn's terms) has assumed that mind and world are distinct. A key aspect of this paradigm is the goal of philosophy to help mind "mirror nature," i.e., to get a clear picture of reality which will then "correspond" to the facts and so count as Truth. That long tradition in Western thought that has sought a definite and universal theory of knowledge based on a correspondence theory of truth (what Rorty labels Philosophy and Epistemology) has failed in its attempt, not least because of mind's failure to mirror nature. Having noted this futile quest for a "representational" Epistemology, Rorty himself insists that he has no specific theory of truth, and rejects any essence or true goal for philosophical activity. He contrasts great systematic philosophers (who seek Truth and engage in Epistemology) with "edifying philosophers" who are more like poets than scientists. "Great systematic philosophers are constructive and offer arguments. Great edifying philosophers are reactive and offer satires, parodies, aphorisms."[20] Just because Philosophy so understood is deeply flawed, Rorty refuses to do Epistemology and claims no special theory of truth. Edifying philosophers such as himself "refuse to present themselves as having found out any objective truth (about, say, what philosophy is). They present themselves as doing something different from, and more important than, offering accurate representations of how things are."[21]

It was open to Rorty, having given this anti-Epistemology argument, to follow the rhetorical fashion of some continental philosophers and claim that he now wanted to engage in "epistemology without Epistemology." When we understand epistemology not as a definite theory of knowledge but as an investigation of the character *and limits* of human knowing (in the tradition of Kant), it is obvious that Rorty continued to work in epistemology for the rest of his career.[22] Instead of making this rhetorical move, however, he claimed that he was simply going to change the subject, not talk about epistemology at all, and replace it with "hermeneutics." He felt other things were more important than philosophy and engaged the larger culture with scintillating essays on politics, art and society. Ironically, he was on his way to becoming the best known philosopher in America.

Rorty left the rarified air of the philosophy department at Princeton, becoming a professor of humanities at Virginia and later of comparative literature at Stanford. It is interesting to compare his career to that of Nelson Goodman's (1906-1998).[23] Like Rorty, Goodman was trained in the tradition of logical pragmatism we discussed earlier. Like him, Goodman adopted a pragmatic theory of truth and Quine's holistic philosophy of language. In a book published in 1978, *Ways of Worldmaking*, Goodman came to pretty much the same conclusions as Rorty did in his book.[24] But Goodman nowhere trumpeted an end to philosophy. He did not seek to change the subject and stop talking about epistemology. Goodman did not take up the whole sweep of Western philosophy à la Heidegger and seek to overcome its deepest flaws. But his book is just as postmodern, just as "radical," as Rorty's own. As such he is another good example of a postmodern analytic philosopher—but one who stayed in his philosophy department.

Since 1979 Rorty has consistently maintained his "post-philosophical" approach to philosophy. A brilliant thinker with a sparkling style and subtle wit, Rorty's essays are always worth reading. He has specifically engaged the larger culture outside of the philosophical guild in a way that is readable, thoughtful and learned. Although he is an analytic philosopher, he came to a conception of philosophy as an open conversation without Truth, Epistemology or fixed rules—a conception at odds with the analytic tradition to say the least. In his book *Contingency, Irony and Solidarity* (1989), Rorty came to identify his attitude toward epistemological theory as characterized by "irony." Because there is a perceived conflict between his argument for the contingency of language, self and community, and his passionate embrace of liberal political values, irony becomes the mediating proposal that allows the liberal intellectual to embrace both contingency and solidarity. The "ironist" fulfills three conditions: (1) "radical and continuing doubts about the final vocabulary she currently uses," (2) a realization "that argument phrased in her present vocabulary can neither underwrite nor dissolve these doubts," and (3) "insofar as she philosophizes about her situation, she does not think that

her vocabulary is closer to reality than others."[25] In this way Rorty continued to insist upon a kind of "metaphysical quietism" in the face of any
nagging questions about epistemology.[26]

Rorty's philosophy has received sustained criticism over the years. His
approach to truth does have serious problems, which critics have not
been slow to point out.[27] To use an analogy from science, Rorty seems
interested only in technology, not in science. In other words, we think
the main problem with his view of truth is his firm embrace of pragmatism. Rorty himself embraces this "just technology" analogy:

> The strong textualist [like Rorty] simply asks himself the same ques-
> tion about a text which the engineer or the physicist asks himself
> about a puzzling physical object: how shall I describe this in order to
> get it to do what I want?[28]

Despite Rorty's throwaway use of the label "physicist" this is *not* how a
natural scientist tends to think: she typically wants to discover the truth
(in a nonpragmatic sense) about the object, not merely get more technology. On the other hand, to be fair to him and so *not* to play the strong
textualist card, some philosophers think Rorty's viewpoint can be rather
easily dismissed as a version of cultural relativism. In fact, Rorty anticipated this objection already in 1979, in his presidential address to the
American Philosophical Association.[29] He considers this question: Why
isn't his version of neopragmatism another kind of epistemological relativism?

> "Relativism" is the view that every belief on a certain topic, or perhaps
> about any topic, is as good as every other. No one holds this view . . .
> The philosophers who get called "relativists" are those who say that
> the grounds for choosing between such opinions are less algorithmic
> than had been thought.[30]

"Relativism" is a disturbing charge, he argued, only if it applies to *real*
theories, that is, not philosophical ones (which we can and should dispense with in favor of what is useful) but important ones on topics like
politics, literature or science. People do, of course, seek larger worldviews
which go beyond specific theories in "real" subjects. "But this holistic
process of re-adjustment is just muddling through on a large scale. It has
nothing to do with the Platonic-Kantian notion of grounding [an Episte-
mology]."[31] Pragmatism and relativism are not the same thing. Since the

pragmatist wants to translate questions of truth into questions of what is useful, she does not believe that all theories or conclusions are equally good. In other words, while Rorty might be a "relativist" on some definition (especially an analytic one), he is not a relativist on a self-critical pragmatic definition.[32]

Rorty's influential and widely discussed work, and that of other postmodern analytic philosophers, has opened up a space for "postanalytic" philosophy in the English speaking world.[33] Intellectuals engaged in this style of philosophy can appreciate the technicalities of the analytic tradition for some tasks, but reject its claim to be the best or only right kind of philosophy. Postanalytic philosophers are multidisciplinary and multicultural. They feel free to use essays, stories, novels and biographies to advance their philosophical conversations. A good example of this kind of move is Ray Monk, who has written a superb intellectual biography of Wittgenstein and a major two-volume biography of Russell.[34] Monk is in fact a professor at the Center for Post-Analytic Philosophy at Southampton University in England.

While Rorty grew less happy with the label "postmodern" in the latter days of his career (like just about every major philosopher), he is nevertheless the best-known example of postmodern analytic philosophy. Rorty attacks modernity in its guise as a quest for Truth in the discourse of Epistemology and Philosophy. He inhabits an important postmodern space in contemporary American philosophy. In this section we have also pointed out that as analytic philosophy made its journey to postmodernity, even mainstream analytic philosophers make some postmodern moves. There are postmodern themes in analytic philosophy in the second half of the twentieth century. Analytic philosophers today take up arguments and positions that look and sound postmodern even while rejecting that label.

Postmodern Themes in Continental Philosophy

The truth is that apart from Lyotard, very few influential philosophers want to be described as "postmodern." The word has simply become so trendy, so loose, so widely used to talk about all kinds of things that it has almost become useless. The problem is that we really have no better umbrella term for thinkers like the ones we will now canvass in French

philosophy. There is enough in common, enough similarity in their gestures of refusal toward modernity, that we are right to group them
together. So in this book the term postmodern does not refer narrowly to
the thought of Lyotard alone, but also to the poststructuralism of Foucault, the deconstruction of Derrida, and the postontological ethical philosophy of Levinas.

Levinas. Emmanuel Levinas (1906-1995) has not always been recognized as the important and influential philosopher he was for French
phenomenology and postmodern philosophy.[35] An early student of
Heidegger and a late student of Husserl, Levinas introduced the work
of Husserl to the French speaking world (including Sartre) in 1930.[36]
His chief philosophical monographs *Totality and Infinity* (1961) and
Otherwise than Being (1974) are now understood to be central statements
of postmodern thought. In moving phenomenology away from Heidegger and toward a postontological ethic of the Other, Levinas played an
important role in the thought of Ricoeur, Lyotard and Derrida, among
others. While not considered a major thinker in Paris until late in his
life, at the end of the twentieth century he became a rather popular figure for serious philosophical engagement. This is a result of his consistent focus on the phenomenology of Heidegger and Husserl (his
teachers), and on the concrete ethical situation, that is, on the true situation of our life with others as a subject for phenomenology beyond
Heidegger's ontology. He thus refused to join the fashionable trends of
French postmodernity. By the end of the century, when these extreme
postmodern trends had played themselves out and phenomenology
continued, the centrality and importance of Levinas' work was rediscovered by continental philosophers.

Levinas was born in Lithuania in 1906 to Jewish parents. In 1923 he
went to the University of Strasbourg to study philosophy and spent a year
(1928-1929) at Freiburg where he was one of the last students of Husserl.
He also studied with Heidegger and was greatly impressed by the newly
published *Being and Time*, a work which he continued to think of as one
of the classics of Western philosophy. After completing his doctorate and
publishing his thesis on Husserl's phenomenology, Levinas moved to
Paris and taught philosophy at a small Jewish institute.[37] After becoming
a French citizen and joining the war effort, he was captured and spent

five years in a Nazi labor camp. During the horrors of the Holocaust, most of his family members, including his mother, father, mother-in-law and brothers, were murdered. Thanks to his friends back in Paris, his wife and children were hidden by nuns in a convent in the south of France, and survived the war.

The Holocaust affected Levinas for the rest of his life, as anyone can understand. He vowed never to set foot in Germany again (even in 1983 when he was awarded the Karl Jaspers prize in philosophy he did not go back—his son accepted it for him). The war, the *stalag*, the Holocaust, Heidegger's involvement with the Nazis—Levinas took all of these things with him into his philosophical labors. These experiences pushed Levinas's thought into closer contact with the embodied, fragile and vulnerable situation of human existence together with others. Some of his central arguments and terminology can be seen already in a small book he began to write in the labor camps: *Existence and the Existents* (1947). But his major philosophical work was yet to come.

After the war Levinas continued to work with Jewish intellectuals in Paris and teach philosophy at a Jewish institution. He studied the Talmud thoroughly with a master, and he published a number of essays on Talmudic, biblical and Jewish subjects. These are his writings "to the Hebrews." In philosophy he continued to use the methods he had learned in phenomenology, although there is often significant overlap between his writings "to the Greeks" (philosophers) and his Jewish-biblical writings. His continued struggle with Heidegger, Husserl and phenomenology soon culminated in his best known work: *Totality and Infinity* (1961). This book also earned him his higher doctorate, and he took up a philosophy chair at a provincial university (Poitiers) soon thereafter. Eventually he became professor of philosophy at the new University of Paris-Nanterre, where he worked with Ricoeur and Lyotard.

In *Totality and Infinity* the central themes of Levinas's philosophy are on display. What is particularly important for Levinas is a phenomenological analysis of the Other as an enigma rather than a phenomenon, an analysis which will provide a new ethical "first philosophy."[38] The face and voice of the Other must not be reduced to the system of the Same, to me and my consciousness. For Levinas, the problem with the phenomenology of Husserl, and even Heidegger, was the focus on the consciousness of the individual, with and to whom the objects (phenomena) of the world appear. He objected to the insularity and self-orientation of this kind of ontology. There is no place for the otherness or "alterity" of the Other in the totalizing metaphysics of Western tradition, including Heidegger's phenomenology: "Western philosophy has most often been an ontology: a reduction of the Other to the same by interposition of a middle and neutral term that ensures the comprehension of being."[39] In place of this totality that obliterates the alterity of the Other, Levinas sought a new approach which would give full weight to the face, the enigma, the presence of the Other (or "neighbor" as this sometimes appears).[40] In order to do this, he struggled to explain the relationship with the Other in a way that did not lead back to classical philosophy or even phenomenology—he sought a relation to the Other that was not a comprehension or a representation.

Levinas developed a kind of proto-ontological analysis of the face and voice of the Other, which he often compared to the transcendence of God. He explicitly refers to Descartes's ontological argument in the third Meditation, where the idea of the Infinite (God) exceeds the capacities of human thought and so must be from outside my mind, outside my world, from God alone.[41] Like the Infinite in Descartes, for Levinas the call and face of the Other creates an infinite ethical obligation upon me. The voice or face of the Other breaks into and interrupts the sameness of my consciousness, of my representation of the world to myself in experience. The Other is the in-breaking of the infinite which is before and beyond human concepts. Levinas translates the transcendence of God into the utterly concrete alterity of the Other in real-life situations. Another model of this for him was the Good in Plato's Republic, which is beyond all concepts and ideas (Forms).[42] This analysis of the absolute alterity of the Other provided Levinas with a kind of postontological analysis of a fundamental relation that transcends human systems of ethics or justice (this transcendent relation is not, however, some kind of classical foundation from which a totalizing system can be built). The Other is an experience which is not an experience, an encounter which is not an event, so that the infinite moral call of the Other upon me cannot be explained away or collapsed back into a system of morality. In other words, face of the Other creates a fissure in the system of the Same. "A calling into question of the Same—which cannot occur within the egoistic spontaneity of the Same—is brought about by the Other. We name this calling into question of my spontaneity by the presence of the Other *ethics*."[43] In Levinas, ethics is not a system of right and wrong: the ethical is an analysis of a disruptive—not conceptual—relation, which breaks into the self-oriented system of my freedom ("spontaneity"). The title of his books speaks to this central theme: the voice of the Other breaks into the totalizing system of my world as the infinite erupting into the finite.

Although some Christians have interpreted personal encounter with the Other in Levinas in terms of a personal encounter with God, Levinas does not follow Buber along this path. True, at one point Levinas characterizes the relationship between the self and the Other as "religion," and even says that "God is the Other."[44] But these sayings are misleading. In *Nine Talmudic Readings* Levinas admits that his philosophy is based on his religion, but only because in both he is interested in "the *approach* to transcendence," not because he conflates theology and philosophy.[45] Indeed, for Levinas God has a double alterity, an excess of otherness, which leaves only a *trace* in our speech and world.[46] God should not be spoken to as You (*pace* Buber), as such a move would undermine the transcendence of the Holy One, bringing God back into the realm of metaphysics (ontotheology). Rather, we address God best by our ethical devotion to the Other; on this point, Levinas is quite antimystical. God is to be approached (*à-Dieu* he sometimes put it) but never reached in human language or situations.[47] The "rupture" of modernity or of law by a face-to-face relationship with the neighbor marks "the approach of an infinite God."[48]

Totality and Infinity increased Levinas's reputation among professional philosophers. In 1964 the relatively unknown younger philosopher, Jacques Derrida, wrote a two-part analysis of Levinas which was the first substantial French discussion of his philosophy.[49] A sign of his new status was his election to a chair in philosophy at the Sorbonne. He retired in 1973, but continued teaching until 1980. During this period he published his second major work, *Otherwise Than Being or Beyond Essence* (1974). In this book Levinas both continues and alters his earlier ethical-philosophical analysis of the enigma of the Other.

In *Otherwise Than Being* Levinas fractures language and phenomenology in his struggle to express the fundamental experience of self and other, a ground or a place (which is not a *locus*) between self and Other. He breaks apart words with hyphens and italics, and uses everyday words in strange, even "barbarous" ways.[50] Most commentators trace at least an aspect of this new approach to the criticism Derrida gave *Totality and Infinity*. Derrida was particularly critical of Levinas's use of language, arguing that in fact it showed he was not making a clean break from the metaphysics of the West and the ontology of the same.[51] In *Otherwise Than Being* Levinas is clearly concerned, from the start, with his language use. This may be why he shifts in his analysis of the situation of the self and the Other from visual to linguistic analogies. The primordial situation of encounter with the neighbor (a term now used more openly) is called Saying; while our conceptual apperception and organization of this responsibility is the Said.[52] In the primordial ethical encounter with the neighbor which is the Saying, Levinas now insisted that even my own self, the "me," is disrupted by the appearance and call of the Other. Earlier in his career, for example in *On Escape* (1935), a meditation written by a Jew in Europe during the rise of fascism, Levinas opens with a more traditional position. He begins with the claim made by traditional Western philosophy that discord between human existence and the brutal facticity of being in the world does not "break up the unity of the 'I'" which "closes on and rests upon itself."[53] Twenty-two years and a bloody war later, one of his main points is the disruption, the fissure, the breakdown of the smooth circularity of the self in the Saying-event, in the face of the Other. He even calls this being taken "hostage" by the neighbor in the Saying-event:

> This book has exposed the signification of subjectivity in the extraordinary death or the being without regard for death. The signification of my responsibility for what escapes my freedom is the defeat or defecting of the unity of transcendental apperception. . . . This book has exposed my passivity, passivity as the-one-for-the-other . . . to the extent of [my] being the-one-being-hostage-for-the-other.[54]

In *Otherwise Than Being* Levinas was, more ever than before, struggling with language and method. He was struggling to bring to expression a basis which is not a foundation, a moment in time which is not a fixed and inevitable point. To do so he wrestles with his language, never sure of just how to put things. We are reminded of the opening lines of the ancient and beautiful Chinese classic, the *Tao Te Ching* (or *Dao de jing*):

The Dao which can be uttered (dao-ed) is not the eternal Dao;

The name which can be named is not the eternal Name;

The Nameless was the beginning of everything.

The Named is the mother of ten thousand things.[55]

The author(s) of this text, named by tradition as Lao Tzu (or Laozi, "ancient teacher") was aware that his language was self-referentially foolish, since he was speaking about that which cannot be brought into language, that which is both Named and Nameless. Levinas must have felt something along these lines. Lao Tzu also knew "One who speaks does not know; one who knows does not speak," thus proving that he knows nothing since he is compelled as teacher to speak.[56] Levinas, too, knew the performative contradictions inherent in his effort to speak of the enigma of the Other which cannot be named.

Levinas died on Christmas Day, 1995, when he was almost ninety years old. A memorial service was held in Paris; the oration was given by Jacques Derrida.[57]

Foucault. One of the reasons for a revival of interest in the work of Levinas at the turn of the century lies in his resistance to the fashionable intellectual trends in Paris during the "radical" days of the "generation of 1968."[58] Michel Foucault (1926-1984) was a captain of that avant-garde, one of the most famous intellectuals in Paris, and one who enjoyed a kind of American rock star status for a time.[59] His wide ranging work was extensively discussed and influential in many disciplines, including law, literature, feminist theory, social theory, history, psychology, sociology, aesthetics, science studies, ethics, politics and philosophy. His name is intimately connected with French postmodern or poststructuralist thought, a viewpoint still dominant in many university departments across the globe.

It is difficult to characterize Foucault's thought. He was not a systematic thinker, and he changed his style, subject and vocabulary over time. He consistently remained interested in the history of social systems and the ways that individuals and institutions functioned within a social space created by often unseen, unconscious codes or systems: "discursive formations" that are independent of the intentions or beliefs of individuals.

Although trained in Marxist and existentialist philosophies, and fully aware of French structuralism, he soon left them all behind to develop his own unique approach—one which was always a work in process, never fixed or complete, never whole. At one point he even wrote about his own writing: "I am no doubt not the only one who writes in order to have no face. Do not ask who I am and do not ask me to remain the same."[60] Like an actor on a stage, each of Foucault's interviews and lectures is a rhetorical performance—and he was brilliant. According to his own philosophy and practice, there is no "real person" behind the *persona,* and Foucault's thought never constituted a fixed philosophical system. We will provide a brief review of his life and work covering three key phases in his historical approach: archaeology, genealogy and the ethics/aesthetics of the self.

Born in Poitiers in 1926 to a middle-class family, Foucault was an outstanding student who studied philosophy in Paris during the high days of Hegel and Marx in French philosophy. Feeling restricted in Parisian society(!), he lectured for years at foreign universities in Sweden and Germany, working on his dissertation. His doctoral thesis is a massive, wide-ranging and brilliant study of the history of madness (1961).[61] The methodology of this book lies in the tradition of the history of the social sciences, or as they say in Paris, *sciences humaines.* In this period of French intellectual life, the human sciences dominated philosophy through the popularity of French structuralism and cultural effects like the new "information age" of the computer.[62] Foucault's *History of Madness* examines the "classical" age (roughly 1650-1800), a time of developing Enlightenment reason in Europe. The book is a challenge to the modern medical conception of the "mentally ill," for he argues that earlier cultures regarded madness not as an illness but as a choice in favor of unreason. Since an enlightened age had no place for people of such unreason, they created institutions to exclude and bind them away from "normal" people.

Foucault followed this work with another study in the history of science, this time medicine: *The Birth of the Clinic* (1963). Already Foucault's methodology changed and became much more structuralist. The subtitle of the volume is "an archaeology of medical perception," and Foucault is interested in the ways that language, society and conceptual structures inscribe and enforce the practice of medicine. He called these structures "epistemes" from the Greek word for science, and they are quite similar to Kuhn's paradigms. He quickly followed it with two more books exploring this new history of paradigms approach or "archaeology": *The Order of Things: An Archaeology of the Human Sciences* (1966) and *The Archaeology of Knowledge* (1969). Foucault assumed that being and the Human (or "Man" as an object of the human sciences) have no fixed essence, no "nature" given to them by God or Reason. His archaeology is a historical examination of the multiple and conflicting ways in which societies and individuals give order to their world and to themselves. This ordering or code is not the product of individual belief or intention: like other structuralists Foucault embraced the death of humanism (especially existentialism) and the end of the Human or "the death of Man." Making reference to linguistics, Levi-Strauss, the logic of Russell and Wittgenstein, the information age and formalism in general, Foucault claimed in a 1966 interview that the new structuralism is "incompatible with humanism" as it was found in Hegel, Marx and Sartre. The classical age "constructed the being of the Human [*l'homme*] as an object of knowledge in the human sciences," as demonstrated in his recent books, but such a concept was no longer relevant (he was speaking in the revolutionary '60s).[63] The surety with which Foucault declares the death of the Human in 1966 is ironic just because the structuralism he is so confident in will soon be dead—and he will be one of its killers.

Foucault's writings and brilliant lectures in the 1960s won him great respect among his fellow French intellectuals. He was a vocal and active member of the radical political left in Paris and a fixture of Parisian cultural life. The faculty of the prestigious Collège de France voted to create for him a new chair in the History of Systems of Thought. Foucault was at the center of the rise of French poststructuralism in the 1970s. While still interested in the ways humans order their world and their selves in historically contingent systems, Foucault's next phase was inspired by Nietzsche. Still very much an historian, he changed his method of analysis from "archaeology" to "genealogy." Abandoning all hope of metaphysics, Truth or an essence to the Human, genealogy traces the way in which power and the body are played out in contingent, local systems of discourse. Power is not in this new phase the result of the individual's choice (capitalism), the State (Hegel) or the class (Marxism): power in this postmodern move is a way of organizing behaviors through communication and observation, which he called "discipline." Discipline in his special sense "trains" the "moving, confused, useless multitudes of bodies and forces them into a multiplicity of individual elements."[64] Discipline makes individuals; it creates the subject by means of communication, discursive practices and "observation." These systems are more concrete and *embodied* than the earlier "episteme," more involved in technical work, institutions, regularization of behaviors and ways of communication that may or may not be verbal. For Foucault is now focusing on systems of power that are embodied, the "biopolitics" which treats the lives/bodies of the masses as a kind of factory.[65]

Foucault makes the radical claim that divisions between truth and untruth, good and evil, pleasure and unhappiness are always already implicit systems of power and individuation. He closely ties the discursive practices of science, ethics, justice and the like to systems of social control. Thus he begins to speak of power/knowledge, not equating them but noting their mutual implications. Genealogy is not merely a tool for understanding, either. It helps us disrupt the system of control in society. "We can give the name 'genealogy' to this coupling together of scholarly erudition and local memories, which allows us to constitute a historical knowledge in contemporary tactics."[66] Genealogy explores the inevitable incoherencies and fissures in the system of knowledge/power, looking to individual and local sources of counter-knowledge to exploit them on behalf of autonomy. It "has to fight the power-effects of any discourse that is regarded as scientific."[67]

Discipline and Punish (1975) is his best example of such a genealogical analysis and questioning of a particular discursive practice: the prison. Undermining the typical narrative of progress in the development of the prison system, Foucault argues that the prison was simply more efficient, more in keeping with the new "disciplinary society" of the eighteenth century—not a moral improvement. His model and metaphor for this kind of surveillance of the self by society is Jeremy Bentham's Panopticon, an "ideal" prison in which the inmates would always be watched and thus their behaviors always monitored. In the Panopticon, "Power has its principle not so much in a person as in a certain concerted distribution of bodies, surfaces, lights, gazes."[68] The surveillance of the disciplinary society, which soon reached far beyond just the prison, he relates to the new sciences of criminology and social psychology; this could be further extended to educational or business theory, which design schools, factories, offices and so on. Changes in systems of thought (new sciences) are intimately caught up with changes in nondiscursive systems of behaviors, especially the modern means of controlling human bodies, images, spaces and the like. Through biopolitics the modern or "normalizing" society inscribes the bodies of the masses through discipline (which is related to the "organism" or individual body) and regimen (related to the "population" or body politic). Foucault soon became interested in the genealogy of sexuality because "sexuality represents the precise point where the disciplinary and the regulatory, the body and the population, are articulated."[69]

He began a set of books *The History of Sexuality* with an introduction in 1976. Foucault rejected the common sense view that male and female are biologically necessary binary opposites. There is a vast multiplicity of sexuality and bodily diversity, and genealogy can uncover these differing and contingent disciplines and regularities. The norm of discipline (toward the body) and the norm of regulation (of the population) have to be studied through genealogy to uncover the various possibilities and technologies of self-expression and social control which are played out in the human body.

This new postmodern understanding of power/knowledge and biopolitics led Foucault to a new theory of government in the late 1970s. Since discipline as power/knowledge creates individuality and subjectivity, so "governmentality" implies a relationship of the self to the self. This new tool or concept in the analysis of power "cover[s] a whole range of practices that constitute, define, organize, and instrumentalize the strategies that individuals can use in dealing with each other."[70] The triad of government-discipline-ethics provides the horizon for Foucault's last approach: an ethics or aesthetics of the self. The normal-science philosophy of the academy has come to an end, but philosophy continues in this "ethical" way in the lives of everyday individuals. "The displacement and transformation of frameworks of thinking, the changing of received values and all the work that has been done to think otherwise, to do something else, to become other than what one is—that, too, is philosophy."[71] Taking up this new approach, Foucault writes the next two volumes of his *History of Sexuality* in a quite different style. *The Use of Pleasure* and *The Care of the Self*, published a few months before his death, provide a genealogy of the "aesthetics of existence" with particular expression to the varying aesthetics of the body and technologies of the self found in ancient Greece and Rome (such as Socrates in *The Symposium*), including early Christian writers like Gregory of Nyssa (e.g., his *Treatise on Virginity*). The personal and political upshot of this study is a new concern for ethics as he understood it. My own body becomes an artistic means of self-expression, especially when I come to grasp the self as project (the "hermeneutics of the self") and so to transgress the discipline and governmentality which seeks to inscribe my body and sexuality.[72]

At the height of his international fame Foucault contracted the new HIV virus and soon began to fail in health. He died in Paris in the summer of 1984. At an impromptu memorial service outside the hospital, his friend, the philosopher Gilles Deleuze, read to the crowd from *The Use of Pleasure*.

Foucault's thought is a radical form of postmodern, poststructuralist philosophy done by means of a "history of the present," an archaeology or genealogy of contemporary social structures, codes and mores. He combined a large number of disciplines in his constant quest to discover the various ways in which humans organize a world without Being. His Nietzschean narratives bring historical-critical analysis to the always contingent, power-laden discourse of discipline, governmentality and the care of the self as a free aesthetics of embodiment, a will to aesthetics in a poetry-of-the-body ("ethics"). Thus Foucault's final philosophy is a struggle "for new practices of freedom, . . . a cry of the spirit."[73]

Foucault never argues for atheism, he simply presumes it, just as he presumes the end of the Human and the absence of any Platonic Truth, any Kantian categorical imperative, or any Romantic experience of the Infinite. These are presuppositions which enter into his history/philosophy, rather than results or conclusions he arrives at through argument. He follows Nietzsche in a transvaluation of values; a valuing of the autonomy of a "hermeneutics of the self" which has to be constructed by the creative individual. In this Nietzschean ethics one does the truth and creates the good through self-expression, transgressing the biopolitics of society through a self-creative aesthetics of one's body. The contrast between this ethic and the way of the cross as a disciple of Jesus could hardly be more stark.

Derrida. If the center of philosophical reflection for the final philosophy of Foucault was the body, for Jacques Derrida (1930-2004) it was the text.[74] After Foucault's death, Derrida was the most influential and world-famous philosopher from France—at least outside Paris, where he did not always fit in with the philosophical elite. Derrida was the philosopher of the sign, the letter, the text, *the written*. As is only fitting, the impact of his thought in other disciplines was first felt in literary theory. While in Paris, Derrida was one philosopher among others, but his fame in North America spread like wildfire in the humanities starting in the 1970s. Derrida frequently came to America to study, then to attend conferences, and finally to lecture at major universities (almost never as a guest of the philosophy departments, however, where analytic philosophy is regnant).

Derrida's overwhelming literary-philosophical *oeuvre* is simply astonishing and very daunting for the beginner.[75] Not least of the problems involved in reading Derrida is his style. As a philosopher with powerful interests in avant-garde literature, art and poetry, possessing a keen sense of rhetoric as well as sensitivity to the event of reading/hearing and the multiple effects they produce, Derrida's style is highly original and aesthetic. He is often flamboyant and almost always difficult to follow. His response to the American philosopher John Searle (an unfortunate set of texts in which both thinkers talk past each other) is a good example of his sometimes bizarre style and "humor" (the whole of *Glas* being another much longer example).[76] Such textual or rhetorical acrobatics usually serve a purpose, however, but on no account should one expect traditional, straightforward academic language and arguments from him. He is usually better in interviews, discussions and orations to the general public (such as memorial lectures). Derrida is capable of perfectly clear prose, as his earliest work testifies. Written for the French philosophical establishment, and all on Husserl, these works develop his method of approach and basic assumptions which he then extended and applied the rest of his career.[77]

Derrida was born a French citizen in Algeria to Sephardic Jewish parents.[78] This heritage made him doubly an outsider in Parisian culture, being Jewish and from a former colony in Africa. The young Jackie (later he changed his first name to Jacques) loved literature and reading, and was an excellent student. He became interested in philosophy listening to a radio program about Camus. He graduated from high school (lycée) in 1948 and moved to Paris to attend a preparatory college in philosophy. He studied at the E. N. S. (École Normale Supérieure), finally passing his state examination in philosophy in 1957. His wrote a master's thesis titled *The Problem of Genesis in Husserl's Philosophy* (1954). A thesis for his first doctorate was an introduction to a new French translation of a fragment from Husserl, *Edmund Husserl's Origin of Geometry: An Introduction* (1962). This work won the young philosopher a prestigious prize in epistemology (the Jean Cavailles Prize). His final Husserl phase was capped by the publication of *Speech and Phenomena* (1967), a book in which he works out the main themes of the philosophical strategies he would then employ for almost forty years.

While working on his second doctorate he taught philosophy at E. N. S. for twenty years and lectured at prestigious American universities (as noted above, he was the guest of humanities, human sciences or literature departments). Derrida's new style did not sit well with the philosophical establishment, and he did not defend his higher doctorate or habilitation until 1980. Meanwhile in the miracle year *(annis mirabilis)* of 1967, his second son Jean was born and he published three books that would establish his new postmodern style: *Speech and Phenomena, Of Grammatology* and *Writing and Difference* (a collection of his early essays). If that were not enough, the year before, Derrida gave a lecture at Johns Hopkins University that launched his career in America. "Structure, Sign and Play in the Discourse of the Humanities" was a powerful deconstruction of then-popular French structuralism (especially Levi-Strauss), written in Derrida's new playful, rhetorical style.[79]

In 1984 Derrida moved to his new position as director of studies at the École des hautes études en sciences sociales (School for Advanced Studies in the Social Sciences). Derrida was never elected to a chair in philosophy in France. As one sign of his ambiguous relationship with the guild of philosophers, there was quite a to-do surrounding his honorary doctorate from Cambridge University in 1992, with philosophers inside and outside the university protesting in private and in print. Such was Derrida's cultural fame that this event earned a paragraph in *Newsweek* under the heading "Doctor deconstructo."[80]

As we have indicated, Derrida's basic approach was worked out philosophically in his early books on Husserl and in his struggle with Heidegger's texts. Although he commented on a vast range of philosophical texts in the Western tradition, Heidegger was his chief mentor. To take two examples, his own philosophical method—which he refused to define or call a method—is generally called "deconstruction," a word he took from Heidegger's *Being and Time*. Another example is his key term *différance*, a concept that is the repetition in the context of French structuralism of what Heidegger called the "ontological difference," the ineffable and inconceivable gap between Being itself and beings.[81] Thus différance is also fundamentally Heideggerian. In the short space left to us we will introduce a few of Derrida's key terms and typical moves which keep repeating and disseminating throughout his writings after the breakthrough of the 1960s. In this way we hope to explain and give context to two of his most outrageous and infamous claims: that writing comes before speech, and that there is nothing outside the text.

Derrida is more than any other thinker a philosopher of the *written*. The influence of poetry, art, literature and film is clear in his many writings on these texts (and yes, buildings, behaviors and film count as "texts" for him). Derrida takes several assumptions from French structuralism into his philosophy. He always understands language as a system of signs, a conception of "system" he uses just as freely on art, film, architecture or ethics. Equally important is that the meaning of any sign is arbitrary and has its place within the system of signs because of its *difference* from other signs. Sounds can be used to communicate by intelligent animals only because the sounds are different. Prairie dogs make a unique sound, different from the others, to signal (sign) that a predator is in the air—run for cover! Letters and sounds are used by humans to communicate only because they are different. The text communicates because its written signs are different from each other. Finally, like other (post-)structuralists, Derrida looks for binary oppositions in the deep structures of human thought/behavior/artifacts.

Any human communication thus takes place through a medium.

There is no immediate communication, no unmediated experience, however sublime. Derrida's word for this mediation is différance, a new word
now found in dictionaries that combines the meanings of differ (as in
different) and defer (as in deferral).[82] This new and special word is different from the normal French word for "differ" only by the letter *a*—a difference in *spelling* which cannot be heard in *oral* French. This is yet one
more sign—if we needed it—that Derrida is a philosopher of the written,
of the graphic, of the sign. By différance Derrida gestures toward the
(Heideggerian) event which is not an event of difference and absence in
the text itself, whose multiple effects inscribe the differences and defer-
ments in the sign. The text or sign is always different from, and takes
place after, that which it signifies. As an artifact, the sign can always be
re-created in new contexts, with very different meanings. Derrida uses
this fact of repetition to great effect, calling it "supplement" and "dissemination." "The same is here called supplement, another name for différance," he wrote, and again "this movement of play . . . is the movement
of supplementarity."[83] It is the goal of deconstruction to uncover the
always, already event of play in the spaces between the signs, in the margins of the text, and so to seek différance in any argument, text, system or
philosophy—and it will always be there.

We have seen several key assumptions in Derrida's philosophical strategy of reading the texts of other philosophers (or poems, or any system
of signs). First, all communication is mediated through signs. One of his
main targets is "logocentrism," the doctrine that thoughts or experiences
can be immediately *present* to the mind or heart or consciousness. The
same error under another name is called "metaphysics," which he understood as any science of presence.[84] As the science of the sign, grammatology (or deconstruction) is the study of presence-in-absence.[85] Second,
any system of signs cannot exist without difference in the signs themselves, and without a temporal gap or absence from the communicator,
speaker or artist. The final move comes when Derrida argues that
because the signs are artifacts (written letters in the case of a text), they
can be endlessly repeated, and they come already loaded with a huge
internal reference to other contexts from the past and to other uses
which they might have in the future. This third point is what Derrida
meant when he concluded in "Structure, Sign and Play" that the text has

no *center,* no transcendental signified which orders and bounds the signs within the text. "The absence of the transcendental signified extends the domain and the play of signification infinitely."[86] No text, just because it is written, can be controlled by the author. Human communication is only possible because of différance, but this same différance makes it impossible to *fix* or *control* the meaning of a text. For this reason Derrida can remark: "the sign is always a sign of the Fall."[87] Perhaps the reader will indulge us in another verse from the *Tao Te Ching?* "As soon as everyone in the world knows that the beautiful are beautiful / There is already ugliness." Ames and Hall comment on this verse: "For the Daoist, dividing up the world descriptively and prescriptively generates correlative categories that invariably entail themselves *and their antinomies.*"[88] Derrida's différance is in accord with this Daoist wisdom.

We can now state the central insight of Derrida's deconstruction or grammatology, by borrowing a term from one of Derrida's teachers, Levinas: the very conditions of the possibility of the text as human communication imply that no text can be totalized from within or from without.[89] No text can be controlled from the center, the margins or the signature at the bottom, because each sign, each trace, carries with it past and future (possible) uses. Consider this dense sentence from his lecture "Différance":

> Différance is what makes the movement of signification possible only if each element of what is said to be "present," appearing on the stage of presence, is related to something other than itself but retains the mark of a past element and already lets itself be hollowed out by the mark of its relation to a future element.[90]

If you can grasp the claims in that sentence you will have come a long way toward understanding Derrida. Now we are in a better position to hear another of Derrida's claims: writing is before oral speech. By "writing" Derrida means any human communication, which as such must be mediated by symbols, even if they are sign-language or facial expressions. As such, speech is impossible without "writing," without the play of différance.

Derrida's many books and articles are a rhetorical avant-garde play, a dancing in the spaces and margins of the texts of others. His work is impossible without other people's texts or communication simply because he refuses to take up a permanent position or system of his own. He endlessly repeats the deconstruction of other great philosophers, showing how différance is at play in the text of their arguments. We might say he lives only by eating the text of others. Perhaps now we are ready for the second infamous aphorism: "there is nothing outside the text."[91] As the larger context of this comment makes clear, and it should be read in context, Derrida is not denying that the "flesh and bones" life of the author is unimportant or uninteresting. His claim is a deeper one: the life of the author does not provide us with an Archimedean point, that is, the life of the author is not a privileged center or fixed external reference from which we can totalize the author's text and fix its meaning. There is also a second level of meaning in this claim: our so-called reality, our experience of and reference to a real world, has the qualities of textuality. This means "every referent, all reality has the structure of a differential trace, and that one cannot refer to this 'real' except in an interpretive experience."[92]

As Derrida matured as a philosopher, and in response to some of his friendly critics, he began to consider ethical and religious issues or texts. For example, his book *The Gift of Death* (1995) is a reading of Kierkegaard's reading of the command to sacrifice Isaac in Genesis. Speaking to a conference on the future of Marxism, Derrida addressed issues of social justice in the new Europe after the fall of the Berlin Wall in his book *The Specters of Marx* (1994). His rhetoric changes with age: absence becomes mourning or death, the memory of the Other, even the haunting of a specter. There was more of an emphasis on what philosophy could still do in the human situation, even given différance. Derrida could even say, "Don't think too quickly that I'm on the side of deconstruction against philosophy."[93] Some have sought to develop this positive side of his later writings.[94] One could seek the assistance of deconstruction, for example, in the cause of theology by seeking to purify its language, worship, liturgy and prayers from idolatry and/or ontotheology. In the cause of justice, deconstruction can help undermine any system of justice or power/knowledge that is totalizing and oppressive, such as sexism, nationalism/colonialism or racism. But just because Derrida always danced with différance, playing in the margins and spaces of the texts of others, his contributions to religion and ethics are rather slim pickings (but some would argue they are worth the work of gleaning).[95]

Given his interest in film and film criticism, we note that Derrida had two films made about him: *Derrida's Elsewhere* (1999) and *Derrida* (2002).[96] On the other hand, his own philosophy and style would preclude him from being the "subject" of a documentary or autobiography, or of such things being relevant to interpreting his *texts* from which as author he is absent. Yet the making of these films is an indicator of his fame outside the normal circles of academic philosophy. Derrida continued in the last decade of his life to lecture and teach throughout the world. He was awarded the Adorno Prize in philosophy by the University of Frankfurt in 2001. He continued a very active life of speaking and publishing until he was diagnosed with cancer in 2003. He died in Paris in October 2004. Jacques Chirac, the president of France, announced his death to the world.

French Feminist Theory and the Postmodern

Derrida's work was discussed, emulated and criticized by many philosophers and intellectuals. One area where Derrida has made an impact, and postmodern philosophy in general has flowered, is in feminist philosophy. Feminist philosophy has a number of important theorists, and they do not all sound alike. Here we must limit ourselves to a few voices.[97] Before we can focus in on French postmodern feminism, it will be helpful to see them in a larger tradition. Thus to look forward we first look back to existentialism and to the mother of feminist theory in the twentieth century, Simone de Beauvoir.

Beauvoir. Simone de Beauvoir (1908-1986) was an existentialist philosopher, literary author and leader in left-bank political movements in France.[98] Born to middle-class parents and raised a Catholic by her mother (her father was an atheist), she was a brilliant student and did exceptionally well in philosophy. She was only the ninth woman to pass the rigorous state examination in philosophy *(agrégation),* and is still the youngest person ever to do so. In her year only Sartre did better on the exam, and it was his second try! Meeting at the Sorbonne, Beauvoir and Sartre became lifelong committed partners, with an open relationship allowing multiple lovers but only one "absolute" partner for life. Beauvoir and Sartre were close colleagues in writing, thinking and politics.[99]

They read each other's work and mutually influenced one another. Despite her academic and literary gifts, Beauvoir always saw Sartre as "the philosopher" because he worked out their ideas in a rigorous phenomenological manner typical of continental thought. After teaching philosophy in some local schools, she decided to write literature, including philosophical novels and several autobiographical books, which develop the existentialism she and Sartre were famous for as well as discussing openly their relationship. In particular, her novels and autobiographies work out a philosophy of interpersonal relationship and the connections between Self and Other that also are important to Sartre's thought (in *Being and Nothingness*, for example).[100] *She Came to Stay* (1943), one of her philosophical novels, was published the same year as *Being and Nothingness;* both books should be considered different modes of expressing the same basic philosophy.[101]

Beauvoir's most famous book was one of her works in social commentary, *The Second Sex* (1949).[102] This massive study of the way women have been treated, thought about and oppressed in Western culture is probably the single most influential book written by any existentialist in the twentieth century. It stimulated the feminist movement worldwide and is the classic text of twentieth-century feminist philosophy. In a synthesis of biology, history, philosophy and the human sciences, Beauvoir shows again and again how men have oppressed women in every dimension of culture, from medicine and psychology to language, religion and politics. The main thesis of the book is that men have treated women as the Other, defining women as distinct from and less important than men. Drawing upon her existentialist understanding of human consciousness, she argues that we become conscious human beings only in concrete encounters with others, with the Other. In this way "the category of the *Other* is as primordial as consciousness itself."[103] But mutuality and equality can be maintained in human relationships only when each is the other and the self in turn, in the development of their self-understanding. Man makes this impossible for Woman. "She is defined and differentiated with reference to man and not he with reference to her; she is the incidental, the inessential as opposed to the essential. He is the Subject, he is the Absolute—she is the Other."[104] She showed that since ancient times women have been forced into a lesser role by men, in a way that is similar to the treatment of slaves by the dominant group. This oppression is not "natural" or based merely in woman's biological nature; rather it is social, educational, cultural and political forces that have kept women "in their place" through the centuries. Biological facts and her role in reproduction do add a factor to the exclusion and subjection of women, but these facts alone are not enough to explain the widespread, multifaceted depreciation of the second-class sex. Social context, symbolic and psychological structures, political and legal oppression all add to the problem. Beauvoir rejects a biological destiny for any person: "One is not born but rather one becomes a woman," she famously stated.[105] Greater political, economic and social equality for women since the nineteenth century in Europe is a real advance, but much more needs to be accomplished.

Beauvoir's proposed solution was as multiple as the problem itself. Women need to create greater community at many levels, including the philosophical and existential. Individual women need to transcend their personal limitations, but political and social freedom is also essential to the freedom of the individual. Not happiness but *freedom* is the key to human fulfillment. Beauvoir stresses at the end of her book the need for women and men to adopt a free and open mutuality of respect, in which both are at once subject and object, self and other. Women need equality in concrete matters, true, but also to develop their own values and way of life that is grounded in their unique experience. "There will always be certain differences between man and woman. . . . To emancipate woman is to refuse to confine her to relations she bears to man, not to deny them to her."[106] She did not advocate a separate but equal policy, but free and emancipated mutual equality and cooperation. She ends her study with this observation: "It is for [humankind] to establish the reign of liberty in the midst of the world of the given. To gain the supreme victory, it is necessary, for one thing, that by and through their natural differentiation men and women unequivocally affirm their brotherhood."

Beauvoir's book is the classic text for feminist philosophy. Other feminists have positioned themselves in relationship to her views, as they develop their own. Feminist theory in France, and in other countries, has grown in conversation with Beauvoir and with the newer philosophical developments. While her language and viewpoint may seem dated from our perspective, acknowledged or not her text provided bricks from which later feminist theory was constructed.[107]

Irigaray and Kristeva. A number of important voices in French philosophy today could be included under a large umbrella of "feminist theory." The names of Luce Irigaray and Julia Kristeva come up most often in English-speaking discussion of contemporary French philosophy; since we must be selective, we will here briefly introduce their work.

Irigaray (1930-) is one of the leading voices in feminist theory worldwide, although she prefers the expression "philosophy of sexual difference" to feminism.[108] Born in Belgium, she is trained in psychoanalysis and studied linguistics and philosophy at Paris. Her theoretical work develops a new symbolic system and semantics which is rooted and grounded in women's bodies, their experience and their sexuality. She earned two doctorates, one in psycho-linguistics and a second one in philosophy. Her second doctoral thesis, *Speculum of the Other Woman* (1974), dared to criticize the patriarch of French psychoanalytic theory, Jacques Lacan (1901-1981), who by all accounts did not play nice with others.[109] She was forced from her position at the University of Paris-Vincennes by Lacan and his minions, but ended up being director of research at the prestigious C. N. R. S. (Centre National de la Recherche Scientifique). She continues to work as a therapist in her retirement, and has been visiting professor at several major universities including Erasmus University (1982) and the University of Liverpool (2007). In 2003 she was awarded an honorary doctorate by the University of London.

Irigaray is a philosopher of sexual difference because in her post-Freudian philosophy she argues that women must create a new discourse, a new metaphysics, a new worldview that takes their being/bodies seriously. The major thesis of *Speculum of the Other Woman* is that Western philosophers from Plato to Hegel (including Lacan) have ignored woman and the feminine, cutting her out of their understanding of reality. Even when science or philosophy speaks in neutral or universal terms—no, *especially* when they do—they exclude the female from the symbolic representation of being.[110] She does not call this "patriarchy" so often as sexual indifference, a serious problem for our world from her point of view. In fact she opens her later work on ethics, *An Ethics of Sexual Difference* (1984), with this claim:

Sexual difference is one of the major philosophical issues, if not the issue, of our age. According to Heidegger, each age has one issue to think through, and only one. Sexual difference is probably the issue in our time which could be our "salvation" if we thought through it.[111]

Her goal of creating such a new discourse and worldview includes a new mythology and the worship of a divine Goddess.[112] Irigaray has also taken up the ancient notion of matter as divined into four basic elements: water, air, fire and earth. These elements or "humors" were also part of ancient psychology, creating a view of four basic psychological types: melancholy (earth), phlegmatic (water), choleric (fire) and sanguine (air). These types were taken up into Jung's psychology among others, which then influenced Irigaray's new symbolic discourse of sexual difference. Each poetic, metaphorical text in the series is also a conversation with a major philosopher of the West. So far in we have *Marine Lover of Friedrich Nietzsche* (1980) and *The Forgetting of Air in Martin Heidegger* (1999).[113] These books contain few worked-out arguments; rather she is exploring new feminist metaphors in conversation with great philosophers of the past, while also exposing the sexism inherent in their texts.

Irigaray's early work in English translation was criticized by feminists for being essentialist or dualist and lacking a strong political-ethical dimension. In her more mature work, such as *An Ethics of Sexual Difference,* she makes it clear that her philosophy is none of these things. Her work with the Italian feminist movement, discussed in some recent books, develops the political side of her thought.[114] Her philosophy of sexual difference does not exclude a consideration and inclusion of males. Yet as a Freudian she finds sexual difference at the root of human being in the world. "That we must go on living and creating worlds is our task. But it can be accomplished only through the combined efforts of the two halves of the world: the masculine and the feminine."[115] While Irigaray supports civil rights for our fellow citizens who are homosexual, it remains an open question whether her philosophy can accommodate a same-sex "world creating" discourse based on lesbian being in the world.[116]

Like Irigaray, Julia Kristeva (1941-) was not born in France.[117] She is from Bulgaria, and first learned Russian and French in a convent school run by French nuns. She moved to Paris to study French literature and

linguistics in the '60s, but remained influenced by Russian formalism, the
Russian literary theorist Mikhail Bakhtin (1895-1975), as well as broad
French-Catholic culture.[118] Her theoretical works bring together psychoanalysis, linguistics and literary theory; she has also authored a number
of novels. Kristeva is interested in the ways in which the ineffable, the
embodied or the female interrupt and make possible the smooth symbolic systems of language in the dominant (patriarchal) culture. Her theories move in the complex relationships between the material and the
symbolic or social-linguistic, with frequent reference to post-Freudian
theory. She seeks to uncover and sustain a focus on the speaking subject,
the embodied self, the "I" that is so easily obscured and reduced by the
languages of modernity and dominant cultural systems.

In her first doctoral thesis on semiotics, Kristeva proposed a distinction between the semiotic and the symbolic using these terms in a
unique, even idiosyncratic, manner.[119] By the symbolic Kristeva means
the social, cultural and linguistic realm of the rule-governed. She first
uses this concept in linguistics, but later applies it to other cultural
domains such as works of art. The symbolic lives in symbiosis with the
semantic, a term she uses to indicate that which is prelinguistic, the
material, the aspects of language that are tone, rhythm, embodied. A
metaphor she uses for the semantic is taken from Plato's myth of creation in the *Timaeus:* the *chora*, that empty void and darkness into which
the Demiurge brought form and reason.[120] In her philosophy of language, the semantic constantly interrupts the symbolic, but it needs the
symbolic to come into language and fullness of being (or in Freudian
terms, maturity). Likewise the symbolic needs the interruption of the
semantic to remain in the process of becoming, thus keeping up with
life and away from static death. The semantic keeps the symbolic close
to the body, to the material, and so keeps it alive. The analysis of this
dynamic symbiosis she called "semanalysis." Much of her theoretical
work shows a continued interest in the ways in which the semantic
makes possible and disrupts the symbolic, including the semantics of
the feminine in a male-dominated symbolic world. By this she means,
in part, that the actual bodies and voices of real women (semantic) keep
interrupting the man-centered systems of meaning (symbolic) which
seek to ignore or obliterate gender difference.

Kristeva became more deeply interested in psychoanalysis through her training in Freudian therapy. She was also active in radical Parisian politics, becoming an associate of the *Tel Quel* review.[121] Eventually she married one of the founding editors, Philippe Sollers. She continued to work on her higher doctorate while training in psychoanalysis, becoming a practicing therapist in 1979. She finished her thesis and published it as *Revolution in Poetic Language* (1974), soon being appointed to a position in linguistics at the University of Paris VII where she taught until retirement (2008). Kristeva has been a regular visiting professor in North America, and was honored with the Hannah Arendt Prize in 2006.

In *Revolution in Poetic Language,* her concern to hear again the speaking subject came to light. She wants linguistics to change its focus from the mere study of language as an objective system to a focus on "poetic language" (a specialized term from the Russian formalists). This term implies a focus on the preverbal aspects of language, including the study of the speech practices involved in semiotic rhythm. In her view, "every language theory is predicated upon a conception of the subject that it explicitly posits, implies, or tries to deny. . . a definite subject is present as soon as there is consciousness of signification."[122] Her analysis seeks the "dialectic" of symbolic and semantic that always, already assumes an embodied speaking subject of some kind.

At the level of the chora—the semantic which as "receptacle" or womb is sexually marked as female—one begins to see the deep-seated function of Freudian theory and hermeneutics on her work. She uses post-Freudian theories to articulate a semantic realm or chora inhabited by Freudian drives, the Id, the unconscious, and the pre-Oedipal phase of psycho-development. What is "revolutionary" about her linguistic analysis is this focus on the embodied, which has a parallel or analogy in the political situation within a given body politic of the oppressed (including the oppression of women). For Kristeva, you will recall, any social structure or symbol system which is law-abiding will count as "the symbolic." The main thesis of *Revolution in Poetic Language* is that avant-garde poetry (and other aspects of art) can be revolutionary.

Poetry has a revolutionary function when it interrupts the self-oriented or narcissistic symbolics of the Same in the discourse of a dominant cultural system. Just as the semiotic can never be brought into the symbolic without rejection and loss, so the marginalized of any society are masked by the symbolic system of its dominant culture. The revolutionary power of avant-garde poetry lies in its "trans-symbolic jouissance" which functions politically to threaten and transgress the "unity of the social realm and of the subject."[123] Kristeva identifies this function with "the ethical," in language that may hearken back to Levinas. Looking at "the ethical function of art in general," she argues that "a practice is ethical when it dissolves those narcissistic fixations (ones that are narrowly confined to the subject) to which the signifying process succumbs in its socio-symbolic realization."[124] Based upon her Freudian understanding of the development of language and the subject-in-process, Kristeva finds that such a "culture of revolt" fulfills a necessary function in society. In any coming to symbolic understanding, both the self and society necessarily must suppress and reject or abject that which is chora, material, maternal, female: the semantic. A culture of revolt set against the symbolic and the Same allows the individual to further develop and realize oneself as autonomous and free. In Freudian terms this is a well-balanced and mature realization of the pleasure principle.

These same dynamics are at work in the political plane, as she explained in 1996.

> Furthermore, on the social level, the normalizing order is far from perfect and fails to support the excluded: jobless youth, the poor in the projects, the homeless, the unemployed, and foreigners, among many others. When the excluded have no culture of revolt and must content themselves with regressive ideologies, with shows and entertainments that far from satisfy the demand of pleasure, they become rioters.[125]

Her point is that after the fall of Marxism in Europe, the new world situation is dominated by capitalism and a consumer society. Those who are excluded in such a society (and any system of laws, any symbolic-cultural world, will have them) need the therapeutic, maturing revolution of artistic expression and culture to give vent to their "semiotic" embodied experience which is preverbal and which (when done with authenticity) will always transgress the dominant symbol-system. A good example of this is the "wall art" common in Latino quarters in major American cities. Lacking such a culture of revolt, numbed by the culture of entertainment, the marginalized have no possible recourse but violent criminal activity or riots.

The revolutionary character of poetry and art is just one sign of the postmodern. We have also looked at the call for a new metaphorical language in Irigaray, and her poetic exploration of new symbols which is anything but an argument. Derrida's jesterlike play with the texts of others in the spaces created by différance is yet another example. This kind of rhetoric is easy to make fun of, but there is a point. These philosophers are seeking to use language itself to disrupt the power-elite of modern global capitalism. Whether this is a futile gesture or "revolutionary poetry" may be in the eyes of the beholder. What is clear is that as the century drew to a close, the extremes of postmodern rhetoric themselves became subject to gestures of refusal by a younger generation that has been steeped in the postmodern. This has led to what we will describe as a new turn to the human in analytic and continental philosophy at century's end. Before we attempt to sketch this newer mood, we must give some space to one major critic of postmodern philosophy.

Jürgen Habermas and the Critique of Postmodern Philosophy

Germany's most important philosopher at the start of the twenty-first century is by all accounts Jürgen Habermas (1929-).[126] Trained in the Frankfurt School of critical theory which early on provided trenchant criticisms of totalitarian discourse and Enlightenment rationalism, Habermas does not fit the mold of "modernist" that is often used to label him. The centrality and importance of his work to philosophy in Germany makes his engagement with French postmodern philosophy particularly important. He is a philosopher of the grand style, developing a systematic approach that draws on numerous disciplines and presents a bold alternative to both modernism and postmodern thought as normally understood. For Habermas sees the Enlightenment as an unfinished project, and while he rejects many aspects of its philosophy, he also seeks to continue and re-found some central themes in order to further political and social progress in Western society.

Early in his career Habermas studied with the founding members of the Frankfurt School, including Theodor Adorno (1903-1969) and Max Horkheimer (1895-1973), and he read carefully the work of other members like Herbert Marcuse (1898-1979). In books like Marcuse's *One-Dimensional Man* (1964) and Adorno and Horkheimer's *Dialectic of the*

Enlightenment (1947) these philosophers in the tradition of Marx were highly critical of the totalitarian regimes of the second World War.[127] As Jews they were forced to flee to America, but they found capitalist democracy just as problematic. According to these philosophers, at the heart of these dehumanizing systems was a penchant for instrumental or bureaucratic reasoning, a kind of goal-oriented "efficiency" they found in fascism and in the superficial consumer culture of American big-corporation capitalism. Habermas, who also studied Heidegger's philosophy with avid interest, inherited this philosophical critique of modernity from his teachers and extended it in his first major work, *The Structural Transformation of the Public Sphere* (1962). This book was well received in German-language social theory and philosophy, and has influenced critical theory since its publication. It traces the historical-social development of a public sphere in Western society since the eighteenth century. These public institutions, various clubs, unions and societies, were neither private (domestic) nor the State (government), and provided a space for rational discussion and debate of the serious issues of the day. The power of instrumental reasoning and bureaucratic capitalism has overwhelmed the public sphere, dominating the State with the concerns of the corporation rather than the public good. A consumer and entertainment culture likewise undermined reasoned and critical public discourse which is so central to open democratic societies. Yet unlike the founders of the Frankfurt School, Habermas held out some hope for reason, free and critical inquiry, and democracy at the end of his book. Thirty years later, having developed a systematic approach to practical reasoning in communicative action, Habermas returned to these themes in *Between Facts and Norms* (1992), still holding out the promise of free and open democratic societies based on public, critical reasoning.

After publishing his habilitation thesis, *Social Transformation,* Habermas spent a few years teaching at Heidelberg before taking the chair in philosophy and social theory at Frankfurt. He spent most of his career there, retiring in 1994, but he remains very active. Long involved in political movements and not afraid to speak his mind in newspapers, magazines, TV and radio, Habermas is the best-known philosopher in the German-speaking world at the start of the twenty-first century.

After 1962 Habermas spent twenty years working out the rationality of the social sciences in works that were critical of the logical positivism still influential in German philosophy. In *The Logic of the Social Sciences* (1970) and *Knowledge and Human Interest* (1968) he sought to ground the rationality of the social sciences in a way quite distinct from positivism and to free scientific reasoning from the scientism of that school. Instead of interest in prediction, control and objectified processes, Habermas grounded rationality and the social sciences on the mutual understanding sought between speakers, on inter-subjectivity and distortion-free communication. Understanding (as in the hermeneutic philosophy of Gadamer) was also not enough, since the practical interests of humans living together in the world demands explanation as well. Thus a pragmatic-linguistic rationality which appreciates human interests has to be developed beyond scientism and positivism. Already in these early works we find his interest in language and communication. "The human interest in autonomy and responsibility is not mere fancy, for it can be apprehended a priori. What raises us out of nature is the only thing whose nature we can know: language."[128]

Habermas's magnum opus is a two-volume presentation of his new understanding of rationality: *A Theory of Communicative Action* (1981). By "communication" Habermas does not mean an infomercial or other superficial speech. Rather, he has in mind a seeking of mutual understanding in a free and open rational conversation, where statements of fact or value are open to investigation: "an ideal speech situation that, on the strength of its formal properties, allows consensus only through generalizable interests."[129] Communicative action is opposed to instrumental action and reason, because the goal of the former is rational agreement about something in the life-world, a goal that still has a practical end of mutual cooperation. Habermas went on to argue that this type of communicative rationality could also ground the values and moral principles of a free society: discourse ethics. "To the highest stage of moral consciousness there corresponds a universal morality, which can be traced back to fundamental norms of rational speech."[130] Habermas states the fundamental principle of discourse ethics as "Only those norms can claim to be valid that meet (or could meet) with the approval of all affected in their capacity as participants in a practical discourse."[131]

With his rejection of modernism and his concern for communication, language, power and discourse ethics, Habermas shared a number of themes with French postmodern philosophers like Foucault, Derrida and Kristeva. Indeed, after some icy exchanges in print, Derrida and Habermas made friends while both were teaching in Chicago and later came together on political and international issues. They even went so far as to publish a joint manifesto on foreign policy in 2003.[132] These were largely political agreements; their philosophical differences remained.

After inviting Derrida to Heidelberg to lecture in 1984, Habermas gave twelve lectures on postmodern philosophy, with two lectures each on Derrida and Foucault, which he later published. In *The Philosophical Discourse of Modernity* he traces their ideas back to Nietzsche and Heidegger, as any German philosopher would, and is critical of them all at key points. For example, Habermas rejects Heidegger's "ontological distinction" between beings and Being, a Heideggerian move so important for later existential and postmodern philosophers. Habermas treats this as an attempt to undermine discursive reasoning, objectifying the world-disclosure aspect of language while turning away from its communicative dimension. In a chapter on the reception of Derrida in literary circles, Habermas likewise is critical of the attempt to turn language into an aesthetic object, ignoring its communicative function (the counter-claim that Habermas focuses too much on language as communication has some validity). His overall objective is to show the ways in which postmodern philosophers are still captured by subject-centered thinking, an either-or false dilemma in which the subject is either a self-grounding Ego or a mere material object. Habermas offers his own communicative rationality as a way out of both subject-centered thinking and the problematics of postmodern thought.

Habermas's critical engagement with postmodern philosophy was hardly effective in turning the popular tide of postmodern thought in the humanities and social sciences in the 1980s, especially in French and English speaking circles. As for his philosophy as a whole, it remains an open question whether communicative action can bear all the philosophical weight he places upon it. But *The Philosophical Discourse of Modernity* is the first major critique by a continental philosopher of international standing who was thoroughly familiar with postmodern thought (despite Derrida's early bleat that Habermas had not read him carefully).[133] It was a signal that the tide of postmodernity may have reached its high-water mark, at least on the continent among philosophers. What tide may come after the postmodern? Despite the hazards attendant upon any such prediction of this type, there may be some indications we can pick up on in a new turn to the human.

Otherwise Than Postmodern

What happens in philosophy after postmodernity? This is a question we have often been asked. The safest answer is "we don't know"; yet there do seem to be some signs or indications—at least among professional philosophers—that movement in, with and through postmodernity is happening today. The extreme rhetoric and grand gestures of apocalyptic tone (the end of the Human, the death of philosophy, the overcoming of metaphysics, etc.) do leave postmodern philosophers open to critique. Advocates of rationalism and scientism have found in the extremes of postmodern rhetoric an easy target for their attacks—most infamously in the "Sokal hoax" of 1996.[134] Our purpose in this short concluding section is to point out several philosophers whose work provides a better model of engagement and critique of postmodern philosophy.

Philosophers who take postmodern thought seriously have also found room for complaint and critique. Style and rhetoric is one obvious place where improvements need to be made. But philosophers have also made more substantial criticisms and suggested new avenues for philosophical investigation that go beyond some of the dead ends found in postmodern philosophy. Here we can only sketch this mood or approach, just because it is quite diverse and tentative. There should be no thought of a school of philosophy here, especially given the wide variety of thinkers we will discuss. Also, we are not arguing for some kind of Hegelian logic, with modernity being the thesis, postmodernity the antithesis, and what we are calling "otherwise than postmodern" a synthesis. Rather we see this third move or attitude as one that is not a simple return to modernity, but is also unhappy with postmodernity. It seeks a way to get beyond the extremes of modern philosophy while also not being postmodern in the way key figures in philosophy have developed that space. The problematic excesses and cul-de-sacs of postmodernity are also pointed out, and there is an attempt to avoid them.

The mood is one of a return to philosophy, rationality, epistemology and ethics without the excessive claims of either modernism *or* the postmodern philosophers of an earlier generation.

One criterion for this new attitude is a thorough knowledge of postmodern philosophy. Too many of the critics of postmodern excess do not appreciate the important points that postmodern thinkers have made. A careful knowledge of postmodern philosophy from Nietzsche and Kierkegaard through Heidegger to Derrida and Rorty is the first sign or signal of this third space in contemporary philosophy. At the same time, key points of significant disagreement will come up. Philosophers in this third mood seek a return to human reason but without rationalism, to ethics without Kant's rational universals, to the human subject without the Cartesian cogito, or to God without the god of the philosophers. The human subject is seen as a subject in community, with a history and a tradition, a narrative that does not allow for the self-grounding subject of the past: but these authors do not trumpet the death of the Human.

Because this is a mood or a space that exists along side of, and only because of, both modernism and the postmodern, the grouping of names and texts has fuzzy boundaries. This is no fixed school of doctrine with a specific agenda. But we have found that the seven examples we mention here have interesting things in common, along with equally important differences. Their work comes from France, England and North America, in a whole variety of traditions including phenomenology, neo-Kantianism, secular humanism, analytic and hermeneutic philosophy. In their own way, each engages and is critical of various aspects of postmodern thought, learns from its critique, and moves on to revive a philosophical discourse that embraces human finitude—but also human promise.

Our first example comes from a philosopher whose work we have already introduced, Paul Ricoeur. In his 1986 Gifford lectures, *Oneself as Another* (1992), Ricoeur takes a new turn to the human self after the critical work of postmodern thought. He seeks to establish a new understanding of the unity of the self as a speaker in philosophy of language, the narrative unity of the self in story and history, and finally the self and the Other together in what Levinas called the ethical. This is not simply a neomodernism, but no more is it just another type of postmodern move either. Something new is being brought forth.

We would also point to a second set of Gifford lectures, this time by Alasdair MacIntyre in 1988. While we introduced his philosophy earlier, we have deferred discussing this text until now. In *Three Rival Versions of Moral Enquiry* MacIntyre surveys the three most important contemporary traditions of moral philosophy, which he names as "encyclopedia," "genealogy" and Thomism.[135] Part of the genius of this lecture series is the examples he picks for each type, each a classic of the nineteenth century: the *Encyclopaedia Britannica* in the famous ninth edition (1875-1889) for modernity; Nietzsche and his genealogical project for postmodernity, and the papal encyclical *Aeterni Patris* for Thomism. MacIntyre is critical of postmodern thought especially in the area of ethics, where he argues that the powerful critical tool of genealogy is overly negative and easily becomes a kind of cultural relativism. His rejection of modernism is equally trenchant. This paves the way for his version of Thomism, which borrows some concepts from the postmodern but also gets beyond genealogy to ground moral principles in a tradition-constituted rationality. The human self for MacIntyre is a self-in-community, not the transcendental ego of modernism.

Another example of a Christian in philosophy who engages the postmodern is Jean-Luc Marion (1946-).[136] He holds chairs at both the Sorbonne and the University of Chicago Divinity School, and is one of the foremost Catholic intellectuals today. Marion is most properly thought of as continuing French postmodern philosophy in the tradition of phenomenology (especially Husserl and Heidegger). His work is not really otherwise than postmodern. Still, his own creative contributions to philosophy and his reaction and response to the way other thinkers have dealt with philosophical themes bordering on the religious, makes his work important for Christian intellectuals seeking to negotiate the postmodern turn.[137] One could say that he is critical of the Nietzschean mood of postmodern thought, and is thus critically engaged with postmodernity. Educated at the Sorbonne and a student of Derrida, Marion engages such faith-friendly philosophical topics as the icon, being given (the gift, grace), revelation and love (charity). His response to other continental philosophers writing on religious subjects, notably Heidegger, Levinas and Derrida, creates a phenomenological philosophy that is friendly to theology. Like Ricoeur, Marion is always careful to insist that he is doing philosophy and not attempting to do theology in disguise. Also like Ricoeur and Gadamer, Marion's thought is engaged with theology as a serious conversation partner.

A very different kind of French philosophy is represented by the work of Vincent Descombes (1943-). He is a professor at the School for Advanced Studies in the Social Sciences in Paris (École de Hautes Études en Sciences Sociales) where he has taught since 1992. His work combines analytic and continental philosophical traditions, but he comes down on the analytic side. As a young intellectual who had spent years studying phenomenology and Heidegger, Descombes publicly broke away from French postmodern thought with his highly witty and personal narrative of French philosophy from 1932-78 that is both informative and critical: *Modern French Philosophy* (1979).[138] This well-known book is a critique of French poststructural thought from someone who learned it from the inside out. In this early book Descombes takes aim at the style of French Nietzschean thought, its excesses and grand gestures, and complains in the end that it leads to a kind of philosophical nihilism in which "there is no meaning proper to words, only figurative meanings, and concepts are therefore only dissembled metaphors; there is no authentic version of a text, there are only translations; no truth, only pastiche and parody."[139] Making good on his implied promise to develop a better philosophy beyond the Nietzschean critique, Descombes has authored a number of elegant philosophical volumes which are learned, professional and make contributions to the field.[140] He continues to develop works in the tradition of Wittgenstein and analytic philosophy that also engage continental thought, and recently has authored an important two-volume work on philosophy of language and philosophy of mind.[141] Descombes's context among the philosophers of Paris means that he is constantly in conversation with continental philosophy, even while going his own way. His concern to keep philosophy close to terms as used in everyday French and in the philosophical tradition, along with his desire to develop a modest metaphysics and a philosophy of mind without the Cartesian cogito, mark him as joining in the new turn to the human.[142]

Known in France for his lifelong study of Heidegger and advocacy of phenomenology is Dominique Janicaud (1937-2002).[143] A professor for many years at Nice until his accidental death at the age of sixty-five, he studied with Heidegger and has been concerned with the rigor and methodological purity of phenomenology. What is clear from works like *Rationalities, Historicities* (1991) and *Phenomenology "Wide Open": After the French Debate* (1998) is that Janicaud wanted to preserve a philosophical understanding of rationality and a careful methodology for phenomenology which goes through and beyond postmodern thought.[144] He is best known in the English speaking world for his three-part analysis, anthology and critique of the recent "theological turn" in French philosophy. He tells us that in fact his anthology is a kind of "postscript" to Descombes's *Modern French Philosophy*, looking at the post-1979 interest in religious themes by philosophers in the tradition of phenomenology.[145] The particular details of this fascinating turn in phenomenology by believing and nonbelieving philosophers makes for very interesting reading.[146] But covering this literature in depth would take us too far into the twenty-first century and distract us from our concluding postscript to twentieth-century postmodernity. The point of discussing Janicaud is his concern for reason, method, clarity and rigor in phenomenology after Heidegger and French postmodernity (a concern shared with Marion among others). In fact in *Powers of the Rational: Science, Technology and the Future of Thought* (1985) he is critical of Heidegger at exactly those points where he argues his texts turn away from the powers of reason. In a kind of follow-up booklet, *On the Human Condition* (2002), he continued his concern with human nature in an age of technology. The concern of this short book is both philosophical and practical: "Man [*sic*] is beginning to doubt his ability to fulfill his own destiny. In view of what he has done to himself and his environment, can he retain confidence in his own abilities to make judgements and assume responsibility?" Our short introduction shows that Janicaud is another example of a philosopher who has engaged the postmodern with appreciation and critique, while moving on to a philosophy that is otherwise than postmodern, especially in the tradition of phenomenology.

Our next examples are a dynamic duo that are currently quite influential in France: Luc Ferry (1951-) and Alain Renaut (1948-). Both came to center stage in French philosophy with a controversial review and critique of "radical" French postmodern philosophy that has its roots in the student revolution of '68. *French Philosophy of the Sixties* (1985) is a trenchant overview and rejection of the style and substance of thinkers like Foucault, Lacan and Derrida. The subtitle gives away their theme: *An Essay on Antihumanism*. They argue that by trumpeting the death of the Human and rejecting liberal democracy, the radical French philosophers of the '60s also rejected the fundamental human rights essential to politics and ethics. As Renaut put this point some years later, "as against individualism, we need to salvage the idea that without common norms there is no conceivable "republic of intersubjectivity." Rejecting any return to premodern divine law or tradition to ground ethics, he states that today we live in "an infinite, open world which, if it is to have meaning, values and norms, can have them only through—and for—the subject."[147] Despite (or perhaps because of) this controversial tract of 1985, Ferry and Renaut did well in their careers. Both are now professors at the Sorbonne, and Ferry even spent a few years as Minister of Education for France. They have both continued to criticize French postmodern thought with anthologies like *Why We Are Not Nietzscheans* (1991) as well as more substantial monographs in which it is clear they seek a kind of postmodern return to Kant.[148] Ferry is an advocate of a return to humanism, as two monographs on aesthetics and ethics make clear (recalling Kant's second and third Critique).[149] Renaut is also interested in a revived concern with Kant in French philosophy, and a postmetaphysical philosophy of the subject. His book *The Era of the Individual: A Contribution to the History of Subjectivity* (1989), for example, begins with Heidegger but *ends* with Kant![150] While both Ferry and Renaut talk about postmodernism, it is clear their philosophies are quite different from what usually goes on in the broad tent of French postmodern thought.

In these brief introductions to philosophers at the end of the twentieth century we have sought to sketch a mood or a space in contemporary philosophy which is neither modern nor exactly postmodern. This is not a school, nor should we think that this mood or strategy is bound to come "after postmodernism." Rather, these philosophers are wrestling with the same cultural phenomena which are usually labeled "postmodern" but doing so with philosophies that are otherwise than postmodern (with the possible exception of Marion). We have called this a "moving on" not because the postmodern is forgotten, but because these philosophers engage and critique the postmodern and so seek to be otherwise than postmodern in their work. We are talking about neither a return to modernity nor another version of postmodernity, but a new mood or approach that draws from both while not fitting into either category. Whether this new space for philosophical reflection is a disjointed collection of philosophical work, a passing fad or an important new direction we shall have to wait and see. While these voices are quite distinct, our best guess is that they can help us negotiate the postmodern turn in Western philosophy. They are certainly a good place for those who wish to read learned and engaging criticisms of the postmodern.

10. CONCLUSION, RETROSPECT AND REFLECTION

Now that our three-volume survey has come to an end, we can look all the way back to the pre-Socratics and marvel at the power and diversity of Western thought. Seeking some kind of overall theme or direction over two millennia is a daunting task, and one we will not attempt. Yet at the end of a long series on philosophy and Christian thought, some general comments on the relationship between philosophy and theology are in order.

Clearly Western philosophy has had a tremendous influence on theology. This powerful influence can be seen in the greatest Christian theologians of the last two millennia, from Origen to Bultmann. Even those like Tertullian or Barth, who seemed to exclude philosophy from their method, nevertheless drew upon philosophical ideas, movements and authors. Is this a bad thing?

From time to time in evangelical circles we encounter the belief that Christian theology should be based upon the Bible and the Bible alone. Any influence from philosophy or science is seen as "polluting" the pure Word of God. Now this notion or feeling should not be confused with a Reformation principle, *sola scriptura*. That principle is properly about our salvation: all we need to know to be saved is found in the Bible, and only in the Bible do we find all we need to know for salvation. But a narrow focus on the Bible alone for theological learning is not and never was part of the method of Luther, Calvin, Wesley and the other great evangelicals of the past. All three of them drew upon history, philosophy and cultural learning in order to develop their ideas. Wherever the idea that *theology* should be based only on the Bible comes from, it certainly cannot be found in the history of serious Christian theology. Even the New Testament authors drew upon not only the Hebrew Bible but philosophical and scientific notions from the larger Greco-Roman world. The use of the Greek term *logos* ("word") in the prologue to the Gospel of John is just one well-known example from a host of others one finds in the biblical texts. After all, academic theology is a good work and should never be confused with our justification which comes from faith in Jesus Christ. We have seen that over and over the best Christian minds have encountered Western philosophy on its own ground, in some cases becoming noted philosophers themselves. Important developments in Christian thought have come not from ignoring philosophy or science, but from a proper and academic engagement with the intellectual culture of the day. Thomas Aquinas and Søren Kierkegaard are quite different but equally stellar examples of this kind of first-class Christian engagement with philosophy. The point of our brief comments here is not that philosophy can or should replace theology, but rather that Christian theology must engage the intellectual culture of the day, including philosophy. Indeed, the very mission of the church and the character of the gospel compel us to preach and teach within each culture and intellectual milieu in every tongue and nation. Doing so in a way that engages the culture without distortion or simplification, while also holding fast to Christ and the gospel, is a significant challenge for us in every age. We hope this overview of two millennia of Western thought from a Christian point of view provides insights and examples for the future, as well as being a guide to the past.

When Colin Brown first published *Philosophy and the Christian Faith* in 1969, evangelical theologians were far less inclined toward positive and open engagement with philosophy. It is to his credit that he was at the vanguard of an evangelical reappraisal of philosophy's contributions and challenges to our theological task. As part of that work he initiated this series and wrote the first volume twenty years ago. In bringing the series to a conclusion, we honor his example and are pleased to follow in his footsteps, as we all follow Christ in the discipleship of the mind.

At the Start of the Twenty-First Century

Looking back over just one century, namely the one that has been our focus in this volume, reveals an apparent jumble of faces and voices in philosophy. The twentieth century has been one of great change, not only among the peoples of the world and within Western thought but also in the rate at which culture has changed. Progress in technology has brought not only a shrinking of the global village but exponential growth in the movement of people and ideas around the world. Although philosophy does move at a more stately pace than, say, pop music, the West has seen as large a variety and diversity of philosophic thought as any comparable period of the past. This makes any attempt to find unifying themes or questions rather difficult. Yet common issues do keep rising to the surface, despite the turbulence of the intellectual waters. Among these are questions of the nature of philosophy itself and its status as a scientific discipline. In addition to these disciplinary questions, issues of language, meaning and human existence are common in the authors we have studied. We have also traced, in various movements, a tendency toward a postmodern critique of key philosophical assumptions and sureties of the past. We can explore these common themes a little more fully in this last chapter.

How can philosophy be scientific? Our century began with an intellectual revolt against the dominant movement known as idealism. Most of this revolution took place in the name of science or rigorous logic. Whether we look to Frege and Husserl or to Russell and Moore, to Peirce or to the Vienna Circle, we find a concern to ground philosophy more strictly upon sound scientific principles. Frege, Russell, Whitehead and Wittgenstein developed a new and rigorous form of symbolic logic, a development which created the analytic movement. At this same time Husserl took the tools of phenomenology in a radical new direction and created a new school of phenomenology on the continent. Like the others we have mentioned, Husserl was concerned to make philosophy a rigorous science, not through deductive logic but through a strict method for the examination of phenomena of human consciousness. Bergson, Dewey and Whitehead, too, in their very different ways, were concerned to bring philosophy into close conversation with the sciences.

The relationship between science and philosophy dominated philosophical methods in the work of major thinkers at the start of the century. This issue did not survive in a robust form through to the end. In various ways the concern to make philosophy objective, neutral and scientific was undermined by those who were trained in these very methods. The grammatical analysis of the later Wittgenstein could never have arisen without his brilliant early work as a student of Frege, Russell and Moore. Likewise the phenomenology of Husserl, with its concern to make philosophy a rigorous science, was a major factor in the development of existentialism on the continent, which took philosophy in a very different direction. The attempt to make philosophy a rigorous science did not succeed, even though it did bring important tools, methods and movements into being. In the main, the philosophy of the twentieth century began with a close association with science, perhaps even with a little bit of science-envy, but this general trend did not long endure. The issue of the relationship of philosophy to human life had a better record of endurance.

What is human being? A consistent and perennial question in philosophy is "what does it mean to be human?" This issue came to the fore in a powerful way with the rise of existentialism, but it can also be seen in structuralism, even though structuralists were highly critical of existential philosophy. The concern to ground language and meaning in human "forms of life" in the later Wittgenstein, as well as in the methods of pragmatism, also show a strong interest in things human. The analytic school has not been interested so much in the "meaning" of human life as in questions surrounding the nature of the human mind, questions of morality and the meaning of ethical language, as well as the relationship between language and practice. This movement has not so much ignored the issue of human existence as focused on a narrower set of topics like the ones just mentioned, which come to the fore given the methods typically used by analytic philosophers. The push back against the postmodern critique, as we saw in the last chapter, can likewise find some common ground in a focus on the human. Of course the question "What does it mean to be human?" is a perennial one for philosophers, and so we are hardly surprised when it shows up in the twentieth century.

While all of these voices and movements show some concern with human being, or what Heidegger called Dasein, none of them gives a consistent answer. Even Heidegger changed his mind on more than one occasion, and his several students each adopted differing points of view. It is hard to find much in common in the philosophies of Sartre, Levinas, Gadamer, Rahner and Derrida, to name just a few prominent Heideggerian scholars, especially when it comes to the question of Dasein. While no consensus emerged, the question itself is a powerful theme in twentieth-century thought.

What about language and meaning? Ever since the work of Russell and Moore, issues of language and logic have been at the heart of the analytic tradition. This was only strengthened in later developments, such as the thought of Wittgenstein, ordinary language philosophy or logical pragmatism. But in a striking parallel between analytic and continental thinkers, language and meaning became equally important to Heidegger and his students as well. Rigorous thinking about Dasein or human existence brought to light issues about language, meaning and communication. Nowhere is this more obvious than in the development of hermeneutic philosophy by Gadamer and Ricoeur. Both structuralism and poststructuralist thinkers like Derrida also developed very powerful interests in language, text and meaning—of course in quite different, even antagonistic ways.

Both symbolic logic and structuralism pushed the philosophy of language in formalist directions. Pushing back against this impulse, several key moves in twentieth century philosophy brought the quest for meaning in language much closer to human life. This is obvious even in the name of ordinary language philosophy, but one sees it as a major shift in the thinking of the later Wittgenstein as well. Heidegger's interest in language in his middle period also connected meaning more fully with human being (Dasein). This minor theme in Heidegger's *Being and Time* was given brilliant expression in the work of Gadamer on hermeneutics. Gadamer's notions of play and horizon, which echo Wittgenstein's "language games" and "forms of life," are good examples of the way that central figures in twentieth-century philosophy responded to the formalism of logical analysis or structuralism. Even the title of Gadamer's magnum opus, *Truth and Method*, sets forth this dichotomy. Similarly, in a way that is typical of his entire approach to philosophy, Ricoeur sought to mediate between this tension in philosophy of language, finding a place for both structuralism and phenomenology in his work.

Given the deep and powerful concern with language and meaning in the last century, there is no doubt that this will continue well into the new century we have just begun. How this interest will take shape is still an open question, but philosophers will have to reckon with and respond to postmodern thought on the topic—this much is clear even now.

What about postmodernity? Our final common issue concerns the postmodern. We have argued that postmodern thought is not merely some form of relativism or nihilism, as too many philosophers still believe. Rather, we agree with those analysts who see the postmodern as taking place within the time of modernity. Perhaps we should simply think of postmodern thought as an attitude or style, a gesture or approach to modern philosophy. If this is right, then the postmodern can only exist with and because of the modern, while also rejecting aspects of it. Postmodern philosophy is vocally critical of some of the central moves of modern philosophy. It is an analysis and response to central values, practices, assumptions and metaphors of Enlightenment reason or Romantic aesthetics. It refuses to ground certainty on the self, any supposed absolute truth or any other transcendent ground. Postmodernity is not only negative, however. It includes a joyous celebration of a new way of being "after" modernity which nevertheless occurs as a space within modern times.

Evangelical scholars have not been particularly good at understanding or responding to postmodern philosophy. Too many take the easy path of a superficial reading of these authors, a reductionist or simplistic analysis, and follow this with complete rejection. Fortunately some evangelical scholars have made it their business to learn about postmodern philosophy with some depth and professional rigor. Their writings help evangelicals to engage postmodern thought with care and sympathy, learning from it while also being critical at appropriate places and points.[1] On the other hand, it is true that some Christian thinkers have so fully embraced postmodern thought that they lose any critical edge. One searches in vain in their writings for a solid critique of, say, Derrida or Foucault or Rorty, whichever guiding light they have chosen to follow. Yet this kind of full and uncritical embrace of postmodernity is very rare in evangelical scholarship. The former problem is a greater one for us.

How rightly to characterize the postmodern remains a significant problem as well. We believe our analysis is defensible, but we hardly think it the one "best" view among a host of competing interpretations. One thing we do reject, to repeat, is the idea that postmodern philosophy is simply a form of relativism. Some unfortunate writers have gone so far as to claim it is a version of nihilism. This kind of simplification does nothing to help us understand contemporary philosophers. But if this view is incorrect, what positive account of postmodern philosophy might we give? Different postmodern thinkers take aim at different aspects of the modern and thus characterize modernity in different ways. Some find modernity in epistemology, a fixed textual meaning or the rationalist quest for certainty. Some find it in notions of the self, consciousness or a transcendental ego as the ground for truth, meaning and ethics (including politics). Still others would point to objectivity, neutrality and universal reason as the key to modernism. In each case what is *post*-modern is a two-step move. The first step is critique of the excesses of modern arguments, virtues, assumptions, practices and metaphors. The second step is an acceptance, even a celebration, of the freedom that comes from abandoning previous confusions, traps for reason and false limitations to human expression. The postmodern is never, therefore, a complete rejection of modernity. Postmodern approaches major on finding problems in the thinking and the works of previous generations, but they do not seek total annihilation of modernity. Rather, their proper goal is to improve life and thought today.

From the perspective of Christian faith, what is key in this type of postmodern move is the critique of rationalism and also of scientism, both all too common in Western thought since the Enlightenment. By bringing into question such commonplace modernist assumptions as (1) there is only one right kind of thinking, one universal human rationality; or (2) that reason and reason alone can lead to truth and goodness; or (3) that faith and/or values will always corrupt the right kind of reasoning, usually associated with natural science; in these and other ways postmodern thinkers do the work of a friend even if disguised as an enemy. Even while recognizing problems in various postmodern philosophers, it is still the case that postmodern thought has made room for Christian scholarship and a place for the voice of faith in our larger culture. This positive gain should not be lightly dismissed by religious critics of the postmodern.

In general a major issue for philosophy in the twenty-first century surrounds the legacy of this postmodern critique and celebration. Some Christian philosophers, Paul Ricoeur among them, have provided us with an excellent model of how to engage with and learn from the postmodern while also being critical of it. Ricoeur's mature philosophical works are enriched by his encounter with the later Heidegger, Gadamer, Derrida and other postmodern thinkers, and adapt key elements of their thought. But he typically finds his own way between the extremes of both modernism and postmodernity—that needs to be our way too. Negotiating the postmodern turn as people of faith and reason is tricky, but rewarding: a good work in many senses.

We hope that this volume has helped students, pastors and intellectuals of all kinds to find their way in the heady streams of twentieth-century thought. We have written a guidebook which does not replace reading the works of these authors, but seeks to stimulate your appetite for thinking, reading and doing philosophy yourself. In this way we can all continue to follow the greatest commandment, namely, to love the Lord our God with our heart, soul, *mind* and strength.

Notes

Introduction
[1] T. S. Eliot, "The Waste Land," part 1, lines 60-65, in *The Complete Poems and Plays, 1909-1950* (New York: Harcourt, Brace and World, 1962), p. 39.

[2] Eliot, "Preludes," in *The Complete Poems and Plays, 1909-1950*, pp. 12-13.

[3] W. B. Yeats, *The Poems: A New Edition*, ed. Richard J. Finneran (New York: Macmillan, 1983), p. 187.

[4] We recommend another InterVarsity Press title for those interested in theological developments: Stanley J. Grenz and Roger E. Olson, *20th Century Theology* (Downer's Grove, Ill.: InterVarsity Press, 1992).

Chapter 1: Science, Philosophy and the Demise of Idealism
[1] For a good introduction to Frege for beginning students, see Anthony Kenny, *Frege* (London: Penguin, 1995). A more advanced introduction is provided by Gregory Currie, *Frege: An Introduction to His Philosophy* (New York: Barnes & Noble, 1982). A useful compilation of important articles on Frege is Hans Sluga, ed., *The Philosophy of Frege*, 4 vols. (New York: Garland, 1993).

[2] For details on Frege's life, see Gottlob Frege, *Conceptual Notation and Related Articles*, trans. and ed. Terrell Ward Bynum (Oxford: Oxford University Press, 1972), pp. 1-55.

[3] In addition to the *Conceptual Notation*, the work of Frege in English translation can be found in the following books: *The Foundations of Arithmetic*, trans. J. L. Austin, rev. ed. (Oxford: Blackwell, 1980); *The Basic Laws of Arithmetic*, trans. Montgomery Furth (Berkeley: University of California Press, 1964); *Posthumous Writings*, ed. Hans Hermes et al., trans. Peter Long and Roger White (Oxford: Blackwell, 1979); *Collected Papers on Mathematics, Logic and Philosophy*, ed. Brian McGuinness (Oxford: Blackwell, 1984). Earlier translations from some of the essays in the *Collected Papers* can be found in *Translations from the Philosophical Writings of Gottlob Frege*, trans. P. T. Geach and Max Black (Oxford: Blackwell, 1952) and *Logical Investigations*, trans. P. T. Geach (Oxford: Blackwell, 1977).

[4] On Gödel and his theorem see Rebecca Goldstein, *Incompleteness: The Proof and Paradox of Kurt Gödel* (New York: W. W. Norton, 2005).

[5] On this topic see Michael A. E. Dummett, *Frege: Philosophy of Language* (London: Duckworth, 1973). Dummett is generally considered the chief Frege specialist in English today. His other books on Frege and attendant subjects (all but one published by Duckworth) are: *Frege: Philosophy of Mathematics* (1991), which is a companion volume to the earlier work; *The Origins of Analytic Philosophy* (1991); and the following collections of essays: *Truth and Other Enigmas* (1978); *The Interpretation of Frege's Philosophy* (1981); and *Frege and Other Philosophers* (Oxford: Oxford University Press, 1991).

[6] See his essay, "Sense and Reference," in *Collected Papers;* also in Geach and Black, eds., *Translations from the Philosophical Writings*.

[7] Frege made this remark in his *Foundations of Arithmetic*, p. 71.

[8] In particular, a full discussion of the collapse of idealism has to include G. E. Moore's famous essay, "A Refutation of Idealism" (1903). This too will be discussed later in the present work.

[9] For an introduction to phenomenology, see Robert Sokolowski, *Introduction to Phenomenology*

(New York: Cambridge University Press, 2000); Dermot Morgan, *Introduction to Phenomenology* (London: Routledge, 2000); or Herbert Spiegelberg, *The Phenomenological Movement*, 2 vols., 3rd ed. (The Hague: M. Nijhoff, 1982) which has a fine section on Husserl. For Husserl and his thought, see the rather long but excellent introduction by David Woodruff Smith, *Husserl* (London: Routledge, 2007); *The Cambridge Companion to Husserl*, ed. Barry Smith and David Woodruff Smith (New York: Cambridge University Press, 1995), which contains a good bibliography; David Bell, *Husserl* (London: Routledge, 1989); Joseph J. Kockelmans, ed., *Phenomenology: The Philosophy of Edmund Husserl and Its Interpretation* (Garden City: Doubleday/Anchor, 1967); or Rudolph Bernet et al., *An Introduction to Husserlian Phenomenology* (Evanston, Ill.: Northwestern University Press, 1993). Some good introductions from Husserl's own work are Edmund Husserl, *Phenomenology and the Crisis of Philosophy*, trans. and ed. Quentin Lauer (New York: Harper, 1965); or some of his *Shorter Works*, ed. Peter McCormick and Frederick A. Elliston (Notre Dame: University of Notre Dame Press, 1981). For a fuller bibliography, see François Lapointe, *Edmund Husserl and His Critics* (Bowling Green: Philosophy Documentation Center, 1980).

[10]Edmund Husserl, *Philosophy of Arithmetic*, trans. Dallas Willard (Dordrecht: Kluwer, 2003).

[11]For more on the relationship between Frege and Husserl, see J. N. Mohanty, *Husserl and Frege* (Bloomington: Indiana University Press, 1982), which contains an English translation of Frege's review.

[12]Edmund Husserl, *Logical Investigations*, trans. J. N. Findlay (London: Routledge, 1970).

[13]Only volume one was published in Husserl's lifetime. The other two volumes were published by the Husserl Archives many years after his death (1952, 1971). There are two English translations of volume one: *Ideas: General Introduction to Pure Phenomenology*, trans. W. R. Boyce Gibson (New York: Macmillan, 1931), and *Ideas Pertaining to a Pure Phenomenology and to a Phenomenological Philosophy: First Book*, trans. F. Kersten (The Hague: M. Nijhoff, 1982). Under the same main title, the other two volumes have also been translated in modern editions: *Second Book* by R. Rojcewicz and A. Schuwer (Dordrecht: Kluwer, 1989), and *Third Book* by Ted E. Klein and William E. Pohl (Dordrecht: Kluwer, 1980). References to this work will be cited as *Ideas* I, II and III according to section number.

[14]An English translation is found in Husserl, *Phenomenology and the Crisis of Philosophy*, and in his *Shorter Works*.

[15]English trans. by Dorion Cairns (The Hague: M. Nijhoff, 1969).

[16]In translation as *Cartesian Meditations*, trans. Dorion Cairns (The Hague: M. Nijhoff, 1960) and *The Crisis of European Sciences and Transcendental Phenomenology*, trans. David Carr (Evanston, Ill.: Northwestern University Press, 1970).

[17]In addition to the German critical editions, a series of English translations of Husserl's collected works has been launched by the Archives and published since 1980 by Kluwer. Beyond those already cited above the following are currently finished: *On the Phenomenology of the Consciousness of Internal Time (1893-1917)*, trans. John Barnett Brough (1990); *Early Writings in the Philosophy of Logic and Mathematics*, trans. Dallas Willard (1994); *Psychological and Transcendental Phenomenology and the Confrontation with Heidegger (1927-1931)*, ed. and trans. Thomas Sheehan and Richard E. Palmer (1997); *The Idea of Phenomenology*, trans. Lee Hardy (1999); *Thing and Space*, ed. and trans. Richard Rojcewicz (1997); *Analyses Concerning Passive and Active Synthesis*, trans. Anthony J. Steinbock (2001). Other translated works not already cited include *First Philosophy*, trans. J. Allen (The Hague: M. Nijhoff, 1978) and *Experience and Judgment*, ed. Ludwig Landgrebe, trans. James S. Churchill and Karl Ameriks (Evanston, Ill.: Northwestern University Press, 1973).

[18]The secondary literature on Husserl is immense (see bibliographies cited above). The following more advanced studies of Husserl's thought and its impact are representative: Theodorus De Boer, *The Development of Husserl's Thought* (The Hague: M. Nijhoff, 1978); James

Edie, *Edmund Husserl's Phenomenology* (Bloomington: Indiana University Press, 1987); Frederick A. Elliston and Peter McCormick, eds., *Husserl: Expositions and Appraisals* (Notre Dame, Ind.: University of Notre Dame Press, 1977); R. O. Elveton, ed. and trans., *The Phenomenology of Husserl* (Chicago: Quadrangle, 1970); Leszek Kolakowski, *Husserl and the Search for Certitude* (New Haven: Yale University Press, 1975); J. N. Moharty, *The Possibility of Transcendental Philosophy* (The Hague: M. Nijhoff, 1985); Maurice Natanson, *Edmund Husserl: Philosopher of Infinite Tasks* (Evanston, Ill.: Northwestern University Press, 1973); Paul Ricoeur, *Husserl: An Analysis of His Phenomenology* (Evanston, Ill.: Northwestern University Press, 1967); Alfred Schutz, *Collected Papers*, vol. 3, *Studies in Phenomenological Psychology* (The Hague: M. Nijhoff, 1975); Robert Sokolowski, *Husserlian Meditations* (Evanston, Ill.: Northwestern University Press, 1974); Elizabeth Ströker, *Husserl's Transcendental Phenomenology*, trans. Lee Hardy (Stanford: Stanford University Press, 1993); Donn Welton, *The Origins of Meaning* (The Hague: M. Nijhoff, 1983); and Dan Zahavi, *Husserl's Phenomenology* (Stanford: Stanford University Press, 2007).

[19]See his "Philosophy as a Rigorous Science," in *Shorter Writings*, pp. 166-97. He works out this program more fully in *Ideas* I.

[20]*Logical Investigations*, 2:701 (Investigation IV, §10), his italics. Husserl's sophisticated realism did not change over the course of the development of his thought. This is clear in many places in his later writing, e.g., *Ideas* I, §55; *Crisis*, pp. 142-47. For Husserl, experience is co-constituted by the thing (later, he would add "life-world") and the knowing subject: this makes idealism impossible for him. For more on Husserl's kind of realism, see John J. Drummond, *Husserlian Intentionality and Non-foundational Realism* (Dordrecht: Kluwer, 1990).

[21]In *Cartesian Meditations*, after rejecting normal "idealism" of various types, Husserl explicitly says that his transcendental idealism is only "an explication of my ego as subject of every possible cognition" (§41, p. 86).

[22]*Ideas* I, §19.

[23]*Ideas* I, §3, omitting his italics.

[24]*Ideas* I, §32.

[25]*Ideas* I, §49.

[26]*Ideas* II, §§2 and 3.

[27]*Crisis*, p. 139.

[28]See Husserl, *On the Phenomenology of the Consciousness of Internal Time*.

[29]*Crisis*, p. 141. For more on the life-world, see *Ideas* II and see further David Carr, *Phenomenology and the Problem of History* (Evanston, Ill.: Northwestern University Press, 1974).

[30]On Husserl's influence see Dermot Moran, *Edmund Husserl: Founder of Phenomenology* (Cambridge: Polity, 2005). We shall discuss the authors named above later, with the exception of Merleau-Ponty (1907-1961). He was an existential phenomenologist and professor of philosophy in Paris, who worked closely with Sartre. Merleau-Ponty followed the phenomenological method of Husserl more closely than Sartre did. For an introduction, see Remigius C. Kwant, *The Phenomenological Philosophy of Merleau-Ponty* (Pittsburgh: Duquesne University Press, 1963).

[31]For a complete listing of works by and about Bergson until 1985, see P. A. Y. Gunter, *Henri Bergson: A Bibliography* (Bowling Green, Ky.: Philosophy Documentation Center, 1986). Gunter also provides some annotations, especially of Bergson's major works.

[32]The following are some good introductions to Bergson's thought: Ian W. Alexander, *Bergson: Philosopher of Change* (New York: Hillary House, 1957); A. R. Lacey, *Bergson* (Boston: Routledge, 1989); and Leszek Kolakowski, *Bergson* (Oxford: Oxford University Press, 1985). Works written before 1936 should be used with caution, as they do not contain a full account of all Bergson's major work. The best introduction to Bergson from his own pen

is a collection of essays, *The Creative Mind: An Introduction to Metaphysics,* trans. Mabelle L. Andison (New York: Philosophical Library, 1946).

[33]On Bergson's influence, see Thomas Hanna, *The Bergsonian Heritage* (New York: Columbia University Press, 1962); and A. E. Pilkington, *Bergson and His Influence* (New York: Cambridge University Press, 1976).

[34]The best source in English for the life of Bergson is still Jacques Chevalier, *Henri Bergson,* trans. Lilian A. Clare (New York: Macmillan, 1928).

[35]The major works of Bergson in English are: *Time and Free Will,* trans. F. L. Pogson (New York: Macmillan, 1910); *Matter and Memory,* trans. Nancy Margaret Paul and W. Scott Palmer (New York: Macmillan, 1911); *Creative Evolution,* trans. Arthur Mitchell (1911; New York: The Modern Library, 1944); and *The Two Sources of Morality and Religion,* trans. R. Ashley Andra and Cloudesley Brereton (1935; New York: Doubleday/Anchor, 1954).

[36]*Creative Mind,* p. 77.

[37]Herbert Spencer (1820-1903) was an English philosopher who was one of the founders of modern sociology. He actually coined the term "survival of the fittest" to describe social conficts, which Darwin later used to describe biological evolution. See further Michael W. Taylor, *The Philosophy of Herbert Spencer* (New York: Continuum, 2007).

[38]In *Bergsonian Heritage,* p. 125.

[39]This is published in English as *Duration and Simultaneity,* trans. Leon Jacobson (Indianapolis: Bobbs-Merrill, 1965).

[40]Harald Höffding, *La Philosophie de Bergson* (Paris: Alcan, 1916), pp. 160-61. Partial English translation in Jacques Maritain, *Bergsonian Philosophy and Thomism,* trans. Mabelle L. Andison (New York: Philosophical Library, 1955), p. 305.

[41]Henri Bergson, *Introduction to Metaphysics,* trans. T. E. Hulme, Library of Liberal Arts, (Indianapolis: Bobbs-Merrill, 1955), p. 27. This oft-quoted essay is also available in a translation by Mabelle L. Andison (New York: Philosophical Library, 1961), reprinted from *The Creative Mind.*

[42]*Introduction to Metaphysics,* p. 24.

[43]A good example of this negative response is Bertrand Russell, *The Philosophy of Bergson* (Chicago: Open Court, 1912). This edition contains a reply to Russell by H. W. Carr, and a rejoinder by Russell. Russell's criticism is overly negative. For a more balanced analysis of Bergson's philosophy of science, see Milič Čapec, *Bergson and Modern Physics* (Dordrecht: Reidel, 1971).

[44]He did write that "If our analysis is correct, it is consciousness or rather super-consciousness[!] that is at the origin of life," *Creative Evolution,* p. 284; but this vague term raises more problems than it solves.

[45]Henri Bergson, *Duration and Simultaneity,* trans. Leon Jacobson, Library of Liberal Arts, (Indianapolis: Bobbs-Merrill, 1965).

[46]In fact a very clear discussion of the *élan vital* is found Henri Bergson, *Two Sources of Morality and Religion,* trans. R. Ashley Audra and Cloudesley Brereton (reprint; Notre Dame: University of Notre Dame Press, 1977), pp. 111-15.

[47]*Two Sources,* chap. 1. Karl Popper adopts this distinction in his own way, in his well-known work, *The Open Society and its Enemies,* 2 vols. (Princeton, N.J.: Princeton University Press, 1963). However, Popper misinterprets Bergson as an "irrationalist" (see, e.g., 2:228-29, 315-16).

[48]*Two Sources* (1977), p. 220.

[49]Criticism of this "process" concept of God will be taken up in a later chapter of this work.

Chapter 2: Logic and Language: Early Analytic Philosophy

[1]For the biography of G. E. Moore, see his "Autobiography" in *The Philosophy of G. E. Moore,* ed. Paul Arthur Schilpp, 2nd. ed. (New York: Tudor, 1952); R. B. Braithwaite,

"George Edward Moore, 1873-1958," in *G. E. Moore: Essays in Retrospect,* ed. Alice Ambrose and Morris Lazerowitz (London: Allen and Unwin, 1970); Thomas Baldwin, "G. E. Moore," *Philosophy* 71 (1996), pp. 275-85; and Tom Regan, *Bloomsbury's Prophet* (Philadelphia: Temple University Press, 1987).

[2]Some good books about Moore (see also the previous note) include: A. J. Ayer, *Russell and Moore* (Cambridge, Mass.: Harvard University Press, 1971); Thomas Baldwin, *G. E. Moore* (London: Routledge, 1990); John Hill, *The Ethics of G. E. Moore* (Assen: Van Gorcum, 1976); E. D. Klemke, ed., *Studies in the Philosophy of G. E. Moore* (Chicago: Quadrangle, 1969) and his *The Epistemology of G. E. Moore* (Evanston, Ill.: Northwestern University Press, 1969); David O'Connor, *The Metaphysics of G. E. Moore* (Dordrecht: Reidel, 1982); Avrum Stroll, *Moore and Wittgenstein on Certainty* (Oxford: Oxford University Press, 1994); and Alan R. White, *G. E. Moore* (Oxford: Blackwell, 1958).

[3]"Autobiography," p. 13.

[4]For more on this group and its influence on Moore (and vice versa), see Paul Levy, *Moore* (New York: Holt, Rinehart and Winston, 1979).

[5]For more on British idealism, see Steve Wilkens and Alan G. Padgett, *Christianity & Western Thought, Volume 2: Faith & Reason in the 19th Century* (Downer's Grove, Ill.: InterVarsity Press, 2000) 2:239-46.

[6]Bertrand Russell, "My Mental Development," in *The Philosophy of Bertrand Russell,* ed. Paul Arthur Schilpp, 3rd. ed. (New York: Harper, 1963), p. 12 (his italics).

[7]G. E. Moore, "The Nature of Judgment." First published in *Mind* 8 (1899): 179-93, reprinted in *G. E. Moore: The Early Essays,* ed. Tom Regan (Philadelphia: Temple University Press, 1986).

[8]"The Nature of Judgment," p. 193 (also in *The Early Essays,* p. 80).

[9]G. E. Moore, *Principia Ethica* (New York: Cambridge University Press, 1903) and "The Refutation of Idealism" in *Mind* 12 (1903): 433-53. The latter is reprinted in his *Philosophical Studies* (New York: Harcourt, 1922). Later essays by Moore are reprinted in his *Philosophical Papers* (London: Allen & Unwin, 1959). His other books are *Ethics* (New York: Holt, 1912) and *Some Main Problems of Philosophy* (London: Allen & Unwin, 1953).

[10]Moore, "Refutation of Idealism," in *Philosophical Studies,* p. 17.

[11]For Messer (whose book summarizes the views of Husserl), see Moore's long book review in *Mind* 19 (1910): 395-409. Moore's lectures on philosophical psychology were "The Subject-Matter of Psychology," *Proceedings of the Aristotelian Society* 10 (1909-10): 36-62. Moore's commentator in the Society, Prof. G. Dawes Hicks, certainly understood this lecture to be in the Brentano tradition (Hicks, "Mr. G. E. Moore on 'The Subject-Matter of Psychology,'" *Proceedings of the Aristotelian Society* 10 [1909-1910]: 232-88). For Moore's views on Brentano's ethics, see the preface to *Principia Ethica,* pp. x-xi, and his review of Brentano's book on ethics in the *International Journal of Ethics* 14 (1903): 115-23.

[12]*Principia Ethica,* p. 154, his italics.

[13]Leonard Woolf, *Sowing* (London: Hogarth, 1960), p. 148. See also John Maynard Keynes, *Two Memoirs* (New York: A. M. Kelley, 1949), pp. 78-103, for more on Moore and the Bloomsbury Club.

[14]"Autobiography," p. 16.

[15]These essays are reprinted in his *Philosophical Studies;* see especially pp. 96 and 163-65.

[16]The original essays are found in *Contemporary British Philosophy,* ed. J. H. Muirhead (London: Allen & Unwin, 1925), pp. 193-223, and *Proceedings of the British Academy* 25 (1939): 273-300. Both are reprinted in Moore, *Philosophical Papers.*

[17]*Philosophical Papers,* p. 150; see also pp. 146-48.

[18]For good, brief introductions to Russell, see his own "My Mental Development," in *The Philosophy of Bertrand Russell,* ed. Paul Arthur Schilpp (New York: Tudor, 1944); see also the

long article on him in the *Encyclopedia of Philosophy,* ed. Paul Edwards, 8 vols. (New York: Macmillan, 1967); A. J. Ayer, *Bertrand Russell* (New York: Viking, 1972); and A. C. Grayling, *Russell* (Oxford: Oxford University Press, 1996). For more advanced discussion of Russell's thought, see Schilpp, ed., *The Philosophy of Bertrand Russell;* Elizabeth Ramsden Eames, *Bertrand Russell's Theory of Knowledge* (London: Allen & Unwin, 1969); A. J. Ayer, *Russell and Moore* (Cambridge, Mass.: Harvard University Press, 1971); E. D. Klemke, ed., *Essays on Bertrand Russell* (Urbana: University of Illinois Press, 1972); David Pears, ed., *Bertrand Russell* (New York: Anchor, 1972); George W. Roberts, ed., *Bertrand Russell Memorial Volume* (London: Allen & Unwin, 1979); and R. M. Sainsbury, *Russell* (London: Routledge, 1979).

[19]Apart from works noted in the next few notes, Russell's chief philosophical writings are: *Philosophical Essays* (London: Longman & Green, 1910); *The Problems of Philosophy* (1912; Oxford: Oxford University Press, 1959); *Our Knowledge of the External World* (Chicago: Open Court, 1914); *Mysticism and Logic* (London: Longman & Green, 1918); *The Analysis of Mind* (London: Allen & Unwin, 1921); *The Analysis of Matter* (New York: Harcourt, 1927); *Philosophy* (New York: Norton, 1927; in the U.K. as "Outline of Philosophy"); *An Inquiry into Meaning and Truth* (1940; London: Penguin, 1962); *A History of Western Philosophy* (London: Allen & Unwin, 1945); and *Human Knowledge: Its Scope and Limits* (London: Allen & Unwin, 1948).

[20]Russell wrote about a great many things, including himself, with style and charm. His *The Autobiography of Bertrand Russell,* 3 vols. (London: Allen & Unwin, 1967-69), is the best source on his life. He also wrote an intellectual biography, *My Philosophical Development* (London: Allen & Unwin, 1959). See also his shorter "My Mental Development" in Schilpp, ed., *The Philosophy of Bertrand Russell.*

[21]The primary and secondary literature on Russell is enormous. For a complete bibliography, see Kenneth Blackwell, *A Bibliography of Bertrand Russell,* 3 vols. (London: Routledge, 1994). This is part of the *Complete Papers of Bertrand Russell* (London: Routledge, 1985) which collects all of his papers and essays, but not all his books. There are shorter bibliographies of Russell's own works in Pears, *Bertrand Russell* and Schilpp, ed., *The Philosophy of Bertrand Russell.*

[22]Besides *Principia Mathematica,* which he wrote with Whitehead and is his greatest work, Russell's chief works in logic and mathematics are: *An Essay on the Foundations of Geometry* (Cambridge: Cambridge University Press, 1897); *The Principles of Mathematics* (New York: Cambridge University Press, 1903); *Introduction to Mathematical Philosophy* (London: Allen & Unwin, 1919); and a collection of essays, *Logic and Knowledge,* ed. Robert Charles March (London: Allen & Unwin, 1956).

[23]*My Philosophical Development,* p. 11.

[24]Two fine historical studies of this early period are Peter Hylton, *Russell, Idealism and the Emergence of Analytic Philosophy* (New York: Oxford University Press, 1990); and Nicholas Griffin, *Russell's Idealist Apprenticeship* (New York: Oxford University Press, 1991).

[25]*Introduction to Mathematical Philosophy,* p. 169. This quote is not found in later editions.

[26]This essay is found in German and English in K. Gödel, *Collected Works,* ed. S. Feferman et al. (New York: Oxford University Press, 1986), 1.144-95.

[27]Russell developed this idea in many places, including two famous papers, "On Denoting" (1905), reprint in *Logic and Knowledge;* and "Knowledge by Acquaintance and Knowledge by Description" (1910), reprint in *Mysticism and Logic.*

[28]"Knowledge by Acquaintance," p. 226.

[29]This was the title of his contribution to *Contemporary British Philosophy,* ed. J. H. Muirhead (London: Allen & Unwin, 1924). See also his *The Philosophy of Logical Atomism,* ed. David Pears (La Salle, Ill.: Open Court, 1985); lectures originally published in *The Monist* (1918) and reprinted in *Logic and Knowledge,* and also in *Complete Papers,* vol. 8 (1986).

[30]City College is part of the City University of New York (CUNY). The facts in this case are recounted by Paul Edwards, Russell's friend and fellow atheist, in the American edition of Russell, *Why I Am Not a Christian and Other Essays on Religion and Related Subjects,* ed. Paul Edwards (New York: Simon and Schuster, 1957).

[31]*Inquiry into Meaning and Truth,* p. 14.

[32]Wayne C. Booth, *Modern Dogma and the Rhetoric of Assent* (Notre Dame: University of Notre Dame Press, 1974). This book and the essay by Brightman (see next note) represent good responses to Russell's views on ethics and religion. The best response to Russell's essay during his own time is H. G. Wood, *Why Mr. Bertrand Russell Is Not a Christian* (London: SCM Press, 1928).

[33]E. S. Brightman, "Russell's Philosophy of Religion," in Schilpp, ed., *The Philosophy of Bertrand Russell,* p. 543.

[34]*Why I Am Not a Christian,* p. 21.

[35]As reported in Wesley Salmon, "Religion and Science," *Philosophical Studies* 33 (1978): 176.

[36]For Russell's views on religion, see: "Proofs of the Existence of God," in *A Critical Exposition of the Philosophy of Leibniz* (New York: Cambridge University Press, 1900); *Religion and Science* (1935; reprint, New York: Oxford University Press, 1961); and the essays collected in *Why I Am Not a Christian,* and also in *Bertrand Russell on God and Religion,* ed. Al Seckel (Buffalo, N.Y.: Promethius, 1986).

[37]See Plantinga, *God and Other Minds* (Ithaca, N.Y.: Cornell University Press, 1967).

[38]Plantinga and his religious epistemology is discussed more fully later in this book; see chapter eight.

[39]*Why I Am Not a Christian,* p. 6.

[40]*Bertrand Russell on God,* pp. 125-26. The debate is also reprinted in the British edition of *Why I Am Not a Christian,* and in John Hick, ed., *The Existence of God* (London: Macmillan, 1964).

[41]For an excellent biography, see Ray Monk, *Ludwig Wittgenstein: The Duty of Genius* (New York: Penguin, 1990); also good on the early Wittgenstein is Brian F. McGuiness, *Wittgenstein, A Life, Volume 1, Young Ludwig: 1889-1921* (London: Duckworth, 1988). Wittgenstein made a tremendous personal impact on those who knew him. His fame and personality have prompted a number of personal recollections. Some of the most interesting are found in: Norman Malcolm, *Ludwig Wittgenstein: A Memoir* (New York: Oxford University Press, 1958); K. T. Fann, ed., *Ludwig Wittgenstein: The Man and His Philosophy* (New York: Dell, 1967); and Rush Rhees, ed., *Recollections of Wittgenstein* (New York: Oxford University Press, 1984).

There are a number of excellent introductions to Wittgenstein's philosophy, including: Anthony Kenny, *Wittgenstein* (Cambridge, Mass.: Harvard University Press, 1973); David Pears, *Ludwig Wittgenstein,* 2nd ed. (Cambridge, Mass.: Harvard University Press, 1986); George Pitcher, *The Philosophy of Wittgenstein* (Englewood Cliffs, N.J.: Prentice-Hall, 1964); Merrill B. Hintikka and Jaakko Hintikka, *Investigating Wittgenstein* (Oxford: Blackwell, 1986); A. J. Ayer, *Wittgenstein* (New York: Random House, 1985); Joachim Schulte, *Wittgenstein: An Introduction,* trans. William H. Brenner and John F. Holley (Albany, N.Y.: SUNY Press, 1992); and P. M. S. Hacker, *Wittgenstein* (New York: Routledge, 1999). William Warren Bartley's work, *Wittgenstein* (Philadelphia: Lippincott, 1973) is controversial and should be avoided by the beginning student.

[42]The literature on Wittgenstein is voluminous, even daunting. A useful, select bibliography is Guido Frongia and Brian McGuinness, *Wittgenstein: A Bibliographical Guide* (Cambridge, Mass.: Basil Blackwell, 1990). A fuller bibliography is found in volume 5 of an important collection of secondary work on Wittgenstein: Stuart Shanker, ed., *Ludwig Wittgenstein: Critical Assessments,* 5 vols. (London: Croom Helm, 1986). This set contains numerous important essays on Wittgenstein. A massive collection of reprinted articles, arranged by

topic, is *The Philosophy of Wittgenstein,* ed. John Canfield, 15 vols. (New York: Garland, 1986). A smaller, excellent collection of essays with a short bibliography is found in *The Cambridge Companion to Wittgenstein,* ed. Hans Sluga and David G. Stern (New York: Cambridge University Press, 1996).

Some of the better advanced discussions of Wittgenstein's philosophy and its importance are: Robert J. Ackermann, *Wittgenstein's City* (Amherst: University of Massachusetts Press, 1988); Cora Diamond, *The Realistic Spirit: Wittgenstein, Philosophy and the Mind* (Cambridge, Mass.: MIT Press, 1991); J. N. Findlay, *Wittgenstein: A Critique* (London: Routledge, 1984); Robert J. Fogelin, *Wittgenstein,* 2nd ed. (London: Routledge, 1987); P. M. S. Hacker, *Insight and Illusion,* 2nd ed. (New York: Oxford University Press, 1986); Saul A. Kripke, *Wittgenstein on Rules and Private Language* (Cambridge, Mass.: Harvard University Press, 1982); David Pears, *The False Prison,* 2 vols. (New York: Oxford University Press, 1987-88); and G. H. von Wright, *Wittgenstein* (Oxford: Blackwell, 1982). Works specifically on the *Tractatus* and the *Philosophical Investigations* are excluded here, but will be found in later notes.

[43]Wittgenstein's publications come in three parts: (1) works he prepared for publication himself, (2) notes of his lectures and conversations written by others and (3) a very large quantity of unpublished work, some of which has only recently been published by Wittgenstein's literary executors. This third part is usually called by the German term *Nachlass.* Here I will list only those publications which relate to the early Wittgenstein.

He published only one book during his lifetime: *Tractatus Logico-Philosophicus,* ed. C. K. Ogden, trans. Ogden and Frank Plumpton Ramsey (London: Kegan Paul, 1922), rev. trans. D. F. Pears and B. F. McGuinness (London: Routledge, 1961). Articles and lectures from this early period are usefully collected in *Philosophical Occasions, 1912-1951,* ed. James C. Klagge and Alfred Nordmann (Indianapolis: Hackett, 1993), including "Some Remarks on Logical Form," *Aristotelian Society,* Supp. Vol. 9 (1929): 162-71 (also reprinted in *Essays on Wittgenstein's Tractatus,* ed. Irving M. Copi and Robert W. Beard [New York: Macmillan, 1966]); and "Wittgenstein's Lecture on Ethics" (1929), *Philosophical Review* 74 (1965): 3-12. Works from his *Nachlass* which are relevant to his early thought are: *Notebooks, 1914-1916,* ed. G. H. von Wright and G. E. M. Anscombe, 2nd ed. (Oxford: Blackwell, 1979); and the *Prototractatus,* ed. B. F. McGuinness, et al. (Ithaca, N.Y.: Cornell University Press, 1971).

[44]For a study of Wittgenstein against the background of Viennese society in his day, see Allan Janik and Stephen Toulmin, *Wittgenstein's Vienna* (New York: Simon and Schuster, 1973). I am particularly indebted to this book for my understanding of the early Wittgenstein. Monk's biography is another good source, especially for his family background (Monk, *Ludwig Wittgenstein*).

[45]They are now found in the *Notebooks, 1914-1916,* appendix 2.

[46]The German edition appeared in the *Annalen der Naturphilosophie* [Leipzig] 14 (1921): 185-262, under the title, "Logisch-Philosophische Abhandlung." There is now a critical edition, with this same title, ed. Brian McGuinness and Joachim Schulte (Frankfurt: Suhrkamp, 1989).

[47]These are collected in Wittgenstein, *Letters to C. K. Ogden,* ed. G. H. von Wright (London: Routledge, 1973).

[48]Three good books on the *Tractatus* are G. E. M. Anscombe, *An Introduction to Wittgenstein's Tractatus* (London: Hutchinson, 1959); Max Black, *A Companion to Wittgenstein's Tractatus* (Ithaca, N.Y.: Cornell University Press, 1964) and H. O. Mounce, *Wittgenstein's Tractatus: An Introduction* (Chicago: University of Chicago Press, 1981). See also Copi and Beard, *Essays on Wittgenstein's Tractatus.*

[49]See his letter to an Austrian publisher (who in the end did not publish the work), "Letters

to Ludwig von Ficker" in C. G. Luckhardt, ed., *Wittgenstein: Sources and Perspectives* (Ithaca, N.Y.: Cornell University Press, 1979), p. 95.

[50]The *Tractatus* is normally cited by the numbered proposition, not the page number: a practice followed here.

[51]Augustine, *On Christian Teaching*, trans. R. P. H. Green, World Classics (New York: Oxford University Press, 1997), p. 10.

[52]For information about Schlick, see the introduction to the English translation of his *General Theory of Knowledge* (Vienna: Springer Verlag, 1974) and *Rationality and Science: A Memorial Volume for Moritz Schlick*, ed. Eugene T. Gadol (Vienna: Springer Verlag, 1982).

[53]For more about the Vienna Circle and logical positivism, see A. J. Ayer, "The Vienna Circle," *Midwest Studies in Philosophy* 6 (1981): 173-87; Jørgen Jørgensen, *The Development of Logical Empiricism*, International Encyclopedia of the Unified Science 2:9 (Chicago: University of Chicago Press, 1951); Victor Kraft, *The Vienna Circle* (New York: Philosophical Library, 1953); and Oswald Hanfling, *Logical Positivism* (New York: Columbia University Press, 1981).

[54]For more on the Berlin society, see Hans Reichenbach, *The Rise of Scientific Philosophy* (Berkeley: University of California Press, 1951); W. C. Salmon, ed., *Hans Reichenbach: Logical Empiricist* (Dordrecht: Reidel, 1979); and R. Jeffrey, "A Brief Guide to the Works of Carl Gustav Hempel," *Erkenntnis* 42 (1995): 3-14.

[55]An English translation of this tract is available in Otto Neurath, *Empiricism and Sociology*, ed. Marie Neurath and Robert S. Cohen (Dordrecht: Reidel, 1973). Neurath (1882-1945) was the major author of the document and an important figure behind the organization of the Circle.

[56]Original publication 1936; 2nd ed. (London: Gollancz, 1946; reprint, New York: Dover, 1952). This text was reprinted in 2001 as a Penguin classic.

[57]For Carnap's life and thought, see his "Autobiography" in *The Philosophy of Rudolf Carnap*, ed. Paul Arthur Schilpp (La Salle, Ill.: Open Court, 1963), with an extensive bibliography. Carnap's many contributions to philosophy include: *The Logical Structure of the World*, trans. Rolf A. George (1928; Berkeley: University of California Press, 1967); *The Logical Syntax of Language*, trans. Amethe Smeaton (London: Kegan Paul, 1937); *Foundations of Logic and Mathematics*, International Encyclopedia of the Unified Sciences, 1/3 (Chicago: University of Chicago Press, 1939); *Meaning and Necessity* (Chicago: University of Chicago Press, 1947); *Logical Foundations of Probability* (Chicago: University of Chicago Press, 1962); and *The Philosophy of Physics* (New York: Basic Books, 1966).

[58]"Autobiography," p. 59.

[59]"Autobiography," p. 57.

[60]See Carnap, "The Methodological Character of Theoretical Concepts," in *Minnesota Studies in the Philosophy of Science*, vol. 1, ed. H. Feigl and M. Scriven (Minneapolis: University of Minnesota Press, 1956), pp. 38-76.

[61]"Replies," in *The Philosophy of Rudolf Carnap*, p. 874; see earlier, "The Old and New Logic," section 9, in Ayer, *Logical Positivism*, p. 145.

[62]Karl R. Popper, *The Logic of Scientific Discovery* (1935; English translation, New York: Basic Books, 1959), p. 36.

[63]Ayer sat in on meetings of the Circle as a young scholar. He taught at London and Oxford, and was eventually knighted. For his own autobiography, see his *Part of My Life* (New York: Oxford University Press, 1978), and his intellectual autobiography in *The Philosophy of A. J. Ayer*, ed. Lewis Edwin Hahn (LaSalle. Ill.: Open Court, 1992), which contains a good bibliography.

[64]*Language, Truth and Logic* (1946 edition), p. 31.

[65]*Language, Truth and Logic*, p. 41.

[66]In Anthony Flew and Alasdair MacIntyre, *New Essays in Philosophical Theology* (London: SCM Press, 1955), p. 99.

[67]An example of this would be R. B. Braithwaite, *An Empiricist's View of the Nature of Religious Belief* (New York: Cambridge University Press, 1955), repr. in Basil Mitchell, ed., *The Philosophy of Religion* (New York: Oxford University Press, 1971).

[68]See John Hick, "Theology and Verification," *Theology Today* 17 (1960): 12-31; reprinted in Mitchell, *Philosophy of Religion.*

[69]See Ian T. Ramsey, *Religious Language* (London: SCM Press, 1957), and his later, influential work, *Models and Mystery* (New York: Oxford University Press, 1964).

Chapter 3: The Meaning of Being: Heidegger and German Existentialism

[1]The work of Dilthey in English is found most fully in the recent set of *Selected Works*, ed. Rudolph A. Makkreel and Frithjof Rodi, 6 vols. [projected] (Princeton: Princeton University Press, 1989-). Two shorter earlier collections edited by H. P. Rickmann are *Selected Writings* (New York: Cambridge University Press, 1976) and *Pattern and Meaning in History* (New York: Harper & Row, 1962). A brief introduction to Dilthey is included in the latter book. Fuller introductions are provided by H. A. Hodges, *Wilhelm Dilthey* (London: Routledge, 1942), and the more up-to-date volume, M. Ermarth, *Wilhelm Dilthey* (Chicago: University of Chicago Press, 1978). Other significant studies of Dilthey in English include: H. A. Hodges, *The Philosophy of Wilhelm Dilthey* (London: Routledge, 1952); Ilse N. Bulhof, *Wilhelm Dilthey: A Hermeneutic Approach to the Study of History and Culture* (The Hague: M. Nijhoff, 1980); Theodore Plantinga, *Historical Understanding in the Thought of Wilhelm Dilthey* (Toronto: University of Toronto Press, 1980); Rudolph A. Makkreel, *Dilthey: Philosopher of the Human Studies*, 2nd ed. (Princeton: Princeton University Press, 1992); and Jacob Owensby, *Dilthey and the Narrative of History* (Ithaca, N.Y.: Cornell University Press, 1994).

[2]Jose Ortega y Gasset, *Concord and Liberty*, trans. Helene Weyl (New York: Norton, 1946), p. 131.

[3]In fact, Dilthey's first significant work (1867) was a biography of Schleiermacher, which has never been translated into English: *Lebens Schleiermachers*, 2nd ed. (Berlin: de Gruyter, 1922).

[4]Dilthey, *Introduction to the Human Sciences*, trans. Ramon J. Betanzos (Detroit: Wayne State University Press, 1988). Another version is also found in the *Selected Works.*

[5]"The Formation of the Historical World in the Human Sciences," in *Selected Writings*, p. 183.

[6]"The Rise of Hermeneutics," in *Selected Works*, 4:236.

[7]*Pattern and Meaning*, pp. 67-68.

[8]"The Rise of Hermeneutics," p. 437.

[9]This is found in English as vol. 3 of his *Selected Works* (2002), and portions of the work are found in *Selected Writings* and in *Pattern and Meaning.*

[10]*Pattern and Meaning*, p. 69, punctuation altered. Cf. *Selected Writings*, pp. 172, 174.

[11]See his paper, "Types of Worldview and their Development in Metaphysical Systems," in *Selected Writings*, pp. 133-54.

[12]*Pattern and Meaning*, pp. 98-99.

[13]Translated by Quentin Lauer, in Husserl, *Phenomenology and the Crisis of Philosophy* (New York: Harper & Row, 1965), esp. pp. 122-47.

[14]See the references to Dilthey in the index to Heidegger's *Being and Time*. There are two editions of *Being and Time* in English, both with good indexes (see below). For an outstanding investigation of the origins of this masterwork, see Theodore Kisiel, *The Genesis of Heidegger's Being and Time* (Berkeley: University of California Press, 1993), who demonstrates that the book has its origins in a long book review of some of Dilthey's philosophi-

cal correspondence. See also C. R. Bambach, *Heidegger, Dilthey and the Crisis of Historicism* (Ithaca, N.Y.: Cornell University Press, 1995), and Rudolph A. Makkreel and John Scanlon, eds., *Dilthey and Phenomenology* (Washington, D. C.: University Press of America, 1987).

[15]For some good introductions to his thought, see William J. Richardson, *Heidegger* (The Hague: M. Nijhoff, 1963); Otto Pöggeler, *Martin Heidegger's Path of Thinking* (Atlantic Highlands, N.J.: Humanities, 1987); Michael Inwood, *Heidegger* (New York: Oxford University Press, 1997); Richard F. H. Polt, *Heidegger* (Ithaca, N.Y.: Cornell University Press, 1999); Hubert Dreyfus and Harrison Hall, eds., *Heidegger: A Critical Reader* (Oxford: Blackwell, 1992); Thomas Sheehan, ed., *Heidegger: The Man and the Thinker* (Chicago: Precedent, 1977); and Charles B. Guignon, ed., *The Cambridge Companion to Heidegger* (New York: Cambridge University Press, 1993). There is an ongoing set of his complete works in German that already numbers over eighty volumes. His major works in English translation are: *Being and Time*, with two English versions (my page references will be to the original German text, cited as *Sein und Zeit*, since these page numbers are found within both the English translations), trans. John Macquarrie & Edward Robinson (New York: Harper & Row, 1962); and trans. Joan Stambaugh (Albany: SUNY Press, 1996); *Basic Writings*, ed. David Farrell Krell (New York: Harper & Row, 1977); *The Basic Problems of Phenomenology*, trans. Albert Hofstadter (Bloomington, Ind.: Indiana University Press, 1982); *Contributions to Philosophy*, trans. Parvis Emad and Kenneth Maly (Bloomington, Ind.: Indiana University Press, 1999); *Discourse on Thinking*, trans. J. M. Anderson and E. Hans Freund (New York: Harper & Row, 1966); *Early Greek Thinking*, trans. David Farrell Krell and Frank A. Capuzzi (New York: Harper & Row, 1975); *The End of Philosophy*, trans. Joan Stambaugh (New York: Harper & Row, 1973); *The Essence of Reasons*, trans. Terrence Malick (Evanston: Northwestern University Press, 1969); *Existence and Being*, ed. Werner Brock (South Bend, Ind.: Gateway, 1949); *Identity and Difference*, trans. Joan Stambaugh (New York: Harper & Row, 1969); *Introduction to Metaphysics*, trans. Ralph Manheim (Garden City, N. J.: Anchor, 1961); *Kant and the Problem of Metaphysics*, trans. James S. Churchill, rev. trans. Richard Taft (Bloomington, Ind.: Indiana University Press, 1962; rev. 1990); *Nietzsche*, 4 vols., trans. and ed. David Farrell Krell et al. (New York: Harper & Row, 1979-82); *On Time and Being*, trans. Joan Stambaugh (New York: Harper & Row, 1972); *On the Way to Language*, trans. Peter D. Hertz and Joan Stambaugh (New York: Harper & Row, 1971); *Pathways*, trans. David Farrell Krell et al. (New York: Cambridge University Press, 1997); *Parmenides*, trans. André Schuwer and Richard Rojcewicz (Bloomington: Indiana University Press, 1992); *The Piety of Thinking*, trans. James G. Hart and John C. Maraldo (Bloomington: Indiana University Press, 1976); *Poetry, Language and Thought*, trans. Albert Hofstadter (New York: Harper & Row, 1971); *The Principle of Reason*, trans. Reginald Lilly (Bloomington: Indiana University Press, 1991); *The Question of Being*, trans. William Kluback and Jean T. Wilde (New York: Twayne, 1958); "The Way Back to the Ground of Metaphysics," trans. by Walter Arnold Kaufmann in his (ed.) *Existentialism from Dostoevsky to Sartre* (Cleveland: World, 1965); *What Is Called Thinking?* trans. Fred D. Wieck and J. Glenn Gray (New York: Harper & Row, 1965); and *What Is Philosophy?* trans. William Kluback and Jean T. Wilde (New Haven: College and University Press, 1958). A complete and current list of Heidegger's works in English has yet to be published, especially since new or revised translations are already on their way.

[16]The secondary literature on Heidegger is vast and found in every European language. Two bibliographies in English provide some help: Hans-Martin Sass, *Martin Heidegger: A Bibliography and Glossary* (Bowling Green: Philosophy Documentation Center, 1982); Joan Nordquist, ed., *Martin Heidegger* and *Martin Heidegger (II)*, 2 vols. (Santa Cruz, Calif.: Reference and Research Service, 1990 and 1996). Heidegger's specialized vocabulary is never easy. For some help see Michael Inwood, *A Heidegger Dictionary* (Oxford: Blackwell, 1999)

or Alfred Denker, *Historical Dictionary of Heidegger's Philosophy* (Lanham, Md.: Scarecrow, 2000). In addition to the works already cited, and also cited below, the following secondary literature is helpful and representative: Jeffrey Andrew Barash, *Martin Heidegger and the Problem of Historical Meaning* (Dordrecht: Nijhoff, 1985); Rodney R. Coltman, *The Language of Hermeneutics* (Albany: SUNY Press, 1998); Hans-Georg Gadamer, *Heidegger's Ways* (Albany: SUNY Press, 1994); Charles Guignon, *Heidegger and the Problem of Knowledge* (Indianapolis: Hackett, 1983); Dominique Janicaud, *Heidegger from Metaphysics to Thought* (Albany: SUNY Press, 1995); Joseph J. Kockelmans, *Heidegger and Science* (Washington, D.C.: University Press of America, 1985); Cristina Lafont, *Heidegger, Language and World Disclosure* (New York: Cambridge University Press, 2000); John Loscerbo, *Being and Technology* (The Hague: Nijhoff, 1981); Frederick A. Olafson, *Heidegger and the Philosophy of Mind* (New Haven: Yale University Press, 1987); Reiner Schürmann, *Heidegger on Being and Acting* (Bloomington: Indiana University Press, 1987); Joan Stambaugh, *Thoughts on Heidegger* (Lanham, Md.: University Press of America, 1991); George Steiner, *Martin Heidegger* (New York: Viking, 1978); Jacques Taminiaux, *Heidegger and the Project of Fundamental Ontology* (Albany: SUNY Press, 1991); and Michael Zimmerman, *Eclipse of the Self: The Development of Heidegger's Conception of Authenticity* (Athens: Ohio University Press, 1981).

[17]An example of this is the 1932 essay by Rudolf Carnap (the logical positivist from the Vienna Circle) which is highly critical of Heidegger and was written partly in response to the latter's published lecture, *What Is Metaphysics?* (1929; English translation in his *Basic Writings* or in *Existence and Being*). Rudolf Carnap, "The Elimination of Metaphysics Through Logical Analysis of Language," in *Logical Positivism*, ed. A. J. Ayer (New York: Free Press, 1959), pp. 60-81.

[18]The standard biography of Heidegger to date is Hugo Ott, *Martin Heidegger* (London: HarperCollins, 1993). Ott is particularly helpful on the early Christian phase of Heidegger's development. A newer biography is Rudiger Safranski, *Martin Heidegger: Between Good and Evil* (Cambridge, Mass.: Harvard University Press, 1998), which has more of a political focus.

[19]Because of the importance of *Being and Time*, historians divide Heidegger's life into three periods. The earliest period is the "young Heidegger," which is also his Christian period. The middle period, during which he published *Being and Time*, is about a decade long, from 1925 to the mid 1930s. This is called the called the "early Heidegger" or Heidegger I. Heidegger II is known as the "later Heidegger." For the young Heidegger, see Ott, *Martin Heidegger;* Kisiel, *Genesis;* John Van Buren, *The Young Heidegger* (Bloomington: Indiana University Press, 1994); and Kisiel and Van Buren, eds., *Reading Heidegger from the Start* (Albany: SUNY Press, 1994).

[20]See Ott, *Martin Heidegger*, pp. 369-71. See also B. Welte, "Seeking and Finding: The Speech at Heidegger's Burial," in Sheehan, ed., *Heidegger*, pp. 73-75.

[21]B. Casper, "Martin Heidegger und die theologische Fakulät Freiburg 1909-1923," *Freiburger Diözesan Archiv* 100 (1980): 541; cited in English in Kisiel, *Genesis*, p. 15. The friend was Engelbert Krebs.

[22]They are found in volume 60 of his *Gesamtausgabe: Phänomenologie des religiösen Lebens* (Frankfurt a. M: V. Klostermann, 1995). The lecture notes published in vol. 60 are: "Introduction to the Phenomenology of Religion," "Augustine and Neoplatonism" and "The Philosophical Basis of Medieval Mysticism." All are from the period 1918-21. For the new English translation, see *The Phenomenology of Religious Life* (Bloomington: Indiana University Press, 2004).

[23]*Phänomenologie des religiösen Lebens*, p. 313.

[24]On the theme of Heidegger and religion, see James Robinson and John Cobb, ed., *The Later Heidegger and Theology* (New York: Harper & Row, 1963), especially the chapter on

Heinrich Ott and its discussion therein; James L. Perotti, *Heidegger and the Divine* (Athens, Ohio: Ohio University Press, 1974); John D. Caputo, *The Mystical Element in Heidegger's Thought* (1978; rev. ed., New York: Fordham University Press, 1986); Caputo, *Heidegger and Aquinas* (New York: Fordham University Press, 1982); Caputo, "Heidegger and Theology" in the *Cambridge Companion to Heidegger;* John Macquarrie, *An Existential Theology* (New York: Macmillan, 1955), and his *Heidegger and Christianity* (New York: Continuum, 1994); George Kovacs, *The Question of God in Heidegger's Phenomenology* (Evanston, Ill.: Northwestern University Press, 1990); Jeff Owen Prudhomme, *God and Being: Heidegger's Relation to Theology* (Atlantic Highlands: Humanities, 1997); and Merold Westphal, *Overcoming Ontotheology* (New York: Fordham University Press, 2001).

[25]This oft quoted phrase comes from Hannah Arendt, who was his student at that time and fell in love with Heidegger. See Arendt, "Heidegger at Eighty," *New York Review of Books* 17 (October 21, 1971), pp. 50-54, repr. in Michael Murry, ed., *Heidegger and Modern Philosophy* (New Haven: Yale University Press, 1978). See further Elzbieta Ettinger, *Hannah Arendt/ Martin Heidegger* (New Haven: Yale University Press, 1995).

[26]From the "Translator's Preface" to *Being and Time,* trans. Macquarrie and Robinson, p. 13.

[27]For some help specifically with *Being and Time,* see Richard Schmitt, *Martin Heidegger on Being Human: An Introduction to Sein und Zeit* (New York: Random House, 1969); Michael Gelven, *A Commentary on Heidegger's Being and Time* (New York: Harper & Row, 1970); Stephen Mulhall, *Routledge Philosophy Guidebook to Heidegger and Being and Time* (London: Routledge, 1996); and the more advanced commentary of Hubert L. Dreyfus, *Being-in-the-World* (Cambridge, Mass.: Harvard University Press, 1991).

[28]*Sein* is the German infinitive "to be," while *da* means "there."

[29]See Heidegger, *Early Greek Thinking,* and his published lectures, *Parmenides* and the *Heraclitus Seminar* (with Eugen Fink), trans. Charles H. Seibert (Evanston, Ill.: Northwestern University Press, 1993).

[30]*Sein und Zeit,* p. 1. Page numbers are to the German edition, *Sein und Zeit.* These page references are found in both English translations. The quotation is from Plato, *Sophist,* 244A.

[31]*Sein und Zeit,* §6.

[32]*Sein und Zeit,* p. 5.

[33]*Sein und Zeit,* p. 7.

[34]*Sein und Zeit,* p. 56.

[35]*Sein und Zeit,* p. 12.

[36]*Sein und Zeit,* §1. The quotation is from Aristotle, *Metaphysics,* 998B.

[37]*Sein und Zeit,* p. 66.

[38]*Sein und Zeit,* p. 98.

[39]*Sein und Zeit,* §38.

[40]*Sein und Zeit,* p. 184.

[41]Heidegger, *History of the Concept of Time: Prolegomena,* trans. Theodore Kisiel (Bloomington: Indiana University Press, 1989), p. 318.

[42]*Sein und Zeit,* p. 19.

[43]*Sein und Zeit,* §79.

[44]K. Löwth, "The Political Implications of Heidegger's Existentialism," in *The Heidegger Controversy,* ed. Richard Wolin (Cambridge, Mass.: MIT Press, 1993), pp. 167-85.

[45]For more on Heidegger and the Nazis (which has become a large literature in itself!), see Ott, *Martin Heidegger,* part 3; Wolin, ed., *The Heidegger Controversy;* Safranski, *Martin Heidegger;* and Victor Farias, *Heidegger and Nazism,* trans. Paul Burrell and Gabriel R. Ricci (Philadelphia: Temple University Press, 1989).

[46]English translation in *Heidegger Controversy,* pp. 29-39.

[47]"But nauseating as they are, Heidegger's gestures and pronouncements during 1933-34

are tractable. It is his complete silence on Hitlerism and the holocaust after 1945 which is very nearly intolerable." This is the judgment of the Jewish intellectual George Steiner, Heidegger's former student, and former husband of Hannah Arendt. Steiner, *Martin Heidegger*, p. 123.

[48]*Introduction to Metaphysics*, p. 166. See also "Overcoming Metaphysics," §XXVI (in Heidegger, *The End of Philosophy*, and also in *The Heidegger Controversy*).

[49]This is found in English in *Existence and Being*, pp. 351-61.

[50]This is found in English as "The Way Back to the Ground of Metaphysics," in Kaufmann, *Existentialism*, pp. 206-21.

[51]"The Way Back," p. 207.

[52]"The Way Back," p. 208.

[53]This is the title of one of his essays, "The End of Philosophy and the Task of Thinking," in *Basic Writings*, repr. from *The End of Philosophy*.

[54]*Basic Writings*, p. 375.

[55]"Overcoming Metaphysics," §III.

[56]"Overcoming Metaphysics," §III.

[57]*The Question Concerning Technology*, p. 28.

[58]"Letter on Humanism," in *Basic Writings*, p. 206.

[59]*Basic Writings*, p. 193.

[60]"Postscript," in *Existence and Being*, p. 360.

[61]*Basic Writings*, pp. 184-85.

[62]*The End of Philosophy*, p. 57.

[63]*On Time and Being*, p. 2.

[64]Heidegger, *Contributions to Philosophy (From Enowning)*, published in German in 1989, contains notes and studies from 1936-38.

[65]*On Time and Being*, p. 41.

[66]See his comments on theology in *The Piety of Thinking*.

[67]The main philosophical work of Buber is *I and Thou*, which has two English translations: one by Ronald Gregor Smith (2nd ed., New York: Scribner, 1958), another by Walter Kaufmann (New York: Scribner, 1970). Both are still in print. I will quote the translation by Smith, but indicate page number from the Walter Kaufmann translation (WK) in parenthesis.

[68]Other than *I and Thou*, the main philosophical works of Buber in English are collected in two books: *Between Man and Man*, trans. Maurice Friedman and Ronald Gregor Smith (New York: Macmillan, 1965) and *The Knowledge of Man*, ed. Maurice Friedman and Ronald Gregor Smith (New York: Harper, 1965). For a good bibliography of works by and about Buber up to 1978, see Willard Moonan, *Martin Buber and His Critics* (New York: Garland, 1981). Out of an extensive list of his publications, the following works are representative of his writings in philosophy of religion: *The Eclipse of God* (New York: Harper, 1957); *The Prophetic Faith* (New York: Harper, 1960); *Two Types of Faith* (New York: Harper, 1961); and *Good and Evil* (New York: Scribner, 1961). Starting with *The Letters of Martin Buber* (1996) Syracuse University Press is publishing a uniform edition of his works in English (series title, The Martin Buber Library), but I will be citing the older and easily available paperback editions.

[69]For some good introductions to Buber as a philosopher, see Maurice Friedman, *Martin Buber: The Life of Dialogue* (New York: Harper, 1960) and the collection edited by Will Herberg, *The Writings of Martin Buber* (New York: Meridian, 1956). For works that focus more on Buber's philosophy of religion and his Jewish/biblical thought, see Greta Schaeder, *The Hebrew Humanism of Martin Buber* (Detroit: Wayne State University Press, 1973); Maurice Friedman, *Martin Buber and the Eternal* (New York: Human Sciences Press, 1986);

Donald J. Moore, *Martin Buber: Prophet of Religious Secularism*, rev. ed. (New York: Fordham University Press, 1996); the new anthology edited by Asher D. Biemann, *The Martin Buber Reader* (New York: Palgrave Macmillan, 2002); and the fine recent study by Steven Kepnes, *The Text as Thou: Martin Buber's Dialogical Hermeneutics and Narrative Theology* (Bloomington: Indiana University Press, 1992).

[70]For the life of Buber, see Maurice Friedman, *Encounter on the Narrow Ridge: A Life of Martin Buber* (New York: Paragon House, 1991) and for the ambitious see Friedman's massive overview of Buber's life and thought in three volumes: *Martin Buber's Life and Work* (New York: Dutton, 1981-83).

[71]The Hasidic school, or Hasidim, was a Jewish mystical movement in Central and Eastern Europe founded by Israel Baal Shem (1700-60).

[72]Buber's artful retelling of the stories of the Hasidim, in English, are collected in three works: *The Legend of Baal-Shem* (Princeton: Princeton University Press, 1995); *Tales of Rabbi Nachman* (New York: Promethius, 1999); and *Tales of the Hasidim*, 2 vols. in 1 (New York: Schocken, 1991). For the introduction mentioned above, see "Spirit and Body of the Hasidic Movement," in *The Martin Buber Reader* (ed. Biemann); also in *The Origin and Meaning of Hasidism*, trans. Maurice Friedman (New York: Harper, 1966), originally published in German in 1922.

[73]I will replace *thou*—so formal and foreign to twenty-first century English—with *you* except in the title of Buber's book. This is in fact closer to his German usage, in which *Du* is the you-familiar.

[74]*I and Thou*, p. 3 (WK, pp. 53-54). In these notes, I first quote the Smith translation, then Kaufmann as WK.

[75]*I and Thou*, p. 18 (WK, p. 69).

[76]*I and Thou*, p. 34 (WK, p. 85), trans. alt.

[77]Martin Buber, "Hasidism and Modern Man," *Martin Buber Reader*, p. 90; also in *Hasidism and Modern Man* (New York: Horizon, 1958).

[78]*Between Man and Man*, p. 219 (rev. ed., 1965).

[79]Given as lectures to the German Academy in 1937, just before being expelled from his philosophy chair by the Nazis: Karl Jaspers, *Philosophy of Existence*, trans. Richard F. Grabau (Philadelphia: University of Pennsylvania Press, 1971). This book makes an excellent introduction to his philosophy. For other introductory books by Jaspers, see *Man in the Modern Age*, trans. Eden and Cedar Paul (Garden City, N.Y.: Anchor, 1957); *Way to Wisdom: An Introduction to Philosophy*, trans. Ralph Manheim (New Haven: Yale University Press, 1954); and *Karl Jaspers: Basic Philosophical Writings*, ed. Edith Ehrlich, Leonard H. Ehrlich and George B. Pepper (Athens: Ohio University Press, 1986). For introductions written by others, see Charles F. Wallraff, *Karl Jaspers* (Princeton: Princeton University Press, 1970) and Sebastian Samay, *Reason Revisited: The Philosophy of Karl Jaspers* (Notre Dame: University of Notre Dame Press, 1971).

[80]The major philosophical books by Jaspers in English (not cited above) are: *Philosophy*, 3 vols., trans. E. B. Ashton (Chicago: University of Chicago Press, 1969-71); *Reason and Existenz*, trans. William Earle (London: Routledge, 1956); *The Perennial Scope of Philosophy*, trans. Ralph Manheim (New York: Philosophical Library, 1949); *The Origin and Goal of History* (New Haven: Yale University Press, 1953); *Philosophical Faith and Revelation*, trans. R. Piper and E. B. Ashton (Chicago: University of Chicago Press, 1967); and *The Great Philosophers*, 3 vols., trans. Ralph Manheim, Edith Ehrlich and Leonard H. Ehrlich (New York: Harcourt, Brace, 1962, 1966, 1993). For a complete bibliography, see Paul Arthur Schilpp, ed., *The Philosophy of Karl Jaspers*, 2nd ed. (La Salle, Ill.: Open Court, 1981).

[81]C. F. von Weizsäcker, "In Memory of Karl Jaspers," in *Karl Jaspers Today*, ed. Leonard H. Ehrlich and Richard Wisser (Washington, D.C.: University Press of America, 1988), p. 27.

[82]Karl Jaspers, *Psychologie der Weltanschauungen*, 6th ed. (Berlin: Springer, 1971), p. x. No English translation currently exists.

[83]Karl Jaspers, *Von der Wahrheit* (Munich: R. Piper, 1947). No English translation currently exists; but see part four, "What Is Truth," in *Karl Jaspers: Basic Philosophical Writings*, ed. Ehrlich and Pepper.

[84]Karl Jaspers, *The Question of German Guilt*, trans. E. B. Ashton (New York: Dial, 1947).

[85]For some representative studies of Jaspers in English, see Paul Arthur Schilpp, ed., *The Philosophy of Karl Jaspers*, which is the best overall volume of interpretive essays; Leonard Ehrlich, *Karl Jaspers: Philosophy as Faith* (Amherst: University of Massachusetts Press, 1975); Leonard H. Ehrlich and Richard Wisser, eds., *Karl Jaspers Today* (Washington, D.C.: University Press of America, 1988); Joseph W. Koterski and Raymond J. Langley, eds., *Karl Jaspers on Philosophy of History and History of Philosophy* (Amherst, N.Y.: Humanity, 2003); Alan M. Olson, *Transcendence and Hermeneutics* (The Hague: M. Nijhoff, 1979); Oswald Schrag, *Existence, Existenz and Transcendence* (Pittsburgh: Duquesne University Press, 1971); Chris Thornhill, *Karl Jaspers: Politics and Metaphysics* (London: Routledge, 2002); Gregory J. Walters, *Karl Jaspers and the Role of "Conversion" in the Nuclear Age* (Lanham, Md.: University Press of America, 1988); Gregory J. Walters, ed., *The Tasks of Truth: Essays on Karl Jaspers' Idea of the University* (Frankfurt: Peter Lang, 1995).

[86]*Man in the Modern Age*, p. 175.

Chapter 4: Being at Paris: French Existentialism

[1]The major philosophical works of Marcel are *The Mystery of Being*, 2 vols. (Chicago: Henry Regnery Company, 1960); *Man Against Mass Society*, trans. G. S. Fraser (Chicago: Henry Regnery Company, 1962); *Being and Having: An Existentialist Diary* (Gloucester, Mass.: Peter Smith, 1976); *Metaphysical Journal*, trans. Bernard Wall (London: Rocliff, 1952); and *The Philosophy of Existentialism*, trans. Manya Harari (Secaucus, N.J.: Citadel, 1956). For significant secondary studies of Marcel's thought and work, consult Seymour Cain, *Gabriel Marcel* (South Bend, Ind.: Regnery/Gateway, 1979); Seymour Cain, *Gabriel Marcel's Theory of Religious Experience* (New York: Peter Lang, 1995); Kenneth T. Gallagher, *The Philosophy of Gabriel Marcel* (New York: Fordham University Press, 1975); Paul Arthur Schilpp and Lewis Edwin Hahn, eds., *The Philosophy of Gabriel Marcel* (La Salle, Ill.: Open Court 1984); and Joe McCown, *Availability: Gabriel Marcel and the Phenomenology of Human Openness* (Missoula, Mont.: Scholars Press, 1978).

[2]*Metaphysical Journal*, p. vii.

[3]*Being and Having*, p. 15.

[4]*Mystery of Being*, 2:10.

[5]*Being and Having*, p. 191.

[6]*Being and Having*, p. 191.

[7]*Metaphysical Journal*, p. 97.

[8]*Mystery of Being*, 1:251.

[9]*Man Against Mass Society*, pp. 90-91.

[10]*Being and Having*, p. 171.

[11]Rene Descartes, *Discourse on Method*, part 6; in *A Discourse on Method*, trans. John Veitch (London: J. M. Dent, 1999), p. 46.

[12]*Being and Having*, p. 164.

[13]*Being and Having*, p. 164.

[14]*Mystery of Being*, 1:127.

[15]*Being and Having*, p. 187.

[16]*Mystery of Being*, 1:264-65.

[17]*Metaphysical Journal*, p. 138.

[18]*Mystery of Being,* 2:197-98.

[19]*Metaphysical Journal,* p. 39.

[20]*Metaphysical Journal,* p. 200.

[21]Some of Camus's major works are *The Stranger,* trans. Stuart Gilbert (New York: Vintage, 1946); *The Plague,* trans. Stuart Gilbert (New York: Modern Library, 1948), *The Fall,* trans. Justin O'Brien (New York: Alfred A. Knopf, 1960); *Notebooks: 1935-1942,* trans. Stuart Gilbert (New York: Vintage, 1972); *The Myth of Sisyphus and Other Essays,* trans. Justin O'Brien (New York: Alfred A. Knopf, 1964); *Resistance, Rebellion, and Death,* trans. Justin O'Brien (New York: The Modern Library, 1960); *Exile and the Kingdom,* trans. Stuart Gilbert (New York: Vintage, 1957); *The Rebel,* trans. Anthony Bower (New York: Alfred A. Knopf, 1961); *Caligula & Three Other Plays,* trans. Stuart Gilbert (New York: Alfred A. Knopf, 1972); and *The First Man,* trans. David Hapgood (New York: Vintage, 1996).

The following secondary sources are useful for understanding his philosophy: Albert Maquet, *Albert Camus: The Invincible Summer,* trans. Herma Briffault (New York: George Braziller, 1958); Jean Onimus, *Albert Camus and Christianity,* trans. Emmett Parker (University: University of Alabama Press, 1965); Richard Kamber, *On Camus* (Belmont, Calif.: Wadsworth, 2002); Emmett Parker, *Albert Camus: The Artist in the Arena* (Madison: University of Wisconsin Press, 1965); and *Camus: A Collection of Critical Essays,* ed. Germaine Brée (Englewood Cliffs, N.J.: Prentice-Hall, 1962). For biographies of Camus, see Olivier Todd, *Albert Camus: A Life* (New York: Alfred A. Knopf, 1997); and Herbert R. Lottman, *Albert Camus: A Biography* (New York: George Braziller, 1980).

[22]This relationship between Sartre and Camus, which had become increasingly strained, finally dissolved with the publication of *The Rebel,* in which Camus relentlessly critiques Communism. He was accused by a review in *Les Temps Modernes* of betraying the political left. Although Sartre did not pen the review, as editor of the publication it was clear that he concurred with this conclusion. When Camus wrote a rebuttal to the review, Sartre became personally involved in the controversy. Sartre's lengthy open letter was highly critical of *The Rebel,* but also included sharp personal attacks on Camus as well. This rift was never healed. However, a month after Camus's death, Sartre wrote a moving "Tribute to Albert Camus," reprinted in *Camus: A Collection of Critical Essays,* ed. Germaine Brée (Englewood Cliffs, N.J.: Prentice-Hall, 1962), pp. 173-75.

[23]*Myth of Sisyphus,* p. 3.

[24]*Myth of Sisyphus,* p. 8.

[25]*Myth of Sisyphus,* p. 55.

[26]*The Stranger,* p. 154.

[27]*Myth of Sisyphus,* p. 121.

[28]*Myth of Sisyphus,* p. 121.

[29]*The Rebel,* p. 5.

[30]Camus, *The Plague,* p. 211.

[31]*The Plague,* p. 213.

[32]Another example of Camus's more conciliatory, but still unyielding, view of Christianity is found when Panaloux tries to convince Rieux that, consciously or not, he was "working for man's salvation" in his acts of mercy. When the atheist doctor rejects this interpretation, Father Paneloux expresses regret that he remains unconvinced. Rieux responds by stating, "What does it matter? What I hate is death and disease, as you well know. And whether you wish it or not, we're allies, facing them and fighting them together. . . . So you see . . . God Himself can't part us now." See *The Plague,* pp. 203-4.

[33]*The Plague,* p. 121.

[34]*The Plague,* p. 154.

[35]*The Plague,* p. 235.

[36]*The Fall,* p. 138.

[37]*The Fall,* p. 131.

[38]*The Plague,* p. 203.

[39]An interesting element has been added to these discussions with the publication of Howard E. Mumma's book, *Albert Camus and the Minister* (Brewster, Mass.: Paraclete, 2000). In the late 1950s, Mumma, a Methodist minister, was pastoring an American church in Paris, where Camus came to attend an organ recital. The two men met and developed a relationship in which they read Scripture together and discussed Christianity. Mumma's book claims that Camus requested baptism, but Mumma hesitated because Camus had been baptized as an infant and he had requested that the baptism remain private. Further conversations between the two never occurred because of Camus's death. Many commentators have raised questions about the veracity of Mumma's memoirs since none of the information had been public for over forty years. On the other hand, given the movements in Camus's thought toward the end of his life, others have found this story quite plausible.

[40]Sartre's major works include *Being and Nothingness,* trans. Hazel E. Barnes (New York: Washington Square Press, 1966); *No Exit and Three Other Plays* (New York: Vintage, 1946); *Existentialism* (New York: Philosophical Library, 1947); *Nausea,* trans. Lloyd Alexander (Norfolk, Conn.: New Directions Paperback, 1964); *The Emotions: Outline of a Theory,* trans. Bernard Frechtman (New York: Philosophical Library, 1948); *What Is Literature?* trans. Bernard Frechtman (San Francisco: Harper & Row, 1965); *Critique of Dialectical Reason: Theory of Practical Ensembles,* ed. Jonathan Rèe, trans. Alan Sheridan-Smith (London: New Left, 1976); and *The Transcendence of the Ego: An Existential Theory of Consciousness,* trans. Forest Williams and Robert Kirkpatrick (New York: Octagon, 1972). Sartre's autobiography is available as *The Words,* trans. Bernard Frechtman (New York: G. Braziller, 1964). Biographical treatments include John Gerassi, *Jean-Paul Sartre: Hated Conscience of His Century* (Chicago: University of Chicago Press, 1989) and Annie Cohen-Solal, *Sartre: A Life* (London: Daedalus, 1987). For additional information on Sartre's philosophy, consult Christina Howells, ed., *The Cambridge Companion to Sartre* (New York: Cambridge University Press, 1992); Norman N. Greene, *Jean-Paul Sartre: The Existentialist Ethic* (Ann Arbor: University of Michigan Press, 1963); Marjorie Glicksman Grene, *Sartre* (New York: New Viewpoints, 1973); Iris Murdoch, *Sartre: Romantic Rationalist* (New York: Viking, 1987); and Dominick La Capra, *A Preface to Sartre* (Ithaca, N.Y.: Cornell University Press, 1978).

[41]*Existentialism,* pp. 60-61.

[42]As an interesting biographical side note, Sartre's maternal grandfather, Karl Schweitzer, was the uncle of the famous missionary doctor, theologian and musician, Albert Schweitzer.

[43]*The Words,* p. 88.

[44]*The Words,* p. 135.

[45]Although highly controversial in its claim that de Beauvoir is the source of the main concepts Sartre develops in his existentialism, Kate Fullbrook and Edward Fullbrook, *Simone de Beauvoir and Jean-Paul Sartre: The Remaking of a Twentieth-Century Legend* (New York: Basic Books, 1994) provides insight into the intellectual relationship between these two figures. Some of their correspondence with each other is found in Jean-Paul Sartre and Simone de Beauvoir, *Quiet Moments in a War: The Letters of Jean-Paul Sartre to Simone de Beauvoir, 1940-1963* (New York: Simon and Schuster, 1993). We discuss de Beauvoir more fully in chapter nine of this book.

[46]*Nausea,* pp. 133-34.

[47]*Nausea,* p. 45.

[48]*Nausea,* p. 19.

[49]*Nausea*, p. 176.

[50]*Nausea*, p. 180.

[51]*Existentialism*, p. 16.

[52]*Existentialism*, pp. 16-17.

[53]*Existentialism*, pp. 18-19.

[54]*Being and Nothingness*, p. 724.

[55]*Being and Nothingness*, p. 101.

[56]*Being and Nothingness*, p. 102.

[57]*Existentialism*, p. 27.

[58]*Being and Nothingness*, p. 87.

[59]*Being and Nothingness*, p. 341.

[60]*Being and Nothingness*, p. 345.

[61]*No Exit*, p. 47.

[62]*Being and Nothingness*, p. 400.

[63]*Existentialism*, p. 61.

[64]*Being and Nothingness*, p. 784.

[65]For a more extensive critique of Sartre, see Steve Wilkens, *Good Ideas from Questionable Christians and Outright Pagans* (Downers Grove, Ill.: InterVarsity Press, 2004), pp. 247-52.

[66]A sampling of biographical treatments includes Francine Du Plessix Gray, *Simone Weil* (New York: Penguin, 2001); Simone Petrement, *Simone Weil: A Life* (New York: Pantheon, 1976); Robert Coles, *Simone Weil: A Modern Pilgrimage* (Reading, Mass.: Addison-Wesley, 1987); and Gabriella Fiori, *Simone Weil: An Intellectual Biography*, trans. Joseph R. Berrigan (Athens: University of Georgia Press, 1989).

[67]Concerning this sense of inferiority, she writes, "At fourteen I fell into one of those fits of bottomless despair that come with adolescence, and I seriously thought of dying because of the mediocrity of my natural faculties. The exceptional gifts of my brother, who had a childhood and youth comparable to those of Pascal, brought my own inferiority home to me. I did not mind having no visible successes, but what did grieve me was the idea of being excluded from that transcendent kingdom to which only the truly great have access and wherein truth abides. I preferred to die rather than live without that truth." See Simone Weil, *Waiting for God*, trans. Emma Craufurd (New York: Perennial, 2001), p. 23.

[68]Some of the key primary sources for Weil's work are *Waiting for God; The Need for Roots: Prelude to a Declaration of Duties Toward Mankind*, trans. Arthur Wills (New York: Octagon, 1979); *Gravity and Grace*, trans. Arthur Willis (New York: Putnam, 1952); *Intimations of Christianity among the Ancient Greeks* (New York: Routledge, 1998); and *Oppression and Liberty*, trans. Arthur Wills and John Petrie (New York: Routledge, 2001). Suggested collections of Weil's works are *Simone Weil Reader*, ed. George A. Panichas (Wakefield, R.I.: Moyer Bell, 1977) and *Simone Weil*, ed. Eric O. Springsted (Maryknoll, N.Y.: Orbis, 1998).

Secondary sources include Alexander Nava, *The Mystical and Prophetic Thought of Simone Weil and Gustavo Gutierrez: Reflections on the Mystery and Hiddenness of God* (Albany: SUNY Press, 2001); Henry Leroy Finch, *Simone Weil and the Intellect of Grace*, ed. Martin Andic (New York: Continuum, 2001); Alexander Nevin, *Simone Weil: Portrait of a Self-Exiled Jew* (Chapel Hill: University of North Carolina Press, 1991); Richard H. Bell, *Simone Weil: The Way of Justice as Compassion* (Lanham, Md.: Rowman & Littlefield, 1998); Diogenes Allen, *Three Outsiders: Pascal, Kierkegaard, Simone Weil* (Cambridge, Mass.: Cowley, 1983); and Rachel Feldhay Brenner, *Writing as Resistance: Four Women Confronting the Holocaust: Edith Stein, Simone Weil, Anne Frank, Etty Hillesum* (University Park: Pennsylvania State University Press, 1997).

[69]*Waiting for God*, p. 26.

[70]*Waiting for God*, p. 27.

[71]*Waiting for God,* p. 89.
[72]*Waiting for God,* p. 107.
[73]*Waiting for God,* p. 104.
[74]*Waiting for God,* p. 109.
[75]*Waiting for God,* p. 103.
[76]*Gravity and Grace,* p. 200.
[77]*Gravity and Grace,* p. 169.
[78]*Waiting for God,* p. 126.
[79]*Waiting for God,* p. 140.
[80]*Waiting for God,* p. 125.
[81]*Waiting for God,* p. 127.
[82]*Waiting for God,* p. 128.
[83]*Waiting for God,* p. 25.
[84]*Waiting for God,* p. 26.
[85]*Waiting for God,* p. 115.
[86]*Waiting for God,* p. 11.
[87]*Waiting for God,* p. 13.
[88]*Gravity and Grace,* p. 78.
[89]*Gravity and Grace,* p. 80.
[90]*Gravity and Grace,* p. 79.

5: Existence and the Word of God: Dialectical Theology and Neo-orthodoxy

[1]A comment usually attributed to the Catholic theologian Karl Adams.

[2]For sources on dialectical theology and its key figures, see Nels Fredrick Solomon Ferre, *Return to Christianity* (New York: Harper & Bros., 1943); Gary J. Dorrien, *The Barthian Revolt in Modern Theology: Theology Without Weapons* (Louisville: Westminster John Knox, 2000); William Hordern, *The Case for a New Reformation Theology* (Philadelphia: Westminster, 1959); Douglas John Hall, *Remembered Voices: Reclaiming the Legacy of "Neo-orthodoxy"* (Louisville: Westminster John Knox, 1998); Stanley Grenz and Roger E. Olsen, *Twentieth Century Theology: God and the World in a Transitional Age* (Downers Grove, Ill.: InterVarsity Press, 1992); Addison H. Leitch, *Winds of Doctrine: The Theology of Barth, Brunner, Bonhoeffer, Bultmann, Niebuhr, Tillich* (Westwood: Revell, 1966); Leonhard Reinisch, ed., *Theologians of Our Time* (Notre Dame: University of Notre Dame Press, 1964); and Philip Edgcumbe Hughes, *Creative Minds in Contemporary Theology* (Grand Rapids: Eerdmans, 1969).

[3]Among Barth's most important primary works are *Church Dogmatics,* ed. and trans. Geoffrey W. Bromiley et al. (Edinburgh: T & T Clark, 1956-77); *Dogmatics in Outline,* trans. G. T. Thompson (New York: Philosophical Library, 1949); *Evangelical Theology: An Introduction,* trans. Grover Foley (New York: Holt, Rinehart and Winston, 1963); *The Epistle to the Romans,* trans. Edwyn C. Hoskyns (London: Oxford University Press, 1933); *Anselm: Fides Quaerens Intellectum,* trans. Ian W. Robertson (Cleveland: World, 1962); *How I Changed My Mind,* introduction and epilogue by John D. Godsey (Edinburgh: Saint Andrew Press, 1969); *Protestant Thought: From Rousseau to Ritschl,* trans. Brian Cozens and H. Hartwell (New York: Harper & Bros., 1959); and *The Word of God and the Word of Man,* trans. Douglas Horton (New York: Pilgrim, 1928). A brief anthology of Barth's writings is available in *A Karl Barth Reader,* eds. Rolf Joachim Erler, Reiner Marquard and Geoffrey W. Bromiley, trans. Geoffrey W. Bromiley (Grand Rapids: Eerdmans, 1986).

The secondary material on Barth is massive. Our suggestions for works on Barth's theology are Hans Urs von Balthasar, *The Theology of Karl Barth,* trans. John Drury (New York: Holt, Rinehart and Winston, 1971); Bruce McCormack, *Karl Barth's Critically Realistic Dia-*

lectical Theology: Its Genesis and Development 1909-1936 (Oxford: Clarendon, 1995); Eberhard Jüngel, *Karl Barth, A Theological Legacy,* trans. Garrett E. Paul (Philadelphia: Westminster, 1986); John Webster, ed., *The Cambridge Companion to Karl Barth* (New York: Cambridge University Press, 2000); Eberhard Busch, *Karl Barth: His Life from Letters and Autobiographical Texts,* trans. John Bowden (Philadelphia: Fortress, 1976); G. C. Berkouwer, *The Triumph of Grace in the Theology of Karl Barth,* trans. Henry R. Boer (Grand Rapids: Eerdmans, 1956); Thomas F. Torrance, *Karl Barth: An Introduction to His Early Theology, 1910-1931* (London: SCM Press, 1962); Herbert Hartwell, *The Theology of Karl Barth: An Introduction* (Philadelphia: Westminster, 1964); and George Hunsinger, *How to Read Karl Barth: The Shape of His Theology* (New York: Oxford University Press, 1991). Geoffrey W. Bromiley, *Introduction to the Theology of Karl Barth* (Grand Rapids: Eerdmans, 1979) provides a very nice summary of the *Church Dogmatics,* which is very helpful to those unfamiliar with Barth's work.

[4]This is one of the chapter titles of *The Word of God and the Word of Man,* in which he speaks of the revolution in his view of Scripture.

[5]*Church Dogmatics,* I/2, pp. 299-300.

[6]*Church Dogmatics,* I/2, p. 282. Some see a decisive shift in Barth's later thought toward an even more positive role for religion as a consequence of his doctrine of election, which we will examine below. In volume IV (*The Doctrine of Reconciliation*) he argues that the Word of God may be spoken by those outside the church (*extra muros ecclesiae*). "We can and must be prepared to encounter 'parables of the kingdom' in the full biblical sense . . . in the secular sphere." See *Church Dogmatics,* IV/3, p. 117. Whether such a shift actually exists, or whether Barth had determined that his doctrine of the Word had been established with sufficient clarity in his earlier writings that he could now safely speak of the positive (though limited) place of religion, is a debate we will leave to others.

[7]*Church Dogmatics,* I/2, p. 301.

[8]Our exposition of Barth's position on natural theology will be considered in the next section on Brunner to illuminate this area of tension between these two giants.

[9]*Church Dogmatics,* I/1, p. 119.

[10]*Church Dogmatics,* I/1, p. 110.

[11]*Church Dogmatics,* I/2, p. 535.

[12]*Church Dogmatics,* I/2, p. 463.

[13]*Church Dogmatics,* I/2, p. 463.

[14]*Church Dogmatics,* I/1, p. 52.

[15]*Church Dogmatics,* I/1, p. 52.

[16]*Church Dogmatics,* I/1, p. 120.

[17]*Church Dogmatics,* I/1, p. 120.

[18]*Church Dogmatics,* I/1, p. 121.

[19]*Dogmatics in Outline,* p. 65.

[20]*Church Dogmatics,* II/1, p. 351.

[21]*Church Dogmatics,* II/1, p. 440.

[22]*Church Dogmatics,* II/2, p. 5.

[23]*Church Dogmatics,* II/2, p. 7.

[24]*Church Dogmatics,* II/2, p. 94.

[25]*Church Dogmatics,* II/2, p. 116.

[26]Among the major primary sources for Brunner's thought are *Man in Revolt: A Christian Anthropology,* trans. Olive Wyon (Philadelphia: Westminster, 1947); *The Divine Imperative,* trans. Olive Wyon (Philadelphia: Westminster, 1947); *Dogmatics,* 3 vols., trans. Olive Wyon, David Cairns, T. H. L. Parker (Philadelphia: Westminster, 1950-62); *Justice and the Social Order,* trans. Mary Hottinger (New York: Harper, 1945); *Revelation and Reason: The Chris-*

tian Doctrine of Faith and Knowledge, trans. Olive Wyon (Philadelphia: Westminster, 1946); *The Mediator: A Study of the Central Doctrine of the Christian Faith,* trans. Olive Wyon (Philadelphia: Westminster, 1947); *The Theology of Crisis* (New York: Scribner, 1929); and *Natural Theology: Comprising "Nature and Grace" and the Reply "No!" by Dr. Karl Barth,* trans. Peter Fraenkel (London: Geoffrey Bles, Centenary, 1946). *Truth as Encounter,* trans. Amandus W. Loos, David Cairns, T. H. L. Parker (Philadelphia: Westminster, 1964) is an enlarged and significantly revised version of *The Divine-Human Encounter,* trans. Amandus W. Loos (Philadelphia: Westminster, 1943). Helpful secondary sources on Brunner's thought are Charles W. Kegley, ed., *The Theology of Emil Brunner,* in *The Library of Living Theology,* vol. 3 (New York: Macmillan, 1962); Paul King Jewett, *Emil Brunner's Concept of Revelation* (London: James Clarke, 1954); Paul King Jewett, *Emil Brunner: An Introduction to the Man and His Thought* (Downer's Grove, Ill.: InterVarsity Press, 1961); and James Edward Humphrey, *Emil Brunner,* Makers of the Modern Theological Mind (Waco: Word, 1976).

[27]*Dogmatics,* 2:252.
[28]*Dogmatics,* 2:240.
[29]*Dogmatics,* 2:240.
[30]*Revelation and Reason,* p. 13.
[31]*Divine Imperative,* p. 61.
[32]*Divine Imperative,* p. 61.
[33]*Dogmatics,* 2:72.
[34]*Man in Revolt,* p. 9.
[35]*Man in Revolt,* p. 9.
[36]*Dogmatics,* 1:15.
[37]*Truth as Encounter,* p. 37.
[38]*Revelation and Reason,* pp. 15-16.
[39]*Revelation and Reason,* p. 16.
[40]*Dogmatics,* 2:27.
[41]*Dogmatics,* 2:47.
[42]*Truth as Encounter,* p. 52.
[43]"Nature and Grace," in *Natural Theology,* p. 24.
[44]Barth, "Nein!" in *Natural Theology,* p. 74.
[45]"Nein!" p. 128.
[46]*Dogmatics,* 1:347.
[47]*Dogmatics,* 1:332.
[48]*Truth as Encounter,* p. 144.
[49]*Dogmatics,* 1:338.
[50]*Dogmatics,* 1:318.
[51]*Revelation and Reason,* p. 145.
[52]*Revelation and Reason,* p. 284.
[53]*Revelation and Reason,* p. 276.
[54]*Dogmatics,* 2:342.
[55]*Revelation and Reason,* p. 169.
[56]*Revelation and Reason,* p. 179.
[57]*Revelation and Reason,* p. 292.
[58]*Revelation and Reason,* p. 132.
[59]For the major works of Bultmann, see *Theology of the New Testament,* 2 vols., trans. Kendrick Grobel (New York: Scribner, 1951, 1955); *Kerygma and Myth: A Theological Debate,* ed. Hans Werner Bartsch, trans. Reginald H. Fuller (New York: Harper & Row, 1961); *The History of the Synoptic Tradition,* trans. John Marsh (Oxford: Basil Blackwell, 1963); *Existence and Faith: Shorter Writings of Rudolf Bultmann,* ed. and trans. Schubert M. Ogden (London:

Hodder and Stoughton, 1961); *Faith and Understanding*, ed. Robert W. Funk, trans. Louise Pettibone Smith (Philadelphia: Fortress, 1987); *Jesus Christ and Mythology* (New York: Scribner, 1958); and *The Gospel of John: A Commentary*, trans. George R. Beasley-Murray (Philadelphia: Westminster, 1971). The following sources represent some of the more significant studies of Bultmann's work: Robert C. Roberts, *Rudolf Bultmann's Theology: A Critical Appraisal* (Grand Rapids: Eerdmans, 1976); Walter Schmithals, *An Introduction to the Theology of Rudolf Bultmann* (Minneapolis: Augsburg, 1968); Charles W. Kegley, *The Theology of Rudolf Bultmann* (New York: Harper & Row, 1966); John Macquarrie, *An Existentialist Theology* (London: SCM Press, 1955); Anthony Thiselton, *The Two Horizons: New Testament Hermeneutics and Philosophical Description with Special Reference to Heidegger, Bultmann, Gadamer and Wittgenstein* (Grand Rapids: Eerdmans, 1980); and Shubert M. Ogden, *Christ Without Myth: A Study Based on the Theology of Rudolf Bultmann* (New York: Harper, 1961).

[60]"Autobiographical Reflections," in *Faith and Understanding*, p. 288.

[61]For a survey of Heidegger's influence on Bultmann, see John Macquarrie, *An Existentialist Theology* (London: SCM Press, 1955).

[62]*Jesus Christ and Mythology*, p. 51.

[63]*Jesus Christ and Mythology*, p. 55.

[64]*Jesus Christ and Mythology*, p. 56.

[65]"New Testament and Mythology," in *Kerygma and Myth*, p. 30.

[66]"The Problem of 'Natural Theology,'" in *Faith and Understanding*, p. 319, his italics.

[67]Bultmann does allow a very limited use of natural theology because to the extent that a person "theorizes philosophically about existence, he knows its historical nature, and to this extent he also knows about God." But this philosophical contemplation reveals only the problem of our existence and, if understood properly, will open us to God's Word. In the end, Bultmann concludes, "the question is not the answer, even though the unbelieving existence always yields to the temptation to interpret it as the answer. Only faith can say that the question is the answer; and when it says this, it banishes 'natural theology.'" See "The Problem of 'Natural Theology,'" p. 323.

[68]*Jesus Christ and Mythology*, p. 65.

[69]*Jesus Christ and Mythology*, p. 40.

[70]"Bultmann Replies to his Critics," in *Kerygma and Myth*, p. 192.

[71]Bultmann makes this distinction since both *Historie* and *Geschichte* translate as "history."

[72]*The History of the Synoptic Tradition*, p. 372.

[73]As an example of Bultmann's view of the irrelevance of the historical facts of Jesus, he states that "Paul is interested only in the fact that Jesus became man and lived on earth. How he was born or lived interests him only to the extent of knowing that Jesus was a definite, concrete man, a Jew, 'being born in the likeness of man and being found in human form' (Phil. 2:7), 'born of woman, born under the law' (Gal. 4:4). But beyond that, Jesus' manner of life, his ministry, his personality, his character play no role at all; neither does Jesus' message." See *Theology of the New Testament*, 1:293-94.

[74]Bultmann goes so far as to state that Jesus' own awareness of his role as Messiah is theologically unimportant. "Only the historian can answer this question—as far as it can be answered at all—and faith, being personal decision, cannot be dependent upon a historian's labor." See *Theology of the New Testament*, 1:26.

[75]"New Testament and Mythology," pp. 11-12.

[76]"New Testament and Mythology," p. 1.

[77]*Theology of the New Testament*, 1:3.

[78]*Theology of the New Testament*, 1:3.

[79]*Jesus Christ and Mythology*, p. 18.

[80]"New Testament and Mythology," p. 3.

[81]"New Testament and Mythology," p. 11.

[82]*Jesus Christ and Mythology*, p. 43.

[83]"New Testament and Mythology," p. 5.

[84]*Jesus Christ and Mythology*, pp. 31-32.

[85]*Theology of the New Testament*, 1:299.

[86]*Theology of the New Testament*, 2:237-38.

[87]Since many of the earliest Christians were present at the crucifixion, the historical event itself was an existential experience that disclosed its meaning to them. However, their historical reports of the event do not allow us to appropriate it as an event with soteriological significance. It is only in our experience of Jesus crucified and risen that the cross assumes meaning for us. See "New Testament and Mythology," p. 38.

[88]"New Testament and Mythology," p. 37.

[89]"New Testament and Mythology," p. 39.

[90]"New Testament and Mythology," p. 39.

[91]*Jesus Christ and Mythology*, p. 71.

[92]John Macquarrie, *An Existentialist Theology: A Comparison of Heidegger and Bultmann* (London: SCM Press, 1955), p. 215.

[93]For key primary sources on Reinhold Niebuhr, see *Beyond Tragedy* (New York: Scribner, 1937); *Christian Realism and Political Problems* (New York: Scribner, 1953); *The Nature and Destiny of Man: A Christian Interpretation*, 2 vols. (New York: Scribner, 1943); *Faith and Politics: A Commentary on Religious, Social and Political Thought in a Technological Age*, ed. Ronald H. Stone (New York: G. Braziller, 1968); *An Interpretation of Christian Ethics* (New York: Seabury, 1979); and *Moral Man and Immoral Society: A Study in Ethics and Politics* (New York: Scribner, 1932). Several collections of Niebuhr's shorter works and essays exist. We recommend *The Essential Reinhold Niebuhr: Selected Essays and Addresses*, ed. Robert McAfee Brown (New Haven: Yale University Press, 1986) and *A Reinhold Niebuhr Reader: Selected Essays, Articles and Book Reviews*, ed. Charles C. Brown (Philadelphia: Trinity Press International, 1992). A good biography on Niebuhr is Richard Fox, *Reinhold Niebuhr: A Biography* (New York: Pantheon, 1985). Recommended secondary sources are Charles W. Kegley and Robert W. Bretall, eds., *Reinhold Niebuhr: His Religious, Social, and Political Thought*, in *The Library of Living Theology*, vol. 2 (New York: Macmillan, 1956); Langdon Gilkey, *On Niebuhr: A Theological Study* (Chicago: University of Chicago Press, 2001); June Bingham, *Courage to Change: An Introduction to the Life and Thought of Reinhold Niebuhr* (New York: Scribner, 1972); Holtan Peter Odegard, *Sin and Science: Reinhold Niebuhr as Political Theologian* (Yellow Springs: Antioch, 1956); and Hans Hofmann, *The Theology of Reinhold Niebuhr* (New York: Scribner, 1956).

[94]For example, Niebuhr states that, "The theological movement initiated by Karl Barth has affected the thought of the Church profoundly, but only negatively; and it has not challenged the thought outside of the Church at all. It defied what was true in Renaissance culture too completely to be able to challenge what was false in it." See *The Nature and Destiny of Man*, 2:159.

[95]Niebuhr, "Intellectual Autobiography," in Kegley and Bretall, *Reinhold Niebuhr*, p. 6.

[96]"Intellectual Autobiography," p. 20.

[97]*The Nature and Destiny of Man*, 1:3.

[98]*The Nature and Destiny of Man*, 1:252.

[99]Niebuhr views sin as a possibility precisely because of freedom, which allows us to transcend the biological functions and limitations of our existence. "Man may lose this virtue [transcendence] and destroy the proper function of his nature but he can do so only by availing himself of one of the elements in that nature, namely his freedom." *The Nature and Destiny of Man*, 1:270.

[100]*The Nature and Destiny of Man*, 1:185.

[101]*Moral Man and Immoral Society*, p. xi.

[102]*The Nature and Destiny of Man*, 1:212.

[103]*The Nature and Destiny of Man*, 1:217.

[104]Epigraph to *Justice and Mercy*.

[105]*The Nature and Destiny of Man*, 1:23.

[106]*The Nature and Destiny of Man*, 1:16.

[107]"Intellectual Autobiography," p. 11.

[108]*The Nature and Destiny of Man*, 1:127.

[109]*Beyond Tragedy*, p. 14.

[110]*Faith and Politics*, p. 17.

[111]"Intellectual Autobiography," pp. 17-18. Niebuhr frequently compares religious myth to the work of the artist, who also uses the physical as a medium for communicating a truth that transcends the created object. A point of comparison also exists in the fact that both art and myth can abuse history and our own experience. "But at their best, both artist and prophet reveal the heights and depths of human experience by picturing the surface with something more and less than scientific exactness" (*Faith and Politics*, p. 27).

[112]*The Nature and Destiny of Man*, 2:50.

[113]*The Nature and Destiny of Man*, 1:263.

[114]*Beyond Tragedy*, p. 290.

[115]*The Nature and Destiny of Man*, 2:294.

[116]For a sample of Tillich's major works, consult *Systematic Theology*, 3 vols. (Chicago: University of Chicago Press, 1951-63); *Theology of Culture*, ed. Robert C. Kimball (New York: Oxford University Press, 1959); *The Protestant Era*, trans. and ed. James Luther Adams (London: Nisbet, 1951); *The Religious Situation* (New York: Meridian, 1956); *The Shaking of the Foundations* (New York: Scribner, 1948); *My Search for Absolutes*, drawings by Saul Steinberg (New York: Simon and Schuster, 1967); *The New Being* (New York: Scribner, 1955); *The Courage to Be* (New Haven: Yale University Press, 1959); *Dynamics of Faith*, ed. Ruth Nanda Anshen (New York: Harper, 1957); and *The Future of Religions*, ed. Jerald C. Brauer (New York: Harper & Row, 1966). An anthology of Tillich's writings is available in F. Forrester Church, *The Essential Tillich: An Anthology of the Writings of Paul Tillich* (New York: Macmillan, 1987).

Helpful secondary sources for Tillich's thought are Charles W. Kegley, ed., *The Theology of Paul Tillich*, in *The Library of Living Theology*, vol. 1 (New York: Macmillan, 1952); Alexander J. McKelway, *The Systematic Theology of Paul Tillich* (Richmond: John Knox, 1964); Kenneth Hamilton, *The System and the Gospel: A Critique of Paul Tillich* (Grand Rapids: Eerdmans, 1967); Walter Eisenbeis, *The Key Ideas of Paul Tillich's Systematic Theology* (Washington D.C.: University Press of America, 1983); and James Luther Adams, Wilhelm Pauck and Roger Lincoln Shinn, eds., *The Thought of Paul Tillich* (San Francisco: Harper & Row, 1985). For a more biographical approach to Tillich's rather colorful life, see Wilhelm and Marion Pauck, *Paul Tillich, His Life and Thought*, vol. 1, *Life* (New York: Harper & Row, 1976) and the memoirs written by his wife, Hannah Tillich, *From Time to Time* (New York: Stein and Day, 1973). For Tillich's own analysis of his life, see Paul Tillich, *On the Boundary: An Autobiographical Sketch* (New York: Scribner, 1966).

[117]*My Search for Absolutes*, p. 48.

[118]*Systematic Theology*, 1:3.

[119]*Systematic Theology*, 1:62.

[120]*Systematic Theology*, 2:13.

[121]*Systematic Theology*, 1:62.

[122]*Biblical Religion*, pp. 11-12.

[123]*Systematic Theology*, 1:22.

[124]*Systematic Theology*, 1:14.
[125]*Biblical Religion*, p. 55.
[126]*Biblical Religion*, p. 51.
[127]*Systematic Theology*, 1:235.
[128]*Systematic Theology*, 1:245.
[129]*Systematic Theology*, 1:252.
[130]*Systematic Theology*, 2:34.
[131]*Systematic Theology*, 2:44.
[132]*Systematic Theology*, 1:135.
[133]*Systematic Theology*, 2:155.
[134]*Systematic Theology*, 1:35.
[135]*Biblical Religion*, p. 4.

Chapter 6: Pragmatism and Process: American Adventures in Ideas

[1]For some one-volume introductions to Dewey, see Richard J. Bernstein, *John Dewey* (Atascadero, Calif.: Ridgeview, 1966); R. W. Sleeper, *The Necessity of Pragmatism: John Dewey's Conception of Philosophy* (New Haven: Yale University Press, 1986); James Campbell, *Understanding John Dewey* (Chicago: Open Court, 1995); J. E. Tiles, *Dewey* (London: Routledge, 1998); or Robert B. Talisse, *On Dewey* (Belmont, Calif.: Wadsworth, 2000).

[2]See the useful collection of essays in *John Dewey: The Essential Writings*, ed. David Sidorsky (New York: Harper, 1977), or the two-volume collection, *The Philosophy of John Dewey*, ed. John J. McDermott (Chicago: University of Chicago Press, 1973). The major philosophical works of Dewey are: *Democracy and Education* (New York: Macmillan, 1916); *Human Nature and Conduct* (New York: Holt, 1922); *Experience and Nature*, 2nd ed. (Chicago: Open Court, 1929); *The Quest for Certainty* (New York: Minton, Balch, 1929); *Art as Experience* (New York: Minton, Balch, 1934); *Logic: The Theory of Inquiry* (New York: Holt, 1938); and *Reconstruction in Philosophy*, enlarged ed. (Boston: Beacon, 1948).

[3]For the life of Dewey, see his autobiographical reflections in "From Absolutism to Experimentalism," repr. in Richard J. Berstein, ed., *John Dewey on Experience, Nature and Freedom* (New York: Liberal Arts Press, 1960). For biographies of Dewey, see "Biography of John Dewey," edited by his daughters, in Paul Arthur Schilpp, ed., *The Philosophy of John Dewey* (New York: Tudor, 1951); Sidney Hook, *John Dewey: An Intellectual Portrait* (New York: John Day, 1939); George Dykhuizen, *The Life and Mind of John Dewey* (Carbondale: Southern Illinois University Press, 1973); and Jay Martin, *The Education of John Dewey: A Biography* (New York: Columbia University Press, 2002). For bibliography, see Milton H. Thomas, *John Dewey: A Centennial Bibliography* (Chicago: University of Chicago Press, 1962); Barbara Levine, *Works about John Dewey* (Carbondale: Southern Illinois University Press, 1996); Jo Ann Boydston, ed., *Guide to the Works of John Dewey* (Carbondale: Southern Illinois University Press, 1970); and the partial bibliography in Schilpp, *The Philosophy of John Dewey*. The works of John Dewey have now been published in a complete edition by Southern Illinois University Press, edited by Jo Ann Boydson et al., under the titles *The Early Works, 1882-1898*, 5 vols. (1967-72); *The Middle Works, 1899-1924*, 15 vols. (1976-83); and *The Later Works, 1925-1953*, 17 vols. (1981-91), which also contains a very useful index volume.

[4]On this early period of Dewey's life, see Neil Coughlan, *Young John Dewey* (Chicago: University of Chicago Press, 1973).

[5]For more on this event in Dewey's life, see X. Zeldin, "John Dewey's Role in the 1937 Trotsky Commission," *Public Affairs Quarterly* 5 (1991): 387-94.

[6]For representative philosophical voices in dialogue with Dewey, see Schilpp, *The Philosophy of John Dewey;* Sidney Morgenbessr, ed., *Dewey and His Critics* (New York: Journal of

Philosophy, 1977); and J. E. Tiles, *John Dewey: Critical Assessments,* 4 vols. (New York: Rout-
ledge, 1992). For some of the many books that discuss aspects of Dewey's thought (in
addition to those cited elsewhere in this section), see Steven Fesmire, *John Dewey and
Moral Imagination* (Bloomington: Indiana University Press, 2003); David Hildebrand,
Beyond Realism and Antirealism: John Dewey and the Neopragmatists (Nashville: Vanderbilt
University Press, 2003); Victor Kestenbaum, *The Grace and the Severity of the Ideal: John
Dewey and the Transcendent* (Chicago: University of Chicago Press, 2002); Thomas Carlyle,
Becoming John Dewey: Dilemmas of a Philosopher and Naturalist (Bloomington: Indiana Uni-
versity Press, 2002); Philip W. Jackson, *John Dewey and the Philosopher's Task* (New York:
Teachers College Press, 2002); and Charlene H. Seigfried, ed., *Feminist Interpretations of
John Dewey* (University Park: Pennsylvania State University Press, 2002).

[7]See *Logic: A Theory of Inquiry,* and the analysis of this work in Sleeper, *The Necessity of Pragmatism;* see further F. Thomas Burke et al., eds., *Dewey's Logical Theory* (Nashville: Vanderbilt University Press, 2002).

[8]*Reconstruction in Philosophy,* p. 121.

[9]By "scientism" I mean a philosophy which sees science as the best, or only, form of reliable knowledge and asserts that a scientific approach will solve any real problems in all
areas of life and thought, if any approach will. For the charge that Dewey adopts a kind of
scientism, see Morton White, *Pragmatism and the American Mind* (New York: Oxford University Press, 1973).

[10]*Quest for Certainty,* p. 81.

[11]*Experience and Nature,* 2nd. ed., p. 4a.

[12]*Existence and Nature,* pp. 71, 70.

[13]*Reconstruction in Philosophy,* p. 177.

[14]For Dewey on democracy, see *Democracy and Education* (New York: Macmillan, 1916) and
The Public and Its Problems (Chicago: Open Court, 1925). See further William Caspary,
Dewey on Democracy (Ithaca, N.Y.: Cornell University Press, 2000).

[15]*A Common Faith* (New Haven: Yale University Press, 1934), p. 42.

[16]As Dewey himself noted, "For what I have called the background and point of departure
seems to be the same for both of us, no matter what deviations may occur later." John
Dewey, "The Philosophy of Whitehead," in Paul Arthur Schilpp, ed., *The Philosophy of
Alfred North Whitehead,* 2nd ed. (New York: Tudor, 1951), p. 645.

[17]For an introduction to process philosophy see Nicholas Rescher, *Process Metaphysics: An
Introduction to Process Philosophy* (Albany: SUNY Press, 1996).

[18]For an introduction to Alexander, see Bertram Brettschneider, *The Philosophy of Samuel
Alexander* (New York: Humanities, 1964).

[19]Samuel Alexander, *Space, Time and Deity,* 2 vols. (1920; repr. New York: Humanities, 1950).

[20]*Space, Time and Deity,* 1:xxiii (from the preface to the 1950 reprint).

[21]In the preface to his important lectures on *Science and the Modern World* (1925; repr. New
York: Mentor, 1948), Whitehead wrote: "It will be obvious to readers that I have found
them [two books, one Alexander's] very suggestive. I am especially indebted to Alexander's great work" (p. vii).

[22]For an excellent overview of Whitehead's life and thought, see Victor Lowe, *Alfred North
Whitehead: The Man and His Works,* 2 vols. (Baltimore: Johns Hopkins University Press,
1985, 1990). For Whitehead's own "Autobiographical Notes," see Schilpp, *The Philosophy of
Alfred North Whitehead,* pp. 3-14. For bibliography, see the partial bibliography in the same
volume, pp. 747-88; and the much fuller Barry A. Woodbridge, *Alfred North Whitehead: A
Primary-Secondary Bibliography* (Bowling Green, Ohio: Philosophy Documentation Center,
1977). His major philosophical works, apart from those in logic and mathematics, are: *Science and the Modern World* (New York: Macmillan, 1925); *Religion in the Making* (New York:

Macmillan, 1926); *The Aims of Education* (New York: Macmillan, 1929); *Process and Reality* (New York: Macmillan, 1929); *Adventures of Ideas* (New York: Macmillan, 1933); and *Modes of Thought* (New York: Macmillan, 1938).

[23]This work is discussed earlier, in the chapter on Russell.

[24]For several of these early papers, see two collections: *The Aims of Education and Other Essays* (New York: Macmillan, 1929) and *The Interpretation of Science,* ed. A. H. Johnson (Indianapolis: Bobbs-Merrill, 1961). See further Malcolm Evans, *Whitehead and Philosophy of Education* (Amsterdam: Rodopi, 1998), and R. M. Palter, *Whitehead's Philosophy of Science,* 2nd ed. (Chicago: University of Chicago, 1970).

[25]These are *An Enquiry Concerning the Principles of Natural Knowledge* (1919; rev. ed., New York: Cambridge University Press, 1925); *The Concept of Nature* (New York: Cambridge University Press, 1920); and *The Principle of Relativity* (New York: Cambridge University Press, 1922).

[26]*Concept of Nature,* p. 3.

[27]*Concept of Nature,* p. 4.

[28]*Concept of Nature,* p. 52.

[29]This is not to suggest that his earlier books were nonmetaphysical, only that this element becomes more dominant in the later books. These are *Science and the Modern World*; *Religion in the Making*; and *Symbolism: Its Meaning and Effect* (New York: Macmillan, 1927).

[30]For a careful study of Whitehead's development in this period, including analysis of *Science and the Modern World,* see Lewis S. Ford, *The Emergence of Whitehead's Metaphysics* (Albany: SUNY Press, 1984).

[31]Students of *Process and Reality* should consult the corrected edition, edited by D. R. Griffin and Donald W. Sherburne (New York: Free Press, 1979). I will cite this work in the notes below, but I include the page numbers to the original 1929 version in brackets. These are also found in brackets within the text of the corrected edition.

[32]*Process and Reality,* p. xii [vi].

[33]Whitehead can be a difficult philosopher to understand. For some introductions to his philosophy, see W. Mays, *The Philosophy of Whitehead* (New York: Macmillan, 1959); Donald W. Sherburne, *A Key to Whitehead's Process and Reality* (New York: Macmillan, 1966), which includes a very helpful glossary; Nathaniel Lawrence, *Alfred North Whitehead: A Primer of His Philosophy* (New York: Twayne, 1974); Ivor Leclerc, *Whitehead's Metaphysics: An Introductory Exposition,* 2nd ed. (Bloomington: Indiana University Press, 1975); and Elizabeth M. Kraus, *The Metaphysics of Experience: A Companion to Whitehead's Process and Reality,* 2nd ed. (New York: Fordham University Press, 1998). For more advanced discussions, see William A. Christian, *An Interpretation of Whitehead's Metaphysics* (New Haven: Yale University Press, 1959) or Victor Lowe, *Understanding Whitehead* (Baltimore: The Johns Hopkins Press, 1962).

[34]*Process and Reality,* p. xiv [x].

[35]*Process and Reality,* p. 3 [4].

[36]*Process and Reality,* p. 3 [4].

[37]*Process and Reality,* p. xiv [x].

[38]*Process and Reality,* p. 17 [27].

[39]*Process and Reality,* p. 18 [28].

[40]*Process and Reality,* p. 88 [135].

[41]For Whitehead's conception of God in his mature philosophy, see *Science and the Modern World,* chap. 11; *Religion in the Making*; and *Process and Reality,* part V, chap. 2. See further the chapters by Charles Hartshorne and Julius Bixler in Schilpp, *The Philosophy of A. N. Whitehead,* pp. 489-559; Charles Hartshorne, *Whitehead's View of Reality* (New York: Pilgrim, 1981); Peter N. Hamilton, *The Living God and the Natural World* (Philadelphia: United

Church Press, 1967); John B. Cobb, *A Christian Natural Theology* (Philadelphia: Westminster, 1965); and Lawrence F. Wilmot, *Whitehead and God: Prolegomena to Theological Reconstruction* (Waterloo, Ontario: Winfred Laurier University Press, 1979).

[42]*Adventures of Ideas* (New York: Macmillan, 1933). Whitehead's mature reflections on Christianity and religion are the scattered throughout this volume, for example.

[43]See Woodbridge, *Alfred North Whitehead: A Primary-Secondary Bibliography.*

[44]For more critical analysis of Whitehead's metaphysics, including the "actual occasion," see Evander Bradley McGilvary, "Space-time, Simple Location, and Prehension," in Schilpp, *The Philosophy of Alfred North Whitehead*, pp. 211-39; Edward Pols, *Whitehead's Metaphysics: A Critical Examination of Process and Reality* (Carbondale: Southern Illinois University Press, 1967); F. G. Kirkpatrick, "Subjective Becoming: An Unwarranted Abstraction?" *Process Studies* 3 (1973): 15-25; and Reto L. Fetz, "In Critique of Whitehead," *Process Studies* 20 (1991): 1-9. The analysis by Fetz is particularly good and is only a partial translation from his larger study, *Whitehead: Prozessdenken und Substanzmetaphysik* (Munich: Vlg. Karl Alber, 1981).

[45]See John Dewey's chapter in Schilpp, *The Philosophy of Alfred North Whitehead*, pp. 641-61.

[46]This is the approach of many Anglo-American philosophers who work in metaphysics today. See, e.g., the first chapter in William Hasker's introduction, *Metaphysics: Constructing a World View* (Downers Grove, Ill.: InterVarsity Press, 1983), and note the two "rules of thumb" that he presses for in evaluating metaphysical claims (pp. 18-25). For a more advanced introduction to metaphysics, see E. J. Lowe, *The Possibility of Metaphysics* (New York: Oxford University Press, 1998) and his *Survey of Metaphysics* (New York: Oxford University Press, 2002).

[47]Here we can agree with George R. Lucas, whose book *The Rehabilitation of Whitehead* (Albany: SUNY Press, 1989) is a plea for contemporary philosophers to read Whitehead with some appreciation and understanding.

[48]One-volume introductions to his thought include Charles E. Raven, *Teilhard de Chardin* (New York: Harper & Row, 1962); Henri de Lubac, *Teilhard Explained* (New York: Paulist, 1968); N. M. Wildiers, *An Introduction to Teilhard de Chardin* (New York: Harper & Row, 1968); and Doran McCarty, *Teilhard de Chardin* (Waco, Tex.: Word, 1976). A very helpful glossary of special terms, with a bibliography, is Sion Cowell, *The Teilhard Lexicon* (Brighton, U.K.: Sussex Academic Press, 2001). For more advanced studies consult Christopher F. Mooney, *Teilhard de Chardin and the Mystery of Christ* (New York: Harper & Row, 1966); Henri de Lubac, *The Religion of Teilhard de Chardin* (London: Collins, 1967); Donald P. Gray, *The One and the Many: Teilhard de Chardin's Vision of Unity* (New York: Herder & Herder, 1969); Thomas M. King, *Teilhard's Mysticism of Knowing* (New York: Seabury, 1981); James A. Lyons, *The Cosmic Christ in Origen and Teilhard de Chardin* (Oxford: Oxford University Press, 1982); and Edward Dodson, *The Phenomenon of Man Revisited: A Biological Viewpoint on Teilhard de Chardin* (New York: Columbia University Press, 1984). For an evangelical assessment, see D. Gareth Jones, *Teilhard de Chardin* (Downers Grove, Ill.: InterVarsity Press, 1970).

The main theological and philosophical works by Teilhard in English are: *The Divine Milieu* (New York: Harper & Row, 1960); *The Heart of Matter* (New York: Harcourt Brace Jovanovich, 1978); *Hymn of the Universe* (New York: Harper & Row, 1961); *The Phenomenon of Man* (New York: Harper & Row, 1959) (retranslated as *The Human Phenomenon* [Brighton, U.K.: Sussex Academic Press, 1999]); and *Science and Christ* (New York: Harper & Row, 1968). For a complete bibliography, see Joseph M. McCarthy, *Pierre Teilhard de Chardin: A Comprehensive Bibliography* (New York: Garland, 1981).

[49]For the life of Teilhard, the standard academic work is still Claude Cuénot, *Teilhard de Chardin* (London: Burns & Oates, 1965). For more contemporary biographies, see Mary

Lukas and Ellen Lukas, *Teilhard* (New York: Doubleday, 1977); or Ursula King, *Spirit of Fire: The Life and Vision of Teilhard de Chardin* (Maryknoll, N.Y.: Orbis, 1996).

[50]Published in English in *Hymn of the Universe*, pp. 13-40.

[51]*Hymn of the Universe*, p. 36.

[52]*Phenomenon of Man*, p. 260.

[53]For a discussion of some criticism from the science side, see H. James Birx, *Interpreting Evolution: Darwin & Teilhard de Chardin* (Buffalo, N.Y.: Prometheus, 1991); his earlier book *Pierre Teilhard de Chardin's Philosophy of Evolution* (Springfield, Ill.: Thomas, 1972) is more descriptive; see also Noel Roberts, *From Piltdown Man to Point Omega: The Evolutionary Theory of Teilhard de Chardin* (New York: P. Lang, 2000). For further evaluations from several disciplines, see Anthony Hanson, ed., *Teilhard Reassessed* (London: Darton, Longman and Todd, 1970).

[54]Hartshorne's major books in philosophy are: *Man's Vision of God and the Logic of Theism* (1941; New York: Harper, 1948); *The Divine Relativity: A Social Conception of God* (New Haven: Yale University Press, 1948); *Reality as Social Process* (Glencoe, Ill.: Free Press, 1953); *Philosophers Speak of God*, with W. L. Reese (Chicago: University of Chicago Press, 1953); *The Logic of Perfection* (La Salle, Ill.: Open Court, 1962); *Anselm's Discovery* (La Salle, Ill.: Open Court, 1965); *A Natural Theology for Our Time* (La Salle, Ill.: Open Court, 1967); *Creative Synthesis and Philosophic Method* (London: SCM Press, 1970); *Whitehead's Philosophy* (Lincoln: University of Nebraska Press, 1972); *Insights and Oversights of Great Thinkers* (Albany: SUNY Press, 1983); *Omnipotence and Other Theological Mistakes* (Albany: SUNY Press, 1984); and *Wisdom as Moderation: A Philosophy of the Middle Way* (Albany: SUNY Press, 1987). For a fuller bibliography, see Lewis E. Hahn, ed., *The Philosophy of Charles Hartshorne* (La Salle, Ill.: Open Court, 1991).

[55]See Hartshorne's short autobiography in Hahn, ed., *The Philosophy of Charles Hartshorne;* and his fuller autobiography titled *Darkness and Light* (Albany: SUNY Press, 1990). For good one-volume introduction, see Alan Gragg, *Charles Hartshorne* (Waco, Tex.: Word, 1973). Some representative studies of his philosophy of religion include W. L. Reese and E. Freeman, eds., *Process and Divinity: The Hartshorne Festschrift* (La Salle, Ill.: Open Court, 1964); George Goodwin, *The Ontological Argument of Charles Hartshorne* (Missoula: Scholars Press, 1978); Colin Gunton, *Becoming and Being* (Oxford: Oxford University Press, 1978); Santiago Sia, *God in Process Thought* (Dordrecht: M. Nijhoff, 1985); Donald W. Viney, *Charles Hartshorne and the Existence of God* (Albany: SUNY Press, 1985); Robert Kane and S. H. Phillips, eds., *Hartshorne, Process Philosophy, and Theology* (Albany: SUNY Press, 1989); Douglas Dombrowski, *Analytic Theism, Hartshorne and the Concept of God* (Albany: SUNY Press, 1996); Edgar A. Towne, *Two Types of New Theism* (New York: P. Lang, 1997); and Douglas Pratt, *Relational Deity: Hartshorne and Macquarrie on God* (Lanham, Md.: University Press of America, 2002).

[56]See two books by Hartshorne, *Anselm's Discovery* and *The Logic of Perfection*.

[57]Hartshorne and Reese, *Philosophers Speak of God*, p. 2.

[58]For representative books by each theologian, see Daniel Day Williams, *The Spirit and the Forms of Love* (New York: Harper & Row, 1968); Shubert Ogden, *The Reality of God* (New York: Harper & Row, 1966); John B. Cobb Jr. and David R. Griffin, *Process Theology* (Philadelphia: Westminster, 1976).

[59]Two excellent book-length criticisms of process theology are Robert C. Neville, *Creativity and God* (New York: Seabury, 1980); and David Basinger, *Divine Power in Process Thought* (Albany: SUNY Press, 1988). See also Ronald Nash, ed., *Process Theology* (Grand Rapids: Baker, 1987).

[60]I develop this criticism further in A. G. Padgett, "Putting Reason in its Place," in Bryan Stone and Thomas J. Oord, eds., *Thy Nature and Thy Name Is Love* (Nashville: Abingdon,

2001); revised and expanded in Alan G. Padgett, *Science and the Study of God* (Grand Rapids: Eerdmans, 2003). See also Clark Pinnock, "Between Classical and Process Theism," in Nash, ed., *Process Theology*.

[61]For a helpful debate between evangelical and process scholars, see John B. Cobb Jr. and Clark H. Pinnock, eds., *Searching for an Adequate God* (Grand Rapids: Eerdmans, 2000).

Chapter 7: Meaning and Analysis: Developments in Analytic Philosophy

[1]For general works about the life and thought of Wittgenstein, see the notes in chapter two on the early Wittgenstein. Here we will list works dealing with his later philosophy. There is a large number of books which have been published by the editors of his papers after his death. The most important of these is of course the *Investigations*. Other important works of the later period include *The Blue and Brown Books* (New York: Harper & Row, 1965); *Culture and Value* (Oxford: Blackwell, 1980); *On Certainty* (Oxford: Blackwell, 1969); *Philosophical Grammar* (Oxford: Blackwell, 1974); *Philosophical Remarks*, 2nd ed. (Oxford: Blackwell, 1975); *Remarks on the Foundations of Mathematics*, 3rd ed. (Oxford: Blackwell, 1978); *Remarks on the Philosophy of Psychology*, 2 vols. (Chicago: University of Chicago Press, 1980); *Remarks on Colour* (Oxford: Blackwell, 1977); and *Zettel*, 2nd ed. (Oxford: Blackwell, 1981). There is a useful collection of other essays and remarks in *Philosophical Occasions, 1912-1952* (Indianapolis: Hackett, 1993).

[2]Introductions to Wittgenstein's philosophy have already been cited in chapter two of this book. The following also include his later period: Anthony Kenny, *Wittgenstein* (Cambridge, Mass.: Harvard University Press, 1973); Robert J. Fogelin, *Wittgenstein* (London: Routledge & Kegan Paul, 1976); P. M. S. Hacker, *Wittgenstein* (London: Routledge, 1999); Merrill B. Hintikka and Jaakko Hintikka, *Investigating Wittgenstein* (Oxford: Blackwell, 1986); David Francis Pears, *Ludwig Wittgenstein*, 2nd ed. (Cambridge, Mass.: Harvard University Press, 1986); and Joachim Schulte, *Wittgenstein: An Introduction* (Albany: SUNY Press, 1992). More advanced studies which focus on his later philosophy include Malcolm Budd, *Wittgenstein's Philosophy of Psychology* (London: Routledge, 1989); Stanley Cavell, *The Claim of Reason* (Oxford: Oxford University Press, 1979); Cora Diamond, *The Realistic Spirit: Wittgenstein, Philosophy and the Mind* (Cambridge, Mass.: MIT Press, 1991); David Francis Pears, *The False Prison*, 2 vols., (Oxford: Oxford University Press, 1986, 1987); P. M. S. Hacker, *Insight and Illusion*, rev. ed. (Oxford: Oxford University Press, 1986); see further the useful collection in Hans Sluga and David G. Stern, eds., *The Cambridge Companion to Wittgenstein* (New York: Cambridge University Press, 1996). Two large collections of secondary essays about Wittgenstein are John Canfield, ed., *The Philosophy of Wittgenstein*, 15 vols. (New York: Garland, 1986) and V. A. and Stuart Shanker, eds., *Ludwig Wittgenstein*, 5 vols. (London: Croom Helm, 1986).

[3]Finally published only after his death as *The Blue and Brown Books* (New York: Harper & Row, 1958).

[4]*Blue and Brown Books*, p. 18.

[5]See n. 1.

[6]*Philosophical Investigations*, trans. G. E. M. Anscombe, 3rd ed. (Oxford: Blackwell, 2001). This work is cited by paragraph number for the first part (§) and page number for the second part (p.). Helpful commentaries on the *Investigations* include Garth Hallett, *A Companion to 'Wittgenstein's "Philosophical Investigations"* (Ithaca, N.Y.: Cornell University Press, 1977); and the massive four volume analytical commentary by Gordon P. Baker and P. M. S. Hacker (Oxford: Blackwell, 1980-92): *Wittgenstein: Understanding and Meaning; Wittgenstein: Rules, Grammar and Necessity;* continued by Hacker alone, *Wittgenstein: Meaning and Mind;* and *Wittgenstein: Mind and Will.*

[7]*Philosophical Investigations*, §43, his emphasis.

[8]*Philosophical Investigations,* §116, his emphasis.

[9]*Philosophical Investigations,* §65.

[10]*Philosophical Investigations,* §66.

[11]*Philosophical Investigations,* §90.

[12]*Philosophical Investigations,* §133, his emphasis.

[13]*Philosophical Investigations,* p. 224.

[14]*Philosophical Investigations,* §188.

[15]Among the numerous books about Wittgenstein, philosophy and religion, see Brian R. Clack, *An Introduction to Wittgenstein's Philosophy of Religion* (Edinburgh: Edinburgh University Press, 1999); Fergus Kerr, *Theology after Wittgenstein,* 2nd ed. (London: SPCK, 1997); and Felicity McCutcheon, *Religion Within the Limits of Language Alone* (Aldershot, U.K.: Ashgate, 2001). For a collection of more critical essays, see *Wittgenstein and Philosophy of Religion,* ed. Robert L. Arrington and Mark Addis (London: Routledge, 2001).

The most important Wittgensteinian philosopher of religion was D. Z. Phillips. See his programmatic book, *The Concept of Prayer* (London: Routledge & Kegan Paul, 1965), and more recently *Belief, Change and Forms of Life* (London: Macmillan, 1987); as well as his collection, *Wittgenstein and Religion* (London: Macmillan, 1993).

[16]*Culture and Value,* p. 85e.

[17]*Culture and Value,* p. 85e.

[18]D. Z. Phillips, *Faith after Foundationalism* (London: Routledge, 1988), p. 218. For further critique of Wittgensteinian approaches to philosophy of religion, see James Kellenberger, *The Cognitivity of Religion* (London: Macmillan, 1985); Gary Gutting, *Religious Belief and Religious Skepticism* (Notre Dame: University of Notre Dame Press, 1982), part 1; Roger Trigg, *Rationality and Religion* (Oxford: Blackwell, 1998); McCutcheon, *Religion Within the Limits;* and several of the essays in Arrington and Addis, *Wittgenstein and Philosophy of Religion.*

[19]See, among many places, D. Z. Phillips, *Religion Without Explanation* (Oxford: Blackwell, 1976), pp. 144-50.

[20]*Concept of Prayer,* p. 12.

[21]*Culture and Value,* p. 83e.

[22]His philosophical works are *How to Do Things with Words,* 3rd ed. (Cambridge, Mass.: Harvard University Press, 1980); *Sense and Sensibilia* (Oxford: Oxford University Press, 1962); and *Philosophical Papers,* ed. J. O. Urmson and G. J. Warnock, expanded ed. (Oxford: Oxford University Press, 1979). For a good introduction, see G. J. Warnock, *J. L. Austin* (London: Routledge, 1989).

[23]See, e.g., Lester K. Little, *Benedictine Maledictions* (Ithaca, N.Y.: Cornell University Press, 1993); or Hugh White, ed., *Speech Act Theory and Biblical Criticism,* Semeia 41 (Atlanta: Scholars Press, 1988).

[24]The major published works of Ryle are *The Concept of Mind* (London: Hutchinson, 1949); *Dilemmas* (New York: Cambridge University Press, 1956); and his *Collected Papers,* 2 vols. (London: Hutchinson, 1971). For a good introduction to his thought, see William Lyons, *Gilbert Ryle* (Brighton, U.K.: Harvester, 1980).

[25]Now found in his *Collected Papers,* vol. 2, chap. 3.

[26]*Concept of Mind,* p. 7.

[27]His major philosophical writings are: *Introduction to Logical Theory* (London: Methuen, 1952); *Individuals* (London: Methuen,1959); *The Bounds of Sense* (London: Methuen, 1966); *Logico-Linguistic Papers* (London: Methuen, 1971); *Freedom and Resentment and Other Essays* (London: Methuen, 1974); *Skepticism and Naturalism* (London: Methuen, 1985); and *Analysis and Metaphysics* (Oxford: Oxford University Press, 1992). This last volume makes a good introduction to his approach (originally given as lectures in France). See also Lewis

Edwin Hahn, ed., *The Philosophy of P. F. Strawson* (La Salle, Ill.: Open Court, 1998).

[28]"On Denoting," *Mind* 59 (1959): 320-44; reprinted in his *Logico-Linguistic Papers*.

[29]*Individuals*, p. 10.

[30]*Skepticism and Naturalism*, p. 27-28.

[31]His major works in philosophy are: *Mind and the World Order* (New York: Scribner, 1929); *Symbolic Logic*, with Cooper Harold Langford (New York: Appleton-Century, 1932); and *An Analysis of Knowledge and Valuation* (La Salle, Ill.: Open Court, 1946). For an introduction to his thought, see Paul Arthur Schilpp, ed., *The Philosophy of C. I. Lewis* (La Salle, Ill.: Open Court, 1968).

[32]For the life of Quine, see his autobiography, *The Time of My Life* (Cambridge, Mass.: Harvard University Press, 1985); and the autobiographical essay in Lewis Edwin Hahn and Paul Arthur Schilpp, eds., *The Philosophy of W. V. Quine* (LaSalle, Ill.: Open Court, 1986). For short introductions to his philosophy, see Roger F. Gibson, *The Philosophy of W. V. Quine* (Tampa: University Presses of Florida, 1982); Lynn Hankinson Nelson and Jack Nelson, *On Quine* (Belmont, Calif.: Wadsworth, 2000); Alex Orenstein, *W. V. Quine* (Princeton: Princeton University Press, 2002); or Gary Kemp, *Quine* (London: Continuum, 2006). There is a fine collection of interpretive essays in Roger F. Gibson, ed., *Cambridge Companion to Quine* (New York: Cambridge University Press, 2004).

[33]His works in symbolic logic (all published in revised editions by Harvard University Press) include: *Mathematical Logic* (1940; rev. 1981); *Elementary Logic* (1941; rev. 1980); *Methods of Logic* (1950; rev. 1982); *Set Theory and Its Logic* (1963; rev. 1971); and *Philosophy of Logic* (1970; rev. 1986).

[34]Their philosophical correspondence is published as Richard Creath, ed., *Dear Carnap, Dear Van* (Berkeley, Calif.: University of California Press, 1990).

[35]Quine's bibliography is extensive; see the list at the end of Hahn & Schilpp, *The Philosophy of W. V. Quine* or in Gibson, *Cambridge Companion to Quine*. His major works apart from symbolic logic (for which see above) are *Word and Object* (Cambridge, Mass.: MIT Press, 1960); *The Web of Belief* (with J. S. Ullian; New York: Random House, 1970); *The Roots of Reference* (LaSalle, Ill.: Open Court, 1974); *Pursuit of Truth* (Cambridge, Mass.: Harvard University Press, 1992); *From Stimulus to Science* (Cambridge, Mass.: Harvard University Press, 1995); and several volumes of collected articles including *From a Logical Point of View* (New York: Harper & Row, 1963); *The Ways of Paradox and Other Essays* (New York: Random House, 1966); *Ontological Relativity and Other Essays* (New York: Columbia University Press, 1969); and *Theories and Things* (Cambridge, Mass.: Harvard University Press, 1981).

[36]For some representative works about Quine and his philosophy, see Hahn and Schilpp, *The Philosophy of W. V. Quine;* Gibson, *The Cambridge Companion to Quine;* Donald Davidson and Jaakko Hintikka, eds., *Words and Objections* (Dordrecht: Reidel, 1975); George Romanos, *Quine and Analytic Philosophy* (Cambridge, Mass.: MIT Press, 1983); Christopher Hookway, *Quine* (Stanford, Calif.: Stanford University Press, 1988); Robert B. Barrett and Roger F. Gibson, eds., *Perspectives on Quine* (Oxford: Blackwell, 1990); and Eve Gaudet, *Quine on Meaning* (New York: Continuum, 2006).

[37]"The Scope and Language of Science" (1954), repr. in *The Ways of Paradox*, p. 215.

[38]Reprinted in *From a Logical Point of View*, chap. 2.

[39]"Two Dogmas," p. 42.

[40]His books of essays are all published by Oxford University Press: *Essays on Actions and Events* (1980); *Inquiries into Truth and Interpretation* (1984); *Subjective, Intersubjective, Objective* (2001); *Problems of Rationality* (2004); *Truth, Language and History* (2005). A good collection with an introduction is *The Essential Davidson*, ed. Ernie Lapore and Kirk Ludwig (Oxford: Oxford University Press, 2006).

[41]Tarski was a Polish-American mathematician and logician whose definition of truth for

formal languages is a biconditional, usually exemplified like this: *P* is true in language *L* if and only if *p* (where *P* is the sentence expressing the proposition *p*). For example, "Snow is white" is true in English if and only if snow is white. For more on Tarski see Anite Feferman, *Alfred Tarski: Life and Logic* (New York: Cambridge University Press, 2004).

[42]See "Truth and Meaning" (1967), in *Inquiries into Truth and Interpretation;* also in *The Essential Davidson.*

[43]"What Thought Requires" (2001), in *Problems of Rationality,* p. 146.

[44]"On the Very Idea of a Conceptual Scheme" (1984), in *Inquiries into Truth and Interpretation,* p. 183; also in *The Essential Davidson.*

[45]"On the Very Idea," p. 198.

[46]See Davidson's reflections on Rorty in the "afterthoughts" to his "A Coherence Theory of Truth and Knowledge," in *The Essential Davidson,* pp. 238-41; also in *Subjective, Intersubjective, Objective.*

[47]For a good introduction to Kripke, see G. W. Fitch, *Saul Kripke* (London: Acumen, 2004). Kripke has published only two books to date: *Naming and Necessity* (Cambridge, Mass.: Harvard University Press, 1980) and *Wittgenstein on Rules and Private Language* (Cambridge, Mass.: Harvard University Press, 1982). Kripke's book on Wittgenstein is not so much an exposition of the other philosopher's work as Kripke's improvisation on Wittgensteinian themes.

[48]"Is there a Problem about Substitutional Quantification?" in Gareth Evans and John McDowell, eds., *Truth and Meaning* (Oxford: Oxford University Press, 1976), p. 416.

[49]See the section on Russell in chapter two of this book.

[50]*Naming and Necessity,* p. 108.

[51]*Naming and Necessity,* p. 41.

[52]See Kripke, *Wittgenstein on Rules and Private Language,* and compare the famous response to Quine's "Two Dogmas" by P. F. Strawson and H. P. Grice: "In Defense of a Dogma" (1956) repr. in Grice, *Studies in the Way of Words* (Cambridge, Mass.: Harvard University Press, 1989).

[53]For an extensive survey of analytic philosophy of religion, see James F. Harris, *Analytic Philosophy of Religion,* Handbook of Contemporary Philosophy of Religion, vol. 3 (Dordrecht: Kluwer, 2002).

[54]For more on MacIntrye see the section on Thomistic philosophy in the following chapter.

[55]*New Essays in Philosophical Theology,* ed. Anthony Flew and Alasdair MacIntyre (London: SCM Press, 1955), p. x.

[56]Ayer and logical positivism are discussed earlier in this book (chapter two).

[57]*Language, Truth and Logic* (1946 ed.), p. 120.

[58]*New Essays,* p. 98.

[59]*New Essays,* p. 99.

[60]For a good introduction to Hick, see *A John Hick Reader,* ed. Paul Badham (London: Macmillan, 1990) and David Cheetham, *John Hick* (Aldershot: Ashgate, 2003). For his life, see his *John Hick: An Autobiography* (Oxford: Oneworld, 2002). Other works about Hick include: Paul Eddy, *John Hick's Pluralist Philosophy of World Religion* (Aldershot: Ashgate, 2002); Harold Netland, *Encountering Religious Pluralism* (Downers Grove, Ill.: InterVarsity Press, 2001); Kenneth Rose, *Knowing the Real: John Hick on the Cognitivity of Religions and Religious Pluralism* (New York: P. Lang, 1996); R. Douglas Geivett, *Evil and the Evidence for God* (Philadelphia: Temple University Press, 1993); C. Robert Mesle, *John Hick's Theodicy* (London: Macmillan, 1991); and Gavin D'Costa, ed., *John Hick's Theology of Religions: A Critical Evaluation* (Lanham, Md.: University Press of America, 1987). A good collection of papers discussing Hick's philosophy is Harold Hewitt Jr., ed., *Problems in the Philosophy of Religion* (London: Macmillan, 1991).

[61]Hick's main books in English are: *Faith and Knowledge*, 2nd ed. (London: Macmillan, 1966); *Philosophy of Religion*, 4th ed. (Englewood Cliffs, N.J.: Prentice-Hall, 1990); *Evil and the God of Love*, rev. ed. (New York: Harper and Row, 1978); *God and the Universe of Faiths*, rev. ed. (London: Macmillan, 1988); *Death and Eternal Life*, rev. ed. (London: Macmillan, 1985); *An Interpretation of Religion*, 2nd ed. (New Haven: Yale University Press, 2004); and *The Metaphor of God Incarnate* (London: SCM Press, 1993). He edited numerous books, including *The Myth of God Incarnate* (London: SCM Press, 1977), and with Paul Knitter, *The Myth of Christian Uniqueness* (Maryknoll, N.Y.: Orbis, 1987).

[62]"Religious Faith as Experiencing-as" (1969), repr. in *A John Hick Reader;* see also *An Interpretation of Religion*, pp. 140-42.

[63]See *Faith and Knowledge*, chap. 8 and his oft-cited paper, "Theology and Verification" (1960), repr. in John Hick, ed., *The Existence of God* (New York: Macmillan, 1964). See further *Death and Eternal Life*, pp. 327-29, for his revised views.

[64]*Evil and the God of Love* (1978), p. 245.

[65]*Evil and the God of Love*, p. 3.

[66]*Evil and the God of Love*, p. 220.

[67]*Faith and Knowledge*, p. 158, his italics.

[68]Hick, *Disputed Questions in Theology and the Philosophy of Religion* (London: Macmillan, 1993), p. 139.

[69]"Jesus and the World's Religions," in Hick, ed., *The Myth of God Incarnate*, p. 178. Several Christian theologians and philosophers of religion have responded to this claim, arguing for the coherence of orthodox Christology. See, for example, Stephen T. Davis, *Logic and the Nature of God* (London: Macmillan, 1983); David Brown, *The Divine Trinity* (London: Duckworth, 1985); Thomas V. Morris, *The Logic of God Incarnate* (Ithaca, N.Y.: Cornell University Press, 1986); Richard Sturch, *The Word and the Christ* (Oxford: Oxford University Press, 1991); or Richard Swinburne, *The Christian God* (Oxford: Oxford University Press, 1994).

[70]"Jesus and the World's Religions," p. 180.

[71]This point can be misunderstood. Alvin Plantinga is a bit unfair to Hick in his criticisms in *Warranted Christian Belief* (New York: Oxford University Press, 2000). For example, Plantinga writes (p. 81) that, for Hick, religious doctrines "are only mythologically true—that is really false." Plantinga ought to have written that the myths are *literally* false; yet that is wholly compatible with them being *really* true.

[72]*An Interpretation of Religion*, p. 348.

[73]For a good introduction to Plantinga's philosophy of religion, see the introduction and papers collected in his *The Analytic Theist*, ed. James F. Sennett (Grand Rapids: Eerdmans, 1998); see further James Beilby, *Epistemology as Theology: An Evaluation of Alvin Plantinga's Religious Epistemology* (Aldershot, U.K.: Ashgate, 2006) with an extensive bibliography, or the older monograph, James F. Sennett, *Modality, Probability and Rationality* (New York: P. Lang, 1992). Collections of papers discussing Plantinga's work include James E. Tomberlin and Peter van Inwagen, eds., *Alvin Plantinga* (Dordrecht: D. Reidel, 1985) which includes an autobiography; Jonathan L. Kvanvig, ed., *Warrant in Contemporary Epistemology* (Lanham, Md.: Rowman & Littlefield, 1996); Michael Beaty, ed., *Christian Theism and the Problems of Philosophy* (Notre Dame: University of Notre Dame Press, 1990); Thomas M. Crisp, Matthew Davidson and David Vander Laan, eds., *Knowledge and Reality: Essays in Honor of Alvin Plantinga* (Dordrecht: Springer, 2006); and Deane-Peter Baker, ed., *Alvin Plantinga* (New York: Cambridge University Press, 2007).

[74]Plantinga's major philosophical books to date are: *God and Other Minds*, 2nd ed. (Ithaca, N.Y.: Cornell University Press, 1990); *The Nature of Necessity*, 2nd ed. (Oxford: Oxford University Press, 1989); *Warrant: The Current Debate* (New York: Oxford University Press, 1993);

Warrant and Proper Function (New York: Oxford University Press, 1993); *Warranted Christian Belief* (New York: Oxford University Press, 2000); and *Essays in the Metaphysics of Modality,* ed. Matthew Davidson (New York: Oxford University Press, 2003). He also edited several books, including *Faith and Rationality* with Nicholas Wolterstorff (Notre Dame: University of Notre Dame Press, 1983). He is currently working on the publication of his second set of Gifford lectures, with the working title of "Science and Religion: Conflict or Concord?"

[75]This sentence concludes part one of the book (p. 111).

[76]J. L. Mackie, "Evil and Omnipotence" (1955), repr. in Marilyn M. Adams and Robert M. Adams, eds., *The Problem of Evil* (New York: Oxford University Press, 1990).

[77]Alvin Plantinga, *The Nature of Necessity* (Oxford: Oxford University Press, 1974), pp. 190-96.

[78]Wolterstorff's significant philosophical work deserves further discussion, but we have to limit ourselves to this brief footnote. A colleague of Plantinga's for many years at Calvin College, Wolterstorff became the Noah Porter Professor of philosophical theology at Yale (he retired in 2001). He is one of the world's foremost Christian philosophers and has contributed widely to metaphysics, epistemology, aesthetics, the philosophy of education and ethics as well as the philosophy of religion. For a good introduction to Wolterstorff, see Andrew Sloane, *On Being a Christian in the Academy* (Carlisle: Paternoster, 2003), with bibliography. One of his most beautiful and moving books is a meditation on the death of his son: *Lament for a Son* (Grand Rapids: Eerdmans, 1987). Some of his main works in philosophy are *Works and Worlds of Art* (Oxford: Oxford University Press, 1980); *Justice* (Princeton: Princeton University Press, 2008); and the following volumes published by Cambridge University Press: *Divine Discourse* (1995); *John Locke and the Ethics of Belief* (1996); and *Thomas Reid and the Story of Epistemology* (2001), based on his Gifford lectures for 1995.

[79]But epistemologies never really die: see Michael R. DePaul, ed., *Resurrecting Old-Fashioned Foundationalism* (Lanham, Md.: Rowman & Littlefield, 2001).

[80]"Reason and Belief in God," in Plantinga and Wolterstorff, *Faith and Rationality,* p. 85.

[81]*Warrant: The Current Debate; Warrant and Proper Function;* and *Warranted Christian Belief.*

[82]*Warranted Christian Belief,* p. 191.

[83]*Warranted Christian Belief,* p. 191, his italics.

[84]See, e.g., the following anthologies: Kvanvig, ed., *Warrant in Contemporary Epistemology,* Crisp, Davidson and Laan, eds., *Knowledge and Reality;* James Beilby, ed., *Naturalism Defeated? Essays on Plantinga's Evolutionary Argument Against Naturalism* (Ithaca, N.Y.: Cornell University Press, 2002); and Baker, ed., *Alvin Plantinga.*

[85]For an introduction to Swinburne, see Alan G. Padgett, ed., *Reason and the Christian Religion: Essays in Honour of Richard Swinburne* (Oxford: Oxford University Press, 1994), which contains his intellectual autobiography. Swinburne's major books in philosophy of religion are, to date: *The Concept of Miracle* (London: Macmillan, 1971); *The Coherence of Theism,* rev. ed. (Oxford: Oxford University Press, 1993); *The Existence of God,* rev. ed. (Oxford: Oxford University Press, 1991); *Faith and Reason* (Oxford: Oxford University Press, 1981); *The Evolution of the Soul,* rev. ed. (Oxford: Oxford University Press, 1997); *Responsibility and Atonement* (Oxford: Oxford University Press, 1989); ed., *Miracles* (New York: Macmillan, 1989); *Revelation* (Oxford: Oxford University Press, 1992); *The Christian God* (Oxford: Oxford University Press, 1994); *Providence and the Problem of Evil* (Oxford: Oxford University Press, 1998); and *The Resurrection of God Incarnate* (Oxford: Oxford University Press, 2003).

[86]*The Coherence of Theism,* p. 291.

[87]The final volume of the trilogy, *Faith and Reason* (1981), considers the nature and rationality of religious belief, including the nature of faith and the value of reason in religion.

[88]*Providence,* p. 15.

[89]*Providence*, p. 15.

[90]His textbook is *Philosophy of Religion: An Introduction* (Belmont: Wadsworth, 1993). The key books by William L. Rowe in philosophy of religion are: *The Cosmological Argument* (Princeton: Princeton University Press, 1975); ed., *God and the Problem of Evil* (Oxford: Blackwell, 2001); and *Can God Be Free?* (Oxford: Oxford University Press, 2004).

[91]William L. Rowe, "The Problem of Evil and Some Varieties of Atheism" (1979), repr. in Marilyn McCord Adams and Robert Merrihew Adams, eds., *The Problem of Evil* (Oxford: Oxford University Press, 1990); also in Rowe, *God and the Problem of Evil*, and many other anthologies on the problem of evil.

[92]For an excellent anthology on this topic, see Daniel Howard-Snyder, ed., *The Evidential Argument from Evil* (Bloomington, Ind.: Indiana University Press, 1996).

[93]Rowe, "The Problem of Evil," in Adams & Adams, *The Problem of Evil*, p. 128. This conclusion is a probable one for Rowe, not a necessary one.

[94]For three fine books in philosophy of religion by Robert Merrihew Adams, all published by Oxford University Press, see *The Virtue of Faith and Other Essays* (1987); *Finite and Infinite Goods* (1999); and *A Theory of Virtue* (2006).

[95]Marilyn McCord Adams, *William of Ockham*, 2 vols. (Notre Dame: University of Notre Dame Press, 1987).

[96]This includes her anthology with Robert Adams, eds., *The Problem of Evil;* her *Horrendous Evils and the Goodness of God* (Ithaca, N.Y.: Cornell University Press, 1999); and her Gifford lectures, *Christ and Horrors: The Coherence of Christology* (New York: Cambridge University Press, 2006).

[97]This is a key thesis in *Horrendous Evils*.

[98]See, e.g., William Wainwright, *God, Philosophy and Academic Culture: A Discussion Between Scholars in the AAR and APA* (Atlanta: Scholars Press, 1996).

Chapter 8: Faith in Philosophy: Thomism, Hermeneutics and Christian Philosophy

[1]For an introduction, see Gerald McCool, *From Unity to Pluralism: The Internal Evolution of Thomism* (New York: Fordham University Press, 1989), or more briefly in his *The Neo-Thomists* (Milwaukee: Marquette University Press, 1990).

[2]Published in English as *The Restoration of Christian Philosophy: Aeterni Patris* (1879; repr. Boston: Paulinist Media, n.d.), p. 21.

[3]*Modernism* in this context denotes the liberal Catholic theology being developed in the late nineteenth century by several theologians, including Alfred Loisy (1857-1940). This kind of Catholic modernism embraced both modern philosophical movements and the newer methods of historical-critical Bible scholarship. It was resisted mightily by Catholic authorities, including Leo XIII. See further Alec R. Vidler, *The Modernist Movement in the Roman Church* (New York: Cambridge University Press, 1934).

[4]His great work is the five-volume *Le point de départ de la metaphysique* [*The Starting Point of Metaphysics*] (Paris: De Brouwer, 1944-49). For English texts see Joseph Donceel, ed., *A Maréchal Reader* (New York: Herder & Herder, 1970).

[5]For good, brief introductions to Maritain, see Ralph McInerny, *The Very Rich Hours of Jacques Maritain* (Notre Dame: University of Notre Dame Press, 2003) and Jude P. Dougherty, *Jacques Maritain* (Washington, D.C.: Catholic University of America Press, 2003). See also the standard biography, Jean-Luc Barré, *Jacques and Raïssa Maritain* (Notre Dame: University of Notre Dame Press, 2005). Other introductions to his philosophy include Brooke W. Smith, *Jacques Maritain* (New York: Elsevier, 1976); William Nottingham, *Christian Faith and Secular Action* (St. Louis: Bethany, 1968); and Charles A. Fecher, *The Philosophy of Jacques Maritain* (Westminster, Md.: Newman, 1958). Maritain wrote a large number of books and articles; his and Raïssa's complete works have been published in French in

fifteen volumes (Fribourg: Ed. universitaires, 1982-95). There is a helpful short list in Smith, *Jacques Maritain*. For a complete bibliography see Jean-Louis Allard and P. Germain, *Répertoire bibliographique sur la vie et l'oeuvre de Jacques et Raïssa Maritain* (Ottawa: J. L. Allard, 1994) or the earlier bibliography in English: Dald Arthur and Idella Gallagher, *The Achievement of Jacques and Raïssa Maritain: A Bibliography* (Garden City, N.Y.: Doubleday, 1962).

The best introduction to Maritain may be Maritain's own writings; see especially his lectures, *On the Uses of Philosophy* (Princeton: Princeton University Press, 1961), or his work on *St. Thomas Aquinas*, rev. ed. (New York: Meridian, 1958). His main philosophical books in English include: *Art and Scholasticism* (London: Sheed & Ward, 1946); *Distinguish to Unite or The Degrees of Knowledge*, rev. ed. (Notre Dame: University of Notre Dame Press, 1995); *A Preface to Metaphysics* (London: Sheed & Word, 1939); *Existence and the Existent* (New York: Pantheon, 1948); and *Moral Philosophy* (New York: Scribner, 1964). The University of Notre Dame Press has undertaken the task of publishing a uniform series of his complete works in English, in twenty volumes (projected).

[6]Shortness of space prevents us from a fuller discussion of the work of Gilson. With Maritain he revived the tradition of Thomistic philosophy in France between the wars. His most important scholarly work lies in the field of medieval philosophy, which he helped to revive and enhance worldwide; but he also wrote on contemporary themes. One of his most influential books is his Gifford lectures, *The Spirit of Mediaeval Philosophy* (New York: Scribner, 1940). For a good introduction see Anton C. Pegis, ed., *A Gilson Reader* (New York: Image, 1957). For an intellectual bibliography, see Francesca Murphy, *Art and Intellect in the Philosophy of Étienne Gilson* (Columbia: University of Missouri Press, 2004).

[7]Jacques Maritain, *Antimoderne* (Paris: E?ditions de la Revue de Jeunes, 1922), preface; English translation from Maritain, *St. Thomas Aquinas*, rev. ed. (New York: Meridian, 1958), p. 15.

[8]*St. Thomas Aquinas*, p. 156, his italics.

[9]*St. Thomas Aquinas*, p. 71.

[10]*Existence and the Existent*, p. 51.

[11]*Degrees of Knowledge* (1995 ed.), p. xi. "First Truth" is a Thomistic term for God.

[12]*Degrees of Knowledge*, p. 7.

[13]*Degrees of Knowledge*, pp. 232-33.

[14]*Degrees of Knowledge*, p. 263.

[15]See further, below, in the section on Christian philosophy.

[16]There exists an extensive secondary literature on Rahner, in many languages. For a good bibliography, see Roman Bleistein and Elmar Klinger, eds., *Bibliographie Karl Rahner* (Freiburg: Herder, 1969). Among many books about Rahner, a few good introductions in English include: Declan Marmion and Mary E. Hines, eds., *The Cambridge Companion to Karl Rahner* (New York: Cambridge University Press, 2005), which has a selective bibliography; Karen Kilby, *Karl Rahner* (London: Routledge, 2004); or Robert Kress, *A Rahner Handbook* (Atlanta: John Knox Press, 1982).

[17]Lonergan's important work as a transcendental Thomist deserves fuller analysis than we have space for here. His major philosophical work was *Insight: A Study of Human Understanding* (New York: Philosophical Library, 1957), a comprehensive exposition of his "generalized empirical method" in epistemology. His other major book, *Method in Theology* (New York: Herder & Herder, 1972), has been widely influential, especially among Roman Catholics in the English-speaking world. For a good introduction to Lonergan, see *The Lonergan Reader*, ed. Mark and Elizabeth Morelli (Toronto: University of Toronto Press, 1997). The University of Toronto has undertaken the project of publishing his collected works.

[18]Rahner wrote most of his theology in essays and lectures, collected in his extensive *Theological Investigations,* 23 vols. (Baltimore: Helcion; New York: Continuum, 1963-92). He also wrote a one-volume summary of his approach to theology, *Foundations of Christian Faith* (New York: Crossroad, 1989).

[19]Rahner, *Spirit in the World* (New York: Herder & Herder, 1968), p. liii.

[20]*Spirit,* p. 57, his italics. We have retained the androcentric character of the English translation for the sake of accuracy.

[21]*Spirit,* p. 67.

[22]*Spirit,* pp. 179-83.

[23]*Spirit,* p. 406.

[24]*Spirit,* p. 406.

[25]*Hearers of the Word* (New York: Herder & Herder, 1969), p. 14.

[26]*Hearers,* p. 22.

[27]*Hearers,* p. 174.

[28]MacIntyre has written numerous articles and books over a long career. Some of his main philosophical books include: *A Short History of Ethics* (New York: Macmillan, 1966); *After Virtue,* 2nd ed. (Notre Dame: University of Notre Dame Press, 1984); *Whose Justice? Which Rationality?* (Notre Dame: University of Notre Dame Press, 1988); *Three Rival Versions of Moral Enquiry* (Notre Dame: University of Notre Dame Press, 1990); *Dependent Rational Animals* (LaSalle, Ill.: Open Court, 1999); and two volumes of selected essays: *The Tasks of Philosophy* and *Ethics and Politics* (New York: Cambridge University Press, 2006). For critical discussions of his philosophy, with bibliography, see John Horton and Susan Mendus, eds., *After MacIntyre* (Notre Dame: University of Notre Dame Press, 1994) and Mark C. Murphy, ed., *Alasdair MacIntyre* (New York: Cambridge University Press, 2003). On MacIntyre and theology, see Jonathan Wilson, *Living Faithfully in a Fragmented World* (Philadelphia: Trinity Press International, 1998).

[29]See the introduction to his *Against the Self-Images of the Age* (London: Duckworth, 1971), pp. vii-x, as well as several of the essays therein.

[30]"A Partial Response to My Critics," in *After MacIntyre,* p. 300.

[31]*First Principles, Final Ends and Contemporary Philosophical Issues* (Milwaukee: Marquette University Press, 1991), repr. in A. MacIntyre, *The Tasks of Philosophy: Selected Essays,* vol. 1 (New York: Cambridge University Press, 2006), p. 145.

[32]We will return to MacIntyre later in his book and discuss his *Three Rival Versions of Moral Enquiry* in conversation with postmodern thought.

[33]Eng. trans. (Boston: Pauline, 1998). Because this text is available in many versions, we will cite section numbers (which are uniform across versions) rather than page numbers. For the work of John Paul II as a philosopher, see John McNerny, *Footbridge Towards the Other* (London: T & T Clark, 2003).

[34]For an overview of this debate in English, see Maurice Nédoncelle, *Is There a Christian Philosophy?* Twentieth Century Encyclopedia of Catholicism, vol. 10 (New York: Hawthorne, 1960). See also Murphy, *Art and Intellect in the Philosophy of Étienne Gilson,* pp. 102-29. A good French discussion and overview is Alexandre Renard, *La querelle sur la possibilité de la philosophie chrétienne* (Paris: École et Collège, 1941). Matthew A. Bloomer, *Judeo-Christian Revelation as a Source of Philosophical Reflection According to Étienne Gilson* (Rome: Appolinare, 2001) is a good if rather uncritical book on Gilson; it is not reliable in some of its statements about other philosophers.

[35]Émile Bréhier, *The History of Philosophy,* vol. 2, *The Hellenistic and Roman Age,* trans. Wade Baskin (Chicago: University of Chicago Press, 1968), pp. 218-50. His point was developed further in an oft-cited article, "Y a-t-il une philosophie chrétienne?" *Révue de Métaphysique et Morale* 38 (1931): 133-62.

[36] *History of Philosophy*, p. 218.

[37] *History of Philosophy*, p. 236.

[38] *History of Philosophy*, p. 225.

[39] For these latter comments, see his article "Y a-t-il une philosophie chrétienne?" cited above.

[40] "La notion de philosophie chrétienne: séance du 21 mars 1931," *Bulletin de la Société française de philosophie* 31 (1931): 37-93. There is a summary of this debate in English in Nédoncelle, *Is There a Christian Philosophy?* chap. 5.

[41] *The Spirit of Mediaeval Philosophy* (1940), pp. 1-41.

[42] *Spirit*, p. 37.

[43] *Spirit*, p. 40.

[44] *Spirit*, p. 36.

[45] See, e.g., Étienne Gilson, *Christian Philosophy* (Toronto: Pontifical Institute of Mediaeval Studies, 1993), pp. 4-5, 21-22, 28, 32, 39, 50, 66, etc.

[46] F. Van Steenberghen, "Étienne Gilson et l'université de Louvain," *Revue philosophique de Louvain* 85 (1987): 5-21, citing p. 12.

[47] Van Steenberghen, "Philosophie et christianisme," *Revue philosophique de Louvain* 89 (1991): 499-505, citing p. 504.

[48] Maritain, *An Essay on Christian Philosophy* (New York: Philosophical Library, 1955), pp. 11-12.

[49] *Essay on Christian Philosophy*, p. 15.

[50] *Essay on Christian Philosophy*, pp. 17-18.

[51] *Essay on Christian Philosophy*, p. 19.

[52] *Essay on Christian Philosophy*, p. 28.

[53] *Essay on Christian Philosophy*, p. 30.

[54] *Essay on Christian Philosophy*, p. 34.

[55] Kuyper was a philosopher, politician, journalist, professor and founder of the Free University of Amsterdam. He founded a school of Dutch Calvinist philosophy which Herman Dooyeweerd and others extended in more theoretical and abstract academic ways in the twentieth century. For the life and work of Kuyper, see James McGoldrick, *God's Renaissance Man* (Darlington, U.K.: Evangelical Press, 2000). The study of Dooyeweerd's thought is a worthwhile journey in Christian philosophy, but a specialized one which we must forego at this juncture. Dooyeweerd's main work in philosophy is his massive *A New Critique of Theoretical Thought*, 4 vols. (1958; rev ed., Lewiston: Edwin Mellen, 1997). For an introduction to his philosophy with some critique, see Ronald H. Nash, *Dooyeweerd and the Amsterdam Philosophy* (Grand Rapids: Zondervan, 1962), or Vincent Brümmer, *Transcendental Criticism and Christian Philosophy* (Franeker: T. Wever, 1961).

[56] Alvin Plantinga, "Advice to Christian Philosophers," *Faith and Philosophy* 1 (1984): 253-71. For an earlier discussion of Christian philosophy by an analytic philosopher, see Arthur Holmes, *Christian Philosophy in the Twentieth Century* (Nutley: Craig, 1969). Holmes also writes in the Reformed tradition. For many years he organized an annual Wheaton Philosophy Conference at Wheaton College; this small meeting provided a seed-bed for the later Society of Christian Philosophers.

[57] "Advice," p. 253.

[58] See note 55 above on Kuyper and Dooyeweerd.

[59] John Wippel, "The Possibility of a Christian Philosophy," *Faith and Philosophy* 1 (1984): 272-90. Another response which ends up being similar to Van Steenberghen's (without knowing it, apparently) is Peter van Inwagen, "Some Remarks on Plantinga's Advice," *Faith and Philosophy* 16 (1999): 164-72. This article is part of a symposium on Plantinga's "Advice."

[60]Wippel, "The Possibility of a Christian Philosophy," p. 288.

[61]Reprinted in Phillips, *Wittgenstein and Religion* (London: Macmillan, 1993).

[62]*Wittgenstein and Religion*, p. 224.

[63]*Wittgenstein and Religion*, p. 225.

[64]*Wittgenstein and Religion*, p. 232.

[65]*Wittgenstein and Religion*, p. 233.

[66]See further, among many works, Arthur Holmes, *All Truth Is God's Truth* (Grand Rapids: Eerdmans, 1977); Nicholas Wolterstorff, *Reason Within the Bounds of Religion* (Grand Rapids: Eerdmans, 1976); Roy Clouser, *The Myth of Religious Neutrality* (Notre Dame: University of Notre Dame Press, 1991); and George Marsden, *The Outrageous Idea of Christian Scholarship* (New York: Oxford University Press, 1997).

[67]Ludwig Wittgenstein, *Zettel* (Oxford: Blackwell, 1967), §455.

[68]By liberal-evangelical we simply mean a moderate and mainstream form of Liberal Protestant theology. It would be hard to prove that this model of implicit Christian faith at work in philosophy is *typical* of liberal-evangelical theology, as contrasted with conservative Catholic or evangelical scholars—but we think it may well be the case.

[69]For a short introduction to Gadamer, see Patricia A. Johnson, *On Gadamer* (Belmont, Calif.: Wadsworth, 2000) or Chris Lawn, *Gadamer* (London: Continuum, 2006). For his life, see his autobiography, *Philosophical Apprenticeships* (Cambridge, Mass.: MIT Press, 1985) or the shorter one that opens Lewis E. Hahn, ed., *The Philosophy of Hans-Georg Gadamer* (LaSalle, Ill.: Open Court, 1997). This volume also contains a very good bibliography of Gadamer's extensive writings. Also very good is *The Cambridge Companion to Gadamer*, ed. Robert J. Dostal (New York: Cambridge University Press, 2002), which opens with a short biography by the editor. Gadamer was an important contributor to the history of philosophy, especially Greek and German thought. See his *The Beginnings of Philosophy* (New York: Continuum, 1998); *Dialogue and Dialectic* [on Plato] (New Haven: Yale University Press, 1980); *Hegel's Dialectic* (New Haven: Yale University Press, 1976); *Heidegger's Ways* (Albany: SUNY Press, 1994); *The Idea of the Good in Platonic-Aristotelian Philosophy* (New Haven: Yale University Press, 1986); and *Plato's Dialectical Ethics* (New Haven: Yale University Press, 1998). Gadamer's main books in philosophy, besides *Truth and Method* (cited below) are *Philosophical Hermeneutics* (Berkeley: University of California Press, 1976); *Reason in an Age of Science* (Cambridge, Mass.: MIT Press, 1981); *The Relevance of the Beautiful and Other Essays* (New York: Cambridge University Press, 1986); and *Hermeneutics, Religion and Ethics* (New Haven: Yale University Press, 1999).

[70]*Truth and Method*, rev. trans. by Joel Weinsheimer and Donald G. Marshall (New York: Continuum, 1989). It is based upon the fifth German edition of *Wahrheit und Methode* (1986), and will be the translation cited here. The earlier English translation of 1975 was inadequate and will not be cited.

[71]Gadamer, *Philosophical Hermenetuics*, p. 50.

[72]*Truth and Method*, p. xxi.

[73]*Truth and Method*, p. 100.

[74]*Truth and Method*, p. 100.

[75]*Truth and Method*, p. 110.

[76]*Truth and Method*, p. 143.

[77]*Truth and Method*, pp. 258-60.

[78]*Truth and Method*, p. 260.

[79]*Truth and Method*, p. 576.

[80]*Truth and Method*, p. 378.

[81]*Truth and Method*, p. 474.

[82]The Gadamer-Habermas debate is helpfully found in English in Gayle Ormiston and

Alan Schrift, eds., *The Hermeneutic Tradition* (Albany: SUNY Press, 1990), pp. 213-96. See further Ingrid Scheibler, *Gadamer: Between Heidegger and Habermas* (Lanham, Md.: Rowman & Littlefield, 2000).

[83]See Diane Michelfelder and Richard Palmer, eds., *Dialogue and Deconstruction: The Gadamer-Derrida Encounter* (Albany: SUNY Press, 1989).

[84]Gadamer, "Hermeneutics and the Social Sciences," *Cultural Hermeneutics* 2 (1975): 307-16, citing 311. See also his article, "Practical Philosophy as a Model of the Human Sciences," *Research in Phenomenology* 9 (1979): 74-85.

[85]For a little more on structuralism, see below.

[86]Key responses to Gadamer can be found in Ricoeur, *Hermeneutics and the Human Sciences*, trans. John B. Thompson (New York: Cambridge University Press, 1981), pp. 270-307 and in *A Ricoeur Reader*, ed. Mario J. Valdés (Toronto: University of Toronto Press, 1991), pp. 216-41.

[87]For an introduction to the life and thought of Ricoeur, see Charles Regan, *Paul Ricoeur* (Chicago: University of Chicago Press, 1996), or the autobiographical chapter which opens *The Philosophy of Paul Ricoeur*, ed. Lewis Edwin Hahn (LaSalle, Ill.: Open Court, 1995), which also contains a bibliography of his extensive publications. Good brief introductions to Ricoeur include Karl Simms, *Paul Ricoeur* (London: Routledge, 2003) and S. H. Clark, *Paul Ricoeur* (London: Routledge, 1990).

Some representative secondary works on Ricoeur include: David M. Kaplan, *Ricoeur's Critical Theory* (Albany: SUNY Press, 2003); James Fodor, *Christian Hermeneutics: Paul Ricoeur and the Refiguring of Theology* (Oxford: Oxford University Press, 1995); Kevin Vanhoozer, *Biblical Narrative in the Philosophy of Paul Ricoeur* (New York: Cambridge University Press, 1990); Mark I. Wallace, *The Second Naivete: Barth, Ricoeur, and the New Yale Theology* (Macon, Ga.: Mercer, 1990); David E. Klemm, *The Hermeneutical Theory of Paul Ricoeur* (Lewisburg, Penn.: Bucknell University Press, 1983); John B. Thompson, *Critical Hermeneutics: A Study in the Thought of Paul Ricoeur and Jürgen Habermas* (New York: Cambridge University Press, 1981); and Don Ihde, *Hermeneutic Phenomenology: The Philosophy of Paul Ricoeur* (Evanston, Ill.: Northwestern University Press, 1971).

Ricoeur's major philosophical works in English include five volumes of collected essays: *History and Truth* (Evanston, Ill.: Northwestern University Press, 1965); *Husserl* (Evanston, Ill.: Northwestern University Press, 1967); *The Conflict of Interpretation* (Evanston: Northwestern University Press, 1974); *Hermeneutics and the Human Sciences* (New York: Cambridge University Press, 1981); and *From Text to Action* (London: Athlone, 1991). Two anthologies of his works on theological themes have been published by Fortress Press: *Essays in Biblical Interpretation* (1980); and *Figuring the Sacred* (1995). His major monographs are: *Fallible Man* (Chicago: Regnery, 1965); *Freedom and Nature* (Evanston: Northwestern University Press, 1966); *The Symbolism of Evil* (New York: Harper & Row, 1967); *Freud and Philosophy* (New Haven: Yale University Press, 1970); *Interpretation Theory* (Fort Worth: Texas Christian University Press, 1976); *The Rule of Metaphor* (Toronto: University of Toronto Press, 1978); *Time and Narrative*, 3 vols. (Chicago: University of Chicago Press, 1984-88); *Oneself as Another* (Chicago: University of Chicago Press, 1992); *The Just* (Chicago: University of Chicago Press, 2000); and *Memory, History, Forgetting* (Chicago: University of Chicago Press, 2004).

[88]*Freud and Philosophy*, p. 9.

[89]*The Symbolism of Evil*, p. 352.

[90]*Freud and Philosophy*, p. 382. See further his article, "The Model of the Text: Meaningful Action Considered as a Text," in *From Text to Action*, pp. 144-67.

[91]For an introduction see Jonathan Culler, *Ferdinand de Saussure* (Ithaca, N.Y.: Cornell University Press, 1986).

[92]Among Claude Lévi-Strauss's many books, a good start is *The Savage Mind* (Chicago: University of Chicago Press, 1966). See further David Pace, *Claude Lévi-Strauss* (London: Routledge, 1983).

[93]For an introduction to the movement, see Peter Caws, *Structuralism* (Atlantic Highlands: Humanities, 1988) or the more advanced, François Dosse, *History of Structuralism*, 2 vols. (Minneapolis: University of Minnesota Press, 1997).

[94]*A Ricoeur Reader*, p. 223.

[95]See Ricoeur, "Structure and Hermeneutics," in *The Conflict of Interpretations*, pp. 27-61.

[96]The four parts were published in 3 vols. (1983-85) and in English translation by the University of Chicago soon thereafter (1985-88).

[97]*Time and Narrative*, 1:ix.

[98]Ricoeur, "Narrative Time," *Critical Inquiry* 7 (1980): 169-90; citing 169.

[99]*Time and Narrative*, 3:100.

[100]*Time and Narrative*, 3:99.

[101]For two collections of his papers on theological themes, both published by Fortress Press, see *Essays in Biblical Interpretation* (1980) and *Figuring the Sacred* (1995). The two lectures given in Edinburgh are published in English in the latter book.

[102]*Oneself as Another*, p. 24.

[103]*Oneself as Another*, p. 24.

[104]*Oneself as Another*, p. 25.

Chapter 9: Journey to Postmodernity

[1]For an introduction to the postmodern in these broad cultural terms, see, e.g., Kevin Hart, *Postmodernism: A Beginners Guide* (Oxford: Oneworld, 2004); Simon Malpas, *The Postmodern* (London: Routledge, 2005) or Steven Connor, ed., *The Cambridge Companion to Postmodernism* (New York: Cambridge University Press, 2004).

[2]So famously Frederick Jamison, "The Cultural Logic of Late Capitalism," (1984) repr. in his *Postmodernism* (Durham, N.C.: Duke University Press, 1991). See also Lee Hardy, "Postmodernism as a Kind of Modernism," in Merold Westphal, ed., *Postmodern Philosophy and Christian Thought* (Bloomington: Indiana University Press, 1999), pp. 28-43. The postmodern is not a complete reversal of the modern.

[3]Agnes Heller and Ferenc Fehér, *The Postmodern Political Condition* (New York: Columbia University Press, 1988), p. 1.

[4]The male-centered focus of Enlightenment rationality in particular, and Western philosophy in general, is one of the criticisms brought out by postmodern feminist theory, as we will see later in this chapter.

[5]On Nietzsche and Kierkegaard, see Wilkens and Padgett, *Christianity and Western Thought*, 2:154-80.

[6]Søren Kierkegaard, *Concluding Unscientific Postscript to Philosophical Fragments*, 2 vols., ed. Howard V. Hong and Edna H. Hong (Princeton: Princeton University Press, 1992), 1:118.

[7]Lyotard, *The Postmodern Condition: A Report on Knowledge* (Minneapolis: University of Minnesota Press, 1984). For an introduction to Lyotard's thought and several of his key essays, see *The Lyotard Reader*, ed. Andrew Benjamin (Oxford: Blackwell, 1989).

[8]*Postmodern Condition*, p. 34.

[9]*Postmodern Condition*, p. 27.

[10]*Postmodern Condition*, p. 37.

[11]*Postmodern Condition*, p. xxiv.

[12]Paul Ricoeur interpreted psychoanalysis as a "hermeneutics of suspicion" in his *Freud and Philosophy* (New Haven: Yale University Press, 1970).

[13]See his *Warranted Christian Belief* (New York: Oxford University Press, 1999), pp. 438-56 for his rather quick criticism of postmodernism (mostly Rorty). For a critical review of Plantinga on Rorty, see G. Elijah Dann, *After Rorty* (London: Continuum, 2006), pp. 109-26.

[14]Thomas Kuhn, *The Structure of Scientific Revolutions*, 2nd ed. (Chicago: University of Chicago Press, 1970). Kuhn continued to interpret and develop the viewpoint of *Structure* in many essays, collected in *The Essential Tension* (Chicago: University of Chicago Press, 1977) and *The Road Since Structure* (Chicago: University of Chicago Press, 2000). For a good, brief introduction to Kuhn's philosophy see Alexander Bird, *Thomas Kuhn* (Chesham: Acumen, 2000).

[15]Kuhn, *Structure*, p. 10.

[16]*Structure*, p. 148.

[17]*Structure*, p. 149.

[18]*The Road Since Structure*, p. 220.

[19]At the time of his death in 2007, Rorty was emeritus professor of comparative literature at Stanford University. For a good, brief but uncritical introduction to his thought see Richard Rumana, *On Rorty* (Belmont, Calif.: Wadsworth, 2000). Even more hagiographic is Alan Malachowski, *Richard Rorty* (Chesham: Acumen, 2002). For a philosophical autobiography, with a bibliography, see the relevant parts of Randall E. Auxier, ed., *The Philosophy of Richard M. Rorty* (LaSalle, Ill.: Open Court, 2008). Rorty's main philosophical books in English are: (ed.) *The Linguistic Turn* (Chicago: University of Chicago Press, 1967); *Philosophy and the Mirror of Nature* (Princeton: Princeton University Press, 1979); *The Consequences of Pragmatism* (Minneapolis: University of Minnesota Press, 1982); *Contingency, Irony and Solidarity* (New York: Cambridge University Press, 1989); and three volumes of philosophical papers, all published by Cambridge University Press: *Objectivity, Relativism and Truth* (vol. 1, 1991); *Essays on Heidegger and Others* (vol. 2, 1991) and *Truth and Progress* (vol. 3, 1998). An important collection of critical responses to Rorty and his replies to them is Robert Brandom, ed., *Rorty and His Critics* (Oxford: Blackwell, 2000).

[20]*Philosophy and the Mirror*, p. 369.

[21]*Philosophy and the Mirror*, pp. 370-71.

[22]See the essays collected in the third volume of his philosophical papers, *Truth and Progress*.

[23]For an introduction to Goodman's philosophy see Daniel Cohnitz, *Nelson Goodman* (Chesham: Acumen, 2006).

[24]Nelson Goodman, *Ways of Worldmaking* (Indianapolis: Hackett, 1978).

[25]*Contingency*, p. 73.

[26]Rorty uses this term for his viewpoint in "Is Truth a Goal of Inquiry?" repr. in *Truth and Progress*.

[27]See, e.g., almost all of the chapters in Brandom, *Rorty and His Critics*, where major philosophers point out problems in his approach to issues of truth, justification and reality.

[28]*Consequences of Pragmatism*, p. 153.

[29]"Pragmatism, Relativism, and Irrationalism" (1979), repr. in his *Consequences of Pragmatism*, pp. 160-75.

[30]*Consequences of Pragmatism*, p. 166.

[31]*Consequences of Pragmatism*, p. 168.

[32]See, e.g., the exchange between Susan Haack and Rorty on "Vulgar Pragmatism" in Herman J. Saatkamp Jr., ed., *Rorty and Pragmatism: The Philosopher Responds to His Critics* (Nashville: Vanderbuilt University Press, 1995), pp. 126-53.

[33]See, e.g., Cornel West and John Rajchman, eds., *Post-Analytic Philosophy* (New York: Columbia University Press, 1985).

[34]Ray Monk, *Ludwig Wittgenstein* (London: Cape, 1990) and *Bertrand Russell*, 2 vols. (London: Cape, 1998, 2000).

[35]For example, Robert Wick, *Modern French Philosophy* (Oxford: Oneworld, 2003) mentions Levinas only in a tiny footnote; and the historical narrative of Vincent Descombes, *Modern French Philosophy* (New York: Cambridge University Press, 1980) does not discuss Levinas except in passing when speaking of Derrida.

[36]For introductions to Levinas see Adriaan Peperzak, *To the Other* (West Lafayette, Ind.: Perdue University Press, 1993); Colin Davis, *Levinas* (Notre Dame: University of Notre Dame Press, 1996); or Simon Critchley and Robert Bernasconi, eds., *The Cambridge Companion to Levinas* (New York: Cambridge University Press, 2002), with a good bibliography of primary and secondary works. For a biography, see Salomon Malka, *Emmanuel Levinas* (Pittsburgh: Duquesne University Press, 2006). Good collections of his key essays are found in Adriaan Peperzak et al., eds., *Emmanuel Levinas: Basic Philosophical Writings* (Bloomington: Indiana University Press, 1996) or in Sean Hand, ed., *A Levinas Reader* (Oxford: Blackwell, 1989).

The main philosophical works of Levinas in English are *Time and the Other* (Pittsburgh: Duquesne University Press, 1985); *Existence and Existents* (The Hague: M. Nijhoff, 1978); *Totality and Infinity* (Pittsburgh: Duquesne University Press, 1969); *Otherwise than Being or Beyond Essence* (The Hague: M. Nijhoff, 1981); *God, Death and Time* (Stanford: Stanford University Press, 2000); and two collections of essays, *Collected Philosophical Papers* (The Hague: M. Nijhoff, 1987) and *Discovering Existence with Husserl* (Bloomington: Indiana University Press, 1988). Levinas wrote a number of books and articles on biblical, Talmudic and Jewish topics, including *Beyond the Verse* (Bloomington: Indiana University Press, 1994); *Difficult Freedom: Essays on Judaism* (Baltimore: Johns Hopkins University Press, 1990); *New Talmudic Readings* (Pittsburgh: Duquesne University Press, 1990); *Nine Talmudic Readings* (Bloomington: Indiana University Press, 1990); and *Of God Who Comes to Mind* (Stanford: Stanford University Press, 1998).

[37]His dissertation, the first study of Husserl's phenomenology in French, introduced phenomenology to French-speaking philosophers and provided French phenomenology with much of its vocabulary (derived, of course, from Husserl and Heidegger's German): *The Theory of Intuition in Husserl's Phenomenology* (Evanston, Ill.: Northwestern University Press, 1995).

[38]See his essay, "Ethics as First Philosophy," in *A Levinas Reader,* pp. 75-87.

[39]*Totality and Infinity,* p. 43.

[40]Sometimes Levinas used the biblical phrase "neighbor" for the Other, e.g., in *Existence and Existents,* p. 95: "the other is the neighbor—but this proximity is not a degradation of, or a stage on the way to, fusion."

[41]*Totality and Infinity,* pp. 48-50, 197-98; see also Rene Descartes, "Third Meditation," in *The Philosophical Writings of Descartes,* ed. John Cottingham et al., 3 vols. (New York: Cambridge University Press, 1984), 2:31-35.

[42]*Totality and Infinity,* pp. 48-51, 102-3; see also Plato, *The Republic,* book 7 (509b).

[43]*Totality and Infinity,* p. 43, my emphasis.

[44]*Totality and Infinity,* pp. 40, 211.

[45]*Nine Talmudic Studies,* p. 182, with the quotation coming from *In the Time of the Nations* (Bloomington: Indiana University Press, 1994), p. 174, his emphasis.

[46]See his essay "The Trace of the Other" in *Deconstruction in Context,* ed. Mark Taylor (Chicago: University of Chicago Press, 1986), pp. 345-59.

[47]See in particular his essay, "God and Philosophy," in *Of God Who Comes to Mind*; also in *Collected Philosophical Papers*.

[48]"Transcendence and Evil," in *Collected Philosophical Papers,* pp. 185-86.

[49]Derrida, "Violence and Metaphysics," now in his *Writing and Difference* (Chicago: University of Chicago Press, 1978). Ten years later Edith Wyschogrod published the first mono-

graph on Levinas in English: *Emmanuel Levinas* (The Hague: M. Nijhoff, 1974).

[50]*Otherwise Than Being*, p. 178.

[51]"Violence and Metaphysics," pp. 108-17.

[52]*Otherwise than Being*, pp. 5-7.

[53]Levinas, *On Escape* (Stanford: Stanford University Press, 2003), p. 49. The short essay goes on to give reasons and experiences which call this opening viewpoint into question.

[54]*Otherwise Than Being*, p. 141.

[55]The book has been translated many times, e.g., by Gia-Fu Feng and Jane English (New York: Vintage, 1989). For the Chinese-English text with translation and commentary see Laozi, *Dao de jing*, trans. and ed. Roger T. Ames and David L. Hall (New York: Ballantine, 2003).

[56]*Tao Te Ching*, chapter 56; in Feng and English, p. 59.

[57]It is one of his more moving texts: Jacques Derrida, *Adieu to Emmanuel Levinas* (Stanford: Stanford University Press, 1999).

[58]This phrase refers to those who lived though and were sympathetic or participated in the leftist student uprisings in Paris in the summer of 1968, often called "the events of May '68." See Peter Starr, *Logics of Failed Revolt: French Theory after May '68* (Stanford: Stanford University Press, 1995).

[59]For a solid and brief introduction to Foucault see Gary Gutting, *Foucault: A Very Short Introduction* (Oxford: Oxford University Press, 2005) together with the biography of David Macey, *Michel Foucault* (London: Reaktion, 2004). Macey has a larger biography too: *The Lives of Michel Foucault* (New York: Pantheon, 1993). *The Foucault Reader,* ed. Paul Rabinow (New York: Pantheon, 1984) is also a good introduction. More extensive discussions and introductions are: Gary Gutting, ed., *The Cambridge Companion to Foucault,* 2nd ed. (New York: Cambridge University Press, 2000), with a good bibliography; David Couzens Hoy, ed., *Foucault: A Critical Reader* (Oxford: Blackwell, 1986); Lois McNay, *Foucault: A Critical Introduction* (New York: Continuum, 1994); or Clare O'Farrell, *Michel Foucault* (London: Sage, 2005).

Foucault's main monographs in English are: *Madness and Civilization* (New York: Pantheon, 1965) or in the far better new translation, *History of Madness* (London: Routledge, 2006); *The Birth of the Clinic* (New York: Vintage, 1973); *The Order of Things* (New York: Random House, 1970); *The Archaeology of Knowledge* (New York: Pantheon, 1972); *Discipline and Punish* (New York: Pantheon, 1977); *History of Sexuality, Volume 1: An Introduction* (New York: Pantheon, 1978); *History of Sexuality, Volume 2: The Use of Pleasure* (New York: Pantheon, 1985); *History of Sexuality, Volume 3: The Care of the Self* (New York: Pantheon, 1984). His views on religion are collected in *Religion and Culture,* ed. Jeremy R. Carrette (London: Routledge, 1999), which also contains some fragments of what would have been volume 4 of *The History of Sexuality* (on chastity and Christianity). His many interviews and shorter writings are now collected in three volumes: vol. 1, *Ethics: Subjectivity and Truth* (1997); vol. 2, *Aesthetics, Method and Epistemology* (1998); and vol. 3, *Power* (2001), all in *The Essential Works of Foucault 1954-84* (New York: New Press, 1997-2001). His original and powerful lectures at the Collège de France [1973-1984] are also in the process of being published in a large set: *Abnormal* [1974-75] (New York: Picador, 2003); *Society Must Be Defended* [1975-76] (New York: Picador, 2003); *Psychiatric Power* [1973-74] (New York: Palgrave Macmillan, 2006); *The Hermeneutics of the Subject* [1981-82] (New York: Palgrave Macmillan, 2006); *Security, Territory and Population* [1977-78] (New York: Palgrave Macmillan, 2007). Just because of his global, multidisciplinary influence, the secondary work on Foucault is enormous, and grows ever larger! For a bibliography up to 1991, see Joan Nordquist, *Michel Foucault,* 2 vols. (Santa Cruz: Research & Reference, 1986, 1992). See also the website <www.foucault.info>.

[60]*Archaeology of Knowledge*, p. 17.

[61]The abridged English edition of 1965, *Madness and Civilization*, has been replaced by a new complete translation, *The History of Madness* (2006). Jacques Derrida's early (1963) critique of this book is worth reading: "Cogito and the History of Madness," repr. in his *Writing and Difference*. Foucault's reply is "My Body, This Paper, This Fire," repr. in his *Aesthetics, Method, and Epistemology*.

[62]We introduced structuralism in an earlier chapter, when discussing Ricoeur.

[63]"L'homme est-il mort?" (1966), essay 39 in *Dits et écrits*, 4 vols. (Paris: Gallimard, 1994), 1:540-44, quoting 540-41. This essay has not appeared in English, but see *The Order of Things*, pp. 248-49, 351-53, 373-87 for similar views expressed with more circumspection and less focus on contemporary politics.

[64]*Discipline and Punish*, p. 170.

[65]See "The Birth of Biopolitics," in *Ethics*, pp. 73-79; *History of Sexuality*, 1:140-45.

[66]*Society Must Be Defended*, p. 8.

[67]*Society Must Be Defended*, p. 9.

[68]*Discipline and Punish*, p. 202.

[69]*Society Must Be Defended*, p. 252.

[70]*Ethics*, p. 300.

[71]*Ethics*, p. 527.

[72]See "About the Beginnings of the Hermeneutics of the Self" (1980), repr. in *Religion and Culture*.

[73]See the study of his ethics by James Bernauer, *Michel Foucault's Force of Flight* (Atlantic Highlands: Humanities, 1990), p. 184.

[74]For some introductions to his philosophy see: Jonathan Culler, *On Deconstruction* (London: Routledge, 1982); Christiana Howells, *Derrida* (Cambridge, Mass.: Polity, 1999); the relevant portions of Richard Kearney, *Debates in Continental Philosophy* (New York: Fordham University Press, 2000); or Mark Dooley and Liam Kavanagh, *The Philosophy of Derrida* (Stocksfield: Acumen, 2007); and from a literary perspective, Nicholas Royle, *Jacques Derrida* (London: Routledge, 2003); or Penelope Deutscher, *How to Read Derrida* (London: Granta, 2005). See also *A Derrida Reader*, ed. Peggy Kamuf (New York: Columbia University Press, 1991). Longer philosophical introductions include John Llewelyn, *Derrida on the Threshold of Sense* (London: Macmillan, 1986); Irene Harvey, *Derrida and the Economy of Différance* (Bloomington: Indiana University Press, 1986); Rodolphe Gasché, *The Tain of the Mirror* (Cambridge, Mass.: Harvard University Press, 1986); and Christopher Norris, *Derrida* (Cambridge, Mass.: Harvard University Press, 1987).

[75]For a helpful annotated bibliography of primary and secondary literature until 1991, see William R. Schultz and Lewis L. B. Fried, *Jacques Derrida* (New York: Garland, 1992), and the more recent listing by Peter Zeillinger, *Jacques Derrida Bibliographie* (Wein: Turia & Kant, 2005) with updates on the author's webpage: <www.univie.ac.at/derrida>; see also the excellent Derrida webpage: <www.hydra.umn.edu/derrida>. The list of his books will continue to grow as posthumous writings are edited and translated.

In addition to his three books on Husserl cited below, Derrida's main works from a philosopher's point of view are as follows (unless otherwise indicated, the publisher is University of Chicago Press): *Writing and Difference* (1978); *Dissemination* (1981); *Margins of Philosophy* (1982); *The Post Card* (1987); *Limited, Inc.* (Evanston, Ill.: Northwestern University Press, 1988); *The Truth in Painting* (1987); *Of Spirit: Heidegger and the Question* (1989); *The Gift of Death* (1995); *Given Time I* (1993); *Specters of Marx* (London: Routledge, 1994); *The Politics of Friendship* (London: Verso, 1997); and interviews and short essays in *Positions* (1981); *Points* (Stanford: Stanford University Press, 1995); and *Negotiations* (Stanford: Stanford University Press, 2002). Derrida's memorial addresses also make for interesting, clear and sometimes moving reading; many are collected in *The Work of Mourning* (2003).

[76]See Derrida, "Limited Inc. a b c . . . " (1977), repr. in *Limited, Inc.* and *Glas* (Lincoln: University of Nebraska Press, 1986). On Searle and Derrida's "debate" see James K. A. Smith, "Limited Incarnation," chap. 6 of Bruce E. Benson, James K. A. Smith and Kevin Vanhoozer, eds., *Hermeneutics at the Crossroads* (Bloomington: Indiana University Press, 2006).

[77]These early works are his master's thesis (published in 1990 but finished in 1954), *The Problem of Genesis in Husserl's Philosophy* (Chicago: University of Chicago Press, 2003); his translation and long introduction to a late fragment by Husserl, *Edmund Husserl's Origin of Geometry: An Introduction*, rev. ed. (Lincoln: University of Nebraska Press, 1989) and *Speech and Phenomena* (Evanston, Ill.: Northwestern University Press, 1973).

[78]See the philosophical bibliography by Jason Powell, *Jacques Derrida* (New York: Continuum, 2007), and for some secondary analysis and autobiography, see Geoffrey Bennington and Jacques Derrida, *Jacques Derrida* (Chicago: University of Chicago Press, 1993).

[79]Now found in *Writing and Difference*, pp. 278-93.

[80]*Newsweek* 119, no. 21 (May 25, 1992): 42. See the letter signed by several important professors of philosophy and the interview with Derrida about this event, in *"Honoris Causa"* repr. in *Points*, pp. 399-421. Even after Derrida's death it still bothered Simon Blackburn, an analytic philosophy professor at Cambridge: see his "Derrida Deserves Some Credit for Trying," in the *Times Higher Education Supplement* 1666 (November 12, 2004): 16.

[81]We discuss Heidegger earlier in this book. That Derrida's différance is a repetition in other terms and contexts of Heidegger's ontological difference is often remarked upon, e.g., Kevin Hart, *The Trespass of the Sign* (New York: Cambridge University Press, 1989), pp. 84-93; Gasche, *Tain of the Mirror*, pp. 177-85.

[82]Derrida uses this word in his early discussion of Husserl, but in a famous lecture introduced it to an audience of professional philosophers: "Différance" (1968), found in both *Speech and Phenomena* and his *Margins of Philosophy*. A helpful anthology devoted to the lecture is *Derrida and Différance*, ed. David Wood and Robert Bernasconi (Evanston, Ill.: Northwestern University Press, 1988).

[83]*Of Grammatology*, p. 150; *Writing and Difference*, p. 289.

[84]"The history of metaphysics . . . is the determination of Being as *presence* in all senses of this word," *Writing and Difference*, p. 279, his emphasis. See also the translator's preface to *Of Grammatology*, trans. Gayatri Chakravorty Spivak, p. xxi.

[85]*Positions*, p. 26; *Of Grammatology*, p. 4.

[86]"Structure, Sign and Play," in *Writing and Difference*, p. 280.

[87]*Of Grammatology*, p. 283.

[88]*Tao Te Ching*, chap. 2; Ames and Hall, *Dao de jing*, p. 80, my emphasis.

[89]See "Structure, Sign and Play," p. 289. See further Kevin Hart, *The Trespass of the Sign*, p. 26, who makes this same point.

[90]*Speech and Phenomena*, p. 142.

[91]*Of Grammatology*, p. 158.

[92]*Limited, Inc.*, p. 148

[93]Derrida, *Ethics, Institutions, and the Right to Philosophy* (Lanham, Md.: Rowman & Littlefield, 2002), p. 51.

[94]See, e.g., David F. Krell, *The Purest of Bastards: Works of Mourning, Art and Affirmation in the Thought of Jacques Derrida* (University Park: Penn State University Press, 2000).

[95]In 1989 Derrida delivered a famous lecture in which he claimed that "justice cannot be deconstructed." For this lecture, "Force of Law," and other essays, see Drucilla Cornell, ed., *Deconstruction and the Possibility of Justice* (New York: Routledge, 1992). For books which develop Derrida's philosophy in terms of social justice and/or ethics, see the introduction by Mark Dooley and Liam Kavanagh, *The Philosophy of Derrida*, chap. 4; see further Rich-

ard Beardsworth, *Derrida and the Political* (London: Routledge, 1996); Simon Critchley, *The Ethics of Deconstruction,* 2nd ed. (West Lafayette, Ind.: Purdue University Press, 1999); or A. J. P. Thomson, *Deconstruction and Democracy* (London: Continuum, 2005). For works on Derrida and theology, see among others Kevin Hart, *The Trespass of the Sign;* John Caputo, *The Prayers and Tears of Derrida* (Bloomington: Indiana University Press, 1997); Yvonne Sherwood & Kevin Hart, eds., *Derrida and Religion: Other Testaments* (London: Routledge, 2005); or Theodore W. Jennings Jr., *Reading Derrida/Thinking Paul* (Stanford: Stanford University Press, 2006).

[96]*Derrida's Elsewhere,* directed by Safaa Fathy, originally produced in Spain under the title *D'ailleurs, Derrida* (1999); *Derrida* (2002) directed by Kirby Dick and Amy Ziering Kofman, distributed on DVD by Zeitgeist Films.

[97]In particular the work of Hélène Cixous and Michèle LeDoeuff deserve more careful exposition that we can provide here. Both find a place, with others, in the *French Feminism Reader,* ed. Kelly Oliver (Lanham, Md.: Rowman & Littlefield, 2000).

[98]For an introduction to her life and thought, including a good bibliography, see Claudia Card, *The Cambridge Companion to Simone de Beauvoir* (New York: Cambridge University Press, 2003). For a brief introduction see Sally Scholz, *On Beauvoir* (Belmont: Wadsworth, 2000). Several biographies of her life have been written, including Deirdre Bair, *Simone de Beauvoir* (New York: Simon & Shuster, 1990).

[99]People who value "technical" academic philosophy see Beauvoir's books as merely illustrating Sartre's more profound thought. Recently some revisionist historians of philosophy have suggested that Beauvoir came up with some of Sartre's ideas first and published them in story form. The historical evidence, including interviews with Beauvoir herself, suggests a greater mutuality than either hypothesis. For a revisionist approach, see Edward and Kate Fullbrook, *Simone de Beauvoir and Jean-Paul Sartre* (New York: Basic Books, 1993). For a viewpoint of mutual interaction (modest revision), see Karen Green, "Sartre and de Beauvoir on Freedom and Oppression," in Julien Murphy, ed., *Feminist Interpretations of Jean-Paul Sartre* (University Park: Penn State University Press, 1999), pp. 175-99, and Max Deutscher, *Genre and Void* (Aldershot, U.K.: Ashgate, 2003), especially pp. xxii-xxxi.

[100]We discuss Sartre's work, including *Being and Nothingness,* earlier in this volume.

[101]Simone de Beauvoir, *She Came to Stay* (London: Flamingo, 1984).

[102]Simone de Beauvoir, *The Second Sex* (New York: Knopf, 1952).

[103]*Second Sex,* p. xvi.

[104]*Second Sex,* p. xvi.

[105]*Second Sex,* p. 267.

[106]*Second Sex,* p. 731.

[107]See, e.g., Toril Moi, *Feminist Theory and Simone de Beauvoir* (Oxford: Blackwell, 1990) or Emily Grosholz, ed., *The Legacy of Simone de Beauvoir* (Oxford: Oxford University Press, 2004).

[108]For an introduction to her thought, see *The Irigaray Reader,* ed. Margaret Whitford (Oxford: Blackwell, 1991); Margaret Whitford, *Luce Irigaray* (London: Routledge, 1992); and the more advanced discussion in Alison Stone, *Luce Irigaray and the Philosophy of Sexual Difference* (New York: Cambridge University Press, 2002). Her main philosophical books in English so far are: *Speculum of the Other Woman* (Ithaca, N.Y.: Cornell University Press, 1985); *This Sex which Is Not One* (Ithaca, N.Y.: Cornell University Press, 1985); *Marine Lover of Friedrich Nietzsche* (New York: Columbia University Press, 1992); *An Ethics of Sexual Difference* (Ithaca, N.Y.: Cornell University Press, 1993); *Sexes and Genealogies* (New York: Columbia University Press, 1993); *The Forgetting of Air in Martin Heidegger* (Austin: University of Texas Press, 1999); *To Speak Is Never Neutral* (London: Routledge, 2002).

[109]For an introduction to Lacan, see Sean Homer, *Jacques Lacan* (London: Routledge, 2005). Lacan's work was important for both Irigaray and Kristeva.

[110]See her *To Speak Is Never Neutral.*

[111]*Ethics of Sexual Difference,* p. 5.

[112]See "Divine Women" (1986) repr. in *Sexes and Geneaologies.* See also her *Prières Quotidiennes: Everyday Prayers* (Paris: Maisonneuve et Larose, 2004).

[113]See *Elemental Passions* (London: Routledge, 1992), a kind of introduction; *Marine Lover of Friedrich Nietzsche;* and *The Forgetting of Air in Martin Heidegger.*

[114]For example, *Democracy Begins Between Two* (London: Routledge, 2001).

[115]*Ethics of Sexual Difference,* p. 127. See also *I Love to You* (London: Routledge, 1996), a recent book on Hegel, ethics and sexual difference.

[116]See, e.g., *Ethics of Sexual Difference,* pp. 101-11.

[117]For an introduction to her thought, see John Lechte, *Julia Kristeva* (London: Routledge, 1990), or two anthologies of her work with introductions and bibliographies: *The Kristeva Reader,* ed. Toril Moi (New York: Columbia University Press, 1986); and *The Portable Kristeva,* ed. Kelly Oliver (New York: Columbia University Press, 1997). Her major theoretical works in English (all published by Columbia University Press) are: *Revolution in Poetic Language* (1984); *Desire in Language* (1980); *Powers of Horror* (1982); *Language, the Unknown* (1989); *Tales of Love* (1987); *In the Beginning Was Love* (1988); *Black Sun: Depression and Melancholy* (1989); *Strangers to Ourselves* (1991); *New Maladies of the Soul* (1995); *The Sense and Non-Sense of Revolt* (2000).

[118]Bakhtin is considered by many to be the most important Russian literary theorist in the twentieth century. See further Gary Saul Morson and Caryl Emerson, *Mikhail Bakhtin: Creation of a Prosaics* (Stanford: Stanford University Press, 1990).

[119]Kristeva, *Séméiotiké* (Paris: Seuil, 1969) has not yet been fully translated, but see *The Kristeva Reader,* pp. 24-87, or *The Revolution in Poetic Language,* pp. 21-24.

[120]Plato, *Timaeus,* §52. *Chora* means place or territory.

[121]The *Tel Quel* circle published a radical magazine during the 1960s in Paris, and the members of the circle were well-known intellectuals involved in left-bank politics and the student uprising in 1968. See Patrick Ffrench, *The Time of Theory: A History of* Tel Quel *(1960-1983)* (Oxford: Oxford University Press, 1995).

[122]*Desire in Language,* p. 124.

[123]*Revolution,* p. 80.

[124]*Revolution,* p. 233.

[125]*Sense and Non-Sense of Revolt,* p. 7.

[126]For good, brief introduction to his thought see James G. Finlayson, *Habermas: A Very Short Introduction* (Oxford: Oxford University Press, 2005). For more substantial discussions see Thomas McCarthy, *The Critical Theory of Jürgen Habermas* (Cambridge, Mass.: MIT Press, 1981); Erik Oddvar Eriksen and Jarle Weigard, *Understanding Habermas* (London: Continuum, 2004); and Stephen K. White, ed., *The Cambridge Companion to Habermas* (New York: Cambridge University Press, 1995), which have good bibliographies (McCarthy's is now dated). The major philosophical books by Habermas in English are (published by MIT Press unless otherwise noted): *The Structural Transformation of the Public Square* (1989); *On the Logic of the Social Sciences* (1988); *Knowledge and Human Interest* (Boston: Beacon, 1971); *Legitimation Crisis* (Boston: Beacon, 1975); *A Theory of Communicative Action,* 2 vols. (Boston: Beacon, 1984); *The Philosophical Discourse of Modernity* (1987); *Moral Consciousness and Communicative Action* (1990); *Postmetaphysical Thinking* (1992); *Between Facts and Norms* (1996); and *Truth and Justification* (2003).

[127]See Herbert Marcuse, *One-Dimensional Man* (Boston: Beacon, 1964); Max Horkheimer and Theodor W. Adorno, *Dialectic of Enlightenment* (New York: Herder & Herder, 1972).

Habermas did not study directly with Marcuse, who moved to the States for good in 1940. See further Martin Jay, *The Dialectical Imagination: A History of the Frankfurt School and the Institute for Social Research 1923-1950* (Berkeley, University of California Press, 1996).

[128]*Knowledge and Human Interest*, p. 314.

[129]*Legitimation Crisis*, p. 110.

[130]*Legitimation Crisis*, p. 95. See further his *Moral Consciousness and Communicative Action*.

[131]*Moral Consciousness*, p. 66, italics removed.

[132]See Lasse Thomassen, ed., *The Derrida-Habermas Reader* (Edinburgh: University of Edinburgh Press, 2006); their joint declaration is on pp. 270-77. See further Giovanna Borradori, ed., *Philosophy in a Time of Terror: Dialogues with Jürgen Habermas and Jacques Derrida* (Chicago: University of Chicago Press, 2003).

[133]See note 9 in Derrida, "Afterword: Toward an Ethic of Discussion," *Limited, Inc.*, pp. 156-58, and note 44 in his *Memories for Paul de Man* (New York: Columbia University Press, 1989), pp. 255-61.

[134]Alan Sokal, a physicist at New York University, published a hoax or joke article in a postmodern journal as an experiment to demonstrate a lack of intellectual rigor and/or integrity. He also publicized the hoax in the magazine *Lingua Franca*. See *The Sokal Hoax*, ed. The Editors of *Lingua Franca* (Lincoln: University of Nebraska Press, 2000); and Alan Sokal and Jean Bricmont, *Fashionable Nonsense* (New York: Picador, 1998) which contains the text of his hoax article.

[135]Alasdair MacIntyre, *Three Rival Versions of Moral Inquiry* (Notre Dame: University of Notre Dame Press, 1990).

[136]Marion made his early mark as a philosopher with significant rereadings of Descartes. See his *Descartes Grey Ontology* (South Bend, Ind.: St. Augustine, 2004); *On Descartes' Metaphysical Prism* (Chicago: University of Chicago Press, 1999); *Cartesian Questions* (Chicago: University of Chicago Press, 1999) and his book on Descartes' theology which should appear soon in English (original title, *Sur la théologie blanche de Descartes* [Paris: Presses univ. de France, 1981]). Marion's best known book in English is *God Without Being* (Chicago: University of Chicago Press, 1991). Among phenomenologists he is best known for introducing the idea of a "saturated phenomena," a notion he uses in his important monograph, *Being Given* (Stanford: Stanford University Press, 2001) and other works. Among his still-increasing number of philosophical books one can find *The Idol and the Distance* (New York: Fordham University Press, 2001); *Prolegomena to Charity* (New York: Fordham University Press, 2002); and *The Erotic Phenomenon* (Chicago: University of Chicago Press, 2007).

[137]See among several works *God Without Being, Being Given* and *Prolegomena to Charity*. On Marion's relationship with theology see Robyn Horner, *Jean-Luc Marion* (London: Ashgate, 2005), and Kevin Hart, ed., *Counter-Experiences: Reading Jean-Luc Marion* (Notre Dame: University of Notre Dame Press, 2007).

[138]The French title is "The Same and the Other: Forty-Five Years of French Philosophy (1933-1978)," a temporal limit which the English title omits: *Modern French Philosophy* (New York: Cambridge University Press, 1980).

[139]*Modern French Philosophy*, p. 182, italics removed.

[140]In addition to the books already mentioned, see *Objects of All Sorts* (Oxford: Blackwell, 1986), which is a kind of sequel to *Modern French Philosophy;* and *The Barometer of Modern Reason* (Oxford: Oxford University Press, 1993).

[141]Only the first volume is currently in English. For more on Descombes, see the translator's forward to his book *The Mind's Provisions: A Critique of Cognitivism* (Princeton: Princeton University Press, 2000). The second volume is *Les Institutions du Sens* (Paris: Minuit, 1996).

[142]See, e.g., *The Mind's Provisions*, pp. 78-83.

[143]His major works in English, to date, are: *Powers of the Rational* (Bloomington, Ind.: Indiana University Press, 1994); *Rationalities, Historicities* (Atlantic Highlands, N.J.: Humanities, 1997); ed., *Phenomenology and the "Theological Turn"* (New York: Fordham University Press, 2000); *Phenomenology "Wide Open"* (New York: Fordham University Press, 2005); and *On the Human Condition* (London: Routledge, 2005).

[144]See in particular the chapters "Philosophy Today and the Question of Rationality," and "After Heidegger," in *Rationalities, Historicities*. See further his *Powers of the Rational*.

[145]Janicaud, *Phenomenology and the "Theological Turn,"* p. 16. Part Three of this series is published as *Phenomenology "Wide Open."*

[146]In addition to the collection by Janicaud, and several books by Marion already cited above, some representative volumes in English are: Michael Henry, *I Am the Truth* (Stanford: Stanford University Press, 2003); Alain Badiou, *St. Paul* (Stanford: Stanford University Press, 2003); Jean-Yves LaCoste, *Experience and the Absolute* (New York: Fordham University Press, 2004); Jean-Louis Chrétien, *The Ark of Speech* (London: Routledge, 2004); and across the water, see the collection edited by two American philosophers, Bruce E. Benson and Norman Wirzba, *The Phenomenology of Prayer* (New York: Fordham University Press, 2005).

[147]Alain Renaut, *The Era of the Individual* (Princeton: Princeton University Press, 1997), p. 23.

[148]Ferry and Renaut, eds., *Why We Are Not Nietzscheans* (Chicago: University of Chicago Press, 1997) and their *Heidegger and Modernity* (Chicago: University of Chicago Press, 1990); see also their individual books cited in the next two footnotes.

[149]Luc Ferry, *What Is the Good Life?* (Chicago: University of Chicago Press, 2005) and *Homo Aestheticus* (Chicago: University of Chicago Press, 1993).

[150]Renaut, *The Era of the Individual*, chaps. 1 and 8. His large study on Kant, *Kant aujourd'hui* (Paris: Aubier, 1997), is not available in English. They have also published a massive five-volume history of political philosophy, parts of which are available in English as *Political Philosophy 1-3* (Chicago: University of Chicago Press, 1990-92).

Chapter 10: Conclusion, Retrospect and Reflection

[1]A key evangelical figure here in America is Merold Westphal. See his *Overcoming Onto-theology* (New York: Fordham University Press, 2001), and the several authors in his edited volume, *Postmodern Philosophy and Christian Thought* (Bloomington: Indiana University Press, 1999). Examples of some readable and reliable works from our publisher, InterVarsity Press, by evangelical scholars on postmodern thought include J. Richard Middleton and Brian Walsh, *Truth Is Stranger Than It Used to Be* (1999); James K. A. Smith, *The Fall of Interpretation* (2000); and Bruce Benson, *Graven Ideologies: Nietzsche, Derrida and Marion on Modern Idolatry* (2002).

Index